Intellectual Property and International Dispute Resolution

IEEM AND INTERNATIONAL INTELLECTUAL PROPERTY LAW

The involvement of the Institute of European Studies of Macau (IEEM) in matters of intellectual property is based on annual conferences that take up topical issues of intellectual property from a comparative perspective with a particular focus on Asia and Europe. The first of these conferences was held back in 2000, and has meanwhile become an annual event complemented by an Intellectual Property School and IP Master Classes. All three venues serve as a platform for academic teaching and discussion on intellectual property awareness and the proper place and function of intellectual property law in the context of society and public interest.

From the very start, the intellectual property conferences, the IP Law School and the Master Classes have enjoyed the support, assistance and commitment of Mr. Gonçalo Cabral, who is an advisor to the Government of Macau, of Ms. Maria do Céu Esteves, past president of the IEEM, and the IEEM's current president Dr. José Luís de Sales Marques. The latter was also instrumental in setting up an IEEM chair for intellectual property law at the Maastricht University in 2004, thereby further contributing to IEEM's academic commitment to the field of intellectual property law. During the five years of its existence, this chair was held by Anselm Kamperman Sanders.

The conference papers, as revised and updated, are edited by Christopher Heath and Anselm Kamperman Sanders as an IEEM Intellectual Property Series the volumes of which are listed at the end of this book.

Intellectual Property and International Dispute Resolution

Edited by

Christopher Heath and Anselm Kamperman Sanders

INSTITUTE OF EUROPEAN STUDIES OF MACAU
澳 門 歐 洲 研 究 學 會
INSTITUTO DE ESTUDOS EUROPEUS DE MACAU

Wolters Kluwer

Published by:
Kluwer Law International B.V.
PO Box 316
2400 AH Alphen aan den Rijn
The Netherlands
E-mail: international-sales@wolterskluwer.com
Website: lrus.wolterskluwer.com

Sold and distributed in North, Central and South America by:
Wolters Kluwer Legal & Regulatory U.S.
7201 McKinney Circle
Frederick, MD 21704
United States of America
Email: customer.service@wolterskluwer.com

Sold and distributed in all other countries by:
Air Business Subscriptions
Rockwood House
Haywards Heath
West Sussex
RH16 3DH
United Kingdom
Email: international-customerservice@wolterskluwer.com

ISBN 978-90-411-9097-0

e-Book: 978-90-411-9113-7
web-PDF: 978-90-411-9112-0

Summary of Contents

Legislation on get-up and plain packaging of cigarettes were challenged in various fora, one of them being ISDS in the context of bilateral investment agreements. The chapter highlights the cases that were brought in this context, and analyses the critique that investors by suing sovereign states were undermining legislation in the field of health or consumer protection.

Australia's Tobacco Plain Packaging legislation was also challenged under the WTO Dispute Settlement System. Five WTO Members brought disputes against Australia's measures alleging inconsistency with the WTO TBT and TRIPS Agreements. This chapter summarises selected IP-related findings from the Panel report circulated in June 2018, some of which have been appealed and are pending before the WTO Appellate Body.

This final chapter analyses the cases brought against plain packaging legislation before the Australian and English courts based on an alleged expropriation of trade mark rights and goodwill.

Preface

When a couple of years ago, intellectual property laws had their first brush with investor-state dispute settlement, the encounter was not considered a particularly welcome one: intellectual property laws operated on the principles of national treatment, transparency (*patere*, Latin for: stay or remain open) and judicial expertise, while ISDS was a specific mechanism open only to foreign investors operating in secret by panels of trade lawyers chosen ad hoc. Unsurprisingly, experts in the field of international trade, and those in the field of intellectual property law that contributed to this book held widely differing views on the merits of ISDS, and whether intellectual property rights should be included as "investments" in bilateral and multilateral investment treaties that envisaged such form of dispute settlement.

Undoubtedly, however, the high profile cases concerning plain packaging laws for tobacco products, and the *Eli Lilly v. Canada* case in the context of NAFTA, have stirred a wider debate on the appropriateness of ISDS particularly amongst developed nations. Trade negotiations of the EU with Canada for the CETA Agreement and with the US for TTIP were accompanied by significant public concerns that foreign investors via ISDS would be allowed to run roughshod over European standards for protecting health, consumers and the environment.

The contributions of this book highlight the different mechanisms of international dispute settlement having particular regard to cases involving intellectual property laws.

The editors gratefully acknowledge the continuing support of the Institute of European Studies (IEEM) in Macao and its president Dr. Sales Marques in the publication of the IEEM Series on Intellectual Property Law.

The Editors

Table of Contents

PART I: GIVING EFFECT TO INTERNATIONAL TRADE AGREEMENTS – HISTORY AND PROCEDURE

About the Authors and Editors

Iveta Alexovičová (1973) is Assistant Professor of International Economic Law at Maastricht University, the Netherlands, focusing predominantly on international trade and investment law. She is a member of the Ius Commune Research School, a fellow of the Institute for Globalisation and International Regulation at Maastricht University and a non-resident fellow at the World Trade Institute in Bern, Switzerland. Since January 2018, Iveta acts as Associate Editor of the International Journal of Public Law and Policy. Iveta holds an LL.M. from Comenius University in Bratislava, Slovak Republic, an LL.M. from Maastricht University, a JUDr. from Charles' University in Prague, Czech Republic and a Ph.D. from Maastricht University. Her previous working experience is both in public service and private sector and includes also various capacity building activities and research projects.

Iveta can be reached by email at i.alexovicova@maastrichtuniversity.nl.

Shahla Ali is Professor and Associate Dean (International) and Deputy Director of the LLM in Arbitration and Dispute Resolution at the Faculty of Law of the University of Hong Kong. Her research and practice centre on questions of governance, development and the resolution of cross-border disputes in the Asia Pacific region. Shahla is the author of *Court Mediation Reform* (Edward Elgar, 2018), *Governing Disasters: Engaging Local Populations in Humanitarian Relief* (CUP, 2016); *Consumer Financial Dispute Resolution in a Comparative Context* (CUP, 2013) and *Resolving Disputes in the Asia Pacific Region* (Routledge, 2010) and writes for law journals in the area of comparative ADR. She has consulted with USAID, IFC/World Bank and the United Nations on issues pertaining to access to justice, peace process negotiation training and land use conflict resolution. She serves as a bilingual arbitrator (English/Chinese) with CIETAC, HKIAC (ADNDRC), SIAC and has served on the IBA Drafting Committee for Investor-State Mediation Rules, the DOJ Mediation Regulatory Committee, the UN Mediation Roster and the FDRC Appointments Committee. Prior to HKU, she worked as an international trade attorney with Baker & McKenzie in its SF office. She received her JD and PhD from UC Berkeley and BA from Stanford University.

Robert Burrell (1973) is Professor of Intellectual Property and Information Technology Law at the University of Oxford and Professor of Law at Melbourne Law School. His previous academic positions include posts at the University of Sheffield, King's College London and the Australian National University. Outside of the academy Robert spent several years working as a registered trade marks attorney and he still consults regularly with Go Trademarks, Brisbane.

Julien Chaisse (1976) is Professor at the City University of Hong Kong, School of Law. He is an award-winning scholar of international law with a focus on the regulation and development of economic globalization. His teaching and research include international trade/investment law, international taxation, international arbitration, and Internet law. Dr. Chaisse has over 15 years teaching experience at universities mainly in Hong Kong, US, and Europe. Dr. Chaisse served as a senior fellow at the World Trade Institute (Switzerland), and as a diplomat for the Embassy of France in New Delhi (India).

Dr. Chaisse has published numerous well-regarded and widely cited books and articles, such as *China's International Investment Strategy* (Oxford University Press, (2019); *The Future of Asian Trade Deals and IP* (Hart, 2019); *International Economic Law and Governance* (Oxford University Press, 2016); 'Maintaining the WTO's Supremacy in the International Trade Order', *Journal of International Economic Law* (2013); and 'Promises and Pitfalls of the European Union Policy on Foreign Investment', *Journal of International Economic Law* (2012).

Dr. Chaisse is also an experienced arbitrator and a sought-after consultant/expert to international organizations, governments, multinational law firms, and private investors. Dr. Chaisse is also an active member of the World Economic Forum (Global Future Council on International Trade and Investment and Tax and Globalization Working Group). He serves as Advisory Board member of the Asian Academy of International Law (AAIL), Director of the Dot Trademark Policy Committee (DTPC), co-founder of the Internet Intellectual Property Institute (IIPI), and he is an active member of the Internet Corporation for Assigned Names and Numbers (ICANN) in which Dr. Chaisse serves on the Working Group on gTLDs' rights protection mechanisms review and the Accountability and Transparency Review program.

Daniel Gervais is the Milton R. Underwood Chair in Law at Vanderbilt University Law School and Director of the Vanderbilt Intellectual Property Program. In 2017–2019, he served as President of the International Association for the Advancement of Teaching and Research in Intellectual Property (ATRIP). He is also "Professor II" at the University of Oslo as part of a research team on the legal aspects of the data economy. In 2018–2019, he held a Chair in Information Law at the University of Amsterdam. Prior to joining Vanderbilt, he was a Full professor and the Acting Dean at the Faculty of Law of the University of Ottawa (Common Law Section). Before he joined the Academy, Prof. Gervais was Legal Officer at the GATT (now WTO); Head of Section at WIPO; and Vice-President of Copyright Clearance Center, Inc. (CCC). In 2012, he was elected to the Academy of Europe. He is a member of the American Law Institute where he serves as Associate Reporter on the restatement of the Law, Copyright project. He studied law at McGill University, the University of Montreal, the Graduate Institute in Geneva, and at the University of Nantes (PhD).

Christopher Heath (1964) studied law at the Universities of Konstanz, Edinburgh and the LSE. He lived and worked in Japan for three years, and between 1992 and 2005 headed the Asian Department of the Max Planck Institute for Patent, Copyright and Competition Law in Munich. Christopher Heath, who wrote his Ph.D. thesis on Japanese unfair competition prevention law, is a Member of the Boards of Appeal at the European Patent Office in Munich.

He can be reached by e-mail at blitzblitzblau@web.de.

Anselm Kamperman Sanders (1968) is Professor of Intellectual Property Law, Director of the Advanced Masters Intellectual Property Law and Knowledge Management (IPKM LL.M/MSc), and Academic Director of the Institute for Globalization and International Regulation (IGIR) at Maastricht University, the Netherlands.

He acts as Academic Co-director of the Annual Intellectual Property Law School and IP Seminar of the Institute for European Studies of Macau (IEEM), Macau SAR, China and is Adjunct Professor at Jinan University Law School, Guangzhou, China.

Anselm holds a Ph.D. from the Centre for Commercial Law Studies, Queen Mary, University of London, where he worked as a Marie Curie Fellow before joining Maastricht University in 1995. He is a member of the European Commission expert group on development and implications of patent law in the field of biotechnology and genetic engineering.

He can be reached by e-mail at a.kampermansanders@maastrichtuniversity.nl.

Flavia Marisi (1987) is Associate at Hanotiau & van den Berg. She is an Italian-qualified lawyer, and worked at the Court of Justice of the European Union, the European Commission, national and international law firms, the Chinese University of Hong Kong, and an environmental NGO. She lectured at different Universities across Europe and Asia, and holds a Ph.D. in Law from Ghent University, an LL.M. from the College of Europe, and a Master of Laws from the University of Milan. Her research interests include International Investment Law, International Litigation and Arbitration, Intellectual Property, Environmental Law, Comparative Civil Procedure, European Union Law, and Theory of Law.

Wolf Meier-Ewert (1969) is Counsellor in the Intellectual Property, Government Procurement and Competition Division of the World Trade Organization (WTO) Secretariat, which is responsible for the administration of the Agreement on Trade-related Aspects of Intellectual Property Rights (TRIPS Agreement). In this capacity he gives legal advice in relation to Intellectual Property and the TRIPS Agreement to Members and Observers of the WTO and assists panels with TRIPS-related dispute settlement cases among WTO Members. He serves as the Secretary to the Council for TRIPS and the negotiating group dealing with TRIPS negotiations under the Doha Round.

Mr. Meier-Ewert is a graduate of the University of Oxford, UK where he studied Politics, Philosophy and Economics (PPE) and holds a Law degree from the Ludwig-Maximilian University in Munich, Germany. Mr. Meier-Ewert was also a researcher at the Max-Planck-Institute for Innovation and Competition in Munich, Germany where he concentrated on copyright law and private international law. He has widely lectured on TRIPS and WTO-related matters.

Wilson Mbugua is a Doctoral Candidate in Law, University of Hong Kong. His research focuses on the current reforms of Bilateral Investment Treaties to safeguard states' right to regulate the environment. Mbugua holds a Master of Laws (LL.M.) from Stockholm University and a Bachelor of Laws (LL.B.) from the University of Nairobi. Mbugua is a qualified advocate of the High Court of Kenya where he previously practiced law. He can be reached by email at juridical25@gmail.com.

Jens Hillebrand Pohl is a doctoral researcher and lecturer in the Department of International and European Law at Maastricht University, the Netherlands, and a Fellow of the Institute for Globalization and International Regulation (IGIR). He is also a practising lawyer qualified in New York, England and Ireland. He worked as a law firm associate in New York for four years, where he was involved in insolvency litigation relating to the Lehman Brothers bankruptcy, and, between 2011 and 2013, he advised EU institutions in connection with the European sovereign debt crisis, including as a seconded expert to the European Financial Stability Facility (EFSF). He holds an LL.M. from Harvard Law School.

Peter Yu is Professor of Law, Professor of Communication and Director of the Center for Law and Intellectual Property at Texas A&M University. Born and raised in Hong Kong, he previously held the Kern Family Chair in Intellectual Property Law at Drake University Law School and was Wenlan Scholar Chair Professor at Zhongnan University of Economics and Law in Wuhan, China. He served as a visiting professor of law at Bocconi University, Hanken School of Economics, Hokkaido University, the University of Haifa, the University of Helsinki, the University of Hong Kong and the University of Strasbourg.

CHAPTER 1

Investor State Dispute Settlement (ISDS) in the Field of Intellectual Property Law and Beyond

Christopher Heath and Anselm Kamperman Sanders

A. INVESTOR STATE LITIGATION AS A CONCEPT OF DISPUTE SETTLEMENT

It is interesting to note that intellectual property lawyers, those who have contributed to this book, just as others, overwhelmingly find it appalling that private investors should be entitled to sue a state behind closed doors, before an ad hoc tribunal of three arbiters of doubtful independence and little idea of the finer points of IP, with no possibility of appeal and with potentially devastating consequences for the state in question. In other words, a state being held hostage and (if bad comes to worse) convicted by three blind men on a donkey. In the ISDS proceedings addressed in this volume, against Australia, Canada and Uruguay, it did not go that far: The state may have been held hostage ("chilling effect", see below), yet ultimately found not liable.

Still, for many experts in international trade law, no such qualms against Investor State Dispute Settlement seem to exist, as is evidenced by the following two chapters in this book, just as regular publications[1] of a small expert group of

1. A journal exclusively dedicated to international arbitration is Transnational Dispute Management (journal) (< www.transnational-dispute-management.com >) (TDM) that already back in 2009 featured a special issue on "The Protection of Intellectual Property Rights through International Investment Agreements" with the following contributions: L. Liberti, Intellectual Property Rights in International Investment Agreements; R.A. Lavery, Coverage of Intellectual Property Rights in International Investment Agreements; V.S. Vadi, Mapping Unchartered Waters: Intellectual Property Disputes with Public Health Elements in Investor-State Arbitration; C.S. Gibson, A Look at the Compulsory License in Investment Arbitration: The Case of Indirect Expropriation; J.D. Mortenson, Intellectual Property as

lawyers perhaps regularly involved in arbitration, be it as counsel or arbitrator.[2] International trade lawyers point to the long tradition of ISDS clauses in international investment agreements and to the fact that otherwise, arbitrary decisions of states frustrating foreign investment could not be remedied.[3] They also point to the fact that outside the controversial field of intellectual property law, ISDS has worked relatively satisfactorily.[4] From the perspective of an investor, "the private investor's chief aim regarding its IP based investment [is] to utilize a new, direct means available through investor-state arbitration for seeking international enforcement of its intellectual property rights".[5]

In most of the publications cited above (perhaps with the exception of Hainbach, *supra* note 1), fundamental critique of the ISDS system is absent. And yet, the ISDS proceedings concerning tobacco packaging seem to have changed something. As the Director General of the WHO, Margaret Chan, observed, "[i]n my view, something is fundamentally wrong in this world when a corporation can challenge government policies introduced to protect the public from a product that kills".[6] A UN Report of

---

Transnational Investment; R. Castro Bernieri, Compulsory Licensing and Public Health: TRIPS-Plus Standards in Investment Agreements; C. Correa, Intellectual Property Rights as Investment: Options for Developing Countries; B. White and R. Szczepanik, Remedies Available under Bilateral Investment Treaties for Breach of Intellectual Property Rights; M. Seelig, Can Patent Revocation or Invalidation Constitute a Form of Expropriation?; M. Perkams and J. Hosking, The Protection of Intellectual Property Rights through International Investment Agreements; A. Anderson and B. Razavi, International Standards for Protection of Intellectual Property Rights Post-TRIPS. A further issue of this journal in 2012 is dedicated to the tobacco plain packaging disputes: P. Henning and L. Shmatenko, Plain Packaging on its Way to Europe; B. McGrady, TRIPS and Trademarks: The Case of Tobacco; id., Revisiting TRIPS and Trademarks: The Case of Tobacco. Further articles: T. Campbell, S. Nappert and L. Nottage, Assessing Treaty-based Investor-State Dispute Settlement (January 2014); UNCTAD, Recent Developments in Investor-State Dispute Settlement (ISDS) (June 2014); March 2016 special issue on CETA: P. Hainbach, The EU's Approach to Investor-State Arbitration in CETA; U. Kriebaum, FET and Expropriation in CETA; R. Cafari Panico and F. Di Benedetto, Recent Developments in the Most Controversial Aspects of EU International Investment Agreements; S. Hindelang, Study on Investor-State Dispute Settlement (ISDS) and Alternatives to Dispute Resolution in International Investment Law. For an in-depth academic analysis of IP and ISDS, the reader may wish to consult S. Klopschinski, Der Schutz geistigen Eigentums durch völkerrechtliche Investitionsverträge, Carl Heymanns 2011.

2. E.g. Gary Born, the arbitrator nominated by Philipp Morris in the ISDS dispute against Uruguay, is one of the leading commentators in this field: Gary B. Born, *International Arbitration: Law and Practice* (Kluwer Law International, Alphen aan den Rijn 2012).
3. See chapters 2 and 3 of this book, and Hindelang, *supra* note 1.
4. L. Nottage and A. Ubilava, Costs, 'Outcomes and Transparency in ISDS Arbitrations: Evidence for an Investment Treaty Parliamentary Inquiry (6 August 2018)', 21 (4) *International Arbitration Law Review* (2018); Sydney Law School Research Paper No. 18/46. Available at SSRN: < ssrn.com/abstract = 3227401 >.
5. Gibson, *supra* note 1, 53/54.
6. Margaret Chan, 'The Changed Face of the Tobacco Industry' (Speech delivered at the 15th World Conference of Tobacco and Health, Singapore, 20 March 2012) < www.who.int/dg/speeches/2012/tobacco_20120320/en/ >.

14 July 2015 presented by Alfred-Maurice de Zayas finds fundamental flaws in the system as such:[7]

> 5. Many observers have expressed concern about certain investor–State dispute settlement arbitrations that have effectively overridden the State's fulfilment of its function to regulate domestic labour, health and environmental policies, and have had adverse human rights impacts, also on third parties, including a "chilling effect" with regard to the exercise of democratic governance. Arbitration tribunals are credible institutions only when they operate in a demonstrably independent, transparent and accountable manner, as required under article 14 (1) of the International Covenant on Civil and Political Rights concerning suits at law. Investor–State dispute settlement tribunals do not operate in a separate legal context, but are bound by the *erga omnes* obligations imposed by the international human rights regime,[8] which permeates all areas of human activity, including by non-State actors. Some observers consider certain arbitration awards frivolous and manifestly ill-founded, yet not appealable....
>
> 15. Among the major threats to a democratic and equitable international order is the operation of arbitral tribunals that act as if they were above the international human rights regime. Investor–State dispute settlement tribunals are made up of corporate arbitrators whose independence has been repeatedly questioned because of conflicts of interest.[9] Admittedly, corporate arbitrators are not natural guardians of the public interest, but of business interests and of a new "industry" that, as experience shows, has privileged investors over the public. The investor–State dispute settlement system entails a completely separate system of dispute settlement, not only outside the domestic court system, but above it, and without appeal. The mind reverts to Juvenal's question *quis custodiet ipsos custodes*? ("who guards the guardians?"). Can a democracy call itself democratic if it allows the creation of separate, non-transparent and non-accountable systems of dispute settlement?
>
> 16. Observers question the legitimacy of tribunals where the investor can sue the State but not vice versa.[10] Interpretations of terms such as "investment",

7. Maurice de Zayas, < www.ohchr.org/EN/HRBodies/HRC/RegularSessions/Session30/_layouts/15/WopiFrame.aspx?sourcedoc = /EN/HRBodies/HRC/RegularSessions/Session30/Documents/A_HRC_30_44_ENG.docx&action = default&DefaultItemOpen = 1 > .
8. Bruno Simma and Theodore Kill, 'Harmonizing investment protection and human rights: first steps towards a methodology', in Christina Binder *et al.* (eds.), *International Investment Law for the 21st Century: Essays in Honour of Christoph Schreuer* (Oxford University Press, 2009).
9. See Pia Eberhardt and Cecilia Olivet, *Profiting from Injustice: How Law Firms, Arbitrators and Financiers are Fuelling an Investment Arbitration Boom* (Corporate Europe Observatory, Brussels, 2012), available from < www.tni.org/sites/www.tni.org/files/download/profitingfrominjustice.pdf > ; < acta.ffii.org/?p = 2118; corporateeurope.org/sites/default/files/annex-2-still-not-loving-isds.pdf > ; < corporateeurope.org/international-trade/2014/07/commission-isds-reform-plan-echo-chamber-business-views > ; < www.bilaterals.org/?investor-to-state-dispute > ; and < www.italaw.com/sites/default/files/case-documents/ita0221.pdf > .
10. See John Hendy, 'A threat to the sovereignty of courts and parliaments', 128 *Graya* (2015), 52–56.

"expropriation" and "fair and equal treatment" have been expansive and difficult to reconcile with the interpretation rules under articles 31 and 32 of the Vienna Convention on the Law of Treaties. Experience shows that arbitrators interpret international investment agreements without human rights or environmental constraints. Their procedures are not transparent and it is not even known how many arbitrations have actually taken place, because most of them are not published. What becomes apparent is the strong business bias of the arbitrators and their feeling of being immune to general principles of law. In a 2012 report, UNCTAD noted that an "expansive interpretation of minimalist treaty language can give rise to a lack of predictability in the application of the standard. This, in turn, may lead to the undermining of legitimate State intervention for economic, social, environmental and other development ends".[11]

17. Spanish arbitrator Fernández-Armesto notes: "When I wake up at night and think about arbitration, it never ceases to amaze me that sovereign states have agreed to investment arbitration at all … Three private individuals are entrusted with the power to review, without any restriction or appeal procedure, all actions of the government, all decisions of the courts, and all laws and regulations emanating from parliament."[12] Indeed, it is disturbing that arbitrators can disregard basic principles such as respect for the "margin of discretion" of States, State legislation and even the judicial pronouncements of the highest domestic courts. The one-way street of investor protection has not contributed to a culture of investor–State cooperation but fuelled an aggressive tendency to litigate and demonstrably generated a "regulatory chill". Arbitration may take place in Washington under the auspices of the World Bank's ICSID, but there is a worrisome degree of forum-shopping, and tribunals may meet before the London Court of International Arbitration, the International Chamber of Commerce, the Stockholm Chamber of Commerce, the Hong Kong International Arbitration Centre or the United Nations Commission on International Trade Law (UNCITRAL). There is a growing number of arbitrations that privilege profit over human rights.[13] According to UNCTAD, many investor–State dispute settlement arbitrations are completely confidential and information is available only regarding some 608 awards.[14]

As is evident from the quote above, the criticism of the ISDS system may not come directly from within the profession of ISDS specialists, but even arbitrators themselves seem to be amazed at the willingness of sovereign states to have their freedom to act curtailed by a group of private individuals that are no more accountable than by the possibility that they may not be nominated to sit in arbitration of a future dispute.

11. *Fair and Equitable Treatment* (United Nations publication, Sales No. E.11.II.D.15), 2.
12. < www.theguardian.com/commentisfree/2013/nov/04/us-trade-deal-full-frontal-assault-on-democracy >.
13. European Centre for Constitutional and Human Rights, 'Human rights inapplicable in international investment arbitration?', available from < www.ecchr.de/worldbank/articles/human-rights-inapplicable-in-international-investment-arbitration.html >.
14. UNCTAD, *IIA Issues Note*, No. 1 (February 2015), available from < unctad.org/en/PublicationsLibrary/webdiaepcb2015d1_en.pdf >.

B. IP AND ISDS

It is certainly correct that our misgivings, and perhaps those of many other IP lawyers, first of all stem from the arbitrability of intellectual property law in the context of free trade agreements. Three arguments speak against IP issues being made subject to ISDS.

I. National Treatment

First, the historical development of intellectual property law based upon the Paris and Berne Conventions and the principle of national treatment as a cornerstone thereof. The notion that intellectual property rights can be obtained and enforced by nationals and foreigners without discrimination is part of IP law's DNA since 1883 or 1886.[15] While an outright expropriation of intellectual property rights has occurred in the context of wars and/or wartime reparations (e.g. the trade mark "Merck" that pre-was was German owned and is now of different ownership in different countries), in peacetime, the discrimination of foreigners in the context of international patent law occurs at a level of sophistication that defies blunt allegations of iniquity: Rules may be introduced that de facto disfavour foreign applicants,[16] but this is where it stops. In other words, in the field of intellectual property law, there is very little that would indicate that foreigners could be jeopardised by unequal or discriminatory treatment and for this reason should have judicial recourses not open to domestic IP owners.

II. Definition of Investment, Expropriation and Legitimate Expectations

Although mentioned as one form of property in many investment agreements, intellectual property becomes a difficult concept when trying to define it in terms of unjustly denied investment. This is due to three reasons.

First, the right as such, even including the efforts to obtain it, under the jurisdiction clause of the ICSID Convention does not qualify as an investment:

> In order to speak of an investment according to the ICSID convention,[17] the foreign investor must have provided a substantive amount of capital or other resources. This can be for example know how that the investor has used in the context of a project.

---

15. Art. 2(1) Paris Convention, Art. 5(1) Berne Convention.
16. C. Heath, 'National Treatment under the Paris Convention', in Kamperman Sanders (ed.), *The Principle of National Treatment in International Economic Law* (Edward Elgar 2014), 223–247.
17. The ICSID Convention in Art. 25 establishes jurisdiction over disputes related to an investment. The interpretation of this term in the context of this Convention may not necessarily correspond to the definition as set out in the BIT, yet is persuasive where the dispute resolution agreed upon falls within the ambit of the Convention. In fact, as is further explained in chapter 2, most dispute resolution proceedings are conducted in accordance with the ICSID Convention, or the UNCITRAL Rules.

> It follows from the dispute settlement case law for Art. 25 (1) ICSID Convention[18] that investments according to the ICSID Convention are complex endeavours with which a certain purpose is pursued. Capital and other resources are but one aspect of such investment and not the investment in itself. Particularly the reading of the dispute *Consorzio Groupment LESI – Dipenta (Italy) v. Algeria* goes in this direction when it states that one could speak of a substantial contribution only when the foreign investor had incurred costs in order to pursue an economic goal. In this case, the investor had used substantial sums of money in order to meet its contractual obligation for the construction of a dike. This contract, and not the capital that was used, was considered the investment under Art. 25 (1) ICSID. The same was held in the case Salini v. Morocco where the Italian investor contributed inter alia his know how for a road building project in order to fulfil a contraction obligation with the Moroccan government. Here, the contract for building a road rather than the know how of the investor was the investment according to Art. 25 (1) ICSID Convention.
>
> In addition, the term "commitment" has a certain finality, in other words, "something is committed for a certain purpose". This becomes even clearer with the term "contribution" that is also used in Art. 25 (1) ICSID.
>
> Where an investor in a certain country owns only intellectual property rights without pursuing a specific project, these objects are no commitment for specific purpose. Properties of the investor are a constituting element of an investment: but in itself, they do not qualify as an investment under Art. 25 (1) ICSID Convention.[19]

In other words, not the IP right represents the investment, but only a specific purpose to be pursued on the basis thereof, e.g. a production facility, a distribution and service network, etc. In the context of intellectual property rights, this is a sensible qualification because it ties the definition of investment to the interests of the host country in local production and commitment.[20]

By way of example, one could think of the case where a foreign investor owns a pharmaceutical patent, yet has set up no local production and only serves the market with (rather expensive) imports. The host state after five years imposes a compulsory licence in favour of a local producer. Under the Paris Convention, this would be acceptable (Art. 5(2)), under TRIPS, discrimination between importation and local production is not permitted (Art. 27), and whether pricing policies of the patentee make the products unavailable to the domestic market would have to be discussed under Art. 31 TRIPS. Yet, frustration of investment under a BIT could

---

18. Art. 25 (1) The jurisdiction of the Centre shall extend to any legal dispute arising directly out of an investment, between a Contracting State (or any constituent subdivision or agency of a Contracting State designated to the Centre by that State) and a national of another Contracting State, which the parties to the dispute consent in writing to submit to the Centre. When the parties have given their consent, no party may withdraw its consent unilaterally.
19. Klopschinski, *supra* note 1, 233, 234.
20. The investment in research and development in order to obtain the right in question (e.g. a patent) cannot qualify when undertaken abroad, and would in any event not be frustrated by denying the patent right locally, because such denial does not impede the right to obtain the patent elsewhere, Art. 4bis Paris Convention.

arguably be not invoked because in the absence of any local production facilities, there is no investment in the first place.

As to trade marks, the investment at issue cannot be the registered mark as such, but only the goodwill the trade mark owner builds up on the basis of such mark, as is pointed out by Robert Burrell in chapter 11 of this book. As to copyright, the investment at issue cannot be the exclusive right as such, but only distribution and service networks (e.g. cinema or software, etc.), or touring, local performance and production (e.g. musical and stage performance, studio or film production and recording, etc.).

The above demonstrates that the link between IP and investment is more complicated than in the case of other proprietary interests.[21]

Second, "expropriation" in the IP field is part of the wear and tear, and often a question of degree.

To take the case of patents: A patent is a right to exclude others. The grant of a compulsory licence is considered by some to be a "taking", as it would allow a third party to use the patent without the patentee's consent.[22] Yet the result is the same when a court refuses to grant injunctive relief against an infringer (e.g. because the patent belongs to a standard, because the patentee did not use the patented technology, or for other reasons). Depending on the jurisdiction, injunctive relief is a right or an equitable remedy. While the label "compulsory licence" has stirred up emotions for more than a century,[23] refusing injunctive relief in some cases has been accepted without much controversy.[24] Both, however, amount to the same thing. The

21. To what extent the above definition of investment is persuasive in other contexts, is an open question, though, in the Canada EU Trade Agreement (CETA) that envisages a different dispute settlement mechanism (see below), the definition of investment is extremely broad: Under Article 8.1 of the CETA, the concept of "investment", for the purposes of that agreement, means:

   "... every kind of asset that an investor owns or controls, directly or indirectly, that has the characteristics of an investment, which includes a certain duration and other characteristics such as the commitment of capital or other resources, the expectation of gain or profit, or the assumption of risk. Forms that an investment may take include:
   (a) an enterprise;
   (b) shares, stocks and other forms of equity participation in an enterprise;
   (c) bonds, debentures and other debt instruments of an enterprise;
   (d) a loan to an enterprise;
   (e) any other kind of interest in an enterprise;
   (f) an interest arising from [certain contracts];
   (g) intellectual property rights;
   (h) other moveable property, tangible or intangible, or immovable property and related rights;
   (i) claims to money or claims to performance under a contract."

22. See the article by Gibson, *supra* note 1.
23. In fact, a good deal of the Lisbon Conference for revising the Paris Convention was dedicated to this issue: S. Ladas, *Patents, Trademarks and Related Rights* (Cambridge Mass. 1975), 320 et seq.
24. Namely in the case of standard essential patents, see e.g. the decisions of the Japanese IP High Court, 16 May 2014, *FRAND Declaration*; US CAFC, *Apple Inc. v. Motorola, Inc.*, 757 F.3d 1286 (Fed. Cir. 2014), CJEU, 16 July 2015, case C-170/13, *Huawei v. ZTE*.

patentee's monopoly can also be dented in other ways: Delays in the grant of a patent (a patent application normally does not give a right to exclude), lengthy infringement proceedings, de facto denial of interim injunctions, etc. – so, when is an exclusive right no longer an exclusive right? A further, but related difficulty is the fact that a specific product is often based on more than one, in the sector of telecommunication and electronics on hundreds or thousands of patents, making the causal link between an individual patent and the marketing of a specific product (or the possibility of excluding others from marketing a competing one) difficult to establish.

In the case of trade marks, the issue of limitations to the use of the mark was extensively discussed in the plain packaging cases. To the extent that the trade mark right is a right that allows the owner to prohibit third parties to use the mark under certain circumstances, there is no case for any expropriation or frustration of investment: The trade mark owner can still prohibit others from using the mark. Yet if the function of a mark is seen in the power to attract customers,[25] or to advertise under the mark, the result may change. In the tobacco cases, the most preferable approach in the context of frustrated investment might have been to analyse whether the measures affected the *goodwill* of the trade mark owner (as Robert Burrell correctly points out in chapter 11 of this book), as only this should be considered the investment.

In addition, intellectual property rights have limits to their scope intrinsic by their function (e.g. exhaustion in the case of patents, non-confusing use in the case of trade marks) or extraneous thereto, e.g. due to considerations of anti-trust: A compulsory licence may be granted under patent law, e.g. for dependent patents, for employee inventors or for prior users, or in light of marketing considerations (abuse of a monopolistic position by patent pooling, or standard-essential patents).

Third, it follows from the above that a definition of frustration of expectations is particularly hard to come by in the IP field. In the *Eli Lilly v. Canada* case (for details, see chapter 8 of this book), the plaintiff/investor based its case on an allegation of state wrongdoing due to the unforeseen change in judicial interpretation of the requirements for sufficient disclosure of an invention. This leads to another specific of intellectual property law: Its justification, foundations, exceptions, scope and limits are far less cast in stone than for real property, and have always been subject to changes in interpretation: It is by no means certain that a patent granted in one country will be granted elsewhere, sufficiency of disclosure being only one of the requirements of patentability; definition and interpretation of technicity, *ordre public*, sufficiency, inventive step and added subject matter have always been subject to change and debate, as have the interpretation of the patented scope (e.g. doctrine of equivalents), the types of infringement (e.g. indirect infringement) and the exceptions (clinical trials, exhaustion). In the field of trade marks, one could point to the rather uncertain issue of protection beyond confusion, in the field of copyrights to the definition of limitations, etc. Changes in jurisprudence in these areas are not infrequent (as was indeed mentioned in the *Eli Lilly v. Canada* dispute with particular reference to the US Supreme Court) and can hardly create legitimate expectations

25. See the discussion in the CJEU case C 129/17 of 25 July 2018 where the court affirmed such additional functions, while other jurisdictions might be more reluctant to do so.

in this field. Particularly in the field of patents, rates of refusals of application or subsequent revocation (with retroactive effect) are beyond 50%, which not only speaks against any expectation that a patent application can indeed be considered a good title for subsequent enforcement against third parties, but also highlights the uncertain nature of intellectual property rights in general.[26]

In her PhD thesis, Aline Larroyed mentions the case of a pipeline patent for Efavirenz for which the Brazilian government issued a compulsory licence, yet it turned out that

> [d]espite having access to all patent information, they were not successful. The active ingredient was finally imported from India, which allowed the manufacture of the drug in Brazil.
>
> Although the reason why India was able to reproduce the active ingredient was its better experience in the production of these substances, if the sufficiency of disclosure is addressed to the person skilled in the art, it is possible to conclude that the content of the patent was not sufficiently disclosed as a detailed description of at least one way of carrying out the invention must be given ... to the person skilled in the art.[27]

In such case, the patent should be revoked in Brazil due to an insufficient disclosure despite the fact that the disclosure might be considered sufficient in other jurisdictions. Yet due to the territorial nature of patents, there cannot be a legitimate expectation that grant of a patent in one country should lead to the grant in other countries as well.

In the field of trade marks, foreign applicants often have inflated perceptions of their mark's recognition abroad, face uncertainties about the scope of rights due to linguistics or face revocation due to non-use in certain or all classes.[28] In other words, IP owners must live with a far higher degree of uncertainty regarding their title than owners of other types of property.

It is for the reasons above that the line between investor frustration that under an investment treaty would allow for a claim of compensation, and inherent limits of the intellectual property system are hard to draw and defy the rather black and white context of traditional cases of expropriation.

---

26. "Even though there are significant differences in national enforcement practice, the general picture is that patentees rarely stand a better-than-even chance of a court finding their patents valid and infringed. High invalidation rates upon review by the patent offices and the courts add a degree of legal uncertainty that in other fields of law would be considered unacceptable": Christopher Heath (ed.), *Patent Enforcement Worldwide* (3rd. edn., 2015), Preface, vii.
27. Aline Larroyed, *Translation Accuracy and Dissemination of Disclosure of Patent Information: An Analysis of Translation and its Influence on Patent Law* (PhD thesis, Maastricht, forthcoming), 183.
28. Only by way of example, one could point to the revocation of the mark McDonald's trade mark "Big Mac" by the European Trade Mark Office (EUIPO) for failure to prove use: Decision of 15 January 2019 (Cancellation No 14 788 C), not yet final.

III. Procedure and Expertise

And it is also for the above reasons that many countries have now set up specialised courts to deal with matters of intellectual property law in the context of the domestic legal order. Not only are such courts better equipped to deal with the finer points of intellectual property law, but they can (and must) also take into account extraneous limits to IP rights, namely issues of competition, health and environmental protection. In this context, particularly Bronckers[29] has advocated that domestic courts should be in a position to give direct effect to the obligations arising under international agreements in order to ensure investor protection in accordance with a state's international obligations, avoid the procedural shortcomings of ISDS and the discrimination of domestic operators. Chapter 5 of this book deals with this approach in more detail and ultimately finds it unwieldly, highly fact-specific and unduly interfering with the domestic legal order.

C. CONCERNS OF ISDS BEYOND IP

I. Chilling Effect

Particularly in regard of ISDS procedures where state measures are based on health or environmental concerns, a chilling effect of such proceedings has been denounced. De Zayas in the UN Report (*supra* note 7) notes the following:

> 5. Many observers have expressed concern about certain investor–State dispute settlement arbitrations that have effectively overridden the State's fulfilment of its function to regulate domestic labour, health and environmental policies, and have had adverse human rights impacts, also on third parties, including a "chilling effect" with regard to the exercise of democratic governance... 8. International investment agreements are not new phenomena in the international arena. Bilateral investment treaties currently number over 3,200. After years of experience with investor–State dispute settlement, the International Centre for Settlement of Investment Disputes (ICSID) and other arbitrations, it has become apparent that the regulatory function of many States and their ability to legislate in the public interest have been compromised. The problem has been aggravated by the chilling effect of certain awards that have penalized States for adopting regulations to protect the environment, food safety, access to generic medicine and reduction of smoking, as required under the WHO Framework Convention on Tobacco Control. The legality of such awards is questionable as contrary to domestic and international *ordre public*, and may be considered, in some cases, *contra bonos mores*.

In cases where states consider legislation in the field of public health or environmental protection, this almost inevitably limits the chances of private market players in unfettered profits, as it entails higher costs and/or limitations to manufacture and marketing. Already the threat of a protracted investor-state litigation with an uncertain

29. M. Bronckers, 'Is Investor-State Dispute Settlement (ISDS) Superior to Litigation before Domestic Courts?', *Journal of International Economic Law* (2015), 655.

outcome may very well scare off smaller countries considering such measures. Given the length of time it took the panel in the *Philip Morris v. Uruguay* dispute to come up with a decision (six years), the plaintiff may have won far more in scaring other countries than it lost in litigation costs.[30]

II. Too Many Bites of the Cherry

As ISDS is an avenue that foreign investors can pursue independently from remedies under the domestic legal order of the host state, the mechanism in effect leads to a discrimination of domestic investors and to several chances of recouping lost investment by way of damages. The Ely Lilly case of Canada (for details, see chapter 8 in this book), and the Vattenfall case in Germany are good examples.

In Ely Lilly, a case brought under NAFTA, Ely Lilly was unhappy with the revocation of two of its patents by the Canadian Supreme Court and argued that the court had misapplied the law in an unforeseeable manner, thereby frustrating investment. The tribunal was essentially asked to act as a further tier of appeal and to review the decision of the Canadian Supreme Court.

Vattenfall is a Swedish energy conglomerate that used ISDS already twice against Germany. According to de Zayas:

> 23. In 2009, the Swedish energy conglomerate Vattenfall sued Germany under the Energy Charter Treaty, demanding 1.4 billion euros in compensation for environmental measures restricting the use and discharge of cooling water into the River Elbe. Only after Germany agreed to lower its environmental standards was settlement reached, with adverse effects on the river and wildlife.[31] Following the Fukushima disaster, the German public demanded the closure of nuclear plants and the Government of Germany decided on a phase-out of nuclear energy. Vattenfall is currently seeking 4 billion in compensation.[32]

By the end of 2016, the German Constitutional Court[33] had decided the constitutional complaint by both RWE and Vattenfall based on an expropriation claim for being denied the chance to supply atomic energy despite having made investments in power plants. The court affirmed expropriation to a limited extent only, and granted damages

---

30. M. Rimmer, 'The Chilling Effect: Investor-State Dispute Settlement, Graphic Health Warnings, the Plain Packaging of Tobacco Products, and the Trans-Pacific Partnership', 17(2) *Queensland University of Technology Review* (2017), 1, 16. Alexovicova in chapter 9 of this book takes a similar position.
31. <www.italaw.com/cases/documents/1655>. Nathalie Bernasconi, 'Background paper on *Vattenfall v. Germany*', IISD; Rechtsanwälte Günther (2012) Briefing Note. The Coal-fired Power Plant Hamburg-Moorburg.
32. <www.fr-online.de/energie/atomausstieg-vattenfall-fordert-milliarden,1473634,21169258.html> Power Shift (2012) Der deutsche Atomausstieg auf dem Prüfstand eines internationalen Investitionsschiedsgerichts? Hintergründe zum neuen Streitfall Vattenfall gegen Deutschland. <www.iisd.org/pdf/2012/powershift_forum_briefing_vattenfall.pdf>.
33. Decision of the First Chamber of 6 December 2016, 1 BvR 2821/11, 1 BvR 321/12, 1 BvR 1456/12.

in an amount that was far less of what the plaintiffs had expected.[34] In doing so, the court took into account the conflicting interests of protecting property and protecting the environment. Vattenfall, dissatisfied with the ruling demands further damages in the context of an ISDS based on a bilateral investment agreement between Sweden and Germany.[35] RWE, the other plaintiff, had no recourse to this avenue because the company is not a foreign investor in Germany, but a domestic company.

Now, neither the Canadian Supreme Court nor the German Federal Constitutional Court are courts suspected for a cavalier attitude towards dispensing justice, begging the question why a foreign investor should get a further recourse in addition to what were undisputedly fair trials. Why should thus liberal democracies with a well-functioning court system such as Canada, the US or the European Union amongst themselves agree on a specific dispute settlement mechanism for foreign investors, in particular because CETA and TTIP are not meant to give foreign investors a higher level of protection, but one corresponding to domestic law.[36] While CETA envisages that investors must withdraw from any domestic proceedings before pursuing an ISDS claim, this only relates to the same subject matter. However, before domestic courts, investors would most likely challenge legislation or lower court decisions in order to have them overturned, rather than in order to obtain damages, making these arguably different claims.[37]

III. Court Structure and Judicial Independence

The third fundamental concern that significantly compounds the other two is the structure and working of the tribunals that decide about investor-state disputes. Both under the UNCITRAL rules or those of the ICSID Convention, panels are composed

34. "3. a) The quantities of energy allocated to power plants by the laws of 2002 and 2010 cannot form a separate object of property, yet are part of the property protection of power plants as relevant quantities of operation.
b) There is no property in approvals under public law. An expropriation under Art. 14(3) of the Constitution requires the removal of property based on a change of property allocation and thus an acquisition. Accordingly, the rules on accelerating the exit from atomic energy as stipulated by the 13th amendment to the Atomic Act of 31 July 2011 do not qualify as an expropriation.
4. Where limitations in the possibilities of use and disposition of property under Art. 14(2) of the Constitution lead to a negation of specific positions of property according to Art. 14(1) 2d sentence of the Constitution, yet without leading to an acquisition, their reasonableness is subject to increased requirements and always pose the question of compensation.
5. The uncompensated revocation by the 13th amendment to the Atomic Act of the extension of the lifespan of nuclear power plants that was stipulated by law in 2010 for an average of 12 years is constitutional in light of he fact that good faith in receiving additional quantities of energy was eroded on several occasions. Even in the absence of new insights regarding dangers the lawmaker could use the nuclear accident of Fukushima in order to accelerate the exit from atomic energy for the protection of the population and the environment."
35. <investmentpolicyhubold.unctad.org/ISDS/Details/467>.
36. Recital 4 of EU Regulation 912/2014 on Establishing a framework for managing financial responsibility linked to investor-state dispute settlement tribunals established by international agreements to which the European Union is a party, [2014] OJ L257/121.
37. As is observed by Hainbach, *supra* note 1, 24.

ad hoc, normally such that both parties nominate one arbiter, while the third (presiding) arbiter is selected by the two, or by the International Centre (ICSID) or the UNCITRAL. When composed according to the rules of the ICSID Convention, there are limitations relating to nationality (different from the defendant state or plaintiff, unless by consent), and previous or current relationship with one of the parties. The arbiters need to sign the following declaration:

> To the best of my knowledge there is no reason why I should not serve on the Arbitral Tribunal constituted by the International Centre for Settlement of Investment Disputes with respect to a dispute between __________ and __________.
>
> I shall keep confidential all information coming to my knowledge as a result of my participation in this proceeding, as well as the contents of any award made by the Tribunal.
>
> I shall judge fairly as between the parties, according to the applicable law, and shall not accept any instruction or compensation with regard to the proceeding from any source except as provided in the Convention on the Settlement of Investment Disputes between States and Nationals of Other States and in the Regulations and Rules made pursuant thereto.
>
> Attached is a statement of (a) my past and present professional, business and other relationships (if any) with the parties and (b) any other circumstance that might cause my reliability for independent judgment to be questioned by a party. I acknowledge that by signing this declaration, I assume a continuing obligation promptly to notify the Secretary-General of the Centre of any such relationship or circumstance that subsequently arises during this proceeding.

While this is meant to guarantee that none of the arbiters has been involved in the same case previously, or has no other conflict of interest regarding to this case, it is clear that the ad-hoc nomination of arbiters and their interest in getting called again may have an influence on their rulings and gives rise to concerns. The more so since the arbiters are regularly chosen amongst a select group of international trade lawyers whose profession it is to serve clients, yet another source of conflicts of interest.[38]

One should note in this regard that both the European Court of Justice and some courts of its member states have set very high standards for judicial independence deriving from both the European Treaty (TFEU) and the European Convention on Human Rights. The CJEU[39] has been very clear in requiring independence of domestic courts:

> 43 The independence of national courts and tribunals is, in particular, essential to the proper working of the judicial cooperation system embodied by the preliminary ruling mechanism under Article 267 TFEU, in that, in accordance with the settled case-law referred to in paragraph 38 above, that mechanism may be activated only by a body responsible for applying EU law which satisfies, inter alia, that criterion of independence.

38. "As long as income-maximizing private adjudicators compete against each other in the market of private dispute resolution for their re-appointment, judicial independence cannot be ensured." Hainbach, *supra* note 1, 23.
39. CJEU, decision (Grand Chamber) of 27 February 2018, Case C-64/16 – *Associação dos Juízes Portugueses.*

> 44 The concept of independence presupposes, in particular, that the body concerned exercises its judicial functions wholly autonomously, without being subject to any hierarchical constraint or subordinated to any other body and without taking orders or instructions from any source whatsoever, and that it is thus protected against external interventions or pressure liable to impair the independent judgment of its members and to influence their decisions (see, to that effect, judgments of 19 September 2006, Wilson, C 506/04, EU:C:2006:587, paragraph 51, and of 16 February 2017, Margarit Panicello, C 503/15, EU:C:2017:126, paragraph 37 and the case-law cited).

> 45 Like the protection against removal from office of the members of the body concerned (see, in particular, judgment of 19 September 2006, Wilson, C 506/04, EU:C:2006:587, paragraph 51), the receipt by those members of a level of remuneration commensurate with the importance of the functions they carry out constitutes a guarantee essential to judicial independence.

Council of Europe Recommendation CM/Rec(2010)12[40] also sees tenure and irremovability as key factors to independence:

> 49. Security of tenure and irremovability are key elements of the independence of judges. Accordingly, judges should have guaranteed tenure until a mandatory retirement age, where such exists.

And the German Constitutional Court in its ruling of 22 March 2018[41] on temporary judges regards irremovability and tenure as cornerstones of public trust in the judiciary. The independence of temporary judges could only be guaranteed where such judges could not be re-appointed[42] and after their appointment would be guaranteed a tenured position as a public servant.

It is surprising, to say the least, that countries agree to be sued in tribunals that fall way short of the requirements of judicial independence mandated for and by their own domestic courts, the more so since tribunals decide about cases that may make such countries liable to damage payment in enormous amounts, without any further legal recourse.

D. REFORMS AND REFORM PROPOSALS

Given the shortcomings of the ISDS system, it is somewhat surprising to the authors that there is still that much support for such undemocratic, secretive and imbalanced mechanism. Some reform is underway, though.

40. Adopted by the Committee of Ministers on 17 November 2010, <search.coe.int/cm/Pages/result_details.aspx?ObjectId=09000016805afb78>.
41. German Federal Supreme Court, decision of 22 March 2018, case 2 BvR 780/16.
42. One of the amendment proposals for the WTO Appellate Body suggests to appoint members for longer terms, yet without any possibility of reappointment in order to avoid that concerns about re-appointment could influence the positions taken in appellate cases. For details, see chapter 4 of this book.

I. Transparency of Proceedings

In 2015, UNCITRAL overhauled its ISDS proceedings to ensure greater transparency of ISDS proceedings. The new UNCITRAL Rules on Transparency in Treaty-based Investor-State Arbitration, General Assembly resolution 68/109[43] - effective as of 1 April 2014 - read as follows (excerpts):

> Article 1. Scope of application
>
> *Applicability of the Rules*
>
> 1. The UNCITRAL Rules on Transparency in Treaty-based Investor-State Arbitration ("Rules on Transparency") shall apply to investor-State arbitration initiated under the UNCITRAL Arbitration Rules pursuant to a treaty providing for the protection of investments or investors ("treaty") concluded on or after 1 April 2014 unless the Parties to the treaty have agreed otherwise.
>
> 2. In investor-State arbitrations initiated under the UNCITRAL Arbitration Rules pursuant to a treaty concluded before 1 April 2014, these Rules shall apply only when:
>
> (a) The parties to an arbitration (the "disputing parties") agree to their application in respect of that arbitration; or
>
> (b) The Parties to the treaty or, in the case of a multilateral treaty, the State of the claimant and the respondent State, have agreed after 1 April 2014 to their application.
>
> *Application of the Rules*
>
> 3. In any arbitration in which the Rules on Transparency apply pursuant to a treaty or to an agreement by the Parties to that treaty:
>
> (a) The disputing parties may not derogate from these Rules, by agreement or otherwise, unless permitted to do so by the treaty;
>
> (b) The arbitral tribunal shall have the power, besides its discretionary authority under certain provisions of these Rules, to adapt the requirements of any specific provision of these Rules to the particular circumstances of the case, after consultation with the disputing parties, if such adaptation is necessary to conduct the arbitration in a practical manner and is consistent with the transparency objective of these Rules.
>
> *Discretion and authority of the arbitral tribunal*
>
> 4. Where the Rules on Transparency provide for the arbitral tribunal to exercise discretion, the arbitral tribunal in exercising such discretion shall take into account:
>
> (a) The public interest in transparency in treaty-based investor-State arbitration and in the particular arbitral proceedings; and
>
> (b) The disputing parties' interest in a fair and efficient resolution of their dispute.
>
> 5. These Rules shall not affect any authority that the arbitral tribunal may otherwise have under the UNCITRAL Arbitration Rules to conduct the arbitration in such a manner as to promote transparency, for example by accepting submissions from third persons.

43. < www.uncitral.org/uncitral/en/uncitral_texts/arbitration/2014Transparency.html > .

6. In the presence of any conduct, measure or other action having the effect of wholly undermining the transparency objectives of these Rules, the arbitral tribunal shall ensure that those objectives prevail.

The UNCITRAL working group III is looking into further improvements of ISDS proceedings in terms of impartiality and independence of arbitrators, costs of proceedings, etc.[44]

The ICSID secretariat on 15 March 2019 published a proposal for amendment of the ICSID Convention in order to ensure greater transparency of proceedings, independence of arbitrators and possibilities of a state counterclaim. The amendments are meant to be discussed in the course of the year 2019.[45]

II. Intra-European ISDS Procedures

In a decision of 6 March 2018, the European Court of Justice held an arbitration clause in an investment agreement between Slovakia and the Netherlands incompatible with EU law and thereby refused the execution of the decision rendered in accordance with ISDS proceedings. The court found that the ISDS mechanism provided in an investment agreement between two EU member states (dispute settlement under UNCITRAL rules) was incompatible with Arts. 267, 344 TFEU. The court reasoned that all EU domestic courts and tribunals had to ensure the full effectiveness of EU law. While an ISDS tribunal might be called upon to interpret or apply EU law, it could not be classified as a court or tribunal of a member state and thus had no power to make a referral to the Court of Justice for a preliminary ruling.[46] The Advocate General and a couple of Member States in observations had taken a different position. The Commission was quick to welcome this decision (although taking a much different position in regard of EU–non-EU BITs, see below for CETA):

> The Commission welcomes EU Member States' commitments on the legal consequences of the *Achmea* judgement and in particular their commitment to terminate all bilateral investment treaties (BITs) between themselves. As the Commission has consistently stated, and as outlined in its July 2018 *Communication on the Protection of intra-EU investment*, the dispute settlement mechanisms provided in these treaties as well as they intra-EU application of the Energy Charter Treaty are incompatible with EU law and discriminate between EU investors. The protection for all EU investors against unlawful interference by Member States is provided by EU law, which ensures that all investors are treated equally. EU investors cannot rely on different intra-EU BITs concluded between two Member States. This was confirmed by the Court of Justice of the European Union in its March 2018 judgment in the *Achmea* case. Following this

44. < www.uncitral.org/pdf/english/workinggroups/wg_3/WGIII-36th-session/149_main_paper_7_September_DRAFT.pdf > .
45. < icsid.worldbank.org/en/amendments > .
46. CJEU (Grand Chamber), decision of 6 March 2018, case C-284/16 *Slowakische Republik v. Achmea*. Comment by C. Contartese and M. Andenas, 56 *Common Market Law Review* (2019), 157.

judgment, the Commission has intensified its dialogue with all Member States. As a result, all Member States committed to terminate all intra-EU BITs.[47]

III. EU Reforms Envisaged in the Context of CETA

Back in 2015, the Commission had still been of the opinion that only investment courts rather than domestic courts should be entrusted with the application of treaty-based applications, as domestic courts would be unfit to deal with treaty-based claims.[48] Under pressure from the European Parliament's Committee on International Trade, and thousands of concerned European citizens taking the streets, the Commission has shifted its position and now advocates a Multilateral Investment Court that indeed would take into account many of the above-mentioned deficits:

> A Multilateral Investment Court, like the approach in the FTAs, would bring the key features of domestic and international courts to investment adjudication.
>
> The idea is that the Multilateral Investment Court would:
> - have a first instance tribunal
> - have an appeal tribunal
> - have tenured, highly qualified judges, obliged to adhere to the strictest ethical standards and a dedicated secretariat.
> - be a permanent body
> - work transparently
> - rule on disputes arising under future and existing investment treaties
> - only apply where an investment treaty already explicitly allows an investor to bring a dispute against a State
> - would not create new possibilities for an investor to bring a dispute against a state
> - prevent disputing parties from choosing which judges ruled on their case
> - provide for effective enforcement of its decisions
> - be open to all interested countries to join.
>
> For the EU, the Multilateral Investment Court would replace the bilateral investment court systems included in EU trade and investment agreements.[49]

In the context of the CETA (Canadian EU Trade Agreement) negotiations, an agreement was reached between the EU and its Member States that CETA should provisionally come into force without the section dealing with ISDS by an investment court.[50] In respect of the dispute settlement aspect, an opinion was asked from the CJEU that the latter issued on 30 April 2019, affirming compatibility of an ISDS mechanism with European law.[51] The decision stresses that the dispute settlement mechanism via

47. < europa.eu/rapid/press-release_MEX-19-483_en.htm > .
48. European Commission, Investment in TTIP and beyond – the path for reform (6 May 2015).
49. European Commission, Directorate General for Trade, < trade.ec.europa.eu/doclib/press/index.cfm?id = 1608 > .
50. Council Decision (EU) 2017/38 of 28 October 2016 on the provisional application of the Comprehensive Economic and Trade Agreement (CETA) between Canada, of the one part, and the European Union and its Member States, of the other part (OJ 2017 L 11, p. 1080).
51. CJEU, Opinion 1/17 of the Court (Full Court), 30 April 2019.

"the tribunals that are established will each have the characteristics of an accessible and independent tribunal." (191).

Regarding the concerns raised in the *Achmea* decision, namely that tribunals could be called upon to rule on issues of EU law without recourse to a referral to the European Court of Justice, the latter in its opinion on CETA states the following:

> 158. It must be added that the jurisdiction of the CETA Tribunal to find infringements of the obligation, laid down in Article 8.10 of the CETA, to accord "fair and equitable treatment" to covered investments is specifically circumscribed, since Article 8.10.2 lists exhaustively the situations in which such a finding can be made.
>
> 159. In that regard, the Parties have concentrated on, inter alia, situations where there is abusive treatment, manifest arbitrariness and targeted discrimination, which reveals, once again, that the required level of protection of a public interest, as established following a democratic process, is not subject to the jurisdiction conferred on the envisaged tribunals to determine whether treatment accorded by a Party to an investor or a covered investment is "fair and equitable".
>
> 160. It is accordingly apparent from all those provisions, contained in the CETA, that, by expressly restricting the scope of Sections C and D of Chapter Eight of that agreement, which are the only sections that can be relied upon in claims before the envisaged tribunals by means of Section F of that Chapter, the Parties have taken care to ensure that those tribunals have no jurisdiction to call into question the choices democratically made within a Party relating to, inter alia, the level of protection of public order or public safety, the protection of public morals, the protection of health and life of humans and animals, the preservation of food safety, protection of plants and the environment, welfare at work, product safety, consumer protection or, equally, fundamental rights.

This is correct from a perspective of law (and the CJEU was asked for an opinion only in this respect), but does nothing to alleviate concerns that investor protection is judged in isolation from the very issues mentioned by the court above (see *infra* 5.).

E. REMAINING CONCERNS

I. Treating Symptoms Rather than the Problem

It is arguable that the above reforms, be it in the context of ICSID, UNCITRAL or the EU, treat some of the symptoms, but not the problem[52] of ISDS which according to Stiglitz is that:

> [t]hese agreements go well beyond trade, governing investment and intellectual property as well, imposing fundamental changes to countries' legal, judicial, and regulatory frameworks, without input or accountability through democratic institutions. Perhaps the most invidious — and most dishonest — part of such agreements concerns investor protection. Of course, investors have to

52. Hainbach, *supra* note 1, 28.

> be protected against the risk that rogue governments will seize their property. But that is not what these provisions are about. There have been very few expropriations in recent decades, and investors who want to protect themselves can buy insurance from the Multilateral Investment Guarantee Agency, a World Bank affiliate (the US and other governments provide similar insurance). ... The real intent of these provisions is to impede health, environmental, safety, and, yes, even financial regulations.[53]

II. In Particular

(1) It is true that in the context of CETA and probably future bilateral free trade agreements, the serious concern about judicial independence and transparency of proceedings has been addressed, but there is still the tantalising question why non-EU investors should be able to rely on a different legal framework than domestic investors, and why the former should receive enforcement avenues not available to the latter.

(2) Why is the asymmetry not addressed that investors can sue states over alleged wrongdoing, but not vice versa? As was mentioned in the de Zayas report (*supra* note 7), alleged cases of expropriation were often the reaction of a state to gross violations of environmental laws that the state in question should accordingly have been able to pursue by way of a counterclaim, or as an independent claim in its own right. The concept of state immunity is put on its head if before investment tribunals, investors are immune (because they cannot be counter-sued), while states are not.

(3) The Opinion rendered by the CJEU on the CETA Agreement[54] highlights that the ISDS Tribunal will only be competent to adjudicate claims in the context of the CETA Agreement, but not "have no jurisdiction to call into question the choices democratically made within a Party relating to, inter alia, the level of protection of public order or public safety". Only thereby can they be reconciled with EU law. This statement is not only Delphic, but it is deeply worrying for two reasons.

In most ISDS cases, investors do not call for the repeal or amendment of laws ("choices democratically made"), but they claim damages because these laws allegedly diminish or expropriate their investments. But it is by the damage claim hanging like a sword of Damocles over a state that the latter may be compelled to repeal such legislation. In other words, the investor does not "call into question" the laws that were enacted, but claims damages for its consequences. In the above case of *Vattenfall v. Germany*, Vattenfall does not ask the ISDS tribunal to order Germany to repeal the law that required an end to nuclear power, but it asks for damages incurred as a consequence of such law. To that extent, the CJEU's opinion only states the obvious, but does not alleviate any of the above concerns regarding chill effect or coercing states to repeal legislation.

The second aspect is equally sinister and concerns the reasons as to why certain legislation is enacted. De Zayas (*supra* note 7) cites the following case:

---

53. < www.project-syndicate.org/commentary/us-secret-corporate-takeover-by-joseph-e--stiglitz-2015-05 >.
54. Opinion 1/17 of 30 April 2019.

> 24. One of the most egregious ICSID arbitrations concerned the case by United States-based Occidental Petroleum against Ecuador concerning the termination of an oil production site in the Amazon, and resulting in an award of $1.76 billion to Occidental ($2.4 billion with interest), which Ecuador accused of multiple human rights violations and environmental destruction.[55]

Neither could Ecuador raise a counterclaim against the plaintiff based on environmental destruction, nor did the tribunal take this aspect into much account. The difference to the subsequent Philip Morris/Uruguay decision is not that domestic legislation was taken into account as such (it was so only in the denial of justice claim), but that a state should be credited with far greater regulatory freedom in pursuing such aspects as protecting health. But even with this increased margin of legislative intervention, the tribunal heavily relied on the fact that the WHO had endorsed and promoted a number of these measures. This is an unusual scenario. There are perhaps no internationally accepted or recommended legislative avenues in the field of environmental protection or human rights violations. This is why for determining the proper justification of a measure, either the state must be credited with a greater freedom to act also in new and upcoming fields, or regard must be had to the domestic legal order of the state in question. Yet the latter is exactly what CJEU would not allow a tribunal to do. But how can a measure such as a compulsory licence be evaluated in terms of alleged expropriation where its justification is based on, say, EU competition law, or access to essential facilities, etc. After all, the justification for certain measures can often only be determined based on the domestic legal order. In this regard, the CJEU's opinion is unclear at best.

F. CONCLUSION

Based on the latest figures released by UNCTAD,[56] ISDS cases are widespread and seem to be on the rise:

- At least 71 treaty-based ISDS cases were initiated in 2018, all but one under old-generation treaties signed before 2012.
- As of 1 January 2019, the total number of known ISDS cases pursuant to international investment agreements (IIAs) had reached 942. To date, 117 countries are known to have been respondents to one or more ISDS claims.
- The new ISDS cases in 2018 were initiated against 41 countries. As in previous years, the majority of new cases were brought against developing countries and transition economies. Developed-country investors brought most of the 71 known cases.

Despite such widespread use, the authors maintain that ISDS is an undemocratic mechanism that should best be abolished.

55. One of the worst aspects of this case is that Ecuador was justified in terminating Occidental's permit under Ecuadorian law and the contract and still the investor–State dispute settlement tribunal penalised Ecuador, < www.citizen.org/documents/oxy-v-ecuador-memo.pdf >.
56. < investmentpolicy.unctad.org/publications/1202/fact-sheet-on-investor-state-dispute-settlement-cases-in-2018 >

PART I:

GIVING EFFECT TO INTERNATIONAL TRADE AGREEMENTS – HISTORY AND PROCEDURE

CHAPTER 2
Dispute Resolution in International and Bilateral Agreements

Shahla Ali[1] *and Wilson Mbugua*

A. BACKGROUND

The legal regime governing arbitration in investor-state dispute settlement (ISDS) is complex and varied. A central pillar of this regime is the International Center for Settlement of Investment Disputes (ICSID), which has been established pursuant to the ICSID Convention. The ICSID Convention does not provide substantive protection for foreign investments; instead, it provides a comprehensive and specified arbitration regime for investment disputes. The ICSID regime will only be triggered when the foreign investor and host state consent to ICSID arbitration. Consent usually takes the form of an arbitration clause contained within an investment contract. It may also be provided in foreign investment law, a bilateral investment treaty or any other treaty. As of October 2016, there were 153 contracting states to the ICSID Convention[2].

Other major multilateral and bilateral treaties governing ISDS include (a) multilateral regional treaties such as the North American Free Trade Agreement (NAFTA), the ASEAN Comprehensive Investment Agreement and treaties in Latin America and Africa; (b) multilateral sectorial treaties like the Energy Charter Treaty; and (c) a network of bilateral investment treaties (BITs)[3].

---

1. The author thanks the Government of Hong Kong's University Grants Committee for its kind support through its HKU GRF Grant (HKU 17604318) and HKU Grant 201611159315.
2. See ICSID, Database of the ICSID Member States, available at <icsid.worldbank.org/apps/ICSIDWEB/about/Pages/Database-of-Member-States.aspx?tab = AtoE&rdo = CSO> (accessed on 31 October 2016).
3. Gary B. Born, *International Arbitration: Law and Practice* (2nd edn., 2015), para. 763.

B. INVESTOR STATE DISPUTE SETTLEMENT: AN OVERVIEW

Investor-State Dispute Settlement (ISDS) is an international arbitration procedure allowing a foreign investor to challenge the host state for damages to the investment caused by a change in law or policy.[4] The goal of ISDS is to protect foreign investors from "indirect expropriation" by the host government through domestic laws, measures or policies which harm the investment.[5] Indirect expropriation refers to the situation where the host state government "takes an action that substantially impairs the value of an investment without necessarily assuming ownership of the investment."[6] Before the existence of ISDS, absent recourse to domestic courts, the most important means by which foreign investors could seek reparation was diplomatic protection.[7] However, the paradigm of diplomatic protection has some serious flaws. First, diplomatic protection is rooted in a state's right to protect its citizens injured by acts of another state and, thus, can only be exercised by a state.[8] In other words, a foreign investor does not have standing to sue a host state directly. This nationality rule "leaves millions of stateless persons without any protection."[9] Second, a state must establish that the injured individual has exhausted all local remedies through the domestic courts of the host state before advancing the claim.[10] Third, when a state acts as a claimant against another state, power differences inevitable affect the resolution of international disputes and developing nations may be unfairly discriminated.[11] Due to these shortcomings, a reform was called for to allow individual investors access to adjudication by international tribunals in their own right. Consequently, the ISDS system was embraced. Governments have put ISDS in treaties for three main reasons: 1) to resolve international investment disputes without creating state-to-state conflict; 2) to protect overseas citizens; and 3) to attract potential investors by promising respect for the rule of law.[12]

---

4. August Reinisch, 'The Scope of Investor-State Dispute Settlement in International Investment Agreements', 21(1) *Asia Pacific Law Review* (2013), 3, 4; Patricia Ranald, 'The Trans-Pacific Partnership Agreement: Reaching behind the border, challenging democracy', 26(2) *The Economic and Labour Relations Review* (2015), 241, 242.
5. Ranald, *supra* note 4, at 248.
6. W. Michael Reisman and Robert D. Sloane, 'Indirect Expropriation and Its Valuation in the BIT Generation', 74 *British Yearbook of International Law* (2003), 115, 121.
7. Won-Mog Choi, 'The Present and Future of the Investor-State Dispute Settlement Paradigm', 10(3) *Journal of International Economic Law* (2007), 725, 726.
8. *Ibid.*
9. *Ibid.*, at 727.
10. *Ibid.*, at 726.
11. *Ibid.*, at 726–727.
12. Office of the United States Trade Representative, *Fact Sheet: Invest-State Dispute Settlement (ISDS)*, at <ustr.gov/about-us/policy-offices/press-office/fact-sheets/2015/march/investor-state-dispute-settlement-isds> (last visited Oct. 13, 2016).

C. HISTORY OF ISDS

ISDS was first implemented in a bilateral trade agreement between Germany and Pakistan in 1959.[13] So far, about 3000 treaties have incorporated the ISDS regime, allowing foreign investors to sue the governments of host countries for violation of property rights.[14] The majority of these are bilateral investment treaties (BITs) numbering about 2700, and a variety of other international investment agreements (IIAs).[15] Two major tribunal systems are used in these treaties: the International Centre for the Settlement of Investment Disputes (ICSID) and the rules of the United Nations Commission on International Trade Law (UNCITRAL).[16] The choice between ICSID and UNCITRAL largely depends on several factors- namely; cost, enforcement mechanism, nationality of the investor or provisions of the BIT.[17] Settling on which rules to adopt in particular a case, will ultimately be determined by a combination of the above factors. Literature suggests that there is no "one size fits all" between ICSID and UNCITRAL rules.[18] However, available data suggests that ICSID has been applied in 55% of the arbitrations compared to 31% that have adopted UNCITRAL rules.[19]

From 1990 through 2014, 676 cases have been submitted to international investment arbitration.[20] The total figure is probably much higher, as many proceedings are not public. Investors from over 70 different host states, mostly US based, have filed for investment arbitration.[21] Arbitration outcomes vary from case to case: investors obtain 30–40% of their initial demands, states prevail more than one-third of the time, and the rest are settled before a judgment.[22]

An important feature on the ISDS landscape is Chapter 11 of the North American Free Trade Agreement (NAFTA).[23] In basic terms, Chapter 11 establishes an *ad hoc* tribunal available to foreign investors (rather than states), when investments are threatened and provides investors with standing to directly proceed against a NAFTA

13. 'The Arbitration Game: Investor-State Dispute Settlement', *Economist* (11 October 2014).
14. Rachel L. Wellhausen, 'Recent Trends in Investor-State Dispute Settlement', 7 *Journal of International Dispute Settlement* (2016), 117.
15. *Ibid.*, at 121.
16. Ranald, *supra* note 4, at 248.
17. < www.acerislaw.com/choosing-icsid-or-uncitral-arbitration-for-investor-state-disputes > (last accessed 3 May 2019).
18. See Leon E. Trakman, 'The ICSID Under Siege', 45 *Cornell Int'l LJ* (2013), 603; Markus Burgstaller and Charles B. Rosenberg, 'Challenging International Arbitral Awards: To ICSID or not to ICSID?', 27(1) *Arbitration International* (2011), 91–108.
19. UNCTAD IIA Issues Note International Investment Agreement- Special Update on Investor-State Dispute Settlement: Facts and Figures, Issue 3 November 2017 at p. 5 referring to arbitrations filed between 1987 and 31 July 2017.
20. Wellhausen, *supra* note 14, at 118.
21. *Ibid.*
22. *Ibid.*
23. Daniel M. Price, 'Chapter 11 – Private Party vs. Government, Investor-State Dispute Settlement: Frankenstein or Safety Valve?', 26 *Canada–United States Law Journal* (2000), 107, 114.

government.[24] An investor can bring a claim based on the following investment obligations imposed on treaty parties under Chapter 11:

(1) National Treatment (Article 1102): A signatory government's obligation to treat other investments or investors from another NAFTA signatory no less favorably than domestic investments or investors in similar circumstances.

(2) Most-Favored Nation (MFN) treatment (Article 1103): A signatory government's obligation to treat investments or investors from another NAFTA signatory no less favorably than any other country.

(3) Minimum standard of treatment (Article 1105): A signatory government's obligation to treat investments or investors from another NAFTA signatory in accordance with international law, including fair and equitable treatment.

(4) Expropriation and compensation (Article 1110): The obligation to not expropriate, or take measures tantamount to expropriation of the the investments of a NAFTA signatory investor without adequate compensation.

(5) Performance requirements (Article 1106): The obligation to not impose certain performance requirements, such as domestic content percentages, in connection with an investment.[25]

As pointed out by Daniel M. Price, a NAFTA negotiator, the ISDS mechanism under Chapter 11 is heavily precedented. In fact, ISDS has been included in every US bilateral agreement, except the Australia–United States Free Trade Agreement (AUSFTA).[26] Canada's BIT with the then-Soviet Union also contained ISDS provisions nearly identical to those in NAFTA Chapter 11.[27] Similar ISDS provisions have been proposed to be included in new multilateral trade agreements including the Trans-Pacific Partnership (TPP), the Canada–EU Trade Agreement (CETA), and the Trans-Atlantic Trade and Investment Partnership (T-TIP).[28]

D. CONSTITUTION OF THE ARBITRAL TRIBUNAL

The constitution of arbitral tribunals in investor-state arbitrations is closely modelled on those in international commercial arbitrations between private parties. In most cases, investor-state arbitrations are heard by a three-person tribunal. Each party nominates one co-arbitrator, and both parties then collectively select the presiding arbitrator. The presiding arbitrator may sometimes also be selected by the co-arbitrators. Where the parties are unable to reach agreement, the appointing authority (usually the ICSID) will appoint the presiding arbitrator.[29] ICSID appointments of

24. NAFTA, Can–Mex–US, Arts. 1105 and 1115, Dec 17, 1992, 32 I.L.M. 289; William L. Owens and R. Andrew Fitzpatrick, 'Investment Arbitration under NAFTA Chapter 11: A threat to Sovereignty of Member States?', 39 *Canada–United States Law Journal* (2015), 55, 56.
25. Owens and Fitzpatrick, *supra* note 24, at 60.
26. Ranald, *supra* note 4, at 248.
27. Price, *supra* note 23, at 107–108.
28. Owens and Fitzpatrick, *supra* note 24, at 55.
29. Born, *supra* note 3 , at para. 808.

presiding arbitrators are made from the ICSID Panel of Arbitrators, consisting of individuals designated by Contracting States or designated by the Chairman of the ICSID Administrative Council.[30]As in commercial arbitration, arbitrators in investment arbitrations are generally subject to obligations of independence and impartiality.

E. STRUCTURE OF ARBITRATION PROCEEDINGS

Procedures in investor-state arbitration are modelled on those in international commercial arbitration. As in commercial arbitration, the guiding principle is party autonomy. If the parties agree to particular procedures, such agreement will be accepted as binding.[31]

In practice, almost all investor-state arbitrations are conducted in accordance with institutional arbitration rules, such as ICSID, UNCITRAL, SCC, ICSID Additional Facility or ICC Rules. Each of these sets of rules establishes a basic procedural framework on the basis of which the arbitration proceedings will be structured. Parties are often left with broad autonomy to agree upon particular timetables or procedures on top of the basic framework. In the absence of agreement, the tribunal has broad discretion to conduct the arbitration.[32]

One of the key organisations involved in the administration of investor-state arbitration is the Permanent Court of Arbitration (PCA). The PCA was established by the 1899 Convention for the Pacific Settlement of International Disputes which was later amended in 1907.[33] The PCA is not a court in the conventional sense, rather, it is an administrative body set up to facilitate international arbitration.[34] The PCA may be called to act as an appointing authority, administrator of ad hoc arbitrations or serve as a secretariat. The PCA has various optional procedural rules that may be adopted by parties depending on the subject matter at hand.[35] The UNCITRAL rules for most part, are the applicable rules in arbitration administered by PCA.

F. TRANSPARENCY AND PUBLIC PARTICIPATION

Transparency is a cornerstone of any judicial process. Investor-state arbitration is a form of judicial process. Transparency lends legitimacy to decisions rendered by adjudicating bodies.[36] Transparency incorporates the ability of the members of the public to follow proceedings and the ability to participate in some form, such as the filing of *amicus curiae.*[37] There has been a sustained momentum for increased

---

30. Article 40, ICSID Convention.
31. Born, *supra* note 3, at para. 808.
32. *Ibid.*
33. <pca-cpa.org/en/about/introduction/history/> (last visited 23 April 2019).
34. Brooks W. Daly, 'Permanent Court of Arbitration', in *The Rules, Practice, and Jurisprudence of International Courts and Tribunals* (Brill Nijhoff, 2012), 39.
35. *Ibid.*
36. Shabtai Rosenne, *Reflections on international arbitration and litigation in the International Court of Justice*, No. 9. (Kluwer Law Intl, 1988), p. 14.
37. Thore Neumann and Bruno Simma, 'Transparency in international adjudication', in Andrea Bianchi and Anne Peters (eds.), *Transparency in International Law* (Cambridge University

transparency in investor-state arbitration, long criticised for being shrouded in secrecy, while the issues being contested are of a public nature. ICSID offers a platform on its website where the awards are published. Also, the Secretary General is obligated to publish all arbitration requests.[38]

In 2006, ICSID Rules and Regulation were amended to allow non-disputing parties to file written submissions.[39] In *Aguas v. Argentina*,[40] the tribunal, in allowing leave for the petitioners to file written submissions, acknowledged that the decision centered on the supply of water and sewerage service, which affects millions of residents in Buenos Aires.[41] In *Biwater v. Tanzania*[42] the tribunal allowed the filing of written submissions pursuant to the 2006 ICSID Rules and Regulations.[43]

The Tribunal in a NAFTA case administered under UNCITRAl rules – *Methanex v. United States,* in allowing amicus curiae stated that the "…arbitral process could benefit from being perceived as more open or transparent: or conversely be harmed if seen as unduly secretive. In this regard, the Tribunal's willingness to receive amicus submissions might support the process in general and this arbitration in particular; whereas a blanket refusal could do positive harm."[44] Another decision that allowed amicus curiae was *United Parcel Service of America v. Canada.*[45]

At the multilateral level, the growing importance of transparency in investor-state arbitration has led to the negotiation and ratification of the United Nations Convention on Transparency in Treaty-based Investor-State Arbitration.[46] The treaty came into force on 18 October 2017.[47] This treaty represents a major stride in promoting transparency in investment arbitration.

G. APPEALS

The finality of awards in investor-state arbitrations varies depending on the treaty under which the arbitration is pursued. In particular, there are significant differences between the status of ICSID and non-ICSID awards.

Press, 2013), 437.

38. ICSID Administrative and Financial Regulations, regulation 22.
39. Rule 37 Rules Of Procedure For Arbitration Proceedings (Arbitration Rules).
40. *Aguas Argentinas, S.A., Suez, Sociedad General de Aguas de Barcelona, S.A. and Vivendi Universal, S.A. v. Argentina* (ARB/03/19) Order in response to a petition for participation as Amicus Curiae 19 May 2005.
41. *Ibid.*, para. 19.
42. *Biwater Gauff (Tanzania) Limited v. United Republic of Tanzania* (ICSID Case No. ARB/05/22).
43. *Ibid.*, Procedural Order No. 5, 2 February 2007.
44. *Methanex v. United States,* Decision of the Tribunal on Petitions from Third Persons to Intervene as "Amici Curiae" 15 January 2001, para. 49.
45. Eugenia Levine, 'Amicus curiae in international investment arbitration: the implications of an increase in third-party participation', 29 *Berkeley J. Int'l L.* (2011), 210.
46. The Mauritius Convention on Transparency.
47. < www.uncitral.org/uncitral/en/uncitral_texts/arbitration/2014Transparency_Convention.html > (last accessed 3 May 2019).

I. ICSID Awards

ICSID awards are subject to a unique, standalone annulment mechanism. Pursuant to the ICSID Convention, a party may challenge an award before an ad hoc annulment committee appointed by ICSID. An ICSID award can only be annulled on certain specified grounds, including (a) improper constitution of the tribunal; (b) manifest excess of authority; (c) corruption involving a member of the tribunal; (d) a serious departure from a fundamental rule of procedure; and (e) a failure by the tribunal to state in the award the reasons on which it is based.[48]

Unlike international commercial arbitration awards, ICSID awards are not subject to annulment proceedings in national courts. Similarly, in recognition proceedings of ICSID awards, national courts are not allowed to review the tribunal's jurisdiction, procedural decisions or other actions, or to consider objections based on local public policy. Rather, pursuant to Article 54 of the ICSID Convention, contracting states are bound to treat awards of pecuniary relief as binding and must recognize them without any judicial review.

II. Non-ICSID Awards

Arbitral awards made in pursuant to treaties other than the ICSID Convention (e.g. BITs and NAFTA) are subject to different review mechanisms. Unlike ICSID awards, they are generally not subject to any internal review mechanism. However, it is possible for a treaty to include a dispute resolution mechanism that provides for ICSID arbitration.[49]

Non-ICSID awards are subject to judicial review in the arbitral seat. National courts can generally apply grounds for setting aside an international commercial arbitration award to set aside an investment award. Some of the common grounds include (a) lack or excess of jurisdiction; (b) procedural unfairness; (c) public policy; and (c) non-arbitrability. Similarly, in recognition proceedings of non-ICSID awards, national courts are entitled to apply the grounds for non-recognition provided under Article V of the New York Convention.[50]

H. POWERS OF THE ARBITRATION TRIBUNALS IN TERMS OF REMEDIES

Remedies can be broadly classified into non-pecuniary and pecuniary remedies. Non-pecuniary remedies typically include (a) the annulling of a governmental measure or decision; (b) injunctions; and (c) declarations in relation the rights and obligations of the parties or legality of particular decisions made by the state. In general, tribunals have limited powers in relation to non-pecuniary remedies. Nonetheless, according to the OECD, arbitrators are increasingly willing to issue provisional injunctions, which restrain the respondent state from taking a particular

48. Article 52, ICSID Convention.
49. Born, *supra* note 3, at para. 811.
50. Born, *supra* note 3, at para. 812.

course of action while the arbitration is taking place.[51] Additionally, some BITs explicitly allow arbitral tribunals to declare that a state party has breached its obligations under a treaty.[52]

Pecuniary remedies remain dominant in investment arbitration. Typical measures include monetary compensation, interest and costs.[53]

I. ENFORCEMENT OF INVESTMENT ARBITRAL AWARDS

According to Article 53 of the ICSID Convention, governments have the obligation to comply with awards issued by the tribunal. Further, as discussed above, Article 54 requires a contracting state to recognize a pecuniary award as if it were a final judgment of a court in that state. However, the ability of parties to enforce awards and judgments against state assets is subject to foreign sovereign immunity and state immunity legislation.[54] This poses a significant impediment to the effective enforcement of ICSID awards. As recognised by Born, execution of non-ICSID awards against foreign state assets is subject to similar limitations.[55]

The enforcement of non-pecuniary awards faces even more difficulties. Some of the primary reasons include (i) the lack of an equivalent of Article 54 in relation to non-pecuniary awards; and (ii) the lack of compliance oversight due to the ad hoc nature of arbitration tribunals.[56] Therefore, some commentators suggest that the tribunal should provide for pecuniary alternatives to non-pecuniary remedies in case of non-performance, such as liquidated damages, penalties or an obligation to pay a certain amount of money.[57]

J. PROTECTION STANDARDS FOR INTELLECTUAL PROPERTY RIGHTS IN INVESTMENT AGREEMENTS

Intellectual property rights are covered by various BITs under the broad category of assets.[58] The widely-used clause to cover intellectual property rights in a considerable

51. OECD, 'Investor-State Dispute Settlement', Public Consultation Paper, 2012, 24.
52. According to the OECD, some treaties concluded by, inter alia, Austria and Mexico, allow tribunals to make statements on breach of treaty obligations.
53. *Supra* note 51.
54. Article 54(3) of the ICSID Convention provides that execution of an award against assets of a state is "governed by the laws concerning the execution of judgments in force in the State in whose territories such execution is sought". Article 55 further provides that enforcement is subject to "the law in force in any Contracting State relating to immunity of that State or of any foreign State from execution".
55. Born, *supra* note 3, at para. 813.
56. Christoph Schreuer, 'Non-pecuniary remedies in ICSID arbitration', 20(4) *Arbitration International* (2004), 325–332 at 332.
57. *Ibid.*
58. Bertram Boie, 'The Protection of Intellectual Property Rights Through Bilateral Investment Treaties: Is There a TRIPS- Plus Dimension?', 4 *NCCR Trade Regulation*, Working Paper No. 2010/19, 2010.

number of BIT's is "every kind of asset".[59] Invoking intellectual property protection through the ISDS has only emerged recently.[60] The prospect of success of intellectual property claims through the ISDS has thus far been considered slim.[61] The very nature of intellectual property regimes lends credence to this view.[62] This section will examine how the tribunals have navigated expropriation and fair and equitable treatment (FET) when rendering awards in disputes touching on intellectual property rights. The choice of the two standards of protection is informed by the publicly available arbitration awards addressing these standards.[63]

K. EXPROPRIATION

Expropriation is a principle of international law that avails sovereign states the right to expropriate property belonging to foreigners on condition that: it is for a public purpose, is in accordance with due process of law, is non-discriminatory and accompanied by compensation.[64] Expropriation takes two forms. direct and indirect expropriation, with the former being a rarity.[65] Indirect expropriation is a subtle form that entails depriving the owner of the economic benefit of its property.[66] The tribunal in *Metalclad v. Mexico*[67] considered expropriation as being "...covert or incidental interference with the use of property which has the effect of depriving the owner, in whole or in significant part, of the use or reasonably-to-be-expected economic benefit of property even if not necessarily to the obvious benefit of the host State."[68] This section will address expropriation on the whole without necessarily drawing a distinction between direct and indirect expropriation.

Generally, to qualify for protection under the intellectual property regime, an investor must make an application to the host state.[69] This applies to trade marks,

59. Chester Brown (ed.), *Commentaries on Selected Model Investment Treaties* (OUP, Oxford, 2013), 23. For a discussion on IP rights as investment, see chapter 7 of this book.
60. Henning Grosse Ruse-Khan, 'Challenging Compliance with International Intellectual Property Norms in Investor–state Dispute Settlement', 19(1) *Journal of International Economic Law* (2016), 241–277 at 242; Susy Frankel, 'Interpreting the Overlap of International Investment and Intellectual Property Law', *Journal of International Economic Law* (2016), 126.
61. Ruse-Khan, *supra* note 60, at 260.
62. Marie Louise Seelig, 'Can Patent Revocation or Invalidation Constitute a Form of Expropriation?', 6(2) *Transnational Dispute Management (TDM)* (2009), 3.
63. As at 20 March 2017.
64. Catherine Yannaca-Small, *"Indirect Expropriation" and the" Right to Regulate" in International Investment Law* (OECD, 2004), 3.
65. Anne Hoffmann, 'Indirect expropriation', *Standards of Investment Protection* (2008), 151.
66. Valentina Vadi, 'Towards a new dialectics: pharmaceutical patents, public health and foreign direct investments', 5(1) *New York University Journal of Intellectual Property and Entertainment Law* (2015), 1-83 at 45.
67. *Metalclad Corporation v. The United Mexican States*, ICSID Case No. ARB(AF)/97/1 (30 August 2000) Award.
68. *Metalclad Corporation v. The United Mexican States*, para. 103.
69. Carlos M. Correa, 'Investment Protection in Bilateral and Free Trade Agreements: Implications for the Granting of Compulsory Licenses', 26 *Mich. J. Int'l L.* (2004), 331 at 340.

patents, industrial designs, protection of plant varieties, etc.[70] This is in line with the TRIPS Agreement which sets out the basic requirements for member states to adopt in their domestic legislation to afford protection of intellectual property rights.[71] There are certain limits to intellectual property rights such as compulsory licensing whereby a patent holders rights may be assigned to third parties for the protection of public health pursuant to Article 31 of the TRIPS.[72] Patents may also be revoked by the host state as we shall see below.

Expropriation was invoked as one of the grounds in the *Eli Lilly v. Canada* case.[73] For details, see chapter 8 of this book. The claimant alleged that revocation of its two patented drugs of Strattera and Zyprexa by Canadian courts amounted to an unlawful expropriation contrary to Article 1110 of NAFTA.[74] Canada on the other hand contended that actions by its court to invalidate the patents could only be litigated before an international tribunal if the actions by its domestic court "amounted to extraordinary circumstance of gross procedural misconduct amounting to a denial of justice, or where court power to make such determinations is exercised in bad faith to mask a violation of international law".[75] Additionally, Canada contended that its actions were in conformity with the TRIPS Agreement.[76]

The tribunal in its analysis chose to address together the minimum standard of treatment (Article 1105 (1) NAFTA) and expropriation and compensation (Article 1110 NAFTA).[77] The tribunal noted that the judiciary is a state organ and its actions are attributable to the state under the principle of international state responsibility which it deemed as uncontroversial.[78] The tribunal was careful in its analysis by clearly spelling out that it was not assuming the mantle of an appellate court to review domestic decisions rendered in Canada.[79] The tribunal reiterated that a "... NAFTA Chapter Eleven tribunal is not an appellate tier with a mandate to review the decisions of the national judiciary."[80] Additionally, the tribunal observed that any form of expropriation should be performed pursuant to due process of law and in exceptional circumstances where there is "clear evidence of egregious and shocking conduct" on the part of the state, which it did not find.[81]

70. *Ibid.*
71. Xu Yi-chong, 'Last chance? Multilateralism, TRIPS and developing countries', *Interpreting and implementing the TRIPS Agreement – Is it Fair* (2008), 46.
72. Christopher Gibson, 'A Look at the Compulsory License in Investment Arbitration: The Case of Indirect Expropriation', 25 *Am. U. Int'l L. Rev.* (2010), 357 at 361–362.
73. *Eli Lilly and Company v. The Government of Canada*, UNCITRAL, ICSID Case No. UNCT/14/2
74. *Ibid.*, Award para. 5.
75. *Ibid.*, Statement of Defence of the Government of Canada, 30 June 2014 para. 9.
76. *Ibid.*, para. 10.
77. *El Lilly v. Canada* Award, *supra* note 73, para. 221.
78. *Ibid.* Also, in *Bilcon v. Canada*, para. 319, the tribunal noted that two arms of government, that is, Nova Scotia and Canadian Federal Government rendered a Joint Review Panel Report on environmental assessment, while their actions were deemed to be attributed to Canada.
79. *Ibid.*
80. *El Lilly v. Canada* Award, *supra* note 73, para. 225.
81. *Ibid.*, para. 224.

The expropriation claim in *Philip Morris v. Uruguay*[82] (for details, see chapter 9 of this book) was centred on the alleged violation of Article 5(1) of the Switzerland–Uruguay BIT. Philip Morris based its claim on the enactment by Uruguay of the Single Presentation Rule (SPR) which required that any brand of cigarette be marketed as one brand without variants and graphic health warnings be increased from 50% to 80% (80/80 Regulation). The claimant asserted that the SPR and 80/80 Regulation effectively expropriated its intellectual property rights associated with its seven brands of cigarettes. On its part, Uruguay contended that the enactment of SPR regulation 80/80 was an act by a sovereign state exercising its mandate to protect the health of its citizens. The tribunal was quick to point out that there was no expropriation of the plaintiff's trade marks as they remained duly registered.[83]

Moreover, the tribunal held that "under Uruguayan law or international conventions to which Uruguay is a party the trademark holder does not enjoy an absolute right of use, free of regulation, but only an exclusive right to exclude third parties from the market so that only the trademark holder has the possibility to use the trademark in commerce, subject to the State's regulatory power."[84] The tribunal also evaluated how Uruguay exercised these regulatory powers and held it did so to protect the public health, hence could not be classified as expropriation.[85] Inasmuch as the measures were geared towards protecting the public health, Uruguay had not adopted them arbitrarily, but did so pursuant to its obligations under the WHO Framework Convention on Tobacco Control (FCTC).[86] Uruguay when ratifying the FCTC had made a declaration highlighting the inherent tension that exist in shaping the trade policy for tobacco industry and maintaining of public health.[87]

Safeguarding public health by enacting packaging regulations in *Philip Morris v. Uruguay* did not amount to indirect expropriation. The tribunal noted that actions by Uruguay did not meet the threshold of what would constitute a *prima facie* showing of indirect expropriation.[88] Though international arbitration in general lacks a doctrine of precedent, this finding was consistent with the findings in *S.D Myers v. Canada*[89] where the tribunal stated that the "general body of precedent does not usually treat regulatory action as expropriation. Regulatory conduct by public bodies is unlikely to be the subject of a legitimate complaint under Article 1110 of the NAFTA…".[90]

A key take away from the award in *Philip Morris v. Uruguay* is the tribunal's recognition that the exercise of police powers by a state to safeguard public order, health or morality has attained the status of customary international law, notwithstanding that such actions may lead to losses in an investor's business.[91] The tribunal

82. *Philip Morris Brands Sàrl, Philip Morris Products S.A. and Abal Hermanos S.A. v. Oriental Republic of Uruguay*, ICSID Case No. ARB/10/7 Award (8 July 2016).
83. *Ibid.*, para. 190.
84. *Ibid.*, para. 271.
85. *Ibid.*, para. 307.
86. *Ibid.*, paras. 395, 401.
87. < treaties.un.org/pages/ViewDetails.aspx?src = TREATY&mtdsg_no = IX-4&chapter = 9&-clang = _en#1 > (last accessed 10 March 2017).
88. *Philip Morris v. Uruguay* Award, para. 276.
89. *S.D. Myers, Inc. v. Government of Canada*, UNCITRAL Partial Award (13 November 2000).
90. *Ibid.*, para. 281.
91. *Philip Morris v. Uruguay* Award para. 295.

also acknowledged that the passage of time has led to this development.[92] Also, when a state is exercising police power it need not make any compensation as long as its actions are "bona fide for the purpose of protecting the public welfare, must be non-discriminatory and proportionate."[93] What this means is that police powers meeting these conditions trump an expropriation claim anchored in a BIT.[94]

In sum, patents and trade marks may be considered forms of property and may be subject to expropriation by the host state. The threshold to determine whether an action amounts to expropriation is dependent on the circumstances surrounding the case. Deference is given to states to take measures that are geared towards protection of public health when compared with other state obligations.[95] The jury is still out as to whether future claimants will succeed in invoking expropriation as a standard of protection to enforce intellectual property rights through BITs.

L. FAIR AND EQUITABLE TREATMENT

Fair and equitable treatment (FET) as an investment protection standard is an ever evolving concept given that its elements are pegged to factual circumstances, which vary from one dispute to the another.[96] It has been employed as a "fail-safe" by claimants as a litigation strategy given that other standards of protection vary in their evidentiary burden of proof, with some being considered difficult to attain.[97] Also, what constitutes "fair and equitable treatment" heavily depends on the treaty at hand given textual nuances and objectives of the treaty under consideration.[98]

The yardstick adopted by tribunals over the years to determine if conduct by a state infringes fair and equitable treatment is whether it runs: "against the international minimum standard required by customary international law; against international law including all sources; [and] against an independent self-contained treaty standard".[99]

92. *Ibid.*, para. 290.
93. *Ibid.*, para. 305.
94. *Ibid.*, para. 306.
95. In matters of the environment, it is still debatable whether expropriation for public purposes will entail an obligation on the host state to pay compensation or not, see Jack Coe and Noah Rubins, 'Regulatory expropriation and the Tecmed case: context and contributions', *International investment law and arbitration: Leading cases from the ICSID, NAFTA, bilateral treaties and customary international law* (2005), 637. This was a finding in *Santa Elena v. Costa Rica* at para. 72, where the tribunal stated that "[e]xpropriatory environmental measures – no matter how laudable and beneficial to society as a whole – are, in this respect, similar to any other expropriatory measures that a state may take in order to implement its policies: where property is expropriated, even for environmental purposes, whether domestic or international, the state's obligation to pay compensation remains."
96. Katia Yannaca-Small, 'Fair and equitable treatment standard: recent developments', *Standards of Investment Protection* (2008), 111.
97. *Ibid.* See J. Mendenhall, 'Fair Treatment of Intellectual Property Rights Under Bilateral Investment Treaties', 6(2) *Transnational Dispute Management (TDM)* (2009), 6.
98. OECD (2004), "Fair and Equitable Treatment Standard in International Investment Law", *OECD Working Papers on International Investment*, No. 2004/03, OECD Publishing, Paris. DOI: < dx.doi.org/10.1787/675702255435 > page 2.
99. *Ibid.*, OECD Working Paper p.9.

Under NAFTA, there have been inconsistencies in the interpretation of FET[100] which led the Free Trade Commission to issue a joint interpretation certain provisions of chapter 11 of NAFTA.[101]

One commentator succinctly summarises the components of FET as:

> [F]air and equitable treatment is interpreted to include the requirement of stability and predictability of the legal framework, consistency in the host State's decision-making, the principle of legality, the protection of confidence or legitimate expectations, procedural due process and the prohibition of denial of justice, the protection against discrimination and arbitrariness, the requirement of transparency, and the concept of reasonableness and proportionality.[102]

From the foregoing, FET has various limbs, with legitimate expectation being frequently invoked by investors.[103] The link between FET and legitimate expectation was pointed out by the tribunal in *Saluka v. Czech Republic*[104] when it held that "[t]he standard of "fair and equitable treatment" is ... closely tied to the notion of legitimate expectations which is the dominant element of that standard ...".[105] A NAFTA tribunal in *Thunderbird v. Mexico*[106] considered what constitutes a breach of legitimate expectation to be "... a situation where a Contracting Party's conduct creates reasonable and justifiable expectations on the part of an investor (or investment) to act in reliance on said conduct, such that a failure by the NAFTA Party to honour those expectations could cause the investor (or investment) to suffer damages."[107]

Legitimate expectation grounds were addressed by the tribunal in *Eli Lilly v. Canada*. Eli Lilly argued that it had a legitimate expectation that its two patents in Zyprexa and Strattera would remain valid for the period for which they were granted, and as such, would be not be nullified by a dramatic change in the utility requirement. Lilly based its argument on the fact that it had already acquired the patents, and on the basis of patent law in Canada and Canadian's international obligations under NAFTA and the Patent Cooperation Treaty (PCT).[108] Further, Eli Lilly asserted that the

100. Yannaca-Small, *supra* note 96, at 114.
101. "Article 1105(1) prescribes the customary international law minimum standard of treatment of aliens as the minimum standard of treatment to be afforded to investments of investors of another Party. The concepts of "fair and equitable treatment" and "full protection and security" do not require treatment in addition to or beyond that which is required by the customary international law minimum standard of treatment of aliens. A determination that there has been a breach of another provision of the NAFTA, or of a separate international agreement, does not establish that there has been a breach of Article 1105(1)." See Charles H. Brower II, Jack J. Coe Jr. and William S. Dodge, NAFTA Chapter Eleven Reports, Volume I: Primary Materials, 139.
102. Stephan W. Schill, *The Multilateralization of International Investment Law*, Vol. 2 (Cambridge University Press, 2009), 80.
103. Michele Potestà; 'Legitimate Expectations in Investment Treaty Law: Understanding the Roots and the Limits of a Controversial Concept', 28(1) *ICSID Review* (2013), 88–122 at 100.
104. *Saluka Investments B.V. v. The Czech Republic*, UNCITRAL Partial Award (17 March 2006).
105. *Ibid.*, para. 302.
106. *International Thunderbird Gaming Corporation v. The United Mexican States*, UNCITRAL Award (26th January 2006).
107. *Ibid.*, para. 147.
108. *El Lilly v. Canada* Award paras. 261–264.

change in the utility requirement was beyond what could be predicted as it was a complete departure from the norm, since Canada applied the new law retroactively.[109] Canada on the other hand, contended that legitimate expectations ought to "(i) be objective, not subjective; (ii) involve a specific assurance or promise by the State to induce the investment, which was relied upon by the investor; (iii) exist at the time the investor decided to make the investment; and (iv) be reasonable in the circumstances, including the political, socioeconomic, cultural and historical conditions prevailing in the host State."[110] Such grounds according to Canada, were not met.

The tribunal in its finding dismissed the claim for the alleged breach of legitimate expectations. The tribunal stated that it was reasonable for Eli Lilly to expect that patents once granted were not absolute and were subject to challenge in Canadian courts. The tribunal concluded that it was not possible to determine in advance how the law on patent utility would evolve, given that it was an outcome of judicial precedent. Judicial precedent by its very nature is gradual.[111]

The other instance where the ground of legitimate expectations was considered was in the case of *Philip Morris v. Uruguay.* The assertion by Philip Morris was that its source of legitimate expectations were the specific investment laws in Uruguay that were geared towards attracting investments.[112] Additionally, the duly registered trade marks according to Philip Morris, were an assurance that it would carry on its business by investing and growing its brand for decades.[113] The tribunal reiterated the standards for what it considered constituted legitimate expectation as being those specific assurances made to an investor to entice them to make an investment.[114] It went on to hold that for an investor to rely on the legitimate expectations ground, prior inquiry must be made before making an investment bearing in mind that the state retains its power to make regulatory changes in exercise of its regulatory mandate.[115]

In a dissenting opinion by one of the arbitrators, Gary Born, on the standard of fair and equitable treatment, noted that the SPR was enacted without any form of consultation, as there was no evidence of any study or consultation carried out with industry stakeholders.[116] This led him to conclude "that the [SPR] is a violation of the *fair and equitable treatment* standard … [and] does not bear a rational relationship to its stated legislative objective, yet disproportionately injures important investor rights."[117]

The two decisions, *Philip Morris v. Uruguay* and *Eli Lilly v. Canada* underpin the notion that the state's regulatory space to protect human health is unfettered by subsisting intellectual property rights such as patents and trade marks. This calls for a debate on TRIPS and its effectiveness given that it offers state parties the freedom to enact domestic legislation.

---

109. *Ibid.*, para. 269.
110. *Ibid.*, para. 301.
111. *Ibid.*, para. 380–385.
112. *Philip Morris v. Uruguay* Award para. 340.
113. *Ibid.*, para. 344.
114. *Ibid.*, para. 426.
115. *Ibid.*, para. 427.
116. *Philip Morris v. Uruguay* (ICSID Case No. ARB/10/7) Dissenting and concurring Opinion Gary Born para. 111.
117. *Ibid.*, para. 129 (emphasis added).

M. CRITIQUES OF ISDS

I. Impediment to the States' Right to Regulate

ISDS has been mainly criticized on the basis of the argument that ISDS threatens signatory states' ability to regulate in the public interest, such as public health and the environment.[118] A frequently cited example is the Philip Morris tobacco company case against the Australian government's 2011 *Tobacco Plain Packing Act.*[119] Philip Morris challenged the constitutionality of the legislation on the ground that "their intellectual property in the form of trademarks had been expropriated on unjust terms in the High Court of Australia.[120] The High Court found the legislation a public health measure based on the WHO Convention on Tobacco Control and ruled against Philip Morris. While Philip Morris was a US-based company and could not use the AUSFTA which contained no ISDS provisions, Philip Morris shifted assets to Hong Kong and used the ISDS provisions in the 1993 Hong Kong-Australia bilateral investment agreement. Pending the outcome of the ongoing Philip Morris Hong Kong case, the New Zealand and UK governments postponed their tobacco plain packaging legislation.[121]

In addition, a US forestry company AbitibiBowater, Inc. brought a NAFTA Chapter 11 ISDS claim against the Canadian federal government and successfully received USD 130 million in compensation for alleged expropriation, where the Canadian province had passed expropriation legislation after AbitibiBowater closed its mill and put about 800 employees out of work.[122] In another case, the Canadian government paid USD 13 million and agreed to reverse the banning of a petroleum additive for health reasons to settle with the US Ethyl Corporation. A Mexican municipal government paid USD 16.2 million in damages to the US Metalclad company for denial of a permit for a toxic waste disposal site for environmental reasons.[123] Invocation of ISDS by corporate entities has imposed significant costs on governments. Damages granted in ISDS cases range up to USD 1.8 billion awarded against Ecuador in 2012.[124] These cases have discouraged governments from regulation and have led to a "regulatory chill" effect.[125]

---

118. Arseni Matveev, 'Investor-State Dispute Settlement: the Evolving Balance between Investor Protection and State Sovereignty', 40 *University of Western Australia Law Review* (2015), 348, 349; See also Shahla F. Ali and Odysseas G. Repousis, 'Investor-State Mediation and the Rise of Transparency in International Investment Law: Opportunity or Threat?', 45(2) *Denver Journal of International Law and Policy* (2018), available at SSRN: <ssrn.com/abstract=3216254>.
119. Ranald, *supra* note 4, at 249.
120. *Ibid.*
121. *Ibid.*, at 250.
122. Thomas Faunce, 'Australia's Embrace of Investor State Dispute Settlement: A Challenge to the Social Contract Ideal?', 69(5) *Australian Journal of International Affairs* (2015), 595, 599.
123. Ranald, *supra* note 4, at 249–250.
124. *Ibid.*, at 250.
125. *Ibid.*

"Regulatory chill" is considered a difficult concept to quantify and measure.[126] It is anchored in the idea that a state may refrain from taking legislative or policy measures due to the imminent threat of an arbitration claim.[127] Notwithstanding the difficulty in measuring "regulatory chill" it is plausible that initiation of an arbitration claim, or the threat to commence one, is a tactic employed by claimants to gain leverage when negotiating with the host state. Amici in *Eli Lilly v. Canada* submitted to the NAFTA tribunal that "Lilly's use of this arbitration proceeding is abusive because it seeks to leverage the proceedings to influence the Canadian Parliament to change the law and limit the interpretation of the utility requirement by judges."[128] In *Bilcon v. Canada*[129] in a dissenting opinion by Professor Donald McRae considered that:

> What the majority has done is add a further control over environmental review panels. Failure to comply with Canadian law by a review panel now becomes the basis for a NAFTA claim allowing a claimant to bypass the domestic remedy ... This is a significant intrusion into domestic jurisdiction and will create a chill on the operation of environmental review panels ... If the majority view in this case is to be accepted, then the proper application of Canadian law by an environmental review panel will be in the hands of a NAFTA Chapter 11 tribunal, importing a damages remedy that is not available under Canadian law.[130]

By the same token, when it comes to developing countries, the nature of their economies make them vulnerable, as is illustrated by the fact that they have been respondents in a majority of investor-state arbitrations.[131] As discussed above, with the costs of arbitration being high, many such countries may not wish to incur such costs and may opt against making any legislative or policy changes that would negatively affect foreign investors.[132]

II. Appointment of Arbitrators

Moreover, critics are concerned about the impartiality of ISDS arbitrators. Due to the *ad hoc* nature of ISDS arbitral tribunals, arbitrators do not enjoy the security of tenure but depend on repeated appointments.[133] Arbitrators are usually lawyers

126. Coe and Rubins, *supra* note 95, 599.
127. *Ibid.*, at 599. See Susan D. Franck, 'Empirically evaluating claims about investment treaty arbitration', 86 *NCL Rev.* (2007), 48.
128. Amicus Curiae submission of Dr. Burcu Kilic, Professor Brook K. Baker, Professor Cynthia Ho and Mr. Yaniv Heled p. 9 available at < www.italaw.com/sites/default/files/case-documents/italaw7146.pdf > (last accessed 1 March 2017).
129. *William Ralph Clayton, William Richard Clayton, Douglas Clayton, Daniel Clayton and Bilcon of Delaware Inc. v. Government of Canada*, UNCITRAL, PCA Case No. 2009-04.
130. *Ibid.*, dissenting opinion para. 48.
131. Lauge N. Skovgaard Poulsen and Emma Aisbett, 'When the claim hits: Bilateral investment treaties and bounded rational learning', 65(2) *World Politics* (2013), 273–313 at 275.
132. Julia G. Brown, 'International Investment Agreements: Regulatory Chill in the Face of Litigious Heat', 3 *WJ Legal Stud.* (2013), 11.
133. Matveev, *supra* note 118, at 351.

who also often serve as lawyers for investors making other ISDS claims.[134] Critics argue that such arbitrators are inherently biased and have a structural incentive "to increase the number of investors interested in launching new cases and enhance the likelihood of being selected for future tribunals."[135] The subject on the choice of an arbitrator, although seemingly an easy one, is a controversial subject. When appointing arbitrators, "...a party's choice of arbitrator involves a forensic decision that is clearly related to a judgment by the appointing party and its counsel of its prospects of success in the dispute."[136] The standard adopted by tribunals when considering a challenge on an appointment of an arbitrator under the ICSID Convection is whether the arbitrator is impartial and independent.[137]

The burden of proof on the party challenging the appointment of the arbitrator is considered a high one.[138] Tribunals recognize the difficulty of assessing and determining the independence and impartiality of an arbitrator as it entails an assessment of the frame of mind of an arbitrator.[139] If one of the arbitrators is privy to some information gathered while sitting in another tribunal this may in and of itself potentially lead to inequality of parties, considering that the arbitrator may not be in a position to erect a "Chinese wall" to distinguish such information.[140] Recent decisions by tribunals suggest that repeat appointments contribute to impairing the impartiality of arbitrators.[141] Whereas the integrity and competence of the arbitrators may not be in doubt, there exists no accountability mechanism over the arbitrators

134. Joel Lexchin and Deborah Gleeson, 'The Trans Pacific Partnership Agreement and Pharmaceutical Regualation in Canada and Australia', 46(4) *International Journal of Health Services* (2016), 597, 602.
135. *Ibid.*
136. *OPIC Karimum Corporation v. The Bolivarian Republic of Venezuela*, ICSID Case No. ARB/10/14 Decision on the Proposal to Disqualify Professor Philippe Sands, Arbitrator para. 47.
137. Various arbitration institutions have set standards for which arbitrator must uphold when carrying out duties of an arbitrator. The ICSID Convention Article 14(1) "Persons designated to serve on the Panels shall be persons of high moral character and recognized competence in the fields of law, commerce, industry or finance, who may be relied upon to exercise independent judgment...". International Court of Arbitration (ICC) Rules Article 11(1) "Every arbitrator must be and remain impartial and independent of the parties involved in the arbitration." Stockholm Chambers of Commerce (SCC) Article 18(1) "Every arbitrator must be impartial and independent". On the other hand, UNCITRAL Arbitration Rules, Article 10(1) "Any arbitrator may be challenged if circumstances exist that give rise to justifiable doubts as to the arbitrators impartiality or independence".
138. James D. Fry and Juan Ignacio Stampalija, 'Forged Independence and Impartiality: Conflicts of Interest of International Arbitrators in Investment Disputes', 30(2) *Arbitr. Int.* (2014), 189-264, at 208.
139. *Suez, Sociedad General de Aguas de Barcelona, S.A.and Vivendi Universal, S.A. v. Argentine Republic*, ICSID Case No. ARB/03/19 Decision on the proposal for the disqualification of a member of the arbitral tribunal (22 October 2007) para. 30.
140. *EnCana Corp v. Ecuador* Partial Award on Jurisdiction 27 January 2004 at para. 45.
141. *Caratube v. Kazakhstan* ARB/13/13, Decision on the Proposal for Disqualification of Mr. Bruno Boesch (20 March 2014); *Blue Bank v. Venezuela* ARB/12/20, Decision on the Parties' Proposals to Disqualify a Majority of the Tribunal, (12 November 2013); *Burlington Resources, Inc. v. Republic of Ecuador* ARB/08/5, Decision on the Proposal for Disqualification of Professor Francisco Orrego Vicuña (13 December 2013).

given that they serve on an *ad hoc* basis.[142] At the extreme end, some critics consider the ISDS system as benefitting lawyers and third party funders who are now facilitating claimants to institute arbitration proceedings.[143]

III. Broad Interpretation of BITs

Since many of the ISDS provisions such as "minimum standards of treatment" and "legitimate expectations" are vaguely worded, arbitrators have significant room to interpret investors' rights in an expansive way and order compensation.[144] The expansive interpretation of the BIT provisions at least in the case of more recent agreements exceeds what state parties to a BIT had contemplated when they negotiated it. This points to why NAFTA Free Trade Commission issued a joint interpretation on certain provisions of Chapter 11 of NAFTA.[145] The binding nature of the joint interpretation was to limit future arbitration tribunals from rendering an expansive interpretation on the standards of fair and equitable treatment and full protection and security.[146]

By extension, there have been instances where disputes arising from the same conduct by the state, or the same treaty, have resulted in different outcomes.[147] This adds to the complexity and unpredictability of the ISDS system. The broad and vague terms will remain in BITs, unless the states modernise them. The Joint interpretation mechanism in NAFTA is not available in the majority of the BITs, though, and governments face difficulties when trying to change the interpretation of such agreements. But see also chapter 9 where the arbitrators in the Philipp Morris/ Uruguay litigation gave the underlying agreement a "modernist" interpretation.

IV. Prone to Abuse

Another criticism of the ISDS system is that it has in some instances been abused. Tribunals do acknowledge that they have an obligation to prevent "manipulation of the system of international investment protection under the ICSID Convection and the BITs".[148] In *Phoenix Action v. Czech Republic,* the tribunal noted that the claimant was merely shifting resources within his family members and purporting to make an

142. <www.afj.org/wp-content/uploads/2015/03/ISDS-Letter-3.11.pdf> (last accessed 1 February 2017) A letter sent by a list of distinguished law professors voicing their opposition to the inclusion of ISDS mechanism in the Trans Pacific Partnership (TPP) and the Transatlantic Trade and Investment Partnership (TTIP).
143. Cecilia Olivet and Pia Eberhardt, 'Profiting from injustice: How law firms, arbitrators and financiers are fuelling an investment arbitration boom, *Transnational Institute* (2012), 27.
144. *Ibid.*
145. <www.sice.oas.org/tpd/nafta/commission/ch11understanding_e.asp> (last accessed 19 February 2019).
146. *Ibid.*
147. <ccsi.columbia.edu/files/2018/11/Inconsistencies_ISDS_Briefing-Note_11.28.18.pdf> (last accessed 19 February 2019).
148. *Phoenix Action, Ltd. v. The Czech Republic,* ICSID Case No. ARB/06/5 Award (15 April 2009) para. 143.

investment to qualify for protection under the Israel–Czech BIT.[149] This gave rise to the question whether the investment was *bona fide* or was motivated to benefit from the ISDS system. The tribunal questioned the rationale of investing in a company that was on its death bed and involved in criminal and civil litigation in the host state.[150]

Similarly, in *Philip Morris v. Australia,*[151] in order to determine whether a corporate restructuring by a claimant was geared to gain access to the ISDS and hence amounting to an abuse, the tribunal adopted the test of whether there was "a reasonable prospect" that a measure adopted by a host state would crystallise into a dispute under a treaty.[152] Australia contended that the restructuring had nothing to do with tax optimisation.[153] The tribunal held " that the main and determinative, if not sole, reason for the restructuring was the intention to bring a claim under the Treaty, using an entity from Hong Kong."[154]

Whilst it is not illegal to restructure investments to bring them under the protection of BITs, tribunals consider the timing of the restructuring to determine whether its sole purpose is to commence an arbitration claim. This was highlighted by the tribunal in *Tokios Tokeles v. Ukraine*[155] when it held that "...[t]he Claimant manifestly did not create Tokios Tokeles for the purpose of gaining access to ICSID arbitration under the BIT against Ukraine, as the enterprise *was founded six years before the BIT between Ukraine and Lithuania entered into force*. Indeed, there is no evidence in the record that the Claimant used its formal legal nationality for any improper purpose."[156]

In the same tribunal, a dissenting opinion by Prosper Wiel noted that the ICSID system was not aimed at allowing nationals to sue their own country through ISDS, effectively taking away the jurisdiction of the local courts.[157] Rather, the tribunals ought to look at "origin of the capital" to determine whether it has jurisdiction.[158] He considered that although there was no evidence of abuse of legal personality by Ukrainian nationals registering an entity in Lithuania, tribunals have discretion to examine each case on its merit to determine whether exercising jurisdiction meets the objective and purpose of the ICSID Convection.[159]

149. Para. 139.
150. *Ibid.*, para. 140
151. *Philip Morris Asia Limited v. The Commonwealth of Australia*, UNCITRAL, PCA Case No. 2012-12 Award in Jurisdiction and Admissibly (17 December 2015).
152. *Ibid.*, para. 554.
153. *Ibid.*, para. 577.
154. *Ibid.*, para. 584.
155. *Tokios Tokelés v. Ukraine*, ICSID Case No. ARB/02/18, Decision on Jurisdiction, April 29, 2004.
156. *Ibid.*, para. 56 (emphasis added).
157. *Tokios Tokelés v. Ukraine*, ICSID Case No. ARB/02/18, Dissenting Opinion Chairman Prosper Weil (29th April 2004) paras. 19–22.
158. *Ibid.*
159. *Ibid.*

V. Reforming BITs

In response to such criticisms, some governments have sought to limit the scope of ISDS. In 2007, Bolivia withdrew from the ICSID Convention and became the first state to do so, followed by Ecuador in 2010[160] and Venezuela in 2012.[161] In 2011, the Australian Government issued a statement that it would no longer agree to the adoption of ISDS in its BITs, but this controversial position was later replaced by a pragmatic treaty-by-treaty approach.[162] Following Australia, a few more countries including Venezuela, Argentina, South Africa, India and Indonesia all announced their intentions to restrict ISDS granting treaties and some of these countries even terminated a number of BITs containing ISDS provisions.[163] Argentina which has one of the highest number of investor-state arbitration claims has maintained its BITs with a few exceptions. These exceptions include a small number of terminations initiated by treaty partners.[164] It would have been expected for Argentina to take the lead in renouncing BITs, however, this has not been the case. Ecuador, on the other hand, after facing numerous investor-state arbitration claims, has terminated the majority of its BITs.

However, a large number of countries still support ISDS.[165] Indonesia for instance, after terminating several BITs, has recently signed a BIT with Singapore.[166] The approach by Indonesia is to discontinue old treaties and gradually negotiate new ones, ostensibly with better terms.[167] In 2014, 27 new investment agreements were concluded, the majority of which contained ISDS provisions.[168] Notably, unlike early BITs, newly concluded BITs commonly restrict investors' access to ISDS by reserving various security exceptions. It is predicted that this new generation of BITs is likely to become more popular.[169]

160. Leon E. Trakman and David Musayelyan, 'The Repudiation of Investor-State Arbitration and Subsequent Treaty Practice: the Resurgence of Qualified Investor-State Arbitration', 31(1) *ICSID Review* (2016), 194, 196.
161. <icsid.worldbank.org/en/Documents/icsiddocs/List%20of%20Contracting%20States%20and%20Other%20Signatories%20of%20the%20Convention%20-%20Latest.pdf> (last accessed 1 February 2019).
162. Trakman and Musayelyan, *supra* note 160.
163. Trakman and Musayelyan, *supra* note 160, at 197.
164. <investmentpolicyhub.unctad.org/IIA/CountryBits/8#iiaInnerMenu> (last accessed 1February 2019).
165. Trakman and Musayelyan, *supra* note 160, at 198.
166. <www.gov.sg/~/sgpcmedia/media_releases/mti/press_release/P-20181011-1/attachment/Press%20release%20on%20signing%20of%20Indonesia-Singapore%20BIT%20on%2011%20Oct%202018.pdf>.
167. Abdulkadir Jailani, 'Indonesia's Perspective on Review of International Investment Agreements', *Rethinking Bilateral Investment Treaties*, 113.
168. Trakman and Musayelyan, *supra* note 160, at 205.
169. Trakman and Musayelyan, *supra* note 160, at 217.

CHAPTER 3

The History of Investment Tribunals and the Protection of IPRs under Investment Treaties

Flavia Marisi and Julien Chaisse[1]

A. INTRODUCTION

International investment has become one of the most dynamic and debated areas of international law in the last decade. This applies in particular when private investors can obtain treaty-based redress via private investor tribunals (so-called investor-state dispute settlement, ISDS) for acts of states that have an adverse effect on their investment, an issue this book is primarily concerned with. The proliferation of treaties and multiplication of disputes largely explain that the stakeholders of this system (i.e. states, investors, and arbitrators) often have diverging views on the lessons to be drawn from the recent ISDS practice and for the best way forward to modernise the regime. It should be borne in mind, though, that the provisions currently governing international investment law are the outcome of a long historical evolution whose roots date back to the first century of the current era.

In the present chapter, it is maintained that the origins of dispute settlement in international investment law have a determining role in shaping the nature of the present international investment regime. This chapter therefore analyses the social and political aspects of such evolution, arguing that the commercial objectives of

1. This research was supported by the General Research Fund (GRF) Project No. 14605915 of the Hong Kong SAR Research Grants Council (RGC). The GRC research projects are subject to a rigorous peer review process via the RGC's five subject panels supported by an international network of expert reviewers.
Since co-writing this Chapter, Dr. Marisi has joined Hanotiau & van den Berg. The views and opinions expressed in this Chapter are those of the author(s) and do not reflect the position of Hanotiau & van den Berg or of any other lawyer in the firm.

capital-exporting countries have shaped the core features of modern international investment law. This is clearly visible from the organisation, principles, ideas, and methods of dispute resolution relies upon or employed in these agreements. By examining the historical scenario, this chapter explores how the main principles of this field of law were developed.

Part B retraces the foundations of international investment law, narrating the history of the protection of foreign investment throughout the centuries. The birth of the Treaties of Friendship, Commerce and Navigation marks the beginning of the era of reciprocity between states in the concessions to foreign merchants and investors. In the early stages, disputes between investors and the host country were solved through diplomacy, with the active engagement of the investor's home country. The development of the Hull Formula and Calvo doctrine allowed the evolution of the concepts of compensated expropriation and national treatment, which were thereafter included in a great part of such treaties.

Part C digs into the development of investment arbitration from State-State to Investor-State, as we know it today, unveils the reasons of its expansive use and outlines the differences with its sibling, commercial arbitration.

Following the outline of the historical and legal framework, Part D focuses on the development of the protection of Intellectual Property Rights under Investment Law, examining how IPRs came to be included in the scope of International Investment Agreements (IIAs): from the first BIT between Germany and Pakistan until more recent treaties. It also provides an overview of Investor-State cases that tackled IPRs and discusses whether investment tribunals are an appropriate forum to determine an alleged frustration of these intangible property rights.

B. THE FOUNDATIONS OF INTERNATIONAL INVESTMENT LAW

Over hundreds of years, individuals and their nations have managed their relations and interactions through a set of international legal regimes[2]. The era of European expansion, a process that manifested itself in several different stages and ways, could be said to have commenced in the first century of the current era[3].

I. Concessions and Investment Protection – The Early Days

In the beginning of the 10th century,[4] various measures to protect foreign direct investment have emerged when merchants from Venice were allowed to anchor their ships in the harbours of the Byzantine Empire free of charge;[5] a similar right was

2. M. Sornarajah, *The International Law on Foreign Investment* (CUP, 1994), 19; C.H. Alexandrowicz, *An Introduction to the History of the Law of Nations in the East Indies (16th, 17th and 18th Centuries)* (OUP, 1967), 997–999.
3. See Andrew William Lintott, *Imperium Romanorum: Politics and Administration* (Routledge, 1993).
4. Jeswald W. Salacuse, *The Law of Investment Treaties* (Oxford University Press, 2010), 80.
5. See generally Richard B. Lillich, *The Human Rights of Aliens in Contemporary International Law* (Manchester University Press, 1984), 7.

later granted to merchants from Genoa.[6] In the 12th century, English kings started to grant similar permits to foreign traders,[7] allowing them to run their activities complying with the laws of their home states.[8]

Even though such measures did not constitute a proper investment agreement, they provide an example of what the initial forms of investment protection were:[9] trade concessions given by a monarch to alien merchants, rather than a treaty signed by two kings for mutual benefits to their citizens in a foreign territory.[10]

Thanks to these concessions, nationals of one country who considered that their rights had been harmed during their stay abroad, could address their sovereign so that the latter would exercise his influence and protect their interests, whereas they were not entitled to claim specific rights against authorities and nationals of the host state.[11]

The legal principle at the basis thereof is the concept of sovereignty, which in the past centuries was deemed to concern the nationals of a specific country, rather than the territory of that country. Therefore, on the one hand a foreigner residing abroad did not enjoy the same rights as the citizens of his residing state, but neither had any specific obligations toward this state. This happened, for instance, when Christian foreigners, both merchants and missionaries, resided in countries in which justice was administered according to different principles compared to those of the Christian tradition.[12]

For regulating this kind of issues, in 1536 Francis I of France and Suleyman I of Turkey signed a treaty which would be taken as a model in subsequent agreements with other countries. The treaty established that the French merchants could settle in Turkey, enjoying individual and religious freedom, and that French civil and penal law would apply to them, administered by consuls appointed by the French monarch. The decisions of these consuls could be enforced in cooperation with the sultan's officers.[13]

This continued until the early stages of the 19th century, when European nations and political institutions managed to manifest their aims and wishes also in regard to cultural impositions; they spread and enforced the European concept of international law and legal conduct over that of native populations.[14]

---

6. *Ibid.*
7. Salacuse, *supra* note 4, at 80; *see also* P. Fischer, *A Collection of International Concessions and Related Instruments* (11 vols., Oceana Publications, New York. 1976–1983).
8. Lillich, *supra* note 5, at 7.
9. Christian Tietje and Freya Baetens, 'The Impact of Investor-State-Dispute Settlement (ISDS)', in *The Transatlantic Trade and Investment Partnership*, Study prepared for the Minister for Foreign Trade and Development Cooperation, Ministry of Foreign Affairs, Netherlands, 2014, < docplayer.net/14338244-The-impact-of-investor-state-dispute-settlement-isds-in-the-transatlantic-trade-and-investment-partnership-study-prepared-for.html > accessed 10 April 2019.
10. Salacuse, *supra* note 4, at 80.
11. Lillich, *supra* note 5, at 9.
12. Edwards A. Van Dyck, *Capitulations of the Ottoman Empire since the Year 1150: Report* (Government Printing Office, Washington 1881), < archive.org/stream/capitulationsot00statgoog/capitulationsot00statgoog_djvu.txt > accessed 10 April 2019.
13. *Ibid.*
14. Antony Anghie, *Imperialism, Sovereignty and the Making of International Law* (Cambridge University Press, Cambridge, 2007), 32–33; Lauren Benton, *Law and Colonial Cultures:*

Therefore, arbitration was initially used only between states,[15] establishing a State-to-State arbitration, because individuals and companies did not have the necessary status to appear before international tribunals.[16] Later, in the second half of the nineteenth century, the first direct Investor-State arbitrations were reported: one of the first was between the Turkish *La Compagnie Universelle du Canal de Suez*, and Egypt, as follows.

In 1864, Egypt issued a law by which it broke an agreement it had signed with the Turkish company, and the latter sought compensation. Although the agreement between Egypt and the company did not include an arbitration clause, the parties agreed to resolve the dispute in arbitration, and appointed Napoleon III as arbitrator.[17] The contested national measure concerned the elimination of forced labour regime, which was essential for the construction works on the Suez Canal. The award was based on the work of an *ad hoc* Commission, composed by French political and legal experts appointed by Napoleon III himself. Completed at Fontainebleau on 6 July 1864, the award, following the recommendation of the Commission's report, found that 84 million francs were to be paid by Egypt to *La Compagnie Universelle du Canal de Suez* in 16 instalments over a period of 15 years.[18]

II. 1700s: Genesis and Spread of Treaties of Friendship, Commerce and Navigation (FCN)

Acts regarding the management and regulation of citizens' economic activities first began to be promulgated by monarchs in writing during the 1600s-1700s as a result of the emergence of Nation-States.[19] The earliest investment protection forms were the treaties signed by two monarchs that outlined how investment and trade protection was to be regulated on their territories.[20]

Towards the end of the 1700s, countries that did not possess colonies began to use a new type of tool devised to protect their economic interests in foreign territories - the Treaties of Friendship, Commerce and Navigation (hereinafter FCNs) not only ensured port access, but also conferred rights to navigate internal waters.[21] In 1778, France and the US signed the first such treaty, which was called Treaty of

Legal Regimes in World History 1400–1900 (CUP, 2002), 10–11.

15. Rudolf Dolzer, Christoph Schreuer *Principles of International Investment Law* (Oxford University Press, Oxford, 2012), 14.
16. M. Sornarajah, *The Settlement of Foreign Investment Disputes* (Kluwer, The Hague, 2000), 151; Zouhair A. Kronfol, *Protection of Foreign Investment: A Study in International Law* (A.W. Sijhoff, Leiden, 1972), 16.
17. *Egypt v. Suez Canal Company* (Award, 1864), cited in Alexander Marie Stuyt, *Survey of International Arbitrations, 1794–1989* (Martinus Nijhoff Publishers, Dordrecht, 1990), 471.
18. Jason Webb Yackee, 'The First Investor-State Arbitration: The Suez Canal Company v Egypt (1864)', 17 *The Journal of World Investment & Trade* (2016), 401–462.
19. Salacuse, *supra* note 4, at 81.
20. *Ibid.*
21. M. Sornarajah *The International Law on Foreign Investment* (Cambridge University Press, Cambridge, 2010), 180–181.

Amity and Commerce[22] and was based on a model developed by John Adams.[23] Even in those early times, the language used in drafting these kinds of treaties was not very different from the language of modern BITs and the principles subsequently described as "MFN"[24] and "FET"[25] already made their appearance. This treaty with France served as the prototype for the bilateral treaties signed by the US with Prussia, Morocco, England, and Spain,[26] and subsequently with countries from Latin America, Africa, and Asia that were open to commercial activities.[27]

These treaties differed from earlier agreements in that they placed more emphasis on reciprocity, ensuring that both parties were fairly protected owing to the relative power balance existing between them.[28] Hence, nationals of the partner state engaged in commercial activities were not only afforded national treatment, but could also initiate legal proceedings in national courts to safeguard their interests.[29]

Nevertheless, their reciprocal character began to diminish as the treaties were established with remote countries which had no choice but to comply with the specifications imposed by their European partners.[30] Furthermore, the treaties

22. Salacuse, *supra* note 4, 84; Treaty of Amity and Commerce between the United States and France, (signed 6 February 1778) <avalon.law.yale.edu/18th_century/fr1788-1.asp> accessed 10 April 2019.
23. Kenneth J. Vandevelde, *Bilateral Investment Treaties: History, Policy and Interpretation* (OUP, 2010), 19.
24. Andreas R. Ziegler, 'Most-Favoured-Nation (MFN) Treatment', in August Reinisch (ed.), *Standards of Investment Protection* (OUP, 2008), 59, 62.
25. Wolfgang Alschner, 'Americanization of the BIT Universe: The Influence of Friendship. Commerce and Navigation (FCN) Treaties on Modern Investment Treaty Law', 5(2) *Goettingen Journal of International Law* (2013), 455, 457.
26. A Treaty of Amity and Commerce between His Majesty the King of Prussia, and the United States of America (signed 10 September 1785), <avalon.law.yale.edu/18th_century/prus1785.asp> accessed 10 April 2019; Treaty of Peace and Friendship, Treaty with Morocco (28 June and 15 July 1786), <avalon.law.yale.edu/18th_century/bar1786t.asp> accessed 10 April 2019; Treaty of Amity Commerce and Navigation, between His Britannick Majesty and The United States of America, by Their President, with the advice and consent of Their Senate ("The Jay Treaty") (signed 19 November 1794), <avalon.law.yale.edu/18th_century/jay.asp> accessed 10 April 2019; Treaty of Friendship, Limits, and Navigation Between Spain and The United States (signed 27 October 1795), <avalon.law.yale.edu/18th_century/sp1795.asp> accessed 10 April 2019.
27. See generally Kenneth J. Vandevelde, 'U.S. Bilateral Investment Treaties: The Second Wave', 14 *Michigan Journal of International Law* (1993), 621, 623.
28. Salacuse, *supra* note 4, 82. *See, e.g.*, Treaty of Friendship, Commerce and Navigation Between Argentina and the United States (signed 27 July 1853), <avalon.law.yale.edu/19th_century/argen02.asp> accessed 10 April 2019; Brazil–US, Treaty of Amity, Commerce, and Navigation (signed 12 December 1828), <avalon.law.yale.edu/19th_century/brazil01.asp> accessed 10 April 2019.
29. Dieter Blumenwitz, 'Treaties of Friendship, Commerce and Navigation', in Rudolf Bernhardt (ed.), *Encyclopaedia of Public International Law,* Vol. IV (North-Holland, 2002), 954–955.
30. Charles Lipson, *Standing Guard: Protecting Foreign Capital in the Nineteenth and Twentieth Centuries* (University of California Press, Berkeley-Los Angeles-London, 1985), 12–14; Anghie, *supra* note 14, 85–86.

became highly biased as investors benefitted greatly from the manner in which the adjudicating authorities interpreted the treaties.[31]

FCN treaties contained the predecessor of the modern "fair and equitable treatment", "most favoured nation" and "national treatment" provisions: they were gradually included in most treaties, and evolved into the standards of protection as we know them today.[32]

In procedural terms, the Treaty of Amity, Commerce and Navigation (known as the Jay Treaty) established between Britain and the US in 1794 introduced a crucial development,[33] namely the creation of mixed commissions responsible for arbitrating the boundary disputes stemming from the damage or seizure that the property of nationals of both countries had suffered during the war. Both disputes between states and between individuals and states entered the jurisdiction of these commissions. This development was a success as during the period 1798–1804, over 500 awards were granted, establishing a direction for future law formulation. Furthermore, the commissions' work was considered to be so satisfactory that arbitration clauses were included in several treaties established during the 1800s.[34] This, in turn, caused a gradual increase in State-to-State arbitration, so that in the first one hundred years, more than a hundred claims were filed.[35]

Despite these advancements, force continued to be frequently used to buttress trade and diplomatic activities. For instance, Japan was coerced to render its commercial infrastructure and ports accessible to European traders following the military incursion of Admiral Perry in 1854,[36] the Boxer Rebellion against foreigners that occurred in China in 1899 was diffused by military means by the Eight-Nation Alliance, and republics in Latin America were obtruded upon by the US Marine.[37]

In a parliamentary speech in 1850, the so-called "gunboat diplomacy" was justified by Lord Palmerston, the Prime Minister of Britain, declaring:

> As the Roman, in days of old, held himself free from indignity when he could say Civis Romanus sum, so also a British subject, in whatever land he may be, shall feel confident that the watchful eye and strong arm of England will protect him against injustice and wrong.[38]

---

31. Lipson, *supra* note 30, 13–14.
32. Blumenwitz, *supra* note 29, 955; Andrea K. Bjorklund, 'National Treatment', in August Reinisch (ed.), *Standards of Investment Protection* (Oxford University Press, Oxford 2008), 29, 31; Salacuse, *supra* note 4, 85.
33. The Jay Treaty, *supra* note 26, Art. 6.
34. Peter Malanczuk, *Akehurst's Modern Introduction to International Law* (Routledge, 1997), 20.
35. David W. Rivkin, 'The Impact of International Arbitration on the Rule of Law', transcript of the 2012 Clayton Utz Sydney University International Arbitration Lecture (2012), at 7 (citing James Brown Scott, *The Hague Peace Conferences of 1899 and 1907*, Volume I (1909), 226).
36. Murray Davies, *Commanding Change: War Winning Military Strategies for Organizational Change* (Praeger, 1962), 43. The Japanese have coined the term "Unequal Treaties" (fuboeki jōyaku) for the agreements they had to enter with Western nations that, inter alia, granted nationals of these countries diplomatic immunity in Japan.
37. Neill H. Jacoby, *Corporate Power and Social Responsibility* (Simon and Schuster, 1973), 116.
38. Piers Brendon, *The Decline and Fall of the British Empire: 1781–1997* (Vintage, 2008), 99.

Regardless of this, however, diplomatic measures continued to be employed on an increasingly regular basis. By the middle of the 1900s, the US and other countries signed additional FCNs to ensure that both individuals and commercial undertakings in foreign countries were safeguarded against any prejudicial action that might have been taken against them. Furthermore, despite the fact that, apart from former colonies, foreign direct investment was not extensive at the time, protection of property against expropriation was a major objective of these FCNs.[39] Notably, one clause in the model FCN prepared by the US stipulated that expropriations required compensation of the owners with a "just compensation", in keeping with the rule of law.[40]

III. 1800s: Emergence of Diplomatic Protection

Foreign investment law emerged during the 1800s in the context of an international law construct called "diplomatic protection of aliens".[41] The general definition of diplomatic protection is that of:

> The invocation by a State, through diplomatic action or other means of peaceful settlement, of the responsibility of another State for an injury caused by an internationally wrongful act of that State to a natural or legal person that is a national of the former State with a view to the implementation of such responsibility.[42]

Thus, diplomatic intervention refers to the measures taken by a country to aid its nationals living in a foreign country when they have not been treated according to the minimum standard of protection.

Customary international law specifies that a state is liable for any damage it has inflicted on a foreigner through illegal measures or negligence and the victim can make recourse to the diplomatic protection instrument to secure compensation. Historically, this has been seen as a state prerogative, as it was considered that the state itself incurred an offence when one of its nationals was mistreated.[43] Therefore, the host country incurred liability for any injury to another state's nationals, while the country of origin could take various measures, including diplomacy and military action, to protect its nationals' rights.[44] Various political and economic factors dictated the course of action that the home country decided upon.[45]

The notion of diplomatic protection was first introduced in 1758 in a declaration made by Emmerich de Vattel, a philosopher, lawyer and diplomat from Switzerland.

39. Salacuse, *supra* note 4, 86.
40. Vandevelde, *supra* note 23, 50–51.
41. Ian Brownlie, *Principles of Public International Law* (Clarendon Press, Oxford, 1998), 524–526.
42. United Nations, *Draft Articles on Diplomatic Protection with commentaries*, 2006.
43. Sornarajah, *supra* note 21, at 138.
44. Chittharanjan Felix Amerasinghe, *State Responsibility for Injuries of Aliens*, (Clarendon Press, 1967), 56.
45. Edwin M. Borchard, *The Diplomatic Protection of Citizens Abroad or the Law of International Claims* (The Banks Law Publishing Company, 1915), 439.

In his *Le Droit des Gens ou Principes de la Loi Naturelle Appliqués à la Conduite et aux Affaires des Nations et des Souverains*[46] he stated that

> Whoever mistreats a citizen, indirectly offends the state, which is bound to protect the citizen; and the sovereign of the latter should avenge his injury, if possible obliging the aggressor to make full reparation; since otherwise the citizen would not enjoy the great end of civil society, which is security.[47]

In 1924, the Permanent Court of International Justice reasserted this notion, stating that

> By taking up the case of one of its subjects and by resorting to diplomatic action or international judicial proceedings on his behalf, a State is in reality asserting its own right, the right to ensure, in the person of its subjects, respect for the rules of international law.[48]

It is evident that this is an overstatement,[49] as attested by the fact that according to the continuous nationality rule, the home state had to prove "that the injured remained its national after the injury itself and up to the date of the presentation of the claim".[50] This rule derived from the conviction that in the past, the individual did not have any rights under international law, and that in order to overcome this disadvantage, it was necessary to have recourse to the fiction that the right to be protected belonged to the home state.

Diplomatic protection could only be instigated when legal solutions in the host country, which would enable the liable state to take reparative action, had been exhausted.[51] The mechanism through which the country of origin of an individual who has incurred damage in a foreign country can take legal action against that country of behalf of its citizen is called *espousal*.[52] Espousal can result in negotia-

46. Emmerich de Vattel, *Le Droit des Gens ou Principes de la Loi Naturelle Appliqués à la Conduite et aux Affaires des Nations et des Souverains*, vol. I (A Leide, 1758), para. 71.
47. Annemarieke Vermeer-Kuenzli, 'Diplomatic Protection as a Source of Human Rights Law', in Dinah Shelton (ed.), *The Oxford Handbook of International Human Rights Law* (OUP, 2013), 250, 251.
48. *Mavrommatis Palestine Concessions* (*Greece v. U.K.*) PCIJ Reports, 1924, Series A, No. 2, p. 12. This dictum was repeated by the Permanent Court of International Justice in the *Panevezys Saldutiskis Railway* case (*Estonia v. Lithuania*) PCIJ Reports, 1939, Series A/B, No. 76, 16.
49. J.L. Brierly, *The Law of Nations: An Introduction to the International Law of Peace* (Clarendon Press, 1963), 276–277.
50. United Nations Draft Articles on Diplomatic Protection with commentaries, *Yearbook of the International Law Commission*, vol. II, part two (2006).
51. *Interhandel* (*Switzerland v. United States of America*), 1959 ICJ Rep. 6, 27.
52. Also the WTO dispute settlement system is a State-to-State adjudication regime, however, different from what occurs in espousal, the WTO system according to Bjorklund focusses "on redressing systemic distortion rather than on compensating an individual claimant". See OECD, Investor-State Dispute Settlement Public Consultation: 16 May – 23 July 2012, 51, <www.oecd.org/daf/inv/investment-policy/ISDSconsultationcomments_web.pdf> accessed 10 April 2019.

tions or litigation between the two states before an international court or arbitral tribunal.[53]

Espousal may fail as a solution for various reasons, as identified by different studies:[54] i) in its desire to maintain good relations with the host country,[55] the home country may refuse to engage in espousal;[56] ii) although the process of submitting a claim in a local court may be costly and lengthy, the home country may resort to espousal only after an unsuccessful exhaustion of local avenues in the host country;[57] and iii) the injured individual has no control over the claim made, as it is in the power of the home country to settle a claim it espouses on its desired terms.[58]

Conversely, customary international law stipulates that if an agreement is reached between an injured individual and the host country to settle their dispute in an arbitration court, the diplomatic protection mechanism can no longer be invoked.[59] However, this rule provides for an exemption: Article 27(1) of ICSID provides:

> No Contracting State shall give diplomatic protection, or bring an international claim, in respect of a dispute which one of its nationals and another Contracting State shall have consented to submit or shall have submitted to arbitration under this Convention, unless such other Contracting State shall have failed to abide by and comply with the award rendered in such dispute.[60]

Further circumstances under which diplomatic protection may continue to be applicable include: i) the lack of an investment treaty or trade agreement with provisions on investment; ii) the lack of ISDS in the presence of such treaties; and iii) the lack of ISDS in such treaties for certain kinds of disputes,[61] e.g. in the case where investment is narrowly defined.[62]

Finally, even if investment agreements grant rights to investors under international law, there are situations in which those rights do not apply to particular subjects or to specific circumstances. For this reason, both ISDS and diplomatic protection may have an important role in the protection of foreign investments abroad.[63]

---

53. Christoph Schreuer, 'The Dynamic Evolution of the ICSID System' (2006), < www.univie.ac.at/intlaw/pdf/cspubl_86.pdf > accessed 10 April 2019.
54. Kenneth J. Vandevelde, 'A Brief History of International Investment Agreements', 12(1) *University of California Davis Journal of International Law & Policy* (2005), 157, 160.
55. Kenneth J. Vandevelde, *United States Investment Treaties: Policy and Practice* (Kluwer Law and Taxation, 1992), 10, 23.
56. Marjorie Millace Whiteman, *Digest of International Law*, U.S. Department of State, 1967, vol. 8, 1216–1219.
57. *Interhandel*, *supra* note 51; Ambatielos Claim (*Greece v. U.K.*) 23 I.L.R. 306, 344 (1956); Whiteman, *supra* note 56, 769.
58. Whiteman, *supra* note 56, 1216–1219.
59. *Banro American Resources v. Democratic Republic of the Congo*, ICSID Case No. ARB/98/7, Award of 1 September 2000, 17 ICSID Rev. – FILJ 232 (2002), paras. 15–21.
60. ICSID Convention, Regulations and Rules, Part A.
61. Ben Juratowitch, 'The Relationship between Diplomatic Protection and Investment Treaties', 23(1) *ICSID Review – Foreign Investment Law Journal* (2008), 27.
62. *Ibid.*, 30.
63. *Ibid.*, 35.

IV. The Hull Formula and the Calvo Doctrine

On the background of economic and political tensions between developed and developing countries during the 1800s, the failure of different developing countries to fulfil their financial duties towards citizens of developed countries made them the target of attacks by European home states of the investors.[64] For example, in support of certain claims brought by French investors against the government of Mexico, Napoleon III authorised an expedition against that country in 1861.[65]

Driven by socialist and communist ideology, Mexico and the USSR undertook the expropriation of vast portions of land as part of their nationalisation program during the late 1800s and early 1900s.[66] The agrarian reform initiated by Mexico during the 1910s to provide land to farmers for cultivation involved expropriation of land under the ownership of US nationals.[67] Likewise, oil investments under the ownership of American nationals underwent nationalisation by the Mexican government in the 1930s.[68]

There were significant differences of opinion between capital exporters and developing and communist states with regard to the matter of expropriation. The former argued that investors had to be compensated if their property was expropriated, while the latter disagreed with this perspective on different legal grounds.

This division of minds is clearly reflected in the manner in which protection of foreigners' property in host countries was interpreted by the then US Secretary of State, Cordell Hull, on the one hand, and the Mexican Ministry of Foreign Affairs, on the other. According to Hull,

> The taking of property without compensation is not expropriation. It is confiscation.[69]

and, in keeping with the case law and literature, investors had to be compensated by a host country if their property was expropriated.[70] The expropriation-related obligations of a country in accordance with customary investment law started to be referred to as the "Hull formula". According to the Hull formula, the home state of the investor did not challenge the expropriation, which was considered a sovereign

64. Manuel R. Garcia-Mora, 'The Calvo Clause in Latin American Constitutions and international Law', 33(4) *Marquette Law Review* (1950), 205.
65. Arthur Nussbaum, *A Concise History of the Law of Nations* (The MacMillan Company, 1947), 211–212.
66. Jan Wouters, Sanderijn Duquet and Nicolas Hachez, 'International investment Law: The Perpetual Search for Consensus', 30 March 2012, 28, <ssrn.com/abstract=2031552> accessed 10 April 2019.
67. Andreas F. Lowenfeld, *International Economic Law* (2nd edn., OUP, 2008) 471–473; J. Wouters, Ph. De Man and L. Chanet, 'The Long and Winding Road of International Investment Agreements', 3 *Human Rights & International Legal Discovery* (2009), 265.
68. Jonathan D. Greenberg and Evan Darwin Winet, 'International Investment Law and Dispute Resolution', in Joseph Mark S. Munoz (ed.), *Handbook on the Geopolitics of Business* (Edward Elgar, 2013), 237.
69. Cordell Hull, Diplomatic Note for the Secretary of State of the United States of America to the Minister of Foreign Affairs of Mexico, 21 July 1938.
70. Lowenfeld, *supra* note 67, 478–479.

act of the host state, but requested that the expropriated investor was rewarded with prompt and adequate compensation.

As stated by Cordell Hull, the government of Mexico was required to offer "prompt, adequate and effective compensation" to affected American investors, with "prompt", meaning "instant" or "rapid" reimbursement, "adequate", meaning "an appropriate valuation of the expropriated property coming close to its full or fair market value",[71] and "effective", referring to a type of payment efficiently "usable by the recipient", with the exception of payments in a currency that could not be converted, for example.[72]

It is obvious that Hull's objective was to warn countries that were considering nationalising American investments.[73]

On the other hand, the stance adopted by the Mexican government later came to be known as the "Calvo Doctrine", after the famous scholar from Argentina, Carlos Calvo. The publication of Calvo's treatise, *Le droit international théorique et pratique*, in France in 1868 coincided with the aftermath of a period of major political unrest in Argentina.[74] The doctrine proposed by Calvo in this treatise was underpinned by the principles that foreign investors had the same rights as nationals and that it was up to national courts to settle investment disputes.[75]

This doctrine stipulated that all countries were sovereign and could self-determine; by having rights and obligations identical to those of nationals, foreign investors had to submit claims against the host country through the same mechanism as nationals, namely, by appealing to domestic courts,[76] the only authorities possessing jurisdiction. Hence, both diplomatic protection[77] and appeals to foreign courts[78] were inaccessible options to foreign investors.

The Calvo Doctrine further specified that non-discrimination was the only obligation that host countries had to uphold with regard to foreign investors under international law. Therefore, foreigners should expect to be treated in the same way as nationals, without recourse to international standards.

Even though the American Secretary of State and the Mexican Ministry of Foreign Affairs did not reach any consensus,[79] the Calvo Doctrine was a major source for legislation regarding foreign investors of many countries in Latin America during

71. PCIJ, *Case Concerning the Factory at Chorzów (Merits)*, 13 September 1928, PCIJ Series A - No. 17, 47.
72. Oscar Schachter, 'Compensation for Expropriation', 78 *American Journal of International Law* (1984), 121.
73. Wouters, Duquet and Hachez, *supra* note 66, 29.
74. OECD, *Latin American Economic Outlook* (2008), 33, 34.
75. Samuel Flagg Bemis, *The Latin American Policy of the United States: An Historical Interpretation* (Harcourt, Brace and Co., 1943), 230–234.
76. Jonathan D. Greenberg and Evan Darwin Winet, 'International Investment Law and Dispute Resolution', in Joseph Mark S. Munoz (ed.), *Handbook on the Geopolitics of Business* (Edward Elgar Publishing, 2013), 237.
77. Mary Helen Mourra, 'The Conflicts and Controversies in Latin American Treaty-Based Disputes', in Mary Helen Mourra and Thomas B. Carbonneau, *Latin American Investment Treaty Arbitration: The Controversies and Conflicts* (Wolters Kluwer, 2008), 8.
78. Andreas F. Lowenfeld, *International Private Investment* (Matthew Bender, 1982), 151.
79. Wouters, Duquet and Hachez, *supra* note 66, 29.

the 1900s,[80] and was incorporated in treaties, municipal law, private contracts with nationals of other countries and the majority of state constitutions in Latin America.[81]

The Calvo Doctrine was included in Article 27 of the 1927 Mexican Constitution, specifying that

> Only Mexicans by birth or naturalization and Mexican corporations have the right to acquire ownership of lands, water and their appurtenance, or to obtain concessions for working mines or for the utilization of waters or mineral fuel in the Republic of Mexico. The Nation may grant the same rights to aliens, provided they agree before the Ministry of Justice to consider themselves as Mexicans in respect to such property, and bind themselves not to invoke the protection of their governments in matters relating thereto, under penalty, in case of non-compliance, of forfeiture to the Nation of property so acquired.[82]

The provision known as the Calvo Clause was part of numerous Investor-State contracts and led to the formulation of the Calvo Doctrine. This clause meant that foreign investors agreed to file claims to the domestic courts of the host country in the event that they incurred damage in that country, whilst relinquishing the right to call on the home country to protect their interests.[83] Although this clause was embraced by countries that imported capital,[84] it did not comprise a full waiver as its scope was rather limited. More specifically, it was just the individuals who renounced their rights, not their home country,[85] which, as a subject of international law, had its own rights vis-à-vis the host state. Hence, the General Claims Commission ruled that the clause simply stated that diplomatic protection could only be invoked once local solutions had been exhausted.[86]

It is noteworthy that more recent international agreements contain stipulations regarding exhaustion of local solutions,[87] which prompted the ironic observation by Schreuer: "*Carlos Calvo* is not alive but he has children and grandchildren that have an uncanny family resemblance to him".[88]

80. Mourra, *supra* note 77, 9.
81. Donald R. Shea, *The Calvo Clause: A Problem of Inter-American and International Law and Diplomacy* (University of Minnesota Press, 1955), 21–27; Subrata Roy Chowdhury, Erik Denters and P.J.L.M. de Waart, *The Right to Development in International Law* (Martinus Nijhoff, 2002), 116.
82. Restatement of the Law (Third), Foreign Relations Law of the United States, Part II Persons in International Law, §202.
83. Nico Schrijver, *Sovereignty over Natural Resources: Balancing Rights and Duties* (CUP, 1997), 178–179.
84. Kate Miles, *The Origins of International Investment Law: Empire, Environment and the Safeguarding of Capital* (Cambridge University Press, Cambridge 2013), 51.
85. F.V. Garcia Amador, Louis Bruno Sohn, and Richard R. Baxter, *Recent Codification of the Law of State Responsibility for Injuries to Aliens* (Oceana Publications, 1974), 74.
86. Decision of the General Claims Commission of Mexico and United States in the North American Dredging Company case. See A.H. Feller, *The Mexican Claims Commissions, 1923–1934* (Macmillan, 1935), 187.
87. Including the ICSID Convention and the BIT between Argentina and Germany.
88. Christoph Schreuer, 'Calvo's Grandchildren: The Return of Local Remedies in Investment Arbitration', 4(1) *The Law and Practice of International Courts and Tribunals* (2005), 3.

C. SETTLING INVESTMENT DISPUTES

The widespread popularity of international investment arbitration has been promoted by a range of reasons, such as Western companies' concern regarding submission to the jurisdiction of the domestic tribunals of the host country;[89] under these circumstances, international arbitration was well-received by both companies and individual investors as it protected them from risks associated with intentional modifications to foreign investment-related legislation.[90] Award implementation is another reason for the popularity of investment arbitration, as in the case of international commercial arbitration. To make sure that awards were acknowledged, binding, and could be implemented across borders, the Convention on the Recognition and Enforcement of Foreign Arbitral Awards (hereinafter: the New York Convention), was established in 1958,[91] and signed by over 145 countries. Given all these considerations, arbitration is currently the tool most often employed to settle investment disputes, as attested by UNCTAD in its 2015 note "Recent developments in ISDS".[92]

Part C. is divided into two sub-sections. The first one addresses the shift from State-to-State to Investor-State arbitration, the establishment of the International Center for the Settlement of Investment Disputes (ICSID) that administers arbitration cases, lays out the statistics proving the vertical rise in the number of cases and reports the data on the outcome of the cases per geographic region. The second sub-section draws the distinction between commercial arbitration, where two private parties claim their interests in court - and investment arbitration, which sees the state as responding party against the investor.

I. Arbitration: From State-to-State to Investor-State

As was highlighted above, if in earlier times a foreign investor had a claim against the host state, the home state of the investor and the host state entered into a State-to-State arbitration.

By contrast, starting from 1959, the considerable proliferation of investment agreements such as BITs has been catalysed by the fact that securing foreign investment has always been the main reason for motivating developing countries to enter into agreements with a clause specifying arbitration as the dispute settlement mechanism.[93] Investors have acquired a range of rights from these types of agree-

89. William H. Knull, II and Noah D. Rubins, 'Betting the Farm on International Arbitration: Is it Time to Offer an Appeal?', 2(4) *American Review of International Arbitration* (2000), 5.
90. Florentino P. Feliciano, 'The Ordre Public Dimensions of Confidentiality and Transparency in International Arbitration', 87(1) *Philippine Law Journal* (2012), 16.
91. Convention on the Recognition and Enforcement of Foreign Arbitral Awards (New York, 1958) < www.uncitral.org/uncitral/it/uncitral_texts/arbitration/NYConvention.html > accessed 10 April 2019.
92. UNCTAD, 'IIA issues note – Recent developments in ISDS' < unctad.org/en/Publications Library/webdiaepcb2014d3_en.pdf > accessed 10 April 2019.
93. Eugenia Levine, 'Amicus Curiae in International Investment Arbitration: The Implications of an Increase in Third Party Participation', *Berkeley Journal of International Law* (2011) 202.

ments, including national treatment, most-favoured-nation treatment, being treated impartially and equitably, ensuring correct expropriation, and the ability to resort to alternative dispute settlement mechanisms like arbitration.[94]

To deal with arbitration-based investment dispute settlement, the World Bank adopted the Convention on the Settlement of Investment Disputes between States and Nationals of Other States ("Washington Convention"), which was first introduced in 1965.[95] Furthermore, to mediate conciliation and arbitration,[96] the Washington Convention created ICSID.[97]

ICSID-managed arbitration has been incorporated in a number of investment agreements as the dispute settlement mechanism of choice, resulting in an increase in the number of parties to ICSID to 144.[98] Before the ICSID, 319 cases had been filed as of June 2010. Registration of 27 new cases led to an increase of 12% in 2010 compared to 2009.[99] The widespread reputation of ICSID has been enhanced by such data as "the leading international arbitration institution devoted to investor-state dispute settlement".[100]

In addition to managing arbitration cases, ICSID provides support to bureaucratic procedures in the context of investment arbitrations in keeping with the UNCITRAL Arbitration Rules ("UNCITRAL Rules"), which are applicable to other arbitration courts as well, including the Stockholm Chamber of Commerce (SCC), the International Chamber of Commerce (ICC) and the Permanent Court of Arbitration (PCA).[101]

In comparison to 1990, there was an increase of over 500% in the number of filed arbitration claims, which reached 550 in 2014.[102] As highlighted by different studies, it is necessary to examine the motives underpinning arbitration claims, the statistics, and the areas with the most numerous arbitration cases.[103] Notably, one study reported that in most cases, the plaintiff was from a developed country while the defendant was a developing country.[104]

---

94. Katia Fach Gómez, 'Rethinking the Role of Amicus Curiae in International Investment Arbitration: How to Draw the Line Favorably for Public Interest', 35 *Fordham International Law Journal* (2012), 524–525.
95. Convention on the Settlement of Investment Disputes between States and Nationals of Other States, 18 March 1965, 17 U.S.T. 1270, 575 U.N.T.S. 159.
96. Washington Convention, Preamble.
97. Washington Convention, Art. 1 "The purpose of the [ICSID] shall be to provide facilities for conciliation and arbitration of investment disputes between Contracting States and nationals of other Contracting States in accordance with the provisions of this Convention".
98. ICSID Annual Report 2010.
99. *Ibid.*, 21.
100. Alessandro Chechi, *The Settlement of International Cultural Heritage Disputes* (OUP, 2014), 179.
101. Gómez, *supra* note 94, 526.
102. Daniel Behn, 'Legitimacy, Evolution, and Growth in Investment Treaty Arbitration: Empirically Evaluating the State-of-the-Art', 46(2) *Georgetown Journal of International Law* (2015), 365; UNCTAD, World Investment Report 2013, Global Value Chain: Investment and Trade for Development 104 (2013), <unctad.org/en/PublicationsLibrary/wir2013_en.pdf> accessed 10 April 2019.
103. Behn, *supra* note 102, 365.
104. *Ibid.*, 404.

Not all defendant countries are developed to the same degree. One study that reviewed 110 cases finalised during the period September 2011 - September 2014 found that 13% of cases with a developed country as defendant were won by the plaintiff, while 30% and 37%, respectively, of cases with an emerging economy and a developing country as defendant were won by the plaintiff.[105] From these figures, it can be inferred that the plaintiff is more likely to win the case if the defendant is a developing country rather than a developed one.

Among all arbitration cases resolved between 2011 and 2014, the plaintiff lost in most cases where the defendant was a West European or North American country. Slovakia and Lithuania[106] were the only two countries that lost their cases as defendant, but they are Eastern European countries that in 2008 were still considered "emerging economies".[107]

There are different factors that can explain this situation. For instance, in comparison with developing countries and emerging economies, developed countries may possess a stronger regulatory framework that minimises the likelihood of treaty violations due to being founded on the principles of non-discrimination, transparency and due process. Another explanation is that the systems of developed countries may be more capable of effectively dealing with legal and financial claims.[108]

II. Similarities and Peculiarities between Investment Arbitration and Commercial Arbitration

There are several key features common to international commercial arbitration and investment arbitration. Consensus is the foundation of both types, but they have different means of conveying consent. Furthermore, in both forms of arbitration, arbitrators specifically chosen by the parties or arbitral institutions approved by the parties are responsible for decision-making and for issuing a definitive and binding award based on implementation of adjudicatory procedures. Additionally, commercial arbitration rules were the inspiration for investment arbitration rules, such as the ICSID Arbitration Rules and the UNCITRAL Rules.[109]

The two types of arbitration differ in certain respects, though. One major difference is that international commercial arbitration occurs between private parties, while investment arbitration occurs between a private party, the investor, and a sovereign country. Hence, state interests and legislative policies can be significantly affected by investment arbitration,[110] the outcome of which thus has implications for the two parties as well as for an extensive portion of the population. Therefore, investment arbitration should not be highly confidential.

105. *Ibid.*, 405-406.
106. *Ibid.*, 406.
107. United Nations Conference on Trade and Development, *Trade and Development Report 2008* (2008), 53.
108. Behn, *supra* note 102, 406.
109. Gary B. Born, *International Arbitration: Law and Practice* (Kluwer Law International, Alphen aan den Rijn, 2012), 503.
110. *Ibid.*, 503-504.

Investment arbitration and international commercial arbitration also differ in that, in the former, just one party can file claims against the other, while in the latter, claims can be brought by both parties.

Compared to international commercial arbitration, investment arbitration is deemed to be "more autonomous" in relation to national law because it falls under a specialised legal framework. The origin of a claim is a supposed treaty provision violation in investment arbitration and a contractual clause violation in international commercial arbitration.[111]

Investment arbitration and international commercial arbitration additionally differ with regard to the legal culture, applicable law, the manner in which the arbitration panel is designated, the jurisdiction, the case management, the manner in which transparency and confidentiality are balanced, how consistent the awards are, the *stare decisis* principle, and the ability to refer to the Court of Justice of the European Union (CJEU).

In terms of legal culture, most institutional arbitration rules in international commercial arbitration specify that arbitrators must take into account customary trade usages, which may differ significantly between regions. Also in investment arbitration, some effects may derive from discrepancies in the legal culture, because of the various tasks fulfilled by states according to their constitution and its practical implementation.[112]

In terms of the applicable law, the New York Convention is the sole treaty applicable to commercial arbitration. By contrast, several public international law treaties, including over 2,000 BITs, multilateral agreements (e.g. ICSID Convention, the Energy Charter Treaty), and regional conventions (e.g. NAFTA, CAFTA, and CETA) may be applicable to investment arbitration.

However, both commercial arbitration and investment arbitration may be subject to European Union Law. For example, commercial arbitration is subject to the EU competition policy.[113] Furthermore, the EU can significantly interfere in investment agreements between its member states and non-EU countries based on the power granted to it by the Lisbon Treaty to finalise new IIAs.[114]

---

111. *Ibid.*, 504–505.
112. Karl-Heinz Böckstiegel, 'Commercial and Investment Arbitration: How Different are they Today?', 28(4) *Arbitration International* (2012), 578–579.
113. The cornerstone of the EU competition legislation are Articles 101 and 102 of the Treaty of Functioning of the European Union, and the Merger Control Regulation. Arbitrability of antitrust rules is undisputed in the EU. See Gordon Blanke and Renato Nazzini. 'Arbitration and ADR of global antitrust disputes: Taking stock (part I)', 1(1) *Global Competition Litigation Review* (2008), 46.
114. Consolidated version of The Treaty on the Functioning of the European Union, [2008] OJ C 115/47, art 207(1) ("The common commercial policy shall be based on uniform principles, particularly with regard to changes in tariff rates, the conclusion of tariff and trade agreements relating to trade in goods and services, and the commercial aspects of intellectual property, foreign direct investment, the achievement of uniformity in measures of liberalisation, export policy and measures to protect trade such as those to be taken in the event of dumping or subsidies. The common commercial policy shall be conducted in the context of the principles and objectives of the Union's external action.").

National law plays different roles in arbitration. For instance, in the context of commercial arbitration, as a consequence of its location, the arbitration is subject to national procedural rules and the law applicable is usually national law. Conversely, in the context of investment arbitration, the applicability of national procedural rules depends on arbitration being under the control of non-governmental institutions (e.g. ICC or SCC), which are required to comply with the law of the arbitration place.

The substantive law applied in investment contracts and investment treaties can be national law as well. In effect, the law of the host country is mentioned alongside the rules of international law in Article 42 of the ICSID Convention regarding ICSID arbitrations.[115]

In terms of arbitrator appointment, the arbitration parties can select the arbitrators according to their competence in relation to different commercial sectors. By contrast, in investment arbitration, the choice of arbitrators typically depends on their level of expertise in public international law, given that the issues under consideration may be narrower and frequently related to expropriation.

Challenges to arbitrators in the two types of arbitration are usually due to different reasons. In commercial arbitration, the nature of the connection that the arbitrators' law firm had or has with the company involved in the dispute may be a source of conflict of interest. In investment arbitration, the previous cases in which the arbitrators were involved and the outcomes of those cases may have a bearing on current cases.[116]

In terms of jurisdiction, commercial arbitration faces fewer jurisdictional difficulties, the main point of concern being the scope of the contractual arbitration clause, particularly how valid the clause is for non-signatory parties among a group of companies. In investment arbitration, on the other hand, the parties' consent is articulated in the investment agreement or investment treaty, and therefore it is usually not an issue. In such circumstances, the Vienna Convention is of relevance. Nevertheless, in certain cases, opposition may be raised to the jurisdiction if, for example, there is evidence that the plaintiff established a company in the surmised home country with the exclusive aim of benefitting from the protection by the BIT with the defendant.[117]

In terms of case management, just a handful of rules (e.g. the principle of due process) are incorporated in the national law or the international treaty for commercial arbitration and investment arbitration, respectively. The arbitration rules comprehensively outline the procedure that must be applied and afford a great deal of discretion to arbitrators, despite differing in terms of how much detail they provide about how proceedings should unfold. Nevertheless, proceedings tend to be longer and more formal in investment arbitration, as one of the dispute parties is a state.[118]

Investment arbitration has been at the core of a vivid debate over the last few years, and several initiatives have been launched for its improvement and reform,

115. *Ibid.*, 579–581.
116. *Ibid.*, 581–583.
117. *Ibid.*, 583–585.
118. *Ibid.*, 584–586.

including on transparency. The UNCITRAL Working Group III on ISDS reform,[119] the Multilateral Investment Court project[120] proposed by the European Commission, the amendment of several sets of procedural rules such as ICSID Rules,[121] the ICC Rules of Arbitration,[122] and the HKIAC Administered Arbitration Rules[123] are just few of the most important fora for discussion and amendment of the perceived flaws in the system of investment arbitration.

D. IPRs, IIAs AND INVESTOR STATE ARBITRATION: UNTANGLING THE TRIANGLE

Intellectual property rights are one of the most precious assets in the international economy.[124] In effect, often most of a company's value consists in its intangible assets such as its IPRs.[125] However, as research stressed, with "great importance and value... comes increased exposure and risk".[126]

Recourse against denial of protection or against infringement is available in most countries under the standards provided by the WTO/TRIPS Agreement,[127] be it due to incorporation into domestic law or by way of direct application.[128] However,

119. United Nations Commission on International Trade Law, UNCITRAL Working Group III on ISDS reform, <www.uncitral.org/uncitral/en/commission/working_groups/3Investor_State.html> accessed 24 April 2019.
120. European Commission, The Multilateral Investment Court project, <trade.ec.europa.eu/doclib/press/index.cfm?id=1608> accessed 24 April 2019
121. ICSID Rule and Regulations Amendment Process, <icsid.worldbank.org/en/amendments> accessed 24 April 2019.
122. New ICC Arbitration Rules and Note take effect, 1 March 2017, <iccwbo.org/media-wall/news-speeches/new-icc-arbitration-rules-and-note-take-effect/>, accessed 24 April 2019.
123. Hong Kong International Arbitration Centre, 2018 Administered Arbitration Rules – 1 November, <www.hkiac.org/news/2018-administered-arbitration-rules-1-november> accessed on 24 April 2019.
124. Lukas Vanhonnaeker, *Intellectual Property Rights as Foreign Direct Investments: From Collision to Collaboration* (Edward Elgar, 2015), 1.
125. Bertram Boie, 'The Protection of Intellectual Property Rights through Bilateral Investment Treaties: Is there a TRIPS-plus Dimension?', World Trade Institute Working Paper No. 2010/19 (2010) <www.wti.org/research/publications/228/the-protection-of-intellectual-property-rights-through-bilateral-investment-treaties-is-there-a-trips-plus-dimension/> accessed 10 April 2019.
126. Julian Davis Mortenson, 'Intellectual Property as Transnational Investment: Some Preliminary Observations', 6(2) *T.D.M.* (2009), 1.
127. Agreement on Trade-Related Aspects of Intellectual Property Rights (TRIPS), 15 April 1994, Marrakesh Agreement Establishing the World Trade Organization, Annex IC, Legal Instruments – Results of the Uruguay Round, 33 *I.L.M.* 1125.
128. Considering the recognition of "direct effect" of the TRIPS Agreement a source of potential confusion, both the European Union and the United States made provisions aimed at denying direct effect. United Nations Conference on Trade and Development, Dispute Settlement, World Trade Organization 3.14 TRIPS, New York and Geneva: United Nations, 2003. See also chapter 5 of this book, which extensively deals with this issue: Christopher Heath, 'The Direct Effect of International IP Agreements before National Courts'.

IP investors can also make use of International Investment Agreements (IIAs) that comprise BITs and Preferential Trade and Investment Agreements (PTIAs).[129]

Part D. consists of three sections. Section I retraces the steps of the presence of IPRs in the oldest treaties and in the first ever concluded BIT between Germany and Pakistan; section II draws attention to the phrasing of the investment definition in the latest treaties; and section III provides an outlook of the Investor-State cases where the challenged State measure was an alleged violation of IP rights.

I. The Protection of IPRs in Early IIAs

It is nothing new for IPRs to be classified as covered investments under the majority of international investment agreements; indeed, this classification goes back to the state-to-state investment agreements established prior to the introduction of BITs. The US Friendship Commerce and Navigation (FCN) Agreements mentioned intellectual property rights before BITs began to proliferate. For example, the 1903 FCN treaty between the US and China already made reference to copyright protection. Furthermore, some treaties included intangible rights under the term "property", whereas others explicitly referred to patents, copyrights and trade marks.[130]

Regarding BITs, an explicit mentioning of patents and "technical knowledge" can be found in the very first BIT that was signed by Germany and Pakistan in 1959:

> GERMANY–PAKISTAN BIT (1959)
>
> *Article 8*
>
> 1) (a) The term "investment" shall comprise capital brought into the territory of the other Party for investment in various forms in the shape of assets such as foreign exchange, goods, property rights, patents and technical knowledge.[131]

Although this provision explicitly refers to patents and technology, a wider interpretation is made possible by the explicit list of what is considered "assets".[132]

IPRs are incorporated in BITs because of the assumption that they can be classified as investments: therefore, they have to satisfy additional treaty-based requirements instead of simply being covered by the formula denoting what can be granted protection. The essential requirements are that IPRs have to fulfil the standard

129. PTIAS include FTAs, regional trade agreements, economic framework agreements, economic partnership agreements, new-age partnership agreements, economic complementation agreements, agreements for establishing a free trade area, and closed economic partnership agreements. UNCTAD, Intellectual Property Provisions in International Investment Arrangements (United Nations 2007) 2.

130. Lahra Liberti, 'Intellectual Property Rights in International Investment Agreements: An Overview', OECD Working Paper on International Investment (2010).

131. Treaty between the Federal Republic of Germany and Pakistan for the Promotion and Protection of Investments, 1959 < investmentpolicyhub.unctad.org/Download/TreatyFile/1387 > accessed 10 April 2019.

132. Liberti, *supra* note 130.

features of an investment,[133] and they have to conform to the laws and rules of the host contracting party.[134]

However, BITs are different from one another: therefore, the degree of protection conferred to IPRs as a consequence of their incorporation in international investment agreements may vary. Furthermore, over time BITs showed changes in the language used to refer to IPRs within the definition of investment. During the period between 1960 and 1990, BITs usually highlighted the difference between "industrial property rights" and "copyrights", and made reference to additional aspects like technical procedures or processes. The latest investment agreements preferably use the all-encompassing term "intellectual property rights".[135]

If incorporated in the relevant BIT, the definition of "intellectual property" has an impact on the degree to which an investor's IP is protected. A clear-cut definition is included in certain international agreements, like the Benin–Ghana BIT: "intellectual property rights, goodwill, technical processes and know-how and all similar rights recognized by the national laws of both Contracting Parties".[136] Indeed, the more precise and limited the definition, the lesser the scope for possible claims based thereupon. Therefore, to diminish accountability for IP claims under a BIT, a state may restrict the protected IP to patents or trade marks registered with the relevant IP bodies at national level.[137]

II. The Protection of IPRs in Recent IIAs

As observed by several researchers, most BITs make explicit reference to IPRs in the classes of property granted protection under the treaty.[138]

Nevertheless, it is expected that IPRs are covered even by agreements that do not directly refer to them, as the list of covered aspects is sufficiently extensive and employs a general language, such as "every kind of assets", "every kind of goods, rights, and interests of whatsoever nature".[139]

133. Bertram Boie, 'The Protection of Intellectual Property Rights through Bilateral Investment Treaties: Is there a TRIPS-plus Dimension?', World Trade Institute Working Paper (2010) <www.wti.org/research/publications/228/the-protection-of-intellectual-property-rights-through-bilateral-investment-treaties-is-there-a-trips-plus-dimension/> accessed 10 April 2019.
134. *Ibid.*
135. UNCTAD, *supra* note 129.
136. Article 1 (a)(iv), Agreement Between the Government Of The Republic Of Ghana And The Government The Republic Of Benin For The Promotion And Protection Of Investments, 2001, <investmentpolicyhub.unctad.org/Download/TreatyFile/442> accessed 10 April 2019.
137. UNCTAD, *supra* note 129.
138. James David Mortenson, 'Intellectual Property as Transnational Investment: Some Preliminary Observations', 6(2) *Transnational Dispute Management* (2009), 4.
139. *Ibid.*, 5; Brian A. White and Ryan J. Szczepanik, 'Remedies Available Under Bilateral Investment Treaties for Breach of Intellectual Property Rights', 6(2) *Transnational Dispute Management* (2009), 3.

Four possible approaches to IPR coverage by a BIT have been discerned by some researchers:[140]

First, the investment agreement may make reference to "property" or "assets" of different kinds, instead of directly to intellectual property, as in the case of the ISD model treaty.[141]

Secondly, the treaty may simply refer to IPRs or "intangible property" with no additional clarification. One example thereof is the Treaty between the Government of the United States of America and the Government of the Republic of Rwanda Concerning the Encouragement and Reciprocal Protection of Investment (2008) which simply states under Article 1: "forms that an investment may take include ... intellectual property rights".[142]

Thirdly, there may be a more specific mentioning of IPRs in the form of a list of the intangible rights covered, regardless of whether the list is deemed exhaustive or not, and whether it does/does not encompass intellectual assets which are usually without coverage as IPRs. Among the latter may be designs that have not been registered.

One of the most recent examples thereof is the Canada Mongolia FIPA 2017, which states:

> *Article 1: Definitions*
>
> ... "intellectual property rights" means copyright and related rights, trademark rights, rights in geographical indications, rights in industrial designs, patent rights, rights in layout designs of integrated circuits, rights in relation to protection of undisclosed information, and plant breeders' rights ...
>
> *Article 11: Transfers*
>
> Each Party shall permit all transfers relating to covered investments to be made freely, and without delay, into and out of its territory. Such transfers include:
>
> ...
>
> profits, dividends, interest, capital gains, royalty payments, management fees, technical assistance and other fees, returns in kind and other amounts derived from the covered investment[143]

Fourthly, international law can draw on domestic law to define property rights: in effect, as stressed by some scholars, "the treaty at stake may either define property

140. Carlos Correa and Jorge E. Viñuales, 'Intellectual property rights as protected investment: How open are the gates?' *Journal of International Economic Law* (2016),19, 91.
141. See Howard Mann, Konrad von Moltke, Luke Eric Peterson, Aaron Cosbey, IISD Model International Agreement on Investment for Sustainable Development (2005) < www.iisd.org/pdf/2005/investment_model_int_agreement.pdf > accessed 10 April 2019.
142. Treaty between the Government of the United States of America and the Government of the Republic of Rwanda Concerning the Encouragement and Reciprocal Protection of Investment, 2008 < ustr.gov/sites/default/files/uploads/agreements/bit/asset_upload_file743_14523.pdf > accessed 10 April 2019.
143. Agreement Between Canada and Mongolia for the Promotion and Protection of Investments, < investmentpolicyhub.unctad.org/Download/TreatyFile/5373 > accessed 10 April 2019.

rights itself or provide for the application of domestic law in light of which the notion will be defined".[144]

According to some researchers, IPRs are deliberately intended to confer protection to both present and future investment, which is why BITs make reference to them in such a broad way, open for new interpretations.[145]

BITs typically address IP rights based solely on investment definition, but further specification is given in some particular cases.[146] One example thereof is the United States–Uruguay BIT 2004: Article 14.5 establishes that national treatment (Article 3) and MFN (Article 4) shall not apply in particular cases as provided under the TRIPS Agreement:

> Articles 3 and 4 do not apply to any measure covered by an exception to, or derogation from, the obligations under Article 3 or 4 of the TRIPS Agreement, as specifically provided in those Articles and in Article 5 of the TRIPS Agreement.

Specific stipulations regarding IPRs are frequently incorporated in PTIAs. Indeed, a whole section is dedicated to IP in some agreements, indicating the substantive obligations that contracting parties must uphold: one example thereof is the North American Free Trade Agreement (NAFTA) whose Chapter Seventeen is entirely focused on Intellectual Property.[147] Inter-party collaboration regarding aspects associated with IP is prioritised by other agreements.[148]

There are often close similarities between treaties ratified by leading economic powers in terms of the IP aspects covered due to the fact that a model agreement generally constitutes the basis of PTIA negotiations. This is the case with the agreements signed by the United States or the European Union.[149] Nevertheless, despite being based on the same model, final agreements may still have discrepancies since negotiation outcomes are determined by a wide range of factors, including the level of negotiating power possessed by the various parties. Furthermore, the occurring discrepancies may have extensive legal ramifications in terms of, for example, National Treatment and Most Favoured Nation duties, which can alter IPR protection in one way or another.[150]

---

144. Lukas Vanhonnaeker, *Intellectual Property Rights as Foreign Direct Investments: From Collision to Collaboration* (Elgar International Investment Law Series, 2015), 31.
145. Yi Shin Tang, *The International Trade Policy for Technology Transfers: Legal and Economic Dilemmas on Multilateralism versus Bilateralism* (Wolters Kluwer, 2009), 124.
146. UNCTAD, *supra* note 129.
147. North American Free Trade Agreement <www.nafta-sec-alena.org/Home/Texts-of-the-Agreement/North-American-Free-Trade-Agreement?mvid = 1&secid = b6e715c1-ec07-4c96-b18e-d762b2ebe511> accessed 10 April 2019.
148. UNCTAD, *supra* note 129.
149. *Ibid.*
150. *Ibid.*

III. Intellectual Property as Investment: A Review of Case Law

As indicated earlier, since the end of the 1960s, stipulations for foreign investors to make direct recourse to international arbitration have been incorporated in the majority of IIAs.[151]

As this is applicable to every aspect covered under the agreements, including IPRs, arbitral claims can be submitted by foreign investors on grounds of violation of IPRs under protection of the relevant IIA.

This has actually occurred in several disputes of significance, like *Philip Morris Asia v. Australia, Philip Morris v. Uruguay* (see chapter 9 in this book), *Eli Lilly v. Canada* (see chapter 8 in this book), *AHS Niger S.A. v. Niger*, and *Shell v. Nicaragua*.

In the case *AHS Niger S.A. v. Niger*, the plaintiff claimed damage to reputation as its successors to airport management continued using the staff uniforms and equipment with its logo, but offered a service of significantly lower quality. However, the arbitration panel decided that it did not possess the authority to judge on the alleged IPR violation.[152]

The case *Shell v. Nicaragua* follows the case *Sonia Eduarda Franco et al. v. Dow Chemical, Shell Oil Company, Standard Fruit, and Dole Food Corporation*[153] which was heard by a Nicaraguan court: former banana workers filed a class action suit, claiming that the banana pesticides allegedly provided by Shell Oil had severely affected their health.

The local court awarded the plaintiffs compensation of USD 489 million under Nicaraguan national law. When the plaintiffs tried to implement the ruling in California, the Central District Court of California refused to recognise or enforce it on the United States territory.[154]

The plaintiffs subsequently tried to enforce the ruling in Nicaragua, resulting in the Shell logo and trade mark being confiscated by a local court. This led to an arbitration case being brought by Shell Brand International AG and Shell Nicaragua SA against the Republic of Nicaragua, on grounds that trade mark confiscation constituted a breach of the stipulations of the relevant BIT.[155] The ruling of the lower court was overturned by the Nicaragua's Court of Appeal in November 2006: the confiscation of the trade mark was revoked, and the two Shell companies dropped their ICSID claim, discontinuing the arbitral proceedings in March 2007.[156]

---

151. Andrew Newcombe and Lluís Paradell, *Law and Practice of Investment Treaties* (Kluwer Law International, 2009), 41–57.
152. *AHS Niger and Menzies Middle East and Africa S.A. v. Republic of Niger* ICSID Case No. ARB/11/11 [2013] <www.italaw.com/sites/default/files/case-documents/italaw3034.pdf> accessed 10 April 2019.
153. *Franco v. The Dow Chemical Company et al.*, CV 03-5094.
154. *Shell Oil Company v. Sonia Eduarda Franco, Franco et al.* (US DC, CD Cal), 10 Nov. 2005, case CV 03-8846 NM.
155. *Shell Brand International AG and Shell Nicaragua SA v. Republic of Nicaragua*, ICSID Case No. ARB/06/14.
156. The ICSID Secretary-General issued an order taking note of the discontinuance of the proceedings pursuant to Arbitration Rule 44 on 12 March 2007, <icsid.worldbank.org/en/Pages/cases/casedetail.aspx?CaseNo=ARB/06/14> accessed 10 April 2019.

Researchers have emphasised that "the case shows that intellectual property may be the targeted object of retaliation measures",[157] but it is also true that the Court of Appeal revoked these measures, acknowledging that the confiscation of the Shell logo and trade mark was tantamount to unlawful expropriation.

E. CONCLUSION

In examining the origins of international investment law, this chapter has discussed the evolution and development of the protection of investors, starting from its origins in the seventeenth to the nineteenth century.

Finding its roots in the era of European commercial exploration, the protection of investors started with the capitulation system, awarded for instance to Venetian merchants in the Byzantine Empire. During the 1600s, the spread of the Treaties of Friendship, Commerce and Navigation (FCN) signalled the start of reciprocal obligations and benefits, with the use of the standards of treatment as we know them today. Conflicts would first be solved by ad hoc commissions in the late 1700s, and later on by diplomatic espousal in 1800s. The use of arbitration to solve investment disputes emerged only in the second part of the 1800s, and at first was a settlement between states. The first Investor-State arbitration registered is the *French Compagnie Universelle du Canal de Suez v. Egypt*. The current framework presents nearly 3,000 Bilateral Investment Treaties and 942 Investor-State cases filed before arbitral tribunals globally,[158] making investment arbitration widely used and still on the rise for the resolution of claims between investors and states.

From a comparative analysis of IIAs, it emerges that many investment treaties include IPRs in the list of assets which define the scope of the term investment. Taking also into account the Investor-State cases that have already dealt with IPRs, and that all took place in the recent years, an increment of such cases is foreseeable in the near future.

It can be argued that investment tribunals are not the ideal forum for the discussion of IPRs because of the lack of specialization of the arbitrators in IP matters. Bearing this concern in mind, excluding IPRs from the scope of the investment definition in investment agreements would force IPR holders to argue their case before a national court, which may even be a specialised IP court[159] more qualified and suitable for judging IP matters.

Another, perhaps more drastic solution would be the carve-out of IPRs from the scope of the treaty, which would ensure that investment tribunals are not burdened with matters out of their rightful competence.

157. Valentina S. Vadi, 'Trade Mark Protection, Public Health and International Investment Law: Strains and Paradoxes', 20(3) *The European Journal of International Law* (2009), 785.
158. UNCTAD Investment Policy Hub, 2019.
159. Including the Unified Patent Court in the European Union and the Intellectual Property and international Trade Court in Thailand. See Jacques de Werra, *Specialised Intellectual Property Courts- Issues and Challenges*, (CEIPI-ICTSD, 2016).

CHAPTER 4

Dispute Resolution under the WTO Regime

Jens Hillebrand Pohl

The WTO Agreement, for the first time in a multilateral agreement, set up a comprehensive - and compulsory - dispute settlement system. This is markedly different from dispute resolution under bilateral trade agreements and is credited with greater transparency, a level playing field (in that complainants and respondents can only be states or customs territories) and a balanced enforcement mechanism. It further provides for an appellate mechanism. This presentation looks at the history of this part of the WTO Agreement, its adjudication and enforcement mechanisms, how it is administered by the WTO, what use has been made of this system hitherto, and whether it has provided a satisfactory answer to non-compliance.

A. INTRODUCTION

Having unsuccessfully challenged Australia's Tobacco Plain Packaging Act 2011 by means of investor-State dispute settlement (ISDS) in *Philip Morris v. Australia*,[1] the global tobacco industry put its remaining hopes to the dispute settlement system of the World Trade Organization (WTO).[2] The cases pending before the WTO (decided in first instance, yet partly appealed, see chapter 10 of this book) illustrate the interoperability between ISDS and WTO dispute settlement and the relative ease with which a dispute can be shifted from one dispute settlement system to the other.

However, the appearance of being alternatives is misleading. The WTO dispute settlement system may be the destination of a complaint arising out of the same facts as an investment treaty claim, but the purpose of WTO dispute settlement, the

1. *Philip Morris Asia Limited v. The Commonwealth of Australia*, PCA Case No. 2012-12.
2. Australia–Tobacco Plain Packaging (Honduras) [DS435], Australia–Tobacco Plain Packaging (Dominican Republic) [DS441], Australia–Tobacco Plain Packaging (Cuba) [DS458], Australia–Tobacco Plain Packaging (Indonesia) [DS467], all decided on 28 June 2018. Only the cases brought by Honduras and the Dominican Republic have been appealed, with the appeals currently pending.

WTO procedure, the WTO substantive law, and the WTO remedies are fundamentally different. More importantly, the WTO dispute settlement system assumes a position of primacy, if not supremacy, in respect of matters arising out of the WTO "covered agreements".[3] With respect to the Australian plain packaging cases further dealt with in chapter 10 of this book, that covered agreement is the Agreement on Trade-Related Aspects of Intellectual Property Rights (TRIPS Agreement).

To date, disputes brought under the TRIPS Agreement have constituted slightly more than 5% of all WTO cases; in a third of these disputes the WTO Member concerned was found to be in violation of the TRIPS Agreement.[4] Although the Australian tobacco cases mentioned above have taken very long time for the panel to issue its report, normally the procedure before the WTO remains both swift and cost effective, albeit decreasingly so.

This chapter examines the dispute settlement system set up by the WTO Agreement and takes stock of its characteristic features for the purpose of comparison with ISDS and dispute settlement under bilateral or regional preferential trade agreements. Under B. below, the chapter investigates how the WTO dispute settlement system came into being, observing that all but one of the characteristic features of that system - multilateral compulsory adjudication, exclusive jurisdiction, non-unilateralism, prospective remedies - derived from the earlier GATT dispute settlement system, while the appellate mechanism emerged as a consequence of efforts to improve and strengthen that earlier system. This is markedly different from dispute resolution under bilateral trade agreements and is credited with greater transparency, a level playing field (in that complainants and respondents can only be states or customs territories) and a balanced enforcement mechanism.

Next, the chapter (under C. below) analyses the design of the WTO dispute settlement system, looking in turn at the adjudication and enforcement mechanisms, how they are administered by the WTO, what use has been made of this system hitherto, and whether it has provided a satisfactory answer to non-compliance. Turning to the experience of the system since its inception (under D. below), its principal achievements are noted, including its satisfactory compliance record, as well as its most important shortcomings and vulnerabilities, as exposed in the current crisis related to appointments of Appellate Body members. Chief among its shortcomings is the institutional imbalance within the WTO, which leaves the dispute settlement system without a political-legal dialectic and exposes it to unfair charges of judicial activism. The principal vulnerability is the risk of Membership disengagement. Under E. below, stock is taken of the reform proposals that have been tabled in an attempt to resolve the current Appellate Body crisis.

The identified key features of the current WTO dispute settlement system are contrasted with ISDS and dispute settlement in bilateral and regional trade agreement

3. Notably the General Agreement on Tariffs and Trade (GATT), the General Agreement of Trade in Services, (GATS), and the other agreements listed in Appendix 1 to the *Understanding on Rules and Procedures Governing the Settlement of Disputes* (the Dispute Settlement Understanding, DSU), itself an annex to the *Agreement Establishing the World Trade Organization*, signed in Marrakesh on 15 April 1994, 1867 UNTS 154 (the WTO Agreement or the Marrakesh Agreement).
4. See < worldtradelaw.net/databases/trips.php > .

(under F. below). The chapter ends with a look to the future of WTO dispute settlement (under G. below) and some concluding reflections (under H. below).

B. THE ORIGINS OF THE WTO DISPUTE SETTLEMENT SYSTEM

The WTO dispute settlement system did not emerge from a blank slate but evolved out of almost half a century of experience with dispute settlement under the General Agreement on Tariffs and Trade, which was negotiated under the auspices of the United Nations Conference on Trade and Employment and signed in Geneva on 30 October 1947 (GATT 1947). The unique features that distinguish the WTO dispute settlement system from other international dispute settlement systems are largely due to the history of the GATT dispute settlement system. To understand the design and practice of the WTO dispute settlement system, it is therefore instructive to examine how these features evolved.

The GATT dispute settlement system is best understood from an evolutionary prism. The blueprint of that system, which emerged from the conclusion of the GATT negotiations in 1947, was incomplete and never quite functioned the way its incomplete design seemed to suggest. Conversely, the characteristic features that came to distinguish GATT disputes in actual practice (the panel system) were not reflected in its original conception. The obvious reason for these "birth defects" was that the GATT was negotiated as a substantive international trade agreement under the framework of a much grander project; the creation of an International Trade Organization (ITO), which was envisaged as a sister organization to the Bretton-Woods institutions.[5] In fact, the GATT was concluded and entered into force on a provisional basis in anticipation of the signing and ratification of the founding treaty of the ITO, the so-called Havana Charter.[6] However, the Havana Charter was never ratified and the ITO was never created.[7] This meant that the GATT, which relied on the institutional framework and bigger picture set forth in the Havana Charter, saw the light of day without a complete dispute settlement mechanism. It is in fact fortunate that any provision at all was included in the GATT referring to dispute settlement, *viz.* Articles XXII and XXIII. On the basis of these provisions, the subsequent decades of dispute settlement practice witnessed the emergence of the GATT panel system and the evolution from diplomatic dispute settlement, with a pragmatic emphasis on finding mutually acceptable solutions in individual cases, towards an ever more structured and adjudicatory procedure.

To explain the evolution of the WTO dispute settlement system design features, this section will address in turn the GATT dispute settlement system as it was originally envisaged (I. below), the emergence and evolution of the panel system (II. below) and

5. For a comprehensive analysis on the history of the GATT and the ITO, see Robert E. Hudec, *The GATT Legal System and World Trade Diplomacy* (2nd edn., 1990).
6. United Nations Conference on Trade and Employment, Final Act and Related Documents, E/CONF.2/78, United Nations publication, Sales No. 1948.II.D.4.
7. The Havana Charter was never formally rejected, but was delayed indefinitely. For an account of the reasons, see William Diebold, *The End of the ITO*, Princeton Essays in International Finance No. 16 (1952).

the crisis of the GATT dispute settlement system that eventually led to the adoption of the DSU at the conclusion of the Uruguay Round (III. below).

I. The GATT Dispute Settlement System as Originally Envisaged

At the inception of the GATT, disputes were meant to be settled pursuant to the elaborately negotiated Havana Charter, which foresaw a system of dispute settlement that would have been truly revolutionary had it come to fruition. That system – the ITO dispute settlement system – was the product of original reflection informed by first-hand experience of the shortcomings of dispute settlement in the Inter-War years and earlier.[8] Before the GATT, trade disputes were principally settled diplomatically through direct negotiation between the states concerned or through the good offices or mediation of a third state, while occasionally states agreed to have their conflict determined by arbitration.[9]

The GATT 1947 not only revolutionised world commerce by creating the first multilateral code of trade conduct,[10] it also radically transformed the settlement of trade disputes. While the GATT 1947 itself in Articles XXII and XXIII only contained minimal provisions for dispute settlement, these provisions were to be understood in the context of the dispute settlement provisions of the Havana Charter, with which they partially overlapped. Importantly, Article XXIII.2 fourth sentence of the GATT provided that in the event of dispute, the legal possibility of a contracting party to retaliate – in the form of the suspension of concessions or other GATT obligations – would be subject to the prior authorization by the Contracting Parties.[11] Although the

8. Cross-border trade prior to the GATT had been regulated on the international plane, if at all, through a web of commercial treaties between two or more states. Such commercial treaties, in US treaty practice often known as Friendship, Commerce and Navigation (FCN) treaties, also often covered navigation (coastal trade) and consular matters and frequently provided for most-favoured-nation (MFN) treatment. See chapter 3 of this book and Lassa Oppenheim, *International Law: A Treatise*, Vol I (2nd edn., 1912), §§ 578–580. Such commercial treaties had a long history, with known antecedents stretching as far back as ancient Greece and Rome, had become more important from the 16th and 17th centuries onwards and proliferated rapidly in the 19th century. Particularly from the mid-19th century, the expanding foreign commerce of the United States had resulted in a determined policy of signing FCN treaties with MFN clauses.
9. Jackson H. Ralston, *International Arbitration from Athens to Locarno* (1929), 153. Agreements to arbitrate were either in the form of arbitration clauses contained in the commercial treaty itself or in the form of submission agreements concluded after the outbreak of a dispute. In the latter case, states were frequently motivated to agree to arbitrate their differences so as to avoid retaliation, a protracted standoff or an endless escalation of retaliation and counter-retaliation (by means of such international legal remedies as retorsion, reprisal (including embargo), pacific blockade or intervention), or even to avoid an escalation into armed conflict. See Lassa Oppenheim, *International Law: A Treatise*, Vol II (2nd edn., 1912), §§ 3, 13, 26–52.
10. Some early multilateral initiatives in the area of international trade were taken by the League of Nations, Economic Committee, Sub-Committee on the Equitable Treatment of Commerce.
11. By convention, the contracting parties or States parties to the GATT are written in capital letters when all of them are referred to collectively.

GATT 1947 did not contain an exclusive jurisdiction clause, the fact that enforcement measures had to be authorised by the Contracting Parties therefore lent itself to the interpretation as both a ban on unilateral enforcement and something akin to *de facto* compulsory and exclusive jurisdiction. However, this need not have been the only available interpretation, as will be further discussed below.

The original dispute settlement system envisaged in the Havana Charter was a multi-tiered system that relied on a combination of negotiation, arbitration, investigation, collective diplomacy and expert advice.[12] Article 92.1 of the Havana Charter expressly committed the ITO Members not to have recourse to any other dispute settlement procedures than those envisaged in the Charter, thus essentially giving the ITO exclusive jurisdiction over such disputes. In Article 92.2, the Members undertook in principle not to have recourse to "unilateral economic measures of any kind contrary to the provisions of the Charter". As discussed above, the essence of these provisions was reflected in Article XXIII.2 fourth sentence of the GATT insofar as the imposition of enforcement measures was concerned.

The procedure for settlement of differences referred to in Article 92 was then outlined in the following Articles 93 through 96, dealing in turn with consultation and arbitration (Article 93), reference to the ITO executive board (Article 94), reference to the ITO plenary conference (Article 95), and reference to the International Court of Justice (Article 96). These procedures coexisted with other specific procedures for consultation and settlement of differences contained elsewhere in the Charter (Article 97).

The consultation provision in Article 93.1 of the Charter was mirrored and retained in Article XXIII.1 of the GATT and was *formulated* as an optional recourse, which nonetheless was a prerequisite for enforcement through retaliation and was therefore *de facto* mandatory. Unlike the GATT provision, Article 93.2 of the Charter provided for binding arbitration as an optional means of dispute settlement.[13] In the event of unsuccessful settlement by consultation, the Havana Charter (similar to Article XXIII.2 of the GATT) provided a mechanism for *authorising* retaliation as a means of enforcement. This was a fundamental novelty compared to previous practice and a departure from general international law, and it remains a prominent feature of the WTO dispute settlement system.[14]

Moreover, the Havana Charter relied on a two-tier procedure before the ITO with an additional possibility of appellate review through reference to the International Court of Justice (ICJ). The GATT only retained the entry tier of the procedure in Article XXIII.2 (Article 94 of the Charter), the first step of which was

12. Chapter VIII (*Settlement of Differences*), containing Articles 92 through 97.
13. Because of the exclusive recourse clause in Article 92.1, arbitration required express authorisation in the Charter to be considered a procedure "envisaged in this Charter" and thus allowed. By contrast, the GATT 1947 neither expressly included nor expressly excluded the possibility that disputing contracting parties agreed to settle their differences through arbitration or any other means. Although never determined by case law, the arbitrability of GATT disputes was asserted in the Uruguay Round negotiations. See MTN. GNG/NG13/W/12, 24 September 1987, at 3.
14. This aspect captured the essence of the exclusive jurisdiction of the ITO dispute settlement system and came to be preserved in the GATT, even though the GATT did not expressly provide for exclusive jurisdiction.

that the Contracting Parties[15] (*cf.* the Executive Board in the Havana Charter, *i.e.* the executive organ of the ITO) investigate the matter. As the next step, the GATT provided that the Contracting Parties "shall make appropriate recommendations to the contracting parties with they consider to be concerned, or give a ruling on the matter, as appropriate". By contrast, Article 94.2 of the Havana Charter provided a more detailed list of possible outcomes.[16]

One pivotal difference between the enforcement provisions of the GATT and the Havana Charter was that, since the GATT was not an organisation, the decision to authorise retaliation had to be agreed by all contracting parties to the GATT acting unanimously, whereas under the Havana Charter, retaliation was decided by the Executive Board or the Conference.[17] Although it could well have been argued that in the context of Article XXIII.2 of the GATT, the term "Contracting Parties" should have been interpreted to exclude the disputants, such an interpretation did not prevail.[18] Instead, the implication under the standalone GATT was that the disputing parties could effectively veto the imposition of any retaliation. This would prove to be one of the principal shortcomings of the GATT dispute resolution system.

Another significant difference between GATT and the Havana Charter was that the latter provided for an appellate mechanism.[19] Article 95 of the Charter provided that the Executive Board, if requested to do so within thirty days by a Member concerned, was obliged to refer to the Conference for its review any action, decision or recommendation by the Executive Board under Article 94.2 or 94.3 of the Charter. While the Conference, similar to the WTO Dispute Settlement Body (DSB), was not an adjudicatory body, the procedure before it importantly provided a right of any Member whose interests were prejudiced by any of Conference decision to have

15. Because the GATT was not an organisation, all dispute settlement tasks under the GATT had to be referred to the Contracting Parties.
16. The Executive Board could: (1) decide that the matter did not call for any action; (2) recommend further consultation to the Members concerned; (3) refer the matter to arbitration upon such terms as may be agreed between the ITO Executive Board and the Members concerned; (4) in the context of "violation complaints", request the Member concerned to take such action as may be necessary for the Member to conform to the provision of the Charter; and (5) in the context of "non-violation complaints" and "situation complaints", to make such recommendations to Members as will best assist the Members concerned and contribute to a satisfactory adjustment. Note that the three types of complaints listed in Article XXIII.1 of the GATT are broadly similar to those in Article 93.1 of the Havana Charter. For simplicity they are referred to here as violation, non-violation and situation complaints.
17. If indeed the Havana Charter had entered into force, the reference to the Contracting Parties in Article XXIII.2 GATT would have been effectively superseded by the references to the Executive Board and the Conference in Articles 94 and 95 Havana Charter, respectively, as the GATT would have been incorporated by reference into the Charter (*cf.* Article 17.3 of the Charter).
18. This interpretation was referred to as "consensus-minus-two". See Mary E. Footer, 'The Role of Consensus in GATT/WTO Decision-making', 17 *Northwestern Journal of International Law & Business* (1997), 653, 671.
19. Modelled on Article XXIX of the Articles of Agreement for the International Monetary Fund and Article IX of the Articles of Agreement of the International Bank for Reconstruction and Development (the World Bank).

the decision submitted for review by the ICJ by means of a request for an advisory opinion (Article 96). The opinion would be considered binding and the relevant Conference decision would be modified accordingly.

II. The Emergence of the GATT Panel System and its Evolution

It appears that when disputes first arose under the GATT 1947, disputants sought to provisionally mimic the procedure envisaged in Articles 92 through 97 of the Havana Charter, as far as possible, being the contextual framework of Article XXII and XXIII of the GATT. However, since the ITO never materialised, such provisional arrangements became *de facto* permanent. Whereas the Contracting Parties "provisionally" took the place of the ITO Conference in exercising plenary powers over the dispute settlement process, disputants looked to the Chair of the Contracting Parties - a diplomat of one of the contracting parties - to "provisionally" assume the dispute settlement system role of the ITO Executive Board.[20] At first, the Chair assumed this role through a series of early "statements" to the Contracting Parties on how a particular dispute ought to be settled.[21] The complexity and importance of the matters at stake made it necessary early on to involve a broader circle of contracting parties in hearing the disputants and seeking to work out a satisfactory settlement. For that purpose, the practice began to convene "working parties" consisting of the disputants and a number of other contracting parties.[22] All participating diplomats, including representatives of the disputants, would attend joint working party meetings, the aim of which were to find a common understanding on the relevant facts and an agreement as to the legal issues involved and to encourage either or both of the parties to compromise.[23] On the basis of the working party deliberations, a report would be drawn up and presented to the Contracting Parties.[24] These reports would therefore sometimes present a settlement that had been agreed during the negotiations within the working party. If no agreement had been reached, the report might *recommend* that the respondent party desist in some objectionable practice. Where it was not possible to reach an amicable resolution, the process aimed at producing an outcome that would nevertheless be accepted and implemented, even if the losing party would dissent with the report's findings. In other cases the report might be inconclusive.

It was apparent early on that some more rigorous method of dispute settlement was required. In 1952, the then Chair of the Contracting Parties decided to establish a "panel" to hear complaints, which brought the task of dispute settlement slightly

20. Andreas F. Lowenfeld, *International Economic Law* (2nd edn., 2008), 151.
21. *Ibid.* These statements were brief and contained minimal motivation or details as to facts and matters of law.
22. Agreed Description of the Customary Practice of the GATT in the Field of Dispute Settlement (Article XXIII.2), Annex to the Understanding Regarding Notification, Consultation, Dispute Settlement and Surveillance, 28 November 1979 (L/4907), para. 6(i).
23. *Ibid.* The working party procedure was essentially a flexible device akin to good offices, mediation and conciliation, depending on the approach taken by the participating contracting parties. The emphasis was on making the disputants' disagreement go away, not on advancing legal interpretations.
24. *Ibid.*

more in line with the envisaged procedure before the ITO Executive Board.[25] Unlike the working party, which included representatives of the disputants, the panel was a group of diplomats, or economists or other experts distinct from the disputants that took the lead in the dispute settlement process and assumed responsibility for issuing the report to the Contracting Parties.[26] The panel would hear the disputants, but would deliberate separately from them. Despite their separation from the disputants, the early panels were not significantly more adjudicatory in the way they operated when compared to working parties. The emphasis was still on reaching mutually acceptable outcomes rather than settling interpretive issues.

While the early panels thus appeared as a moderate elaboration of the working party system, subsequent panels became steadily more like arbitral tribunals. However, an important difference between GATT panel proceedings and arbitration was that the former was a multilateral form of dispute settlement. Similar to arbitration, the establishment of panels to hear a dispute required the consent of the disputants. This was not because of any formal agreement, such as an agreement to arbitrate, but simply followed from the multilateral nature of the proceedings. Nor was such consent inherent in the GATT; the panels were essentially convened *ad hoc*. Panels were established by the Contracting Parties, which, as it was not organ of any organisation, could only act by unanimous consent, meaning that all contracting parties had a veto. Moreover, very much unlike normal arbitration, once the disputants had consented to have their case heard by a panel (or, in practice, had not objected to it), they were not bound to accept the panel's findings. Rather, the Contracting Parties would only adopt the panel's report by consensus. A disputant who was dissatisfied with the panel report could therefore block its adoption by objecting to it.

Another manifestation of the multilateral nature of the panel proceedings was that, unlike arbitration, the disputants were not free to bilaterally modify the procedure and decide on procedural issues; indeed the panel answered not to the disputants but to the Contracting Parties. Also in other respects the panel procedure differed from normal arbitral procedure. For example, unlike a typical arbitral tribunal, the panel would interact with the disputants and would discuss a draft of its report with them in quite an informal manner. For all these reasons, even though arbitration can take many forms and even though the panel procedure had certain similarities with arbitration (and also to conciliation), the panel procedure that emerged through practice was a distinct, *sui generis* form of international adjudication.

III. Crisis of the GATT Dispute Settlement System

A trend that can be discerned from the period beginning in the mid-1960s through the end of the Uruguay Round was that the major trading powers – being, as they were, "repeat litigants" in a small, closed dispute settlement system – gradually adapted, learned from each other and refined their litigation strategies in light of

25. Report of the Panel, *Treatment by Germany of Imports of Sardines*, (31 Oct. 1952), GATT BISD 1st Supp. (1953), at 53.
26. Agreed Description of the Customary Practice of the GATT in the Field of Dispute Settlement, *supra* note 22, para. 6(ii).

their opponents' arguments and litigation tactics.[27] The direction of this adaptation was towards ever more factually granular and precise submissions and ever more complex legal argumentation. As a result, further "legalisation" of disputes led to increased "judicialisation" of the dispute settlement process.[28]

This process of "judicialisation" first materialised in the GATT normative framework through the 1979 Understanding on Disputes.[29] However, what was clear at the outset of the Uruguay Round was that, unlike a "real" litigation system, the GATT dispute settlement system was essentially optional (being non-binding in practice due to the consensus requirement) and rested on the good will and the good faith of the disputants.[30]

1. First Phase: The Limitations of the GATT Panel System Exposed

The initial success of the GATT dispute settlement system was largely due to the mutual willingness on the part of disputants to settle their differences amicably, even if at times this meant accepting painful compromises. As the decades went on, that original dose of goodwill slowly dissipated. That change of sentiment is not difficult to understand when one considers the profound changes that occurred among the Contracting Parties during the first two decades of the GATT. In 1947, the United States exerted an unrivalled hegemony amongst the 23 original signatories to GATT who were engaged in the Geneva negotiations.[31] Although the United States would continue to dominate the GATT for decades to come, the original group of

27. For a narrative of the successive US–EEC litigation experience under the GATT in the 1960s and 1970s, see Robert E. Hudec, *Enforcing International Trade Law: The Evolution of the Modern GATT* (1993), 47–99.
28. While it might be tempting to blame GATT/WTO adjudicators for "judicialising" trade disputes, it appears that they no more than responded to the increasingly legalistic or "judicial" submissions by litigants in the disputes before them. However, the core legal provisions of the GATT 1947 remained and still remain unchanged (in the form of GATT 1994). As a result, the adjudicators, being obliged to rule on the issues before them, were pushed by disputants to clarify in ever-greater detail the constructive ambiguities (intentional or not) left behind in the GATT 1947.
29. Understanding Regarding Notification, Consultation, Dispute Settlement and Surveillance, 28 November 1979 (L/4907), GATT BISD 26th Supp. [1980] at 210 (1980) [hereinafter the 1979 Understanding].
30. Although Article XXIII GATT could be interpreted to create a *de facto* exclusive jurisdiction over GATT disputes since enforcement measures required the consent of the Contracting Parties, that jurisdiction was in practice not compulsory, because the consensus requirement also applied to the establishment of panels and adoption of panel reports. It is in light of this "defect" that the use by the United States of retaliation in the form of Section 301 of the Trade Act should be considered, as is further described below.
31. Europe (seven signatories: Belgium, Czechoslovakia, France, Luxembourg, the Netherlands, Norway and the United Kingdom) was still in ruins and dependent on the aid of the US Marshall Plan. Much of Asia and most of Africa was still under colonial rule. China was caught up in a bloody civil war. British India, all of which had just become independent (India, Pakistan, Burma and Ceylon), had large populations living in abject poverty, a sizeable proportion of which were internally displaced due to the 1947 partition of India. The remaining signatories were made up of the *de facto* independent British Dominions

representatives for the contracting parties, who had participated in the Geneva negotiations, would gradually be replaced by other diplomats without such first-hand experience. The contracting parties would also be joined by many new signatories, particularly during the wave of decolonialisation in the 1960s. By the close of the Kennedy Round in 1967, the contracting parties had more than tripled to 71,[32] equal to an annualised growth rate of nearly 6 per cent since 1947. After that initial surge, the number of accessions continued at a pace of approximately 1.5 per cent until the start of the Tokyo Round in September 1973 (83 contracting parties),[33] with 92 contracting parties at the start of the Uruguay Round in September 1986,[34] until it reached 95 by on the 40th anniversary of GATT in November 1987.[35]

The difficulty of exerting hegemony over such a large and diverse group of countries was exacerbated by the gradually shifting economic relations between primarily the United States and Europe in the form of the emerging power of the EEC (later, the EC, and today, the EU).[36] It was the disputes between the United States and the EEC/EC that came to shape the "judicialisation" of the dispute settlement system.[37]

By 1971, the United States faced its most severe economic situation since the Second World War with high unemployment, high inflation, a balance of payments deficit and bulging public debt.[38] Fearing that the US dollar was overvalued compared to the official gold exchange rate of USD 35 dollar per ounce, US trading partners increasingly began to demand dollar conversion into gold. Under the threat of a run on the US gold reserves, President Nixon enacted a series of emergency measures consisting of a suspension of the US convertibility to gold, freezing interest rates and wages, and imposing a 10% "surcharge" on imports.[39] What became known as the "Nixon Shock" was followed by a decade of economic upheavals, notably in the

(Australia, Canada, New Zealand and South Africa) plus Brazil, Chile, Cuba, Lebanon and Syria.

32. GATT press release (GATT/981), 7 March 1967 (<docs.wto.org/gattdocs/q/GG/GATT/981.PDF>).
33. GATT press release (GATT/1133), 9 September 1973 (<docs.wto.org/gattdocs/q/GG/GATT/1133.PDF>).
34. GATT press release (GATT/1393), 1 September 1986 (<docs.wto.org/gattdocs/q/GG/GATT/1393.PDF>).
35. GATT press release (GATT/1423), 30 November 1987 (<docs.wto.org/gattdocs/q/GG/GATT/1423.PDF>).
36. Generally see Derek Aldcroft, *The European Economy 1914–1990* (3rd edn., 1994), 132–138.
37. The first more prominent controversy between the two trading powers came in the form of the famous "Chicken War" of the 1960s, which had its roots in the EEC's Common Agricultural Policy. Although that standoff was resolved pragmatically and followed by a period of decline in the use of dispute settlement, the scene was set for a more combative approach to address trade disputes. See Lowenfeld, *supra* note 20, 153.
38. The situation had grown steadily worse during the preceding decade due to profligate public spending on everything from public welfare to the Cold War arms race, the Vietnam War, and the Apollo lunar expedition, and a deteriorating trade balance as the economic output of Western Europe, notably West Germany, and Japan recovered strongly. See generally Peter M. Garber, 'The Collapse of the Bretton Woods Fixed Exchange Rate System', in Michael D. Bordo and Barry Eichengreen, *A Retrospective on the Bretton Woods System: Lessons for International Monetary Reform* (1993), 461–494.
39. *Ibid.*, 465.

form of the two Oil Shocks of 1973 and 1979, which further drove up inflation and worsened the US current account deficit. All this led to a hardening of economic relations among the Western nations. It was in this context that the next phase of the GATT dispute settlement system unfolded.

Breaking with previous practice, the United States now adopted a more proactive approach to GATT enforcement and began to challenge various trade restrictions or discriminatory measures that it considered non-compliant with GATT. The prime target of these challenges was the EEC. The EEC responded to these early challenges by refusing to consent to the US requests for panels in the GATT Council;[40] and without consensus among the Contracting Parties, a panel could not be established. A way to unlock GATT dispute settlement presented itself in 1973 as the US introduced tax incentives to encourage exports in the form of "Domestic International Sales Corporations" or "DISCs", which prompted the EEC itself to lodge a complaint.[41] The EEC requested a panel, which the United States would only agree to if the EEC *reciprocally* accepted the panel to hear a US complaint against EEC tax law. After more than two years of negotiation, the panel was eventually established. However, once the panel reported back, the EEC blocked its adoption in the GATT Council and the United States blocked it to the extent the EEC would not consent to it. After another four years of negotiations, the parties agreed to unblock the panel report.

The discouraging experience of the DISC case placed dispute settlement reform firmly on the reform agenda for the on-going Tokyo Round negotiations, which resulted in the 1979 Understanding on Dispute Settlement.[42] While the principal problem with the panel system was that the establishment of panels was frequently and rather unpredictably blocked, in the cases where it was possible to establish panels the compliance record was actually quite good, with over 80% of panel reports being adopted.[43] Moreover, even though there are no reliable statistics for the extent to which adopted reports remained unimplemented, only once did the Contracting Parties actually authorise retaliation.[44]

Although it did not bring about an automatic right to panels, the 1979 Understanding nevertheless appears to have resulted in fewer blocked panel appointments.[45] However, the number of blocked appointments remained high as the caseload more than doubled in the period between the end of the Tokyo Round and the end of the Uruguay Round.[46] Yet, it seems that the preferred method of obstruction after the 1979 Understanding shifted from blocking panel appointments to blocking the adoption of panel reports, which sent the number of unadopted panel reports soaring.[47]

---

40. Lowenfeld, *supra* note 20, 154.
41. *Ibid.*
42. *Supra* note 29.
43. Hudec, *supra* note 27, 395–608.
44. *US–Suspension of Obligations (1952)*, Working Party Report, Netherlands Action under Article XXIII:2 to Suspend Obligations to the United States, 8 November 1952 (L/61).
45. Hudec, *supra* note 27, 395–608.
46. *Ibid.*
47. *Ibid.*, 145–164.

2. *Second Phase: Section 301 and the Demise of the Old GATT Panel System*

Driving the wave of GATT disputes during the Uruguay Round was US dissatisfaction with the EEC's Common Agricultural Policy, which it regarded as strongly trade restrictive and which it was not successful in curtailing during the Tokyo Round. The EEC response to these challenges was predominantly to take up the challenges in panel proceedings, but to object to the adoption of unfavourable panel reports.[48] With respect to the adoption of panel reports, deals had to be struck whereby a losing party agreed to unblock a panel report in exchange for the winning party agreeing to unblock a panel report in a case where it had lost. The "deal making" may not have been explicit, but reciprocity seemed to have been the only workable principle during that period. However, mutually agreeing to the establishment of panels and to unblocking panel reports still left open the ultimate *implementation* of the reports' findings. Once panel reports had been adopted, GATT contracting parties might still not comply in reasonable time with the reports. Non-implementation of panel reports became the final way to evade enforcement; a practice that proliferated in the 1980s.[49]

Against this background, the United States enacted the Omnibus Trade and Competitiveness Act of 1988, which amended Section 301 *et seq*. of the Trade Act of 1974.[50] Although the Act itself had been in place since the 1970s, it was only after the 1988 amendment that Section 301 began to be vigorously made use of. It rarely needed to be enforced; the mere threat of unilateral retaliation was often sufficient to bring the trading partner concerned to the negotiation table.[51] Among the actions authorised was the so-called "Super 301" in the area of intellectual property, which before the conclusion of the Uruguay Round fell outside the range of disciplines associated with the GATT.[52]

The broad scope of Section 301 and the manner in which it was applied appeared as an authorisation to engage in unilateral trade retaliation contrary to Article XXIII.2 fourth sentence, of the GATT. Section 301 thus appeared to bypass the fundamental premise of the GATT that retaliation required the authorisation of the Contracting Parties.[53]

---

48. *Ibid.* Indeed, as the EEC became a more frequent claimant, the EEC found itself willing to agree on panel appointments in cases brought against it by the United States, "in exchange" – to a lesser or greater extent – for the United States accepting to establish panels requested by the EEC.
49. Lowenfeld, *supra* note 20, 158.
50. 19 U.S.C. §§ 2411–2420 and 2242. The essence of this Act was to authorise the US government to take action where "the rights of the United States under any trade agreement is being denied" including where "an act, policy, or practice of a foreign country violates, or is inconsistent with, the provisions of" such agreement or "is unjustifiable and burdens or restricts United States commerce".
51. Lowenfeld, *supra* note 20, 159.
52. Petros C. Mavroidis, *Dispute Settlement in the WTO: Mind over Matter*, EUI Working Papers RSCAS 2016/04, 3.
53. Lowenfeld, *supra* note 20, 196.

3. *The Birth of WTO and a New Dispute Settlement System*

The new US policy of aggressively applying Section 301, which - ostensibly at least - appeared to address shortcomings in the GATT dispute settlement and enforcement, had an immediate and profound effect on the EEC's (from 1993, the EC's) and other contracting parties' willingness to consider US demands for dispute settlement reform, including an automatic right to panels. Already by the end of 1988, agreement had been reached in principle on several key issues.[54] After further negotiations, in 1990 a formula was found that would be memorialised in a new dispute settlement agreement, the DSU, whereby there would be a right to a panel, panel reports would be adopted by "reverse consensus", and a procedure would be put in place for retaliation if a panel report was not implemented within a reasonable period of time.[55] Because panel reports were to be adopted by reverse consensus - and thus in practice automatically - the possibility of ex post "correction" of reports by the GATT Council would effectively be lost.[56] Instead, an appellate body of some sort was foreseen to review panel reports and if appropriate modify them.

C. THE DESIGN OF THE WTO DISPUTE SETTLEMENT SYSTEM

The chief improvement of the DSU over the GATT dispute settlement system was to clarify the nature of the jurisdiction and provide for a procedural framework for panel and appellate body proceedings, as well as for the implementation and enforcement of panel and appellate body reports. In what follows, these innovative aspects will be discussed with reference also as to how they relate to dispute settlement under the previous GATT framework.

Compared to the Havana Charter, the DSU did not provide the exclusive and compulsory jurisdiction of its dispute settlement system in similarly unambiguous language. Rather, the wording of Article 23 (*Strengthening the Multilateral System*) of the DSU reflects the tortuous compromises that gave rise to it.[57] On its face, the

54. GATT BISD 36th Supp. [1990], 61.
55. To its defenders, Section 301 served as a final enforcement mechanism in situations where the United States had exhausted its legal remedies under the GATT dispute settlement system, but had been denied prompt and effective relief, either because the respondent had opposed the establishment of a panel or the adoption of a panel report unfavourable to it, or because it had failed to implement the report's recommendations or rulings in reasonable time. Lest the conclusion be drawn that the GATT disciplines were merely hortatory in nature, they would ultimately have to lend themselves to effective enforcement. According to this argument therefore, while the retaliation authorised under Section 301 were unmistakably unilateral, states are permitted under customary principles of state responsibility to take enforcement measures unilaterally without first obtaining authorisation from other states. See, e.g., MTN.GNG/NG13/23/23 (24 Oct. 1990).
56. As originally negotiated, the Dispute Settlement Understanding (DSU) was not premised on the creation of the WTO, but was conceived within the framework of GATT 1947. This may have been a reason why ITO dispute settlement provisions of Chapter VIII of the Havana Charter did not serve as an immediate blueprint.
57. Article 23.1 provides that Members "shall have recourse to, and abide by, the rules and procedures of this Understanding" and "[i]n such cases, Members shall not make a

exclusivity of DSU jurisdiction is limited to "such cases", i.e. where the Members (in fact) have recourse to the dispute settlement system. Yet, does having recourse to the dispute settlement system necessarily exclude also having recourse to *other* means of enforcement? Fortunately, any such ambiguity was early on extinguished in WTO case law. In the seminal case *US–Section 301 Trade Act (2000)*, the panel confirmed that Members are obliged to bring any dispute arising under the covered agreements to resolution within the WTO dispute settlement system. The ruling held that Section 301, which on its face contradicted the exclusive nature of the WTO dispute settlement system, in the event was compliant with the DSU on the basis of policy assurances by the United States to the effect that Section 301 would be applied in conformity with the DSU.[58] In the end, the DSU, just like Article 92 of the Havana Charter, ensures both the exclusivity of the WTO dispute settlement system in relation to other international dispute settlement mechanisms and enjoins Members from taking unilateral action to enforce the covered agreements.[59]

Like the Havana Charter, but unlike most other international adjudication systems, the DSU foresees an appellate mechanism. The DSU retained the requirement in Article 93 of the Havana Charter and Article XXIII.1 of the GATT that any authorisation for retaliation be preceded by an attempt at negotiated settlement in the form of consultation. It preserved the panel system that had evolved under the GATT, but added an appellate mechanism.

The DSU strengthened the consultation process, clarifying that consultations must have been attempted before the matter can advance to panel proceedings and imposing strict timelines for responding to a request for consultation (Article 4 of the DSU). Importantly, consultations offers an opportunity for a kind of pre-litigation discovery.[60] On the basis of each party's factual submissions and legal arguments, the parties can at that point negotiate an agreed settlement.[61] Another vital aspect of consultations is that the request for consultation bears upon the panel request, which in turn defines the scope of the dispute and delimits the panel's jurisdiction.[62]

The panel system of the old GATT dispute settlement system was essentially preserved in the DSU. The main innovations of the panel process in the DSU have

---

determination to the effect that a violation has occurred, that benefits have been nullified or impaired or that the attainment of any objective of the covered agreements has been impeded, except through recourse to dispute settlement in accordance with the rules and procedures of this Understanding, and shall make such determination consistent with the findings contained in the panel or Appellate Body report adopted by the DSB or an arbitration award rendered under this Undertaking".

58. See Panel Report, *US–Section 301 Trade Act (2000)*, paras. 7.125–7.126.
59. See Panel Report, *EC–Commercial Vessels (2005)*, para. 7.193.
60. Peter Van den Bossche, *The Law and Policy of the World Trade Organization* (4th edn., 2017), 266.
61. *Ibid.*, para. 267. Depending on whether the consultations are conducted on the basis of Article XXII or XXIII of the GATT (or their equivalents in other covered agreements), the consultation may or may not include third parties.
62. Appellate Body Report, *Brazil–Aircraft (1999)*, para. 132. See also case law cited in Van den Bossche, *supra* note 60, 267. While the challenged measures and claims of WTO inconsistency identified in the request for consultation and the panel request do not need to be precisely and exactly identical, the *essence* of the challenge and claims must not have changed.

already been mentioned.[63] Although stricter timelines were imposed and more clarity achieved as to panel appointments (Article 8 of the DSU), rules on third party participation (Article 10 of the DSU) and confidentiality (Article 14 of the DSU), the difference between the DSU and the previous GATT panel system is not significant as regards the function and formal elements of the panel proceedings (Articles 11 and 12 of the DSU).[64]

However, the introduction of an appellate mechanism profoundly reshaped the dispute settlement system as it had existed before the WTO. The Appellate Body was originally intended merely as a way to ensure that panel reports could be "corrected" in the exceptional event of a legally errant panel report (the so-called "rogue" panel scenario).[65] Since panel reports were now to be adopted by reverse consensus, some way had to be found to review and amend them if necessary. The Appellate Body has been described as an "afterthought",[66] necessary to compensate for giving up the possibility to "correct" panel reports once the adoption of panel reports became automatic. The drafters of the DSU appear not to have anticipated the full judicial role that the Appellate Body as designed necessarily would have to assume. Nor did they seem to have considered the likelihood that a legislative counterweight to the Appellate Body would develop - or perhaps even the essential importance of such a counterweight - which would have ensured that the substantive WTO law continued to reflect the evolving political opinion among the WTO Membership.

Interestingly enough, the "rogue" panel scenario is merely a consequence of a "holy cow" in the Uruguay Round negotiations: retaining the essentially non-judicial composition of GATT panels, which in turn harks back to the diplomatic origins of trade dispute settlement. The fear that panellists - who were, and often still are, economists or government officials (but not necessarily legally trained), rather than lawyers - might come up with a ruling or recommendation that in some crucial respect is legally erroneous, could of course have been addressed differently. Instead of "professionalising" the panels or replacing them with a permanent world trade court, the Appellate Body was to be created as a permanent body composed of seven full-time international judges, each appointed for a four-year term with the possibility

63. Article 6.1 of the DSU gives complainants a right to have a panel established at the latest at the DSB meeting following that at which the request first appeared as an item on the DSB's agenda, unless at that meeting the DSB decides by consensus not to establish a panel (reverse consensus). Article 16.4 of the DSU establishes that panel reports shall be automatically adopted by reverse consensus unless any of the disputants lodges an appeal. These two provisions ensure that panel proceedings are compulsory.

64. See Petko D. Kantchevski, 'The Differences Between the Panel Procedures of the GATT and the WTO: The Role of GATT and WTO Panels in Trade Dispute Settlement', 3 *Brigham Young University International Law & Management Review* (2006), 79, at 137.

65. See Robert Howse, 'The World Trade Organization 20 Years On: Global Governance by Judiciary', 27 *European Journal of International Law* (2016), 9, at 26. Because panel reports prior to the DSU required adoption by consensus, Contracting Parties in the GATT Council could, and often did, modify panel reports to reflect the consensus view. By replacing the consensus requirement in the GATT Council with the reverse consensus requirement in the DSB, another way to correct panel reports had to be devised.

66. Peter Van den Bossche, 'From Afterthought to Centrepiece: The Appellate Body and Its Rise to Prominence in the World Trading System', in Giorgio Sacerdoti et al. (eds.), *The WTO at Ten: The Contribution of the Dispute Settlement System* (2006), 289.

of reappointment once. The appointments are made by the DSB by consensus, i.e. with each WTO Member wielding a veto. Panels, by contrast, are normally composed of three members, who are appointed *ad hoc*, either by agreement between the complainant and respondent, or by the Director General of the WTO.

The reform of the GATT dispute settlement system would have been incomplete without a mechanism to ensure that panel reports (and Appellate Body reports) were properly implemented, and, if needed, enforced.[67] By making the panel process truly compulsory, the drafters of the DSU would have been right to suppose that implementation and enforcement mechanisms of the dispute settlement system also needed to be reinforced. The DSU therefore introduced a structured process of surveillance and implementation in Article 21 DSU, which required the losing party to inform the DSB within 30 days after the adoption of the relevant panel or Appellate Body report of its intentions as to implementation. Members need not comply immediately but are entitled, pursuant to Article 21.3 DSU, to a "reasonable period of time" to implement the report's recommendations and rulings.[68] The next step at the implementation and enforcement stage is to determine whether the Member concerned indeed has implemented the report's recommendations and rulings within the previously determined "reasonable period of time".[69]

If, following the expiration of the relevant reasonable period of time, the losing party has failed to implement the relevant report and thus failed to bring an inconsistent measure into compliance, the last resort is enforcement. While enforcement was rare under the old GATT,[70] it has been used, or at least requested, somewhat more frequently under the DSU.[71] Article 22 DSU provides for remedies in the form of compensation or retaliation (suspension of concessions). The DSU provides scant detail on how the level of compensation is to be determined, as it is voluntary, except

---

67. The final years of the old GATT dispute settlement system had shown that, even where contracting parties – balancing their opposing interests – would agree not to block the establishment of panels and subsequently agree not to block certain unfavourable panel reports (as *quid pro quo* for having favourable reports unblocked), the ultimate uncertainty was whether panel reports would eventually be implemented. During the 1980s, the problem had shifted away from blocking panel appointments and panel report adoptions and was instead one of non-implementation. The 1979 Understanding did not offer concrete guidance, but merely stated in Section 22 that "[i]f the Contracting Parties' recommendations are not implemented within a reasonable period of time, the contracting party bringing the case may ask the Contracting Parties to make suitable efforts with a view to finding an appropriate solution".
68. The length of that period may depend on a multitude of factors, including the complexity of the factual matters involved. Unless the period proposed by the Member concerned is approved by the DSB, it has to be mutually agreed between the disputants, failing which the matter will be determined by binding arbitration. These steps must comply with strict timelines.
69. Based on pre-WTO experience, this could also be a contentious point. The losing party might insist that it had implemented the report, while the winning party might disagree. For this eventuality, Article 21.5 DSU provides that the matter shall then be referred back to the dispute settlement procedures, and where possible to the original panel, for final decision.
70. Only once did the Contracting Parties actually authorise retaliation. Cf. above fn 44.
71. For recent statistics, see Van den Bossche, *supra* note 60, 204.

that it must be mutually acceptable and consistent with the covered agreements. In practice, compensation has infrequently been agreed upon.[72] Instead, the principal (and only true) enforcement measure is retaliation, which mainly takes the form of suspension of concessions to a level equivalent to the level of nullification or impairment resulting from the inconsistent measure that is the subject matter of the dispute (Article 22.4 of the DSU).

D. THE WTO DISPUTE SETTLEMENT SYSTEM IN PRACTICE

The WTO dispute settlement system has often been referred to as the crowning achievement of the Uruguay Round or the "jewel in the crown" of the WTO.[73] Indeed, the first two decades of the new system proved to be a great success. At the apex of this widely lauded system was the Appellate Body which managed to thoroughly "judicialise" trade dispute settlement and, in a stroke, remedy the shortcomings of the previous GATT dispute settlement system which had plagued the multilateral trading system for the better part of its existence.

Yet, over the course of the decades since the inception of the DSU, trouble has been brewing. Grievances about the functioning of the dispute settlement system and in particular of the Appellate Body's jurisprudence have steadily accumulated. A crisis has been looming since the second decade of the 21st century. It is not without historical irony that it is the architect of the system who harbours these grievances: the United States.

Since 2017, this crisis has become acute with the United States consistently having refused to consent to the appointment (or reappointment) of Appellate Body members. As their terms of office have expired, the Appellate Body members have fallen in number from the ordinary seven down to four at the end of 2017 and three at the end of 2018. On 10 December 2019, the terms of two of the three remaining members will expire and the Appellate Body will be down to one member. With three judges being the minimum number to hear a case, the Appellate Body will then cease to operate. Because rulings of first instance WTO panels cannot take effect while appeals are pending, panel rulings that are appealed will be stuck in a stationary queue and remain unenforceable for an indefinite period of time. The entire WTO dispute settlement system will therefore be paralysed.

I. The First Two Decades

From the very beginning, the United States showed the way by not hesitating to make use of the appellate mechanism, and other Members soon followed.[74] Within the first decade, the number of disputes brought under the WTO dispute settlement system exceeded the total number of complaints filed during the 47 years of the old

---

72. *Ibid.*
73. See e.g. Ernst-Ulrich Petersmann, 'The "Crown Jewel" of the WTO has been Stolen by US Trade Diplomats – And They Have No Intention of Giving it Back', in Denise Prévost, Iveta Alexovičová and Jens Hillebrand Pohl (eds.), *Restoring Trust in Trade: Liber Amicorum in Honour of Peter Van den Bossche* (2018), 105.
74. *US–Gasoline* (1996).

GATT dispute settlement system.[75] Of these cases, almost every second panel report was appealed and an Appellate Report was issued.[76] It was clear that the Appellate Body was called upon not just in the odd "rogue" panel case, but generally (as often as not) when one of the disputants took issue with a panel report. Appeals quickly became commonplace, not exceptional. The Members, through their litigation conduct, expressed their trust in the Appellate Body and their clear preference for it to replace the panels as the centrepiece of the new dispute settlement system.

The Appellate Body, on its part, rose to the challenge and almost from the outset went about asserting, first, its judicial primacy and then its judicial independence. One important step was to clarify the role of precedent,[77] as well as the role, significance and bearing upon WTO law of non-trade values and interests.[78] A point of controversy in these early years that appeared to signify the Appellate Body's broad conception of its mandate was the admissibility and use of *amicus curiae* briefs which the DSU neither restricted nor expressly provided for.[79] In the end, crisis could be averted.[80] It took a good part of the first decade for the Appellate Body to establish its independence and fend off criticism as to its legitimacy.

The caseload continued to expand in the DSU's second decade of operation. The number of disputes brought under the WTO dispute settlement system reached 500, generating over 200 Appellate Body reports, exceeding by far the number of reports issued under the old GATT dispute settlement system.[81] While expanded trade volumes during the 1990s and early 2000s and an expanded Membership – notably by the accession of China in 2001 – could have been expected to account for an increase in caseload, it also clear that the new system offered something that was unavailable under the old, namely a true adjudication mechanism that was capable of swiftly and reliably delivering acceptable outcomes.

The Members' acceptance of the decisions of the WTO dispute settlement system is rarely expressed verbally – on the contrary, as just shown, open criticism has been commonplace[82] – but it is an acceptance, or common consent, expressed in the only form that really matters in international relations: as a general pattern of conduct – or practice. With 90% of all reports being implemented, a large majority of

75. Supachai Panitchpakdi, 'The WTO at Ten: Building on Ten Years of Achievements', in Sacerdoti et al., *supra* note 66, 8.
76. *Ibid.* Currently two-thirds of panel reports are appealed (< www.wto.org/english/tratop_e/dispu_e/dispustats_e.htm >).
77. *Japan–Alcoholic Beverages II (1996)*, linking prior GATT *acquis* to the notion of legitimate expectations. With respect to Appellate Body reports, the matter was further clarified in *US–Stainless Steel (Mexico) (2008)*.
78. *US–Gasoline* (1996) and *US–Shrimp* (1998).
79. This controversy is described in Van den Bossche, *supra* note 60, 260.
80. A special meeting was convened by the General Council, exercising its plenary authority, to discuss the issue of *amicus curiae* submissions. The conclusion of the discussions was that the Appellate Body was advised to "exercise extreme caution in future cases until Members had considered what rules were needed" to regulate the issue of *amicus curiae* briefs. General Council, Minutes of Meeting held on 22 November 2000, WT/GC/M/60, dated 23 January 2001.
81. See < worldtradelaw.net/databases/basicfigures.php > .
82. Also, with the launch of the Doha Round, critique subsided. See Howse, *supra* note 65, 42.

which involved a mutual agreement among the disputants as to the "reasonable period of time" for implementation, the WTO dispute settlement system has successfully managed to achieve compliance.[83]

The practice of compliance has been general, but not uniform. There have been exceptions to the general pattern of compliance, but none so protracted as the issue relating to "zeroing".[84] The effect of "zeroing" is to increase the frequency of situations that indicate dumping and to inflate the dumping margin. To date, more than a dozen cases relating to "zeroing" has been working their way through the WTO dispute settlement system. The Appellate Body, which initially was careful in not ruling out the legality of zeroing categorically,[85] was pressed towards finally declaring it inconsistent with the Anti-Dumping Agreement.[86] However, rather than complying with Appellate Body rulings, the United States strongly resisted this case law, arguing that the Appellate Body had misinterpreted its mandate by declaring inconsistent a measure which is not expressly disallowed under WTO law. In spite of vocal opposition and dragged-out Article 21.5 DSU compliance proceedings, the Appellate Body has held firm, not being inclined to be seen as vulnerable to an individual Member's pressure and influence. Meanwhile, more and more disputes were brought against the United States involving its continued use of zeroing. The United States lost these cases but was reluctant to bring itself into compliance, which resulted in extensive and in some cases repetitive compliance proceedings.

It might appear surprising how something so technical and arcane as zeroing could give rise to such a vigorous resistance on the part of the United States. The question of zeroing is certainly a matter of principle, but not in an intellectual sense. Regardless of what might be the theoretically best way to calculate a dumping margin, the principle at stake is the general conception and place of WTO law and its relation to domestic trade law. The Appellate Body's rejection of zeroing had the effect of significantly reducing the scope of application for domestic trade remedies and thus

83. Only in around 10% of cases to date have compliance proceedings had to be initiated, retaliation has been requested in around 5% and authorization to retaliate has been granted in less than 2% of cases. See Van den Bossche, *supra* note 60, 200, 204, 206 and 289. Of course, it could be argued that this general practice of compliance was not entirely due to the good will and intentions manifested in the Marrakesh Agreement and not totally free from the influence of peer pressure and extraneous considerations – unrelated to the persuasiveness of Appellate Body legal reasoning – of the effect that non-compliance might have on the Members' complex and multifaceted relationships. Nevertheless, such dynamics, however difficult their existence might be to prove, may frequently be at play in motivating states to pursue a particular general practice.

84. "Zeroing" refers to the methodology used to determine the existence of dumping (an unfair trade practice against which Members may apply trade remedies under domestic law) as well as the extent of dumping (dumping margin). The distinguishing feature of the methodology is that it ignores from the determination (sets equal to zero) instances not indicative of dumping (i.e. where the normal value of a product does not exceed its export price).

85. See e.g. *EC–Bedlinen* (2001), *US–Corrosion Resistant Steel Sunset Review* (2004), *US–Softwood Lumber V* (2004).

86. See e.g. *US–Zeroing* (EC) (2006), *US–Zeroing* (Japan) (2007), *US–Continued Zeroing* (2009).

the ability of the US government to take action against "unfair trade" practices, specifically dumping.[87]

The "Zeroing Saga" generated significant bitterness on the part of the United States and contributed to a hardening attitude towards the WTO dispute settlement system in general and the Appellate Body in particular. The United States applied "relentless pressure" on the Appellate Body, which backfired.[88] Having lost its duel with the Appellate Body over zeroing, the United States appeared to turn its attention to the Appellate Body itself, both in the form of open criticism and in focusing its attention on its composition and the appointment of its members. First, the United States criticised the US member of the Appellate Body at the time, Jennifer Hillman, for not defending US perspectives and refused to support her reappointment in 2011.[89] Two years later, the United States went a step further by refusing to agree to the first-term appointment of James Gathii of Kenya, which led to a deadlock in the DSB until the following year.[90] This was widely perceived as serving to undermine the perception of judicial independence of the Appellate Body and drew severe criticism.[91]

However, when the United States in 2016 blocked the reappointment for a second term of Seung Wha Chang of South Korea, expressly on grounds of his involvement in three cases which the United States thought were wrongly decided, condemnation followed with a widespread sense that the United States had gone too far.[92] Unlike the previous cases of blocked appointments, the blocking of Chang's reappointment implied that *serving* Appellate Body members' independence from extraneous considerations in carrying out their judicial mandates might be compromised by their interest of securing support for their reappointment. In other words, Appellate Body members might be perceived to be at risk of being "bribed" into ruling in favour of a mighty Member so as to be appointed for another term. Such perceptions would be seriously damaging for the legitimacy and credibility of the Appellate Body.

II. The Appellate Body Crisis

The dispute settlement system, still shaken by the Chang controversy, was thrown into a much deeper crisis in 2017, when following the early departure of one Appellate Body member and the expiry of the second term of two other members, the United States refused to initiate the appointment procedures for all three of these vacancies.[93]

87. This was always unlikely to go down well with US trade lawyers who make their living by enforcing US anti-dumping laws, but was, more importantly, also difficult to defend politically at home, especially following the financial crisis of 2008–09 when being told by a "foreign" court that it was unable to go after "unfair foreign trade" appeared politically intolerable.
88. Howse, *supra* note 65, 71.
89. *Ibid.*
90. *Ibid.*, 72.
91. *Ibid.*
92. Manfred Elsig, Gregory Pollack and Mark Shaffer, 'The U.S. is causing a major controversy in the World Trade Organization. Here's what's happening', *Washington Post*, 6 June 2016 (< www.washingtonpost.com/news/monkey-cage/wp/2016/06/06/the-u-s-is-trying-to-block-the-reappointment-of-a-wto-judge-here-are-3-things-to-know/?utm_term = .77a8a91d8eb4 >).
93. 'America holds the World Trade Organisation hostage', *The Economist*, 23 September 2017.

With only four members left, the Appellate Body became dangerously close to the minimum three members required to hear a case,[94] a level which was reached in August 2018 when yet another Appellate Body member's term expired.

To the frustration of many, the United States has not fully explained its refusal to consent to initiating appointment procedures for replacement of Appellate Body members, apart from asserting its disagreement with a provision in the Appellate Body working procedures that permits retired members to complete the disposition of appeals after the expiry of their terms. While there has been speculation whether the United States would intend to condition the appointment procedures upon a broader renegotiation of the DSU, no such proposals have been made official. This in turn has fuelled speculation that the blocking of appointments might be meant to express US distrust in the Appellate Body at a more fundamental or conceptual level, to discredit it or even to render the dispute settlement system as a whole inoperable.[95]

Appellate Body appointments do indeed appear to be an Achilles' heel of the design of the DSU. Decisions on appointments in the DSU must be made by consensus without recourse to voting.[96] By the continued blocking of appointments, the Appellate Body could fall below three members in December 2019, which would mean that it could no longer decide new cases. Yet, even with its current three members (*i.e.* four vacancies), the Appellate Body greatly struggles to handle all pending cases and is incurring significant delays. Moreover, the effect is not limited to the Appellate Body. Because disputants have an unrestricted right to appeal panel reports, the panel system would also be paralyzed in case the Appellate Body were incapable of deciding cases.[97] A losing party would simply lodge an appeal and rest assured that the matter would not proceed any further, and could thus block implementation and enforcement, knowing that the case would never be concluded. In the end, the enforceability of WTO legal obligations would be effectively suspended.

E. PROPOSED REFORMS OF THE WTO DISPUTE SETTLEMENT SYSTEM

In addition to not giving a comprehensive explanation for its vetoing of efforts to appoint Appellate Body members, the United States has also not communicated any proposals to address its non-elaborated "concerns" with the Appellate Body. Rather, the United States has resigned itself to let other WTO Members come up with ideas and present proposals.

In November 2018, two groups of WTO Members, including the EU, China, India, Canada, South Korea and Mexico, published proposals on dispute settlement reform. The first proposal was presented on behalf of the EU, China, Canada, India, Norway,

94. See Article 17.1 of the DSU.
95. Manfred Elsig, Gregory Pollack and Mark Shaffer, 'Trump is fighting an open war on trade. His stealth war on trade may be even more important', *Washington Post*, 27 September 2017 (< www.washingtonpost.com/news/monkey-cage/wp/2017/09/27/trump-is-fighting-an-open-war-on-trade-his-stealth-war-on-trade-may-be-even-more-important/?utm_term = .08f0dc29df82 >).
96. Footnote 3 to Article IX.1 of the Marrakesh Agreement.
97. See Article 16.4, second sentence, of the DSU.

New Zealand, Switzerland, Australia, South Korea, Iceland, Singapore and Mexico.[98] It set forth proposed amendments of the DSU addressing the following subjects:

(1) transitional rules for outgoing Appellate Body members, aimed at codifying in the DSU the current transitional rule 15 of the Working Procedures for Appellate Review which allows retiring Appellate Body members to finalise their work on cases pending at the expiration of their terms;
(2) enhanced consultation and transparency obligations to address situations where appellate cases cannot be resolved within 90 days;
(3) clarification that the Appellate Body's review of panel findings does not include a review as to the meaning of domestic legislation, which remains an issue of fact to be determined by panels and which is not subject to appeal;
(4) amendment of the scope of review so that the Appellate Body no longer shall address each of the issues raised on appeal by the parties, but only to the extent necessary for the resolution of the dispute; this is aimed at countering the criticism that the Appellate Body "overreaches" its mandate; and
(5) introduction of a "channel of communication" in the form of annual review meetings between the Appellate Body and the Dispute Settlement Body to discuss systemic issues or trends in the jurisprudence; this is meant to address criticism about the precedential value of Appellate Body case law.

The second reform proposal of November 2018 was presented on behalf of the European Union, China and India.[99] It proposed a set of additional amendments of the DSU addressing:

(6) the enhancement of the independence of Appellate Body members, by proposing one single but longer term (6–8 years) that would be non-renewable, which would be aimed at ensuring that Appellate Body members would not be pressured to compromise their independence in the hope of being re-appointed for a second term;
(7) the increase of the number of Appellate Body members from seven to nine, in order to better handle the case load and to provide an improved geographical balance of the Appellate Body;
(8) providing that Appellate Body membership should be an exclusive occupation and not be compatible with side activities inconsistent with the function as an Appellate Body member;
(9) stipulating that outgoing Appellate Body members should continue discharging their duties until their places have been filled, but not longer than for a period of two years following the expiry of their term; and
(10) providing that the procedure to replace outgoing Appellate Body members should be initiated automatically, without a veto possibility for WTO Members.

The November proposals did not receive a positive response from the United States, or indeed any formal response. Instead, Honduras published a number of communications in January and February 2019, expressing what was widely considered a

98. WT/GC/W/752.
99. WT/GC/W/753.

proxy for the US perspective.[100] These communications did not address the November proposals head-on. Nor did they present a coherent set of alternative proposals. Instead, the Honduras communications took stock of a number of reform issues and listed several alternative solutions, lending support to some and not to others. If anything, the Honduras communications could be seen as qualified rejections of the November proposals and perhaps the next stage in what might turn out to be lengthy multilateral negotiations.

However, what is clear from reading the November proposals and the Honduras communications together is that the positions are sufficiently far apart that any amendment of the DSU would unlikely be concluded in time for the appointment of new Appellate Body members by December 2019, when the number of members fall below three. This then leads to the conclusion that if any ambitious reform proposal is pursued, which would require a DSU amendment, a period during which the Appellate Body will be dormant must be expected.

Possibly with this in mind, Taiwan, Brazil, Japan and Australia published moderate proposals in spring 2019, which would not require a DSU amendment, but instead could be implemented by an authoritative interpretation or guidelines adopted by the WTO General Council. These proposals would either not have the same scope or the same binding force as the proposed amendments of the DSU. Even though these limited proposals could be more swiftly implemented, they are clearly insufficient to address the fundamental criticism of the Appellate Body that is widely attributed to the United States. While they offer an escape route - or chance to save face - the limited proposals nevertheless amount to a climb-down by the United States.

F. THE WTO DISPUTE SETTLEMENT SYSTEM COMPARED TO ISDS AND OTHER BILATERAL OR REGIONAL FORA

The WTO dispute settlement system evolved out of the GATT dispute settlement system and without taking much inspiration from alternative international adjudication systems. By the time the DSU was negotiated, what is often regarded as the first ISDS case was decided,[101] although ISDS clauses had been included in bilateral investment treaties since 1969.[102] Rather than being influenced by ISDS, efforts were contemplated to integrate investments under the WTO regime.

In the two decades following the creation of the WTO, there has been ample opportunity to compare the practical operation of the WTO dispute settlement system with ISDS. Such comparison must take account of at least four principal differences.

First, WTO obligations under the DSU are only prospectively enforceable and thus do not give rise to responsibility for injury incurred in the period before enforcement is authorised, while the level of retaliation is limited to the level of

100. WT/GC/W/758, WT/GC/W/759, WT/GC/W/760, and WT/GC/W/761.

101. *Asian Agricultural Products Ltd. v. Republic of Sri Lanka*, ICSID Case No. ARB/87/3.

102. Chad–Italy bilateral investment treaty (1969). Note that the first bilateral investment treaty, signed in 1959 between Germany and Pakistan did not include an ISDS clause. For an historical account, see Andrew Newcombe and Lluis Paradell, *Law and Practice of Investment Treaties* (2009), 45.

nullification or impairment of benefits which an inconsistent measure continues to incur.[103] By contrast, responsibility for breach of investment treaty obligations is by no means limited to the prospective benefits that the relevant investor might derive from the treaty, but also includes damages for injury incurred in the past as a result of a treaty breach.

Second, the WTO dispute settlement system is obviously strictly limited to inter-WTO Member disputes. This does not prevent Members from enacting domestic legislation that obliges the Member to investigate alleged WTO inconsistencies and, where such inconsistencies are found, to actively pursue dispute settlement before the WTO. Such a solution overcomes many of the disadvantages of not allowing individual traders access to the WTO dispute settlement system, including unequal opportunity to petition the government of the relevant Member to take appropriate action. At the same time, it creates a more level playing field in the dispute settlement process, since all participants in the WTO dispute settlement system are Members, *i.e.* states (or customs territories).

Third, another obvious difference is the absence of an appellate mechanism in ISDS, although in CETA,[104] provision has been made for an appellate mechanism and an eventual world investment court (a multilateral investment court system, sometimes abbreviated MIC or ICS). WTO experience shows that "rogue rulings" are a real problem of relying on *ad hoc* tribunals, which appellate review can aptly address. As discussed under C. above, the "rogue" panel risk is also related to the lay composition of panels. This is a point of difference with investment tribunals which are normally composed of jurists. A well-designed permanent investment court could arguably be sufficient without the need for an appellate mechanism to rein in errant lay adjudicators.

Fourth, there is a different balance struck between the need for transparency and confidentiality in the proceedings. While far from being as transparent as could be wished from a domestic legal perspective, the DSU managed to strike a "fair"

103. This can be explained by the purpose of retaliation, which is not to obtain "full reparation" in line with general principles of state responsibility, but to serve as a sanction to induce compliance. The DSU effectively "contracted out" of customary principles on state responsibility. See Van den Bossche, *supra* note 60, 208. This question had been dealt with by GATT panels in the 1980s, which recommended retrospective remedies in line with customary principles in the context of reimbursement of illegal antidumping duties. However, the United States and the EEC did not support these findings in the discussions on this matter during the Uruguay Round. See Mavroidis, *supra* note 52, 7, 17; MTN.GNG/NG13/W/32 of 14 July 1989. This leaves the possibility that the Member who violates its WTO obligations chooses to accept the retaliation against it instead of complying. See Howse, *supra* note 65, 20. Another problem associated with retaliation as a remedy is that its effectiveness depends on the economic prowess of the injured Member and the additional injury that retaliation would inflict on the retaliating Member itself. Suffering retaliation from a very small Member may do little to encourage compliance, while imposing retaliation may harm the Member imposing it. See Marco Bronckers and Freya Baetens, 'Reconsidering financial remedies in WTO dispute settlement', 16 *Journal of International Economic Law* (2013), 281, at 300, 303.
104. Articles 8.28 and 8.29 of the Canada–EU Comprehensive Economic and Trade Agreement (CETA).

balance that appears to have satisfied Members and civil society alike to a degree. ISDS by contrast has only recently moved in the direction of improved transparency.

These differences aside, there is a significant overlap and scope for interoperability between ISDS and WTO dispute settlement insofar as trade disputes may be reformulated as investment disputes and vice versa. It is indeed also possible to shift disputes from the WTO system to bilateral or regional trade agreements. However, the Appellate Body has taken a restrictive line against such "forum shopping" by emphasising the exclusive nature of its jurisdiction under Article 23 of the DSU.[105] The effect is that where WTO law is involved, the jurisdiction of the WTO dispute settlement system has primacy. This leaves open the possibility that accommodating a ruling under a bilateral or regional trade agreement or an ISDS arbitration award might conflict with WTO law and result in a dispute under the WTO dispute settlement system. To be sure, complying with such rulings would not necessarily constitute an inconsistent measure that would be actionable under WTO law. Rather, the point is that where there is a substantive overlap between an obligation under a WTO covered agreement and an obligation under a bilateral or regional trade agreement or an investment treaty, a dispute arising out of an alleged breach of such an overlapping obligation would likely be perceived as a WTO dispute by a WTO panel or the Appellate Body. If so, the act of settling such a dispute outside the WTO dispute settlement system would be a violation of Article 23 of the DSU.

Even though, due to its claim for primacy, the WTO dispute settlement system cannot be regarded as an alternative to ISDS or dispute resolution under bilateral or regional trade agreements, there nevertheless are practical characteristics that set it apart. Perhaps the most notable of those is the speed (and cost efficiency) of WTO cases. Although the *Australia – Tobacco Plain Packaging* cases were very time consuming, lasting 50 months between panel composition and circulation of the panel report, normally panel proceedings currently take on average 18 months to conclude,[106] while Appellate Body proceedings take 123 days.[107] These timeframes exceed the maximum permitted under the DSU – 9 months and 90 days, respectively – which indeed is a cause of concern, particularly in view of the lack of retrospective remedies and the resulting importance to settle disputes promptly. Nevertheless, these timeframes are still very moderate compared to those of comparable international fora and fall well below the average case duration at such fora.[108] Even the WTO cases that are clear outliers in terms of case duration, like the *Australia – Tobacco*

105. *Brazil–Retreaded Tyres* (2007), *Peru–Agricultural Products* (2015).
106. See < www.worldtradelaw.net/databases/paneltiming.php > , accessed on 25 April 2019.
107. *Ibid.*
108. At the Court of Justice of the European Union, in 2018, first-instance proceedings before the General Court took on average 20.0 months to conclude, while appeal cases before the Court of Justice took on average 13.4 months, see *Annual Report 2018: Judicial Activity*, Court of Justice of the European Union (2019), 134, 241. The average duration of an investment arbitration is around 4 years, see *Proposals for Amendment of the ICSID Rules – Working Paper*, Vol. 3, Schedule 9, (ICSID Secretariat, International Centre for Settlement of Investment Disputes, 2018), 898 (< icsid.worldbank.org/en/Documents/ Amendments_Vol_3_Schedule%209.pdf >).

Plain Packaging cases or the Boeing and Airbus cases (*US – Large Civil Aircraft* and *EU – Large Civil Aircraft*), have lasted no longer than an average ISDS case.[109]

G. THE FUTURE OF THE WTO DISPUTE SETTLEMENT SYSTEM

Is there a serious risk that the WTO dispute settlement system will cease to operate as a result of blocked appointments? While further disruption cannot be ruled out, there are several possible workarounds that would allow WTO Members to at least "muddle through" until a political solution is reached. *First*, it has been suggested that the Appellate Body could amend its working procedures so as to be able to effectively reject appeals, so that the panel reports could be implemented and enforced.[110] This is meant to ensure that WTO dispute settlement could continue to operate at the panel level and not be blocked by appeals that cannot be heard. The proposal has sustained some criticism, but remains plausible.[111] *Second*, Members could agree not to appeal. This would serve the same purpose of retaining the functioning of the panel level. Such an agreement was concluded by Indonesia and Vietnam in March 2019 relation to *Indonesia – Safeguard on Certain Iron or Steel Products*.[112] A crucial problem with this approach is that it requires an agreement not to appeal. It may be unrealistic to expect such agreements. *Third*, Members could activate arbitration, a possibility left open in Article 25 DSU, as a means of recreating appellate review on an interim basis until the appointments crisis has subsided.[113] This also requires an agreement between disputants to arbitrate, which may not be forthcoming. *Fourth*, the WTO General Council, as a plenary organ, could intervene and bypass the crisis by making the appointments by voting.[114] However, this would be an extraordinary step, which may result in WTO Members leaving the organization. It is also legally doubtful, since Appellate Body appointments are the responsibility of the DSB and not subject to voting.[115]

In the event that the Appellate Body crisis is not resolved in time, the immediate consequences of a dispute settlement breakdown may not be all that dramatic. Even if no new Appellate Body members are appointed before the number falls below

---

109. *Ibid.*

110. Steve Charnovitz, 'How to Save WTO Dispute Settlement from the Trump Administration', *International Economic Law and Policy Blog*, 3 November 2017 (<worldtradelaw.typepad.com/ielpblog/2017/11/how-to-save-wto-dispute-settlement-from-the-trump-administration.html>).

111. Tetyana Payosova, Gary Clyde Hufbauer and Jeffrey J. Schott, *The Dispute Settlement Crisis in the World Trade Organization: Causes and Cures* (Peterson Institute for International Economics, Policy Brief No 18-5, 2018).

112. WT/DS496/14.

113. Jens Hillebrand Pohl, 'A Blueprint for a Plurilateral WTO Arbitration Agreement under Article 25 of the Dispute Settlement Understanding', in Prévost et al., *supra* note 73, 139.

114. Pieter Jan Kuijper, 'Guest Post from Pieter Jan Kuijper on the US Attack on the Appellate Body', *International Economic Law and Policy Blog*, 15 November 2017 (<worldtradelaw.typepad.com/ielpblog/2017/11/guest-post-from-pieter-jan-kuiper-professor-of-the-law-of-international-economic-organizations-at-the-faculty-of-law-of-th.html>).

115. This follows from footnote 3 to Article IX of the Marrakesh Agreement. See Pohl, *supra* note 113, 140.

three, the outgoing Appellate Body members will be able to finalise the appeals pending at that time. Moreover, pending panel proceedings would continue. Panels could continue to be composed in respect of new WTO cases and panel reports could continue to be circulated. More generally, just because the dispute settlement system would be blocked, it does not follow that the body of substantive WTO law would not remain legally binding. The breakdown of the dispute settlement system would not itself excuse performance.

However, the Appellate Body will not be able to hear new appeals from the moment there are no longer three Appellate Body members. This means that, although panel proceedings may continue and new panel reports may be circulated, a backlog of appealed disputes will begin to build. The incentive to appeal and thus avoid an adverse panel report entering into force, may then prove irresistible. This backlog may build for some time without necessarily prompting WTO Members to lose confidence in the eventual revival of the dispute settlement system or of the WTO legal system. However, if the backlog of appealed cases grows sufficiently daunting and if the prospects for a political solution fade, then the risk of general breakdown of confidence may become acute.

This leaves open the real possibility of a dispute settlement breakdown leading WTO Members to abandon the WTO legal system *en masse*. However, the probability of such a scenario may be exaggerated. Rather than concluding that the Marrakesh Agreement and the WTO legal system it creates *as a whole is no longer is enforceable*, the dispute settlement breakdown engages the possibility of concluding that *the enforcement mechanism of the DSU is no longer enforceable*. In the choice between, on the one hand, suspending the operation of the Marrakesh Agreement, including GATT, GATS, TRIPS, DSU and all other covered agreements, and, on the other hand, suspending the obligation in Article 23 DSU to seek authorization before retaliation, the latter would appear the more measured conclusion.

In this respect, public international law indicates the way forward. Article 60(2)(b) of the Vienna Convention on the Law of Treaties (VCLT) provides that a material breach of a multilateral treaty by one of its parties entitles a party specially affected by the breach to invoke it as a ground for suspending the operation of the treaty in whole or in part in the relations between itself and the defaulting state. Article 60(4) VCLT provides that this is without prejudice to any provision in the treaty applicable in the event of a breach. Can this provision be invoked in case a WTO Member materially breaches its WTO obligations? Since the right to suspend treaty obligations is without prejudice to the "provision in the treaty applicable in the event of breach" – i.e. the DSU, and specifically Article 23 DSU which provides for prior authorisation before retaliation – it follows that a WTO Member would in principle not be able to rely on suspension of treaty obligations instead of complying with Article 23 DSU. However, would this conclusion hold if the Appellate Body is dormant due to a WTO Member's veto? In that situation, could the "provision in the treaty applicable in the event of breach" itself be the relevant treaty obligation that would be suspended?

Another view is that, even if Article 23 DSU could not be lawfully suspended, the fact that the dispute settlement system is paralysed might entitle a WTO Member to invoke a circumstance precluding wrongfulness in order to excuse a suspension of Article 23 DSU which would otherwise be unlawful.[116] It could be argued that countermeasures taken in accordance with the Draft Articles on the Responsibility of States for Internationally Wrongful Acts 2001 (DARSIWA) could constitute such a circumstance, but Article 50(2)(a) DARSIWA subjects such countermeasures to the obligations "under any dispute settlement procedure applicable". Whether this nevertheless is a possible route may boil down to whether Article 23 DSU is "intransgressible", i.e. on par with peremptory norms.[117] In any event, provisional suspension or non-performance of Article 23 DSU would arguably be less radical and more readily excused than non-performance of substantive WTO obligations. While the latter certainly would nullify or impair the benefits under the WTO agreements, the former may be the only remaining means to attain the objectives of those agreements. In fact, the prospect of such suspension may be exactly what is needed to entice Members to conclude arbitration agreements or agreements not to appeal.

If the possibility remains to suspend Article 23 DSU, if only provisionally, credible incentives will exist for WTO Members to agree not to appeal or to arbitrate. This may prove sufficient to salvage adjudicatory dispute settlement in the multilateral trading system. The obvious alternative is that multilateralism gives way to regionalism and that existing and new regional trade agreements, such as the Comprehensive and Progressive Agreement for Trans-Pacific Partnership (CPTPP), the Canada–EU Comprehensive Economic and Trade Agreement (CETA) or other EU-centered trade agreements, will replace the WTO legal system and with it the multilateral dispute settlement system.

H. CONCLUSIONS

The DSU ushered in a new era in world trade relations, transforming settlement of inter-State economic disputes within a compulsory and comprehensive system of collective – i.e. multilateral – dispute resolution, and not merely a way for disputing parties to bilaterally resolve their differences on a case-by-case basis. However, after nearly 25 years of experience, the most prominent shortcoming and vulnerability of this system is its absence of an institutional balance. Without a healthy dialectic between legislature and judiciary, the Appellate Body is liable to be accused of judicial activism, as it will necessarily have to address ambiguous points of law in order to settle disputes. Simply relying on the Appellate Body to exercise judicial self-restraint and self-regulation cannot work as an effective substitute for institutional checks and balances. Members must be prepared to act collectively as a legislature, engage in debate and dare to make use of the voting arrangements of the Marrakesh Agreement, even at the risk of being outvoted. Notably, Members wishing to modify Appellate Body case law must consider proposing authoritative interpretations of the covered agreements as a "political filter".[118]

Perhaps the most serious and lasting concern of the appointments crisis is that it is the latest manifestation of a development – beginning in earnest with the

116. Iain Cameron, 'Treaties, Suspension', in *Max Planck Encyclopedia of Public International Law* (2007), § 12.
117. Commentary (10) to Article 50 DARSIWA.
118. Cf. Article IX.1 and IX.2 of the Marrakesh Agreement.

"Zeroing Saga" and continuing through the blocking of the Hillman, Gathii and Chang appointments - which points in the direction of US disengagement from the WTO dispute settlement system and perhaps from the WTO project as a whole. Having championed the "judicialisation" of dispute settlement in the multilateral trading system, the United States seems to have concluded that it was all a mistake and that it would have been better off embracing power politics and power-based diplomacy, rather than the rule of law, at the international plane. This in turn begs the question whether the WTO could survive without US leadership or even its active membership and constructive engagement. Would a transition from US hegemony to a truly multipolar world economy result in the demise of the institutions created by the hegemon? The answer to those questions are not institutional and legal, but political and historical.

CHAPTER 5
The Direct Application of International IP Agreements Before National Courts

Christopher Heath

A. INTRODUCTION

I. The Problem

> The debate on ISDS illustrates that there is a need to have an informed debate about the desired effect of international law in the EU legal order. The implications of this debate obviously go way beyond investment protection ... When investors (or other private stakeholders) are seeking full protection against domestic regulations under an international treaty, they will want to have the possibility of arguing such regulations actually violate a treaty rule. In those cases, private stakeholders are asserting the right to base a claim on an international agreement ...[1]

This chapter deals with the question whether the direct application of the provisions of an international agreement can be a means to ensure the proper application of international obligations on the plane of domestic law. If so, it could be an attractive alternative to cumbersome State to State litigation before the WTO (discussed in chapter 4), or proceedings before special investor dispute settlement mechanisms (discussed in chapters 2 and 3).

The direct application of international agreements in domestic disputes before domestic courts may be regarded as an alternative route to the direct application of international law by investor-state tribunals or the WTO dispute settlement procedure. While investor-state tribunals as a matter of course apply the international agreement that gives the investor a standing to sue, domestic courts first and foremost

1. Marco Bronckers, 'Is Investor-State Dispute Settlement (ISDS) Superior to Litigation Before Domestic Courts?', 18 *Journal of International Economic Law* (2015), 655, 664.

apply domestic law. Where international agreements have not been implemented, imperfectly implemented or wrongly implemented, the mere application of domestic law by domestic courts would however be insufficient for a private party to avail itself of the provisions of an international agreement. It is this inconsistency between domestic law and international obligations that makes a direct application of an international agreement look attractive.

II. Scenarios

In the context of intellectual property rights, the following case scenario may serve as an example:

Contrary to its international obligations, WTO Member State X does not implement the provisions of the TRIPS Agreement on the minimum period of patent protection (20 years from the filing date, Art. 33), and under domestic patent law only grants patent protection for 17 years from the filing date. A corresponding request to extend the patent to 20 years made by patentee Y was thus refused by the domestic Patent Office.

If this case was brought before the WTO by a Member State, the outcome could be that Member State X was found not to comply with the WTO/TRIPS Agreement and be obliged to change its domestic legislation. Even if this happened, it is unlikely that such amendment would be made with retroactive effect, if implemented at all.[2]

If this case was made the object of an investor dispute settlement dispute (in case such obligation was found in an agreement that provided for such a kind of dispute resolution), the outcome could be that State X was found to have unfairly frustrated the investment made by the patentee and should indemnify the investor.

If this case came before a domestic court in Member State X and the court decided that Art. 33 WTO/TRIPS Agreement (or the respective provision of a bilateral or multilateral investment treaty) could be directly applied and should prevail over domestic law that was inconsistent with this provision, the court could order the Patent Office to extend the patent right for a further three years.

Such avenue would be open to foreign patentees only, however. In the same way as investment treaties, the fabric of international IP agreements only allows foreigners to invoke them. Both the Paris Convention[3] and the TRIPS Agreement[4] are agreements that confer benefits to nationals of other member states. To that extent, a direct application would confer the same preferential treatment to foreign nationals as would an investor settlement dispute, and to that extent give a more favourable treatment to foreign nationals.

2. E.g., the US never complied with the findings in WT/DS160 United States – Section 110(5) of US Copyright Act.
3. Art. 2(1) Paris Convention specifies that the beneficiaries of the Convention are nationals of other countries of the Union.
4. Art. 3(1) TRIPS Agreement: "Members shall accord the treatment provided in this Agreement to the nationals of other Members."

III. Issues to be Addressed

Arriving at the direct application of a certain provision in an international agreement by a domestic court involves a complex analysis of both domestic and international law and requires an answer to a number of questions that are analysed in part B:

I. What is the position of international law on the direct effect of international agreements? *This question must be answered under international law alone.*

II. Does domestic law in general allow international agreements to be given direct effect, and if so, what is the relationship between treaty-based obligations and domestic legislation? *This question must be answered under domestic law alone.*

III. Does the agreement in question contain explicit rules as to how it should be given effect, or can any such rules be inferred from the agreement, from the drafting or the implementing process? *This question, and the following one, must be answered by interpreting the agreement in question. Particularly for the WTO/TRIPS Agreement, this is highly controversial issue.*

IV. Can the specific provision of the agreement be directly applied and can it form the basis of a claim?

V. Can a Treaty-friendly interpretation lead to the application of general principles laid down in the Agreement? *This question requires the interpretation of the agreement in question, and an interpretation under domestic law.*

In the course of the following Part B, the above questions are specifically addressed for the Paris Convention, and for the TRIPS Agreement. These are not only fundamental agreements on intellectual property rights, but have also been subject to the question of direct applicability in a number of contexts and countries.

B. DIRECT APPLICATION OF INTERNATIONAL AGREEMENTS

I. What is the Position of International Law on the Direct Effect of International Agreements?

In the traditional understanding, agreements between states can only create rights and obligations between the contracting parties, that is, between states. Even though individuals might benefit from certain treaty obligations, these could and should be enforced by way of espousal (see Chapter 3 of this book). The reason for this rule is "the respect for the sovereignty and jurisdiction of the state competent to deal with the question through its judicial organs."[5] Yet on three occasions starting in 1928, the International Court of Justice (or its predecessor) dealt with the question whether – if intended implicitly or explicitly – agreement provisions could also be invoked by private parties. The court affirmed this on all three occasions. In the first case concerning an agreement between the City of Danzig and Poland, certain provisions of the agreement concerned the protection of railroad officials referred

5. Jimenez de Arechaga, 'International Responsibility', in Max Sørensen (ed.), *Manual of Public International Law* (1968), 584.

to as the *Beamtenabkommen*. Asked for an advisory opinion, the Permanent Court of International Justice held:

> The wording and general tenor of the *Beamtenabkommen* show that its provisions are directly applicable as between the officials and the Administration ...[6]

While treaties in the field of human rights often stipulate express obligations regarding access to justice, an agreement may also implicitly create rights for individuals, as was reaffirmed in two more recent cases[7] in regard of the right of detained foreigners to consular notification.[8] The court in the latter two cases established that the particular wording of Art. 36 Vienna Convention created individual rights, that such individual rights could be invoked in domestic courts, and that a violation of Art. 36 Vienna Convention should in the future lead to a review of the conviction (in the *LaGrand* case a review was no longer possible, as the death penalty had already been executed). The court however refrained from any concrete order as to how the decision should be implemented.

One should note that such implied rights for individuals are exceptions, though:

> Although for some treaties there will be an implied right for individuals to invoke the treaty in national courts, a standard treaty interpretation analysis may lead to a conclusion that a right of access to national courts should not be implied ... At present, there is no obligation under general international treaty law, customary international law, or general principles of international law for a state to open its courts for invocation by individuals of treaty norms ... There is no such obligation under the Vienna Convention on the Law of Treaties (VCLT), whether as a component of pacta sunt servanda or any other general norm of treaty law.[9]

In other words, unless bound by the provisions of the agreement itself, states under their domestic law are free to determine as to how international agreements should be given effect and in which manner a state meets its international obligations.

II. Does Domestic Law Allow International Agreements to be Given Direct Effect?

1. *Theory*

The question about the effect of international agreements on the plane of domestic law is not determined by international law (see above I) and thus foremost one of domestic law. One first of all needs to distinguish a number of steps in the making of an international agreement: Signature, exchange of instruments constituting a

---

6. Jurisdiction of the Courts of Danzig, Advisory Opinion, 1928 P.C.J.J. (sec. B) no. 15.
7. *Germany v. United States*, 2001 I.C.J. 456 – *"LaGrand", and Mexico v. United States*, 2004 I.C.J. 12 – *"Avena et al."*.
8. The right invoked was Art. 36 Vienna Convention on the Law of Treaties 1969.
9. Sean D. Murphy, 'Does International Law Obligate States to Open Their National Courts?', in David Sloss (ed.), *The Role of Domestic Courts in Treaty Enforcement* (Cambridge University Press, 2009), 105, 118, 63.

treaty, ratification, acceptance, approval or accession. These are further defined in Arts. 11 – 16 of the Vienna Convention.[10]

Of relevance here are, first, the signature to an international agreement, normally after a new agreement has been negotiated. The signature can be likened to a declaration of intent by a state to accede to the agreement, normally by a representative of a national government. Such signature is not binding on the signatory state, yet may give rise to certain rights that subsequent signatory states do not enjoy (for example an automatic right to become member to an international agreement for the original signatory states, while other states that want to accede later may have to fulfil certain conditions).[11]

Second, the ratification of an agreement. In most countries, ratification requires an act of legislature whereby the international agreement in some form becomes part of domestic law and subsequently binds the state. In most countries, (formal) ratification is the act of signature of the agreement by the representative of state. The agreement thereby becomes binding on the state, while an exchange or deposition of the instrument of ratification also creates an international obligation to be bound by the agreement. Yet, in a number of countries, notably the UK and its former colonies, agreements are ratified by government and do not become binding upon ratification, but only upon transformation into domestic law.

This difference is referred to as the difference between *monism* and *dualism*:

> 37. Even though the distinction between monism and dualism is a simplification which masks important differences between the systems which form part of one or the other camp, (reference) the fact remains that one characteristic of dualism lies in the fact that the provisions of international treaty law are not directly applicable nationally, because their legal effects, within the domestic legal order, depend on domestic legislative or regulatory acts intended to ensure their implementation (transformation). It is, however, on account of the existence of an international source that the interpretation of the internal provisions in question is governed by the principle of "treaty friendly interpretation" in order to prevent, in so far as possible, any conflict between the national provision and an obligation under a convention.[12]

However, even where a country "in theory" follows the monistic approach, this by no means answers the question whether an international agreement or a specific provision of an agreement is indeed directly applicable. For this reason, even the theoretical significance of this distinction is increasingly questioned.[13]

---

10. Vienna Convention on the Law of Treaties 1969.
11. For example in the case of the Lisbon Arrangement for the Protection of Appellations of Origin (1958), the following countries have signed the agreement, but never ratified it: Greece, Morocco, Romania, Spain and Turkey: <www.wipo.int/treaties/en/ShowResults.jsp?lang=en&treaty_id=10>.
12. Citation from the Opinion of Advocate General Jääskinen delivered ion 8 May 2014 in joined cases C-401/12P to C-403/12P, *Council of the European Union v. Vereiniging Millieudefensie et al.*, para. 37.
13. Butzer/Haas, in: Schmidt-Bleibtreu/Klein, *Grundgesetzkommentar*, 14th edition 2018, Art. 59 para. 111.

While the dualist approach can already stop at the question as to whether international agreements can produce an effect on the domestic order (they cannot), the monist approach must deal with two subsequent issues. First, although the monist approach recognises the effect of international agreements on the domestic order, this does not automatically mean that such an international agreement produces any direct effect in that it can be invoked by individuals, and, second, what the position of such international agreement is within the domestic order of constitutional law, ordinary law or lower ranking rules and regulations. These additional two questions are very much intertwined with the first and make an analysis of the question of direct effect rather more complicated.

2. *The Dualist Approach*

The *dualist approach* as taken under the law of the **UK** and some of its former colonies does not allow international agreements, even when ratified, to have direct effect. The reason is that in the UK, it is the prerogative of the Crown to ratify international agreements, yet the prerogative of Parliament to grant, amend or withdraw individual rights. Thus, as the legislature is not involved in the process of ratification, an act of Parliament is necessary so that the provisions of the agreement are given domestic effect.

The UK Supreme Court revisited this issue *in extenso* in the course of the Brexit litigation[14] and cited with approval its position previously taken in the Tin Council decision:[15]

> It is axiomatic that municipal courts have not and cannot have the competence to adjudicate upon or to enforce the rights arising out of transactions entered into by independent sovereign states between themselves on the plane of international law ...
>
> As a matter of the constitutional law of the United Kingdom, the Royal Prerogative, whilst it embraces the making of treaties, does not extend to altering the law or conferring rights upon individuals or depriving individuals of rights which they enjoy in domestic law without the intervention of Parliament. Treaties, as it is sometimes expressed, are not self-executing. Quite simply, a treaty is not part of English law unless and until it has been incorporated into the law by legislation. So far as individuals are concerned, it is res inter alios acta [i.e. something done between others], from which they cannot derive rights and by which they cannot be deprived of rights or subjected to obligations; and it is outside the purview of the court not only because it is made in the conduct of foreign relations, which are a prerogative of the Crown, but also because, as a source of rights and obligations, it is irrelevant.

14. UK Supreme Court, *R (on the application of Miller and another) (Respondents) v. Secretary of State for Exiting the European Union (Appellant)* 24 January 2017, [2017] UKSC 5 (The *"Brexit"* Case).
15. UK House of Lords, *J.H. Rayner (Mincing Lane) Ltd v. Department of Trade and Industry* [1990] 2 AC 418, at 499E-500D (The *Tin Council* Case).

The position in the UK is thus clear: While the ratification of an international agreement is within the sovereign powers of the administration, such ratification cannot create (alter; remove) any rights for individuals. Only acts of Parliament can do so, and private individuals can subsequently only rely on these rather than the international agreement as such. The same was held for Canada:

> An international agreement does not have force of law in internal law unless it is incorporated into internal law by the legislative body having jurisdiction under the Constitution. Quebec's implementation Acts set out a statement of fact and enunciate a truism with respect to legislative competence. They do not express an intent to make the free trade agreements part of Quebec's domestic law, and such an intent could not be inferred from their text ... The trial judge correctly ruled that the international free trade agreements had not been incorporated into Quebec law and could not, therefore, be invoked to invalidate the section.[16]

3. *The Monist Approach*

a) *Strongly Monist Countries: The Netherlands and Poland*

In regard of the three questions as mentioned under above 1., **the Netherlands** in its Constitution follows a very structured approach:

Under unwritten constitutional law, the validity of properly ratified international treaties does not depend on any further implementing legislation. This corresponds to the monist approach and has been good law in the Netherlands since a Supreme Court decision in 1919.[17] Art. 93 of the Dutch Constitution mandates the direct application of treaty provisions "which may be binding on all persons by way of their contents" – in other words, where a provision can be directly applied (see below III), it should be directly applied. As to the third question, Art. 94 of the Dutch Constitution provides that "Statutory regulations in force within the Kingdom shall not be applicable if such application is in conflict with provisions of treaties that are binding on all persons or of resolutions of international institutions." This clarifies that international treaties (provided that they have passed the second hurdle) take precedence over domestic law enacted either before and after the treaty came into force.[18]

In **Poland**,[19] Art. 9 of the 1997 Constitution provides that "the Republic of Poland shall respect international law binding on it." This includes a treaty-friendly interpretation of domestic laws.[20] When properly ratified (Art. 89 of the Constitution),

16. *UL Canada Inc. v. Quebec* (Attorney General), 2003 R.J.Q. 2729. The case concerned the direct application of a trade agreement in order to disapply a provision of Canadian domestic law.
17. Dutch Supreme Court, decision of 3 March 1919, NJ 1919, 371. The case concerned reliance by a private person on an international agreement between the Netherlands and Prussia.
18. This is also true for Switzerland. Directly applicable international agreements prevail over ordinary laws even if these have been enacted after the agreement came into force: Decision of the Federal Supreme Court, 27 June 1996, BGE 122 II 234, 239.
19. Lech Garlicki, Małgorzata Masternak-Kubiak and Krzysztof Wójtowicz, 'Poland', in Sloss (ed.), *supra* note 9, 370.
20. Polish Constitutional Court, 11 May 2005, case K 18/04.

international agreements are directly applicable (Art. 91 para. 1) if the provision in question is formulated in a self-executing manner. According to Art. 91 para. 2, treaties shall have precedence over statutory law if the international agreement cannot be reconciled with the latter. On the domestic plane, international treaties therefore take precedence over ordinary laws.

b) *Hybrid Monist Jurisdictions: Germany, the European Union and the US*

(1) In **Germany**, the common principles of international law apply even without ratification and stand above ordinary law (but not on par with the Constitution), Art. 25 German Constitution (Grundgesetz). Yet international agreements normally do not represent such common principles: Rather, such principles are generally considered those expressed in the Vienna Convention, e.g. the principle of *pacta sunt servanda*. In case of a conflict between such common principles and domestic law, courts should refer the matter to the Constitutional Court, Art. 100 (2) German Constitution. The Constitutional Court also regards itself as a gatekeeper to the interpretation and application of other international agreements, though:

> the Federal Constitutional Court is also competent to prevent and remove, if possible, violations of public international law that consist in the incorrect application or non-observance by German Courts of international law obligations and may give rise to an international law responsibility on the part of Germany ... In this, the Federal Constitutional Court is indirectly responsible for enforcing international law and in this way reduces the risk of failing to comply with international law. For this reason it may be necessary, deviating from the customary standard, to review the application and interpretation of international law treaties by the ordinary courts.[21]

In general, international agreements after ratification become part of German law, Art. 59 German Constitution, although it is not clear under which legal construct (transformation theory, application theory; order for application):[22] Most commonly, it is assumed that by its ratification, the international agreement becomes executable and the agreement domestically comes into force.

The question of whether domestically binding agreements produce direct effect and can be invoked by individuals has been generally affirmed, although there is no specific decision to this end. In the decisions referred to under III. below, the question was only whether the concrete provisions can produce direct effect either in regard of the international agreement, or the concrete provision in question. If so, the provisions were directly applied.

The status of international agreements within the domestic legal order has been subject to a recent case of the Constitutional Court.[23] The case concerned the

21. German Constitutional Court, 14 October 2014, BverfGE 111, 307 (328).
22. Butzer/Haas, in: Schmidt-Bleibtreu/Klein, *Grundgesetzkommentar*, Art. 59 paras. 111–114. In practice, "Tensions between the transformation theory and the execution theory are largely irrelevant to the concrete analysis of the impact of international treaties to domestic affairs": Andreas L. Paulus, 'Germany', in Sloss (ed.), *supra* note 9, 222.
23. German Constitutional Court, 15 December 2015, BverfGE 141, 1.

effect of a bilateral double-taxation agreement concluded with Turkey in 1985. The agreement had been properly ratified and contained a provision whereby a German resident for taxation purposes was not required to declare income from Turkey. This provision conflicted with a subsequently enacted provision of the German Income Tax Act whereby income gained in countries with which Germany had concluded a double-taxation treaty, had to be declared and was taxed unless the German resident could demonstrate that such income had already been taxed in the country of source, or the source country had declared that no tax had to be paid thereupon. The provision of the double taxation treaty with Turkey was thus more favourable than the domestic Income Tax Act. As the local tax authorities had applied the Income Tax Act also to cases where income had been gained in Turkey, the Federal Tax Court referred the case to the German Constitutional Court, as it found the provision of the Income Tax Act unconstitutional to the extent it contradicted an international agreement that Germany had ratified. The case was contested even amongst the judges of the court and decided by a majority of 7:1.

The majority opinion held that unless general principles of international law (Art. 25 German Constitution, see above) were at stake, a properly ratified international agreement according to Art. 59(2) German Constitution had the same status as a domestic law. A conflict between such agreement and domestic legislation had thus to be resolved by applying the principles for resolving conflicts between different domestic laws. One of these principles was the *lex posterior* whereby a later law that conflicted with an earlier one should be given precedence as it implicitly abrogated the former one. This was a simple consequence of democratic discontinuity in that Parliament was sovereign to repeal or override earlier laws within constitutional limits. This being so, the earlier double-taxation treaty to the extent that this specific provision was concerned should be considered overridden by the subsequent provision of the Income Tax Act. That Germany was bound by its treaty obligation was an issue between the member states to the treaty, but not in the context of domestic legislation. Any other result would mean that German Parliament in the future could no longer legislate in an area where an international agreement applied, which contradicted the principle of democracy and the sovereignty of Parliament. If anything else had been intended, the German Constitution had not used the construct of ratification by way of implementing legislation in order to apply an international treaty.

The minority opinion agrees that international agreements when properly implemented obtain the same status as a domestic law, and that Parliament should be in a position to amend such law, yet sees a need to balance this principle of democracy with the rule of law. The latter requires legislature not to simply override treaty obligations, but first to explore whether a termination or modification of the agreement is possible. In other words: While the democracy principle allows Parliament to override international obligations, parliamentary liberty is limited by the rule of law that requires a "treaty friendly" behaviour that in the case at issue would have meant to instruct government to terminate or renegotiate the agreement in question.

While the majority opinion is certainly correct from a formalistic point of view, the outcome is somewhat disconcerting from the point of view of comity (including a treaty friendly behaviour as a general principle of international public law according to Art. 26 Vienna Convention, see above) and international legal order. The latter is a principle that under Art. 25 German Constitution enjoys precedence over ordinary laws and should, as the minority opinion proposes, be invoked in order to ascertain whether a way can be found to abrogate an internationally binding obligation without breaching it. Parliament would not be prevented from overriding an internationally binding obligation, but would be required first to explore whether this can be done in a treaty friendly fashion.

(2) Also the **European Union** in principle follows the hybrid monist approach:

> 30. Generally speaking, it appears to have been accepted since *Haegeman*,[24] a judgment given in 1974, that a monist approach underlies Article 216 TFEU (ex Article 300(7) EC), pursuant to which "agreements concluded by the Union are binding upon the institutions of the Union and on its Member States", (references) thus entailing "automatic incorporation", (references) with the result that international agreements, as such, are sources of EU law.
>
> 32. In accordance with the monist approach, the provisions of conventions thus produce effects within the legal order of the European Union even in the absence of any legislative or regulatory act adopted in order to implement those provisions.[25]

This principle has been subsequently qualified in that the approach now largely depends on the kind of agreement concerned, see below III.

(3) According to the Restatement (Third) on the Foreign Relations Law of the **United States** (1987),

> International agreements, even those directly benefitting private persons, generally do not create private rights or provide for a private cause of action in domestic courts, but there are exceptions with respect to both rights and remedies. Whether an international agreement provides a right or requires that a remedy be made available to a private person is a matter of interpretation of the agreement.[26]

As one would expect, details are far more difficult. Although Art. VI clause 2 of the US Constitution stipulates that "all Treaties made, or which shall be made, under the Authority of the United States, shall be the supreme Law of the Land",[27] court decisions have often denied such supremacy with the argument that the treaty or provision in question is not self-executing.[28] The position in regard of IP agreements

24. ECJ, case 181/73, EU:C:1974 – *Haegemann*.
25. Citation from the Opinion of Advocate General Jääskinen delivered ion 8 May 2014 in joined cases C-401/12P to C-403/12P, *Council of the European Union v. Vereiniging Millieudefensie et al.*, paras. 30, 32.
26. Restatement (Third) on the Foreign Relations Law of the United States § 907 ctm. a (1987).
27. Note that "treaties" are only those approved by a two-thirds majority vote in the Senate. All other international agreements binding upon the US are called sole executive agreements (concluded by the President only) or congressional-executive agreements (approved by a majority vote in Congress).
28. Namely the US Supreme Court decision *Medellin v. Texas*, 128 S.Ct. 1346 (2008) in regard to Art. 94 UN Charter. The presumption against individually enforceable rights in effect shields governments from judicial review of government compliance and appears a method

seems to be that, either, they have been properly implemented into domestic law and no recourse to them is necessary (Paris Convention), or that they are explicitly exempt from direct application (WTO/TRIPS).

III. Does the Agreement in Question Contain Explicit Rules as to How it Should be Given Effect, or Can any Such Rules be Inferred from the Agreement, from the Drafting or the Implementing Process?

In the area of intellectual property rights, discussions about this point have mainly been wielded in regard of the Paris Convention, and the TRIPS Agreement. While both are international agreements with a huge membership, the agreements differ in nature in that the Paris Convention is not reciprocal (as one of its fundamental principles is national treatment rather than reciprocity), while the WTO/TRIPS Agreement is "based on the principle of negotiations undertaken on the basis of 'reciprocal and mutually advantageous arrangements'"[29] Furthermore, different from the WTO/TRIPS Agreement, failure of a Member State to comply with the obligations under the Paris Convention are not justiceable.[30]

1. The Paris Convention[31]

a) The Paris Convention in Art. 25 (formerly Art. 17) contains a provision that reads:

> Every State, party to this Convention, undertakes to adopt, in accordance with its constitution, the measures necessary to ensure the application of this Convention.
>
> It is understood that at the time an instrument of ratification or accession is deposited on behalf of the State, such State will be in a position under its domestic law to give effect to the terms of this Convention.

---

not limited to the US. In a case from Japan, the courts denied direct applicability of certain norms, yet arguably meant to say that international agreements in principle should not be directly applied "since international law by its nature regulates relations between States [and] legal subjectivity in principle is recognised for States, not for individuals ..." Tokyo High Court, 8 February 2001, 2002 JAIL 142.

29. European Court of Justice, *International Fruit Co. v. Produktschap voor Groenten en Fruit*, Joined cases 21–24/72, [1972] ECR 1219, 1227.
30. Several attempts were made at the Revision Conferences of the Hague 1925, London 1934 and Lisbon 1958 to introduce a provision whereby states could bring a dispute between them and related to the implementation of the Paris Convention before the International Court of Justice in the Hague. This proposal was always opposed by the United States, however: S. Ladas, *Patents, Trademarks and Related Rights*, vol. I (Cambridge 1975), 237. The provisions of the Paris Convention are now actionable to the extent that they have become part of the TRIPS Agreement, though: WTO Dispute Settlement (DS) 176 "US – Section 211 Appropriations Act", where Art. 8 Paris Convention was invoked.
31. The most detailed account of this problem is provided by Ladas, *supra* note 30, chapter 9 ("Relation of the Convention to the National Law of the Member States"), 206–242 and *idem*, 'The self-executing character of International Conventions on Industrial Property and their effects on substantive rights', 36 *Trademark Bulletin* (1941), 5.

This provision clearly concerns the effect the provisions of the Convention should have under domestic law. Yet, and this refers back to the discussion under above II, it is a matter of domestic law to what extent international law is given effect. Only under the monist theory can there by a direct effect. But even in prevalently monist countries (e.g. the US and Germany), there is no uniform picture on the application of the Paris Convention, also because the issue is often dealt together with the question whether a specific provision, or whether a general principle can be directly applied.

b) The US Supreme Court first denied direct applicability of the Paris Convention,[32] then subsequently affirmed it.[33] While it now appears settled case law that the Paris Convention can be directly applied in the US,[34] there is no case where any of its provisions was indeed found to be self-executing. In fact, the prevailing view in the US seems to be that the Paris Convention creates neither a federal cause of action nor additional substantive rights (see below 3). There are also decisions to the contrary, however.[35]

c) The German Federal Supreme Court found it so self-evident that the Paris Convention was directly applicable that it did not even discuss the issue. It expressly held the provisions of Arts. 2, 4(2) and 6bis self-executing.[36]

2. *The WTO TRIPS Agreement*

a) The TRIPS Agreement much more than the Paris Convention confers minimum standards of protection, affirms that intellectual property rights are private rights and requires Member States to introduce effective enforcement mechanisms. Good prerequisites for a direct application, one might think. On the other hand, the TRIPS Agreement as part of the WTO framework provides a mechanism whereby lack of compliance can be litigated in the context of a State to State dispute settlement mechanism (see above chapter 4 of this book), which might speak against opening up an avenue for private litigants before domestic courts.

The question of the direct application of TRIPS has been mostly argued in the context of European Union law (the EU is an independent member to the WTO Agreement) (b), and its interaction with the law of individual member states (c). Yet, there are also noteworthy decisions from Brazil and India in this regard (d).

b) Apart from its Member States, also the European Union is a Member to the WTO/ TRIPS Agreement, a competence which it has under Arts. 216 and 217 Treaty of the

---

32. US Supreme Court, *Cameron Septic Tank Co. v. City of Knoxville* (1913), 227 US 39, 48–49.
33. US Supreme Court, *Bacardi Corp. v. Domenech* (1940), 311 US 150. This case concerned the Inter-American Convention for Trademark and Commercial Protection 1929, though. The wording of this Convention is similar to that of the Paris Convention as far as the provisions for conferring protection are concerned, however.
34. E.g. most recently US Court of Appeals of the Fourth Circuit, *Belmora LLC v. Bayer Consumer Care et al.* (2016), where following the TTAB the Court found the Paris Convention applicable, yet Art. 6bis not self-executing.
35. US Court of Appeals of the 11th Circuit, *International Café v. Hard Rock Café,* 252 F. 3rd 1274 (2001).
36. German Federal Supreme Court, 2 April 1969, 1 IIC 272 (1970) – *"Recrin"*.

Functioning of the European Union (TFEU). Normally, an accession is effectuated by way of a council decision, in the case of the WTO by Council Decision [94/800/EEC]. In addition to the EU, also all its Member States are members to the WTO. This first of all gives rise to the question which law should be relied upon in order to determine direct effect, EU law, or the law of its Member States. Prior to the TFEU coming into effect (negotiated as the so-called Treaty of Lisbon, signed in 2007 and effective as of 2009), domestic law applied to those fields that had not been legislated by EU law, namely the area of patents.[37] Since that time, TRIPS has become the exclusive domain of the EU under Art. 207 TFEU ("commercial aspects of intellectual property")[38] which would mean that also for the question of direct application, Member States must apply EU law (with the consequence that there is no direct application, see below).[39]

Traditionally, the EU has followed the monist theory about the application of international agreements (see above), yet qualified this approach later on as follows:

> 31. In *Kupferberg*,[40] a judgment given in 1982, the Court confirmed the incorporation of international agreements into the Community legal order, whilst making clear that "the effects within the Community of provisions of an [international] agreement ... may not be determined without taking account of the international origin of the provisions in question", and that "[i]n conformity with the principles of public international law [the contracting parties] ... [may] agree ... what effect the provisions of the agreement are to have in the internal legal order of the contracting parties". The Court explained that the institutions which have the power to negotiate and conclude an agreement with a non-member country are free to agree what effect the provisions are to have in the internal legal order. Only if that question has not been settled by the agreement does it fall for decision by the Court.[41]

In other words, the first qualification of the monist theory stems from the effect that the EU wants to give to a specific agreement.

The second qualification was made in a decision rendered in 1972 and concerns the nature of the agreement:

37. European Court of Justice, decision of 11 September 2007, case C-431/05 - *Merck Genericos*. See below for the decisions of Portugal, Austria and Poland.
38. European Court of Justice (now CJEU), decision of 18 July 2013, case C-414/11 - *Daiichi Sankyo*.
39. The impact of the *Daiichi Sankyo* decision on the domestic intellectual property system of Member States is discussed by G. Tritton, in *Tritton on Intellectual Property in Europe* (4th edn., 2014), 1-67–1-69. One consequence of this decision is that individual Member States are now also bound by TRIPS under EU law and already for this reason have to interpret domestic IP laws in the light and purpose of TRIPS.
40. European Court of Justice, decision of 26 October 1982, case C-104/81, EU:C:1982:362 - *Kupferberg*.
41. Citation from the Opinion of Advocate General Jääskinen delivered on 8 May 2014 in joined cases C-401/12P to C-403/12P, *Council of the European Union v. Vereiniging Millieudefensie et al.*, para. 31.

> 19 It is also necessary to examine whether the provisions of the General Agreement confer rights on citizens of the community on which they can rely before the courts in contesting the validity of a community measure.
>
> 20 For this purpose, the spirit, the general scheme and the terms of the General Agreement must be considered.
>
> 21 This Agreement which, according to its preamble, is based on the principle of negotiations undertaken on the basis of "reciprocal and mutually advantageous arrangements" is characterized by the great flexibility of its provisions, in particular those conferring the possibility of derogation, the measures to be taken when confronted with exceptional difficulties and the settlement of conflicts between the contracting parties.
>
> 27 Those factors are sufficient to show that, when examined in such a context, Article XI of the General Agreement is not capable of conferring on citizens of the community rights which they can invoke before the courts.[42]

In the act of ratification of the WTO/TRIPS Agreement by the European Union, the last recital reads:[43]

> Whereas, by its nature, the Agreement establishing the World Trade Organization, including the Annexes thereto, is not susceptible to being directly invoked in Community or Member State courts.

Further, and following its previous case law, the ECJ in the decision C-149/96 took the view that the WTO Agreement, just like GATT, should be qualified as a reciprocal agreement and that a direct application "would deprive the legislative and executive organs of the Community of the scope for manoeuvre enjoyed by their counterparts in the Community's trading partners".[44] Exceptions could apply where a specific legal measure was taken in order to comply with a WTO obligation, or where domestic or Community legislature made express reference to a WTO provision.[45] As a consequence, "all the provisions of the TRIPS Agreement cannot have direct effect ... regardless of whether or not [they are] sufficiently precise, unconditional and [do] not require the adoption of any subsequent implementing measure."[46]

This position was affirmed in a subsequent decision:[47]

42. European Court of Justice, decision of 12 December 1972, joined cases 21–24/72, *International Fruit Co. NV v. Produktschap voor Groenten en Fruit.*
43. Council Decision of 22 December 1994 concerning the conclusion on behalf of the European Community, as regards matters within its competence, of the agreements reached in the Uruguay Round multilateral negotiations (1986–1994) (94/800/EC).
44. European Court of Justice, decision of 23 November 1999, case C 149/96, *Portuguese Republic v. Council.*
45. *Ibid.*
46. AG Cosmas, opinion of 11 July 2000 for cases C-300/98 and 392/98, *Parfums Christian Dior v. Tuk Consultancy,* endorsed by the decision rendered on 14 December 2000.
47. European Court of Justice, decision of 30 September 2003, case C-93/02, *in re Biret International,* paras. 52, 53.

> 52. As the Court of First Instance observed in paragraph 61 of the contested judgment, given their nature and structure, the WTO agreements are not in principle among the rules in the light of which the Court is to review the legality of measures adopted by the Community institutions (see *Portugal* v *Council*, paragraph 47; the order in *OGT Fruchthandelsgesellschaft*, paragraph 24; and the judgments in *Omega Air and Others*, paragraph 93, and Case C-76/00 P *Petrotub* and *Republica* v *Council* [2003] ECR I-79, paragraph 53).
>
> 53. It is only where the Community has intended to implement a particular obligation assumed in the context of the WTO, or where the Community measure refers expressly to the precise provisions of the WTO agreements, that it is for the Court to review the legality of the Community measure in question in the light of the WTO rules (see, as regards GATT 1947, *Fediol* v *Commission*, paragraphs 19 to 22, and *Nakajima* v *Council*, paragraph 31, and, as regards the WTO agreements, *Portugal* v *Council*, paragraph 49).

The ECJ denied a direct effect in the above case even though the EU had been found to be in breach of the WTO Agreement and had been required to change its law.[48]

In fairness, one should add that most of the opinions delivered by the Advocates General of the ECJ took a critical stance on the ECJ doctrine of division of powers.[49] Further, the EC Council in one case argued that the existence of an autonomous system for the settlement of disputes would simply leave no room for the national courts to directly apply the rules of the agreement.[50]

The UK Patents Court in a case decided in 1997 regarded it as "*acte claire*" that in the context of EU law, TRIPS could not have a direct effect.[51]

---

48. As is mentioned further below, this does not affect the stance of individual member states unless (as is now the case) precluded by Union law: CJEU 14 December 2000, *Parfums Christian Dior SA and Tuk Consultancy BV* and *Assco Gerüste GmbH, Rob van Dijk and Wilhelm Layher GmbH & Co. KG, Layher BV*, Joined Cases C-300 at paras. 43–48: "[o]n the other hand, in a field in respect of which the Community has not yet legislated and which consequently falls within the competence of the Member States, the protection of intellectual property rights, and measures adopted for that purpose by the judicial authorities, do not fall within the scope of Community law. Accordingly, Community law neither requires nor forbids that the legal order of a Member State should accord to individuals the right to rely directly on the rule laid down by Article 50(6) of TRIPs or that it should oblige the courts to apply that rule of their own motion."
49. E.g. AG Ruiz-Jarabo Colomer, opinion of 23 January 2007 for case C-431/05 *Merck Genericos v. Merck et al.*, paras. 68, 75, 78.
50. Cited in AG Saggio's opinion in case C-149/96 *Portuguese Republic v. Council*, 25 February 1999, para. 23.
51. UK Patents Court, *Lenzing AG's European Patent* (UK), 22 May 1997, [1997] RPC 245, 269: "So, in the face of the fact that TRIPS (one of its Annexes) is an agreement which all member States explicitly considered (through the recital) not to create direct effect, it is said that the Court of Justice may nonetheless hold otherwise. I think that is fantastic. And it is highly fantastic when one considers that the predecessor of the WTO Agreement, namely the 1947 General Agreement on Trade and Tariffs (GATT) was held by the ECJ not to create directly enforceable rights, *International Fruit Co. NV v. Produktschap voor Groenten en Fruit* [Joined cases 21–24/72, see note 42]".

c) The direct application of TRIPS was argued and affirmed in three European countries: **Austria**,[52] **Poland**[53] and **Portugal**.[54] According to the Austrian Supreme Court, (1) the fact that the ECJ refused direct application could not prevent national courts from holding otherwise, (2) parliament when ratifying the WTO Agreement did not issue an implementing reservation. Further:

> Accordingly, pursuant to the judicial practice of the Administrative Court …, in the event of doubt it is to be assumed that the Agreement is directly applicable. No subjective of objective reasons that could refute this assumption can be found. Firstly, there is no apparent common intention of the parties to the Treaty directed at its inapplicability; on the contrary, this question was disputed and was therefore left to the national law of the Member States …

In Germany, there is no case law on this point, but an indication that the agreement should be directly applicable.[55]

d) As to countries outside Europe,

(1) it is clear that the TRIPS Agreement is not directly applicable in the **US** due to a legislative provision.[56]

(2) There was a significant discussion about the direct applicability in **India** in the course of a lawsuit that concerned the provisions of Arts. 27, 65 and 70(8) TRIPS,[57] in particular whether the newly inserted sec. 3(d) Indian Patent Act was compliant with Art. 27 TRIPS Agreement. The Madras High Court[58] denied direct applicability of TRIPs due to the existence of a specifically established, exhaustive and mandatory

52. Austrian Supreme Court, 26 August 2008, 41 IIC 598 – *"Losartan"* (2010).
53. Polish Administrative Supreme Court, decision of 8 February 2006, reported by: Andrzej Pinikiewski, 'Poland – Direct effect of certain provisions of the TRIPS Agreement', in *Building and Enforcing Intellectual Property Value* (2007), 210–212.
54. Portuguese Supreme Court, 15 November 2007, 41 IIC 614 – "Patent Term Extension/ Enalapril" (2010). The court gave no reasons other than that each country was sovereign to determine the direct application of international agreements.
55. Bundestagsdrucksache 12/7655, 345 (Draft law on the implementation of the WTO Agreement as submitted to Parliament): "In addition, the obligations under the TRIPS Agreement should be accounted for by directly applying those of its provisions that by their wording can be considered in this respect. This is the case for example for the obligation of national treatment and most-favoured nation treatment, and the provisions formulated as absolute rights for right owners." Of course, the above is a suggestion by government and not an expression of an intention by Parliament.
56. 19 U.S.C. § 3512(a)(1)(2000): "No provision of any of the Uruguay Round Agreements, nor the application of any such provision to any person or circumstances, that is inconsistent with any law of the Unites States shall have effect."
57. The history of the lawsuit is clearly set out in the respective decision of the Indian Supreme Court of 1 April 2013 concerning related appeals *Novartis AG v. Union of India, Natco Pharma v. Union of India and M/S Cancer Aid Association v. India*, accessible under < www.juris.nic.in/supremecourt >.
58. Madras High Court, *Novartis AG v. Union of India*, case MANU/TN/1263/2007. An overview of the litigation is provided by R. Parthasarathy and H. Goddar, 'Patentability of Pharmaceutical Products in India – The *Novartis* Case', 40 *IIC* (2009), 38.

dispute settlement mechanism under the WTO regime. Only in this context could compliance of domestic law with TRIPS be argued.

(3) The question of a direct application of TRIPS provisions also came up in **Brazil**. The case refers to a long-running dispute between the Brazilian Patent Office (INPI) on the one hand side, and a number of patent proprietors on the other, over the duration of patents granted before the new Industrial Property Code (Law no. 9279 of 14 May 1996 - IPC 1996) came into force on 15 May 1997. Under the old Industrial Property Code 1971 (Law no. 5772 of 21 December 1971), the lifespan of patents was calculated as 15 years from the date of filing, while this was changed under the new IPC 1996 to 20 years from filing or ten years from grant, whichever was longer (Sec. 40). According to an opinion commissioned by the ABPI (Brazilian Association of Intellectual Property Rights),[59] TRIPS entered into force in Brazil on 1 January 1995 due to the fact that the Brazilian Government failed to avail the country of the possibility offered by Art. 65.2, that is, to defer the effects of TRIPS for five years in view of Brazil's status as a developing country. This, so the argument went, would mean that Brazil had to comply with TRIPS by 1 January 1995, and that pending or granted patents should run for 20 years from the filing date in accordance with TRIPS Art. 33, or be extended accordingly in compliance with Art. 70.2 that makes the TRIPS provisions applicable to subject matter existing at the date of application. However, such line of argument could only be invoked before the courts where TRIPS was found to directly apply. The Federal Appeal Court ultimately denied this in two decisions.[60] In the first, the court reasoned as follows:

> The first essential point that was dealt with only marginally in the previous decisions concerns the limits of the applicability of TRIPS in terms of its addressees. In effect, until today the Federal Appeal Court has affirmed an extension of the protection period for patents based on the implicit understanding that TRIPS, after having been implemented into domestic law, is capable of direct application to specific legal relationships, one of these being the beneficiaries of the rights over an invention. It is important to clarify that when the Federal Appeal Court discussed the question of extending the patent term of 15 years as granted under the previous IP Code 5771/71 to twenty years based on the TRIPS Agreement, it was taken for granted and not called into question that once TRIPS had been implemented, it would have direct effects on private legal relationships, and also on those patents still in force. But this is far from settled. While this has been little examined, it is a necessary prerequisite that in order to request a term extension of five years, the TRIPS Agreement must directly confer such right in the first place.
>
> When asked this way, the question - that already in itself would be a sufficient reason to subject the TRIPS Agreement to a further examination by this Bench - shows that the precedents mentioned above cannot be sustained. TRIPS is not

59. Cited by Dannemann/Siemsen, *Propriedade Intelectual no Brasil* (Rio d.J. 2000), 97.
60. Decision of the Federal Appeal Court, 15 April 2009 (Extraordinary Appeal No. 960.728 - RJ 2007/0134338-8) *E. I. Du Pont de Nemours and Company v. INPI*, 41 IIC 601 (2010) - "Patent Term Extension I", and Decision of the Federal Appeal Court (2nd and 3rd Section), 28 April 2010 (REsp 642213/RJ) *E. I. Pont Du Nemours v. INPI*, 41 IIC 612 (2010) - "Patent Term Extension II".

> a uniform law. In other words, it is not a treaty that was drafted in a manner to allow its literal application to relationships between private persons in each of its Member States that in such case would be limited to the ratification of the treaty in an appropriate manner (in Brazil by way of a Legislative Decree). There are, however, treaties that establish a complete legal framework for a certain subject matter. These contain legal subject matter that can be applied to certain legal relationships, and one can call the provisions of these treaties "self-executing". Other treaties, however, are restricted to setting obligations that can only be complied with by the individual member states, although in essence they deal with questions of private law. Actually, the ambit of these treaties is to furnish guiding posts in order to bring domestic legislation of each country in line with the treaty (see Denis Borges Barbosa, 'Propriedade intelectual: a aplicaçao do Acordo TRIPS'. Lumen Juris, 2nd ed. Rio d. J. 2005, 18 et seq.).
>
> In this respect, Maristela Basso, who has published a specific article on this subject ('A data de aplicaçao do TRIPS no Brasil', 30 Revista de Direito Constitucional e Internacional, Jan-March 2000) thought it impossible for there to occur a contradiction between the rules of TRIPS and the old Industrial Property Code ...
>
> In the same vein, Ricardo Sichel informs us that the possibility of directly applying the TRIPS Agreement to legal relationships between the citizens of one of the Member States of the WTO "has been denied by the European Court of Justice" ('TRIPS', in: Revista De AJUFE, year 20, number 68, p. 311 et seq.). Apart from that, according to Denis Borges Barbosa, "*such proposal, that is, the direct application by private parties, was explicitly discussed and rejected during the negotiations of the agreement. Even more, as has been reiterated by the European Court of Justice, the direct application of TRIPS would deprive Member States of one the most important rights guaranteed to them by the WTO system, that is, to negotiate and grant compensation in cases of non-compliance with the rules as established by the TRIPS Agreement*" ('Propriedade Intelectual – A aplicaçao do Acordo TRIPS', Rio de Janeiro: Lumen Juris, 2nd. ed. 2005, 85).
>
> The above is one of the unexamined avenues of the problem that in itself it is already sufficient to force a change in the jurisprudence of this court in order to establish that the TRIPS Agreement does not directly create rights and obligations to private persons and that therefore this Agreement cannot be used as a basis for requesting an alteration of the term of patents currently in force.

Now that Member States to the EU can no longer autonomously decide on the direct application of agreements that concern international trade, it would appear that no country is prepared to give direct effect to the TRIPS Agreement, this being due to the WTO Agreement's nature as a reciprocal and mutually advantageous trade agreement directed only at Member States.

IV. Can the Provision Relied upon be Directly Applied and Can it Form the Basis of a Claim?

1. International agreements even when considered to be directly applicable often contain a number of very different provisions: Administrative provisions related to the functioning of the agreement, to the setting up of certain structures, or to

create and maintain laws. Such provisions are addressed to the Member States. Also substantive provisions that create or guarantee certain rights may not be directly applicable because they require fine tuning by domestic laws or further administrative provisions: Domestic courts would find it difficult to affirm rights of priority (Art. 4 and 5*bis* Paris Convention), or the right of an inventor to be named (Art. 4*ter* Paris Convention) in the absence of any legal provisions. After all, "[t]he condition of direct effect is [only] satisfied where the provision relied on contains a clear and precise obligation which is not subject, in its implementation or effects, to the adoption of any subsequent measure."[61] In the context of intellectual property law, this has been discussed for Arts. 6bis and 10bis Paris Convention, and a number of TRIPS provisions, namely Arts. 32 and 33 TRIPS Agreement.

2. The US decision *Grupo Gigante*[62] denied direct application of Arts. 6bis and 10bis **Paris Convention** on the following grounds:

The Paris Convention claims:

> The district court properly held that Grupo Gigante's claim for "use of a well-known mark" under Article 6 *bis* of the Paris Convention is duplicative of its claim that, because the Gigante mark is well-known, that mark is entitled to protection under the Lanham Act. The district court also properly rejected Grupo Gigante's claim for unfair competition under Article 10 *bis* of the Paris Convention.
>
> There has been some understandable confusion among the district courts with respect to whether the Paris Convention, implemented in § 44 of the Lanham Act, creates substantive law or a right of action applicable to international trademark disputes. *Compare Mattel, Inc. v. MCA Records, Inc.*, 28 F.Supp.2d 1120, 1158 (C.D.Cal.1998) (holding that the Paris Convention does not create a right of action separate and distinct from those available under the Lanham Act), *with Maison Lazard et Compagnie v. Manfra, Tordella & Brooks, Inc.*, 585 F.Supp. 1286, 1289 (S.D.N.Y.1984) (holding that the Paris Convention creates a distinct cause of action for unfair competition). That confusion results from the interplay between Article 10 *bis* and § 44 of the Lanham Act. As discussed above, Article 10 *bis* requires member countries "to assure to nationals of [other member countries] effective protection against unfair competition." Paris Convention, art. 10 *bis*, 21 U.S.T. at 1648. Section 44 of the Lanham Act implements Article 10 *bis* by extending Lanham Act protection to foreign nationals to the extent necessary to satisfy the United States' treaty obligations:
>
> Any person whose country of origin is a party to any convention or treaty relating to trademarks, trade or commercial names, or the repression of unfair competition, to which the United States is also a party, or extends reciprocal rights to nationals of the United States by law, shall be entitled to the benefits of this section under the conditions expressed herein to the extent necessary to give effect to any provision of such convention, treaty or reciprocal law, in

61. ECJ, case 12/86, decision of 30 September 1987 *Meyram Demirel v. Stadt Schwäbisch Gmünd*, EU:C:1987:400, paragraph 14. Also UK Patents Court, 22 May 1997, *Lenzing AG's European Patent* (UK), [1997] RPC 245, 273: "unconditional and sufficiently precise".

62. US Court of Appeals, 9th Circuit, *Grupo Gigante SA v. Dallo & Co.*, 391 F. 3d 1088 (2004).

> addition to the rights to which any owner of a mark is otherwise entitled by this chapter ...
>
> Grupo Gigante uses the phrase "in addition to the rights to which any owner of a mark is otherwise entitled to by this chapter" to argue that § 44 of the Lanham Act implements certain additional substantive rights created by international treaties. Although that may be true as a general matter, Article 10 *bis* itself does not create additional substantive rights. Rather, "[t]he Paris Convention ensures that 'foreign nationals should be given the same treatment in each of the member countries as that country makes available to its own citizens' as to trademark and related rights." *Int'l Cafe, S.A.L. v. Hard Rock Cafe Int'l, Inc.*, 252 F.3d 1274, 1277 (11th Cir.2001) (quoting *Vanity Fair Mills, Inc. v. T. Eaton Co.*, 234 F.2d 633, 640 (2d Cir.1956)).
>
> As we held in *Kemart Corp. v. Printing Arts Research Laboratories, Inc.*, 269 F.2d 375, 389 (9th Cir.1959), "the Paris Convention was not intended to define the substantive law in the area of 'unfair competition' of the signatory countries." More recently, we concluded that the interaction between § 44 of the Lanham Act and Article 10 *bis* of the Paris Convention simply results in equal treatment of foreign and domestic parties in trademark disputes:
>
> A foreign national is entitled to the same effective protection against unfair competition to which an American is entitled, Paris Convention, art. 10bis, and in turn, the American gets the same right that the foreign national gets ... But [a party] has no claim to a nonexistent federal cause of action for unfair competition. As said, the Paris Convention provides for national treatment, and does not define the substantive law of unfair competition.
>
> *Mattel*, 296 F.3d at 908. *See also Int'l Cafe*, 252 F.3d at 1278 (holding that the Paris Convention "only requires 'national treatment'").
>
> Because the Paris Convention creates neither a federal cause of action nor additional substantive rights, the district court properly dismissed Grupo Gigante's Paris Convention claims.

As mentioned above, the German courts found Arts. 2, 4(2) and 6bis self-executing.[63]

3. In the case of **TRIPS**, direct application was affirmed for a number of provisions:

   - Art 33 (duration of patents) by the Portuguese Supreme Court:[64]
     "Finally, Art. 33 TRIPS is precise and unconditional, prerequisites for its direct application. This has already been so held by a decision of this court in 1999 ..."

63. German Federal Supreme Court, 2 April 1969, 1 IIC 272 (1970) – *"Recrin"*. Ladas (Ladas, *supra* note 30, chapter 9 ("Relation of the Convention to the National Law of the Member States"), 209) advocates a convention-friendly interpretation and also finds the following provisions of the Paris Convention self-executing: Arts. 4, 4bis, 4ter, 4quater, 5A(1), 5A (2) and (3), 4(B), (C) and (D), 5bis, 5ter, 5quater, 6, 6bis, 6ter, 6quater, 6quinquies, 6sexies, 6septies, 7, 8, 9, 10 and 10bis(3).
64. Portuguese Supreme Court, 15 November 2007, 41 IIC 614 – *"Patent Term Extension/ Enalapril"* (2010). The Polish Administrative Supreme Court held the same: Polish Administrative Supreme Court, decision of 8 February 2006, reported by Pinikiewski, *supra* note 53, 210–212.

- The same provision was thought not to be directly applicable by AC Colomer, however:

  "Art. 33 of the TRIPS Agreement, because it is subject to the power of the national legislature to fix the exact duration of the protection granted to patents in its own legal order, does not have direct effect."[65]

  This example highlights an interesting quandary that adds another layer of difficulty to the subject: The divergent interpretation of treaty provisions by national courts.[66]

- The Austrian Supreme Court affirmed direct application of Arts. 27(1) in connection with 70(2), and also Art. 13 TRIPS:

  Secondly, the provisions of relevance here [Arts. 27(1) in connection with 70(2)] – like Art. 13 of TRIPS, the direct applicability of which has already been confirmed by this Court [citation omitted] – contain a sufficiently specific content such that they can be the basis for acts of enforcement even without specific implementation ...[67]

V. Treaty Friendly Interpretation

1. General Considerations

In many cases, see above III, international norms cannot be directly applied even where the agreement as such is held directly applicable, because the norms are not precise or unconditional. However, these norms may express general principles that can be used to interpret domestic laws. Examples are the general principles contained in the Paris Convention and the TRIPS Agreement, namely the right of priority, the independence of rights, national treatment and most-favoured nation treatment. In such case, a domestic court needs to determine whether and how to apply such general principles. In this respect, Art. 26 Vienna Convention[68] requires a performance of treaties in good faith ("pacta sunt servanda"), which implies a treaty-friendly interpretation of domestic law even in the absence of a direct effect. There are examples in the IP field of a direct application of general principles (under 2.), or of a treaty-friendly interpretation in the absence of direct effect (under 3.)

2. Direct Application of General Principles

There is some case law in particular for taking into account the principle of territoriality as specified in the Paris Convention when interpreting domestic law.

There are examples from Germany:

65. AG Colomer in *Merck Genericos v. Merck, supra* note 49, para. 95. It is difficult to understand how the Portuguese Supreme Court (Portuguese Supreme Court, 15 November 2007, 41 IIC 614 – *"Patent Term Extension/Enalapril"* (2010)) that actually referred this case to the ECJ, failed to take this argument into account, let alone mention it.
66. For further study: Helmut Philipp Aust and Georg Nolte, *The Interpretation of International Law by Domestic Courts: Uniformity, Diversity, Convergence* (Oxford, 2016).
67. Austrian Supreme Court, 26 August 2008, 41 IIC 598 – *"Losartan"* (2010).
68. Vienna Convention on the Law of Treaties (1969).

> These principles alone suggest that also in the case of a prior use *abroad* knowledge alone is not sufficient to establish unfairness. But the decisive point is that a different interpretation of the law would not be in accord with the system of international protection of trademarks as it was developed on the basis of the Paris Convention and the Madrid Trademark Agreement. Since this system is based on the territorial limitation of trademark protection, it takes for granted that the same mark may be used simultaneously in different countries by different owners for goods of the same kind. To decide that the application in Germany for a trademark used in a foreign country by an applicant who has knowledge of the foreign use, constitutes by itself (without further circumstances) an act of unfair competition, would thus mean to extend the protection of a national trademark beyond national borders.[69]

And from the United States:

> But the facts of this case implicate another well-established principle of trademark law, the "territoriality principle." The territoriality principle, as stated in a treatise, says that "[p]riority of trademark rights in the United States depends solely upon priority of use in the United States, not on priority of use anywhere in the world." ... The problem with this is that treating international use differently is what the territoriality principle does. This interpretation of the exception would effectively eliminate the territoriality principle by eliminating any effect of international borders on protectability. We would end up treating foreign uses of the mark just as we treat domestic uses under the *Tea Rose-Rectanus* doctrine, asking in both cases whether the use elsewhere resulted in secondary meaning in the local market.
>
> We would go too far if we did away with the territoriality principle altogether by expanding the famous-mark exception this much. The territoriality principle has a long history in the common law, and at least two circuits have described it as "basic to trademark law." That status reflects the lack of a uniform trademark regime across international borders. What one must do to acquire trademark rights in one country will not always be the same as what one must do in another. And once acquired, trademark rights gained in other countries are governed by each country's own set of laws. Furthermore, we are arguably required by the Paris Convention, of which the United States is a signatory, to preserve the territoriality principle in some form. Thus, we reject Grupo Gigante's argument that we should define the well-known mark exception as merely an inquiry into whether the mark has achieved secondary meaning in the area where the foreign user wishes to assert protection.[70]

69. German Federal Supreme Court, 2 April 1969, 1 IIC 270 (1970) – Recrin.
70. *United States Grupo Gigante SA DE CV v. Dallo & Co., Inc.* 391 F.3d 1088 (2004). A further analysis of the interplay between the principles of the Paris Convention and the Lanham Act is provided by James Faris, 'The Famous Marks Exception to the Territoriality Principle in American Trademark Law', 59(2) *Case Western Reserve Law Review* (2009), 451; and Andrew Cook, 'Do as we say, not as we do: A Study of the Well-Known Marks Doctrine in the United States', 8 *J. Marshall Rev. Intell. Prop. Law* (2009), 412.

Yet there are also US cases where not much heed was paid to the general principles of the Paris Convention (here: national treatment).[71]

3. Treaty Friendly Interpretation

The principle of treaty-friendly interpretation of domestic law should also apply in cases where the international agreement is not directly applicable, because (see above), treaty-friendly interpretation is a general principle of international public law as it helps to avoid conflicts between international obligations and the plane of domestic law.[72] Although the European Court of Justice has consistently denied the direct application of the TRIPS Agreement (see above II.), it has nonetheless applied the agreement in order to interpret domestic law in a treaty-friendly manner:

> 28. It is true that the measures envisaged by Article 99 and the relevant procedural rules are those provided for by the domestic law of the Member

71. An obvious case of discrimination were the so-called *Hilmer* rules in the US whereby a foreign filing could not count as prior art reference (while a US filing could) (*In re Hilmer I*, CCPA, 359 F.2d 859 (1966)), and that under the first-to-invent system, proof of prior conception could only be furnished for inventions made in the US, while for inventions made abroad, the filing date would count rather than abroad (*In re Hilmer II*, CCPA, 424 F.2d 1108 (1970).
72. This should be clear for monist or hybrid monist states, yet is also recognised by the courts in dualist jurisdictions. The Canadian Supreme Court held that "Since the purpose of [domestic law] is to implement the underlying Convention, the Court must adopt an interpretation consistent with Canada's obligation under the Convention. The wording of the Convention and the rules of treaty interpretation will therefore be applied to determine the meaning of [the Treaty provision] in domestic law." Canadian Supreme Court, *Pushpanathan v. Canada*, [1998] 1 SCR 98, and for the UK: *Sidhu v. British Airways*, [1997] All E R 193, 201. On the other hand, there is an opinion expressed by the Advocate General in case C-401/12P that wants to limit such rule to cases where the international agreement is directly applicable:
    a) 100. In accordance with settled case-law, an international agreement must be interpreted by reference to the terms in which it is worded and in the light of its objectives. Article 31 of the Vienna Convention of 23 May 1969 on the Law of Treaties and Article 31 of the Vienna Convention of 21 March 1986 on the Law of Treaties between States and International Organisations or between International Organisations, which express general customary international law on the matter, state that a treaty is to be interpreted in good faith in accordance with the ordinary meaning to be given to its terms in their context and in the light of its object and purpose ...
    b) 135. It is settled case-law that provisions of EU law must be interpreted, as far as is possible, in the light of the wording and purpose of the international agreements to which the European Union is party. ... In the case of international law, such a "conciliatory reading" ... has one limitation, namely that that principle "applies only where the international agreement at issue prevails over the provision of Community law concerned". (159)

    It is difficult to agree with this position, as the direct application of an international agreement no longer requires a treaty-friendly interpretation of domestic law, because direct recourse can be had to the agreement.

> State concerned for the purposes of the national trade mark. However, since the Community is a party to the TRIPS Agreement and since that agreement applies to the Community trade mark, the courts referred to in Article 99 of Regulation No 40/94, when called upon to apply national rules with a view to ordering provisional measures for the protection of rights arising under a Community trade mark, are required to do so, as far as possible, in the light of the wording and purpose of Article 50 of the TRIPS Agreement (see, by analogy, Case C-286/90 *Poulsen and Diva Navigation* [1992] ECR I-6019, paragraph 9, and Case C-61/94 *Commission* v *Germany* [1996] ECR I-3989, paragraph 52).[73]

C. RESUMÉ

The above analysis started from the question whether the direct application of an international agreement containing provisions on intellectual property rights could be a possible alternative to or substitute for the application of domestic law provisions inconsistent with such agreement.

I. In General

The above analysis has shown that the direct application of international agreements not only finds no international consensus, but the details thereof are in dispute regarding almost every angle of the question:

1. Which agreements should be eligible for direct application? There is a certain understanding that agreements that only and clearly protect fundamental human rights may very well be directly applicable, while this is disputed for give-and-take agreements that regulate trade relations and that in many cases contain an explicit set of rules for dispute resolution.
2. Which treaty norms may be eligible for direct application? Would the treaty provision protect an individual right, and be reasonably precise to be directly applied?
3. In which context could the provision be applied, and regarding which remedies? Could a treaty provision be invoked in an action against the state (as was the case in the patent extension litigations), or also in a litigation between private parties (e.g. in cases where a remedy such as destruction, or a procedural right such as the right of inspection is only contained in the agreement)? In such case, how should the court deal with the argument of legitimate expectations of defendants in the application of domestic law?
4. What would be the relationship between treaty provisions and other rules of domestic law? Should the court for example extend a patent right based on TRIPS, what about good faith provisions of third parties? This issue is particularly problematic in regard of the sovereignty of states and the fact that both state-to-state dispute resolution and investor-state dispute resolution would at the most order a state to indemnify the agreed actors, but refrain from what amounts to a change in legislation.

73. European Court of Justice, decision of 16 June 1998, case C-53/96, *Hermès*.

II. On the Direct Application of the TRIPS Agreement in Particular

A number of further arguments speak against the direct applicability of TRIPS in particular.

1. There is the implementing history that for the EU and the US quite clearly expresses the intention that TRIPS should not find direct application.
2. The fact that the TRIPS Agreement already provides for a rather elaborate mechanism of dispute settlement meant to address the missing, incorrect or incomplete implementation or application of the agreement under domestic law points to an interpretation that issues of compliance should be left to a more competent forum. Given the complexity of grace periods, mailbox systems, interplay between the GATT and TRIPs Agreements, etc., one can reasonably argue that these issues should not be brought before domestic courts. The counter position is that direct application could be complementary and thus alleviate the burden of the WTO panels.[74] Yet, as mentioned above, direct application represents a far more severe intrusion of international law into the plane of the domestic legal order and may thereby unduly prejudice other actors in this field and thereby disregard the respect for the sovereignty of the competent state to find a solution on the plane of domestic law.
3. Further, while TRIPS recognises IP rights as private rights, the agreement does so in the context of a trade agreement. The rights are not private rights as such, but trade-related private rights. They are granted and must be interpreted in the context of and in accordance with the principles of international trade. In other words, TRIPS rights are subject to WTO rules and not vice versa. AG *Colomer* is correct when he observes[75] in the Portuguese referral case *Merck* that "it is difficult to put – without incongruities – minimum standards of protection, such as the duration of patents, on the same footing as rules which, for example, require the reduction or withdrawal of customs tariffs in order to facilitate the access of products to the market" (para.83). But to the extent that the WTO Agreement makes this linkage (and there are good reasons to doubt the logic of TRIPS that IP rights are trade-related, and in some cases such as geographical indications one can even doubt that these are private rights), these issues must be put on the same footing, for better or worse. If international trade agreements such as the WTO are regarded as legal instruments of trade policy, TRIPS as part of such an agreement, cannot be interpreted but in the same way.[76] And for such interpretation,

74. J. Drexl, 'Das TRIPS Abkommen und seine Anwendung in der Europäischen Gemeinschaft', *GRUR Int.* (1994), 785.
75. AG Ruiz-Jarabo Colomer, opinion of 23 January 2007 for case C-431/05 *Merck Genericos v. Merck et al.*, paras. 68, 75, 78.
76. According to Petersmann, 20 *Common Market Law Review* (1983), 397, 424, 435, the principle of reciprocity is a purely political rather than legal principle and thus irrelevant for legal analysis. This is a valid and forceful argument. Yet due to its nature as a trade agreement, its addressees are clearly member states that should be sovereign in how to implement the agreement's obligations, or not. Default of implementation, as is argued in

bodies that regularly interpret international agreements such as the WTO panels may be the more suitable forum.

4. A further argument is that IP rights are a different cup of tea from, say, human rights. An international convention requiring Member States to abolish the death penalty is directly applicable in that it only defines a relationship between an individual and the state.[77] The commons is not affected where a death penalty is not executed. This is different for intellectual property rights. They are a burden to society, conceded in order to stimulate inventive (or creative) activity and only when certain conditions are met. An ex-post extension of patents (or other rights, for that matter) for inventions made in the expectation of a lesser reward fails to fulfil any meaningful incentive, and on the contrary frustrates the expectation of the public in being able to work the invention after a term established at the time of filing. A direct application of TRIPS thereby disadvantages the commons (competitors, the general public) in that it deprives legislature of acting as an intermediary to balance the rights of inventors with the interests of competitors and the general public. An extension of the patent term may, for example, be balanced by introducing a requirement of inventive step (as was the case for Turkey or for India), or certain exceptions for governmental use in the health sector, etc.[78] Particularly patents due to their strong linkage with industrial policy are imbedded in a system of checks and balances that a unilateral, direct application of TRIPS would frustrate.[79]

---

the last section of this chapter, should lead at most to a damage claim against the State, but not to a direct application. In the same vein ECJ, decision of 30 September 2003 in case C-93/02 Biret *International v. Council,* where the EU had failed to implement a WTO Settlement order to allow the importation of hormone-treated beef.

77. The same holds true for Association Agreements or other treaties where these define personal liberties rather than trade relations.
78. Note Art. 1(1) TRIPS Agreement according to which "Members shall be free to determine the appropriate method of implementing the provisions of this Agreement within their own legal system and practice."
79. There are also good arguments for the position that TRIPS should be directly applicable: J. Drexl, 'Das TRIPS Übereinkommen und seine Anwendung in der Europäischen Gemeinschaft', *GRUR Int.* (1994), 777, 785 et seq. According to him, (1) the Agreement itself does not preclude its direct application, (2) the subject matter of TRIPS concerns rights of individuals, (3) the existence of a dispute resolution mechanism does not preclude direct application, as national and international mechanisms of dispute settlement/enforcement should be applied cumulatively.

CHAPTER 6

The Pathways of Multinational Intellectual Property Dispute Settlement

Peter K. Yu[1]

A. INTRODUCTION

Multinational intellectual property dispute settlement is fraught with challenges. While most right holders have relied on domestic litigation in countries in which they invest or conduct business – or host states in investment lingo – the arrival of new international trade, investment and intellectual property agreements have provided alternative mechanisms for settling these disputes.

For instance, the Berne Convention for the Protection of Literary and Artistic Works (Berne Convention) and the Paris Convention for the Protection of Industrial Property (Paris Convention) provide state parties with an optional mechanism to settle disputes through the International Court of Justice. Although individual intellectual property right holders cannot file complaints on their own, they can lobby their home governments, or other governments, to intervene on their behalves. The World Trade Organization (WTO) also has instituted a mandatory process to settle state-to-state disputes arising from WTO agreements, including the Agreement on Trade-Related Aspects of Intellectual Property Rights (TRIPS Agreement).

Apart from state-to-state dispute settlement (SSDS), many international trade or investment agreements now provide investor-state dispute settlement (ISDS) mechanisms to help foreign investors to resolve disputes with host states. Taking advantage of these agreements, foreign intellectual property right holders can now take grievances to independent arbitral panels. Examples of international instruments offering such dispute settlement mechanisms are Chapter 11 of the North American

1. This chapter draws on research the author conducted for earlier articles in the *American University Law Review*, the *Loyola University Chicago Law Journal* and a volume collecting presentations at the ALAI Congress 2018.

Free Trade Agreement (NAFTA) and Chapter 9 of the Trans-Pacific Partnership (TPP) Agreement, which has now been incorporated into the Comprehensive and Progressive Agreement for Trans-Pacific Partnership (CPTPP).[2]

To deepen our understanding of the different pathways of multinational intellectual property dispute settlement, this chapter assesses three distinct mechanisms addressed in this volume: (1) domestic litigation in host states; (2) SSDS; and (3) ISDS. This chapter begins by identifying the various challenges multinational intellectual property right holders encounter when they seek to resolve foreign disputes. It then highlights the improvements provided by international intellectual property agreements and the agreements' mixed success in alleviating the right holders' challenges. The chapter further reviews the strengths and limitations of SSDS and ISDS, discussing each dispute settlement mechanism in turn. It concludes with three observations, aiming to improve multinational intellectual property dispute settlement.

B. DOMESTIC LITIGATION IN HOST STATES

When multinational intellectual property right holders secure protection or establish businesses abroad, they inevitably encounter disputes with local firms or host state governments. To address these disputes, they rely on domestic litigation in host states. Although national courts provide logical avenues for redress, the failure of *some* host states, in particular those in the developing world, to adequately protect intellectual property rights has frustrated multinational right holders. At times, these right holders have also found local courts inefficient, corrupt, xenophobic and prone to local protectionism.

This section discusses the problems that are inherent in host state litigation. In view of the voluminous literature on adjudication by national courts, this section does not re-evaluate the strengths and limitations of this dispute settlement mechanism; instead, it focuses on why multinational intellectual property right holders have found it unsatisfactory to resolve disputes in national courts alone. This section then examines the various improvements provided by international intellectual property agreements. It further discusses the agreements' mixed success in improving multinational intellectual property dispute settlement.

I. Problems

As far as multinational right holders are concerned, the biggest problem with host state litigation is the lack of adequate standards in local laws. The textbook examples are the many inadequacies found in intellectual property laws in developing countries. Owing to different economic and technological backgrounds, these countries often do not protect intellectual property rights to the same extent as their counterparts in the developed world.

2. On the CPTPP, see Peter K. Yu, 'Thinking about the Trans-Pacific Partnership (and a Mega-Regional Agreement on Life Support)', 20 *SMU Science and Technology Law Review* (2017), 97, at 104–106.

To complicate matters, some of these countries lag behind in legal development. As a result, their laws do not align with international standards, such as those found in the latest international intellectual property agreements. Without appropriate laws, local courts are of limited use to foreign right holders. Worse still, these courts may be underdeveloped or highly inefficient.[3] Judges in these courts may also lack adequate training,[4] especially in relation to highly technical matters such as intellectual property. Even in developed countries, many foreign litigants remain reluctant to try highly specialized intellectual property cases in courts that rarely handle them.

To exacerbate the challenge for foreign right holders, some courts and judges may be beholden to powerful local interests and may therefore issue biased decisions.[5] Many of these right holders also worry about corruption[6] and the high political risks involved in foreign investment.[7] For jurisdictions with armed conflicts or civil strife, efforts to resolve foreign disputes through local means could indeed be highly dangerous.[8]

Moreover, local governments may enjoy sovereign immunity,[9] which prevents foreign right holders from suing the host state governments in the first place. Some local judges may also be reluctant to invalidate local laws, regulations or administrative actions. Although foreign commentators often blame unfavourable decisions on anti-foreign bias, some of these decisions could be attributed to local variations. After all, the judges' life experiences inevitably colour their perception of legal problems and available remedies.

In sum, multinational intellectual property right holders have remained highly reluctant to litigate in host states. Such reluctance has raised questions about whether these right holders would have better chances litigating at home or in third states instead. While intellectual property right holders have had some success in suing local firms outside the host states, especially when these firms have assets abroad, their ability to sue host state governments at home or in third states remains limited. As *Andrea Bjorklund* explained in the European and US contexts:

3. Andrea K. Bjorklund, 'Private Rights and Public International Law: Why Competition among International Economic Law Tribunals Is Not Working', 59 *Hastings Law Journal* (2007), 241, at 259; Charles N. Brower and Stephan W. Schill, 'Is Arbitration a Threat or a Boon to the Legitimacy of International Investment Law?', 9 *Chicago Journal of International Law* (2009), 471, at 479.
4. Peter K. Yu, 'From Pirates to Partners: Protecting Intellectual Property in China in the Twenty-first Century', 50 *American University Law Review* (2000), 131, at 214.
5. Daniel C.K. Chow, 'Organized Crime, Local Protectionism, and the Trade in Counterfeit Goods in China', 14 *China Economic Review* (2003), 473; Li Yiqiang, 'Evaluation of the Sino-American Intellectual Property Agreements: A Judicial Approach to Solving the Local Protectionism Problem', 10 *Columbia Journal of Asian Law* (1996), 391.
6. Brower and Schill, *supra* note 3, at 479.
7. Lone Wandahl Mouyal, *International Investment Law and the Right to Regulate: A Human Rights Perspective* (Routledge, Abingdon, 2016), 8; Surya P. Subedi, *International Investment Law: Reconciling Policy and Principle* (2nd edn., Hart Publishing, Oxford, 2012), 87.
8. Peter K. Yu, 'The Investment-Related Aspects of Intellectual Property Rights', 66 *American University Law Review* (2017), 829, at 847.
9. Bjorklund, *supra* note 3, at 254; Brower and Schill, *supra* note 3, at 479; Cynthia M. Ho, 'Sovereignty under Siege: Corporate Challenges to Domestic Intellectual Property Decisions', 30 *Berkeley Technology Law Journal* (2015), 213, at 232; Yu, *supra* note 8, at 846–847.

> Municipal courts in the home state of the investor will often be unavailable either for lack of jurisdiction over the host state, or because foreign sovereign immunity protects the host government. All the western European nations, and many beyond, have adopted the restrictive theory of sovereign immunity, holding that foreign governments do not enjoy immunity when they are acting *jure gestionis* (in a private capacity), but that they retain immunity when acting *jure imperii* (in a public capacity). The United States followed the lead of the European countries and codified the restrictive theory of immunity in the Foreign Sovereign Immunities Act of 1976. In the investor-state dispute settlement context, foreign states sometimes act in a private capacity, but very often act in a public capacity as they enact a government measure with deleterious effects on a foreign investor or his investment.[10]

Finally, regardless of the venue, multinational intellectual property right holders may face complicated legal questions that are commonly found in private international law, such as those regarding jurisdiction, applicable law and enforcement and recognition of judgements. Although there is nothing wrong with local courts applying their preferred laws and procedures – usually the law of the forum (*lex fori*)[11] – these right holders understandably hope that courts would embrace legal standards that are most familiar to them as well as those that strongly support their business and competition models.

In sum, this section has explained why multinational intellectual property right holders have found it unsatisfactory to resolve disputes in national courts alone – whether at home, in host states or in other states. Obviously, any analysis from the right holders' perspective will have to be taken with a large grain of salt, as this type of analysis frequently overstates the problems of local courts and judges. Such analysis is also prone to stereotypes, especially in relation to developing countries. As Chapter 5 has shown, national courts can provide promising avenues for redress, especially when these courts are willing to give effect to obligations under international agreements. Regardless of the strengths and limitations of national courts, however, the analysis in this section has provided useful insights into why multinational right holders and their supportive governments have actively negotiated new international trade, investment and intellectual property agreements to establish alternative dispute settlement mechanisms. This analysis, in turn, will pave the way for the chapter's later discussions of SSDS and ISDS (see also Chapters 2 to 4).

II. Partial Improvements

To address problems confronting multinational intellectual property right holders, countries have entered into a wide variety of multilateral agreements. These agreements are beneficial in four ways. First, they include national treatment provisions that prevent countries from discriminating against foreign authors or inventors. Article 5(3) of the Berne Convention states that "when the author is not a national of the country of origin of the work for which he is protected under this Convention,

10. Bjorklund, *supra* note 3, at 254.
11. *Ibid.* at 255.

he shall enjoy in that country the same rights as national authors". Likewise, Article 2(1) of the Paris Convention declares:

> Nationals of any country of the Union shall, as regards the protection of industrial property, enjoy in all the other countries of the Union the advantages that their respective laws now grant, or may hereafter grant, to nationals; all without prejudice to the rights specially provided for by this Convention. Consequently, they shall have the same protection as the latter, and the same legal remedy against any infringement of their rights, provided that the conditions and formalities imposed upon nationals are complied with.

Although neither provision was designed to target anti-foreign bias and local protectionism, requiring state parties, and their courts and administrative agencies, to offer the same protection to foreign and domestic right holders is an important step towards the development of a fair multinational dispute settlement environment.

Second, multilateral intellectual property agreements, such as the Berne and Paris Conventions, include international minimum standards for substantive protection. While the Berne Convention protects artistic and literary property, the Paris Convention covers industrial property, such as trademarks, patents, utility models and industrial designs. Although multinational intellectual property right holders remain dissatisfied with the overall levels of protection and enforcement, the existence of international minimum standards addresses the problems caused by non-existent or inadequate laws. Greater harmonization also helps to reduce questions about applicable law.

Third, multilateral intellectual property agreements include dispute settlement mechanisms that allow state parties to resolve disputes with other state parties. In identical language, Article 33(1) of the Berne Convention and Article 28(1) of the Paris Convention declare:

> Any dispute between two or more countries of the Union concerning the interpretation or application of this Convention, not settled by negotiation, may, by any one of the countries concerned, be brought before the International Court of Justice by application in conformity with the Statute of the Court, unless the countries concerned agree on some other method of settlement.

This state-to-state arrangement is the precursor of the WTO dispute settlement process, which will be discussed in greater depth in the next section. Compared with that process, the dispute settlement mechanism under the Berne and Paris Conventions suffer from two major defects: first, the arrangement is available only to state parties, not private intellectual property right holders; second, the use of this mechanism is *optional* and requires the consent of the relevant state parties.[12] These two major limitations largely explain why no multinational intellectual property dispute has ever been brought before the International Court of Justice. To a large

12. Article 36(1) of the Statute of the International Court of Justice states: "The jurisdiction of the Court comprises all cases which the parties refer to it and all matters specially provided for in the Charter of the United Nations or in treaties and conventions in force."

extent, the lack of disputes has raised questions about whether the Berne and Paris Conventions are de facto unenforceable.[13]

Finally, although these two Conventions contain some rare and piecemeal enforcement provisions – such as those relating to the seizure of goods upon importation, the institution of infringement proceedings, and the right to obtain appropriate legal remedies[14] – these provisions do not seek to reshape courts or improve their enforcement capabilities. Indeed, significant improvements in this area do not emerge until after the establishment of the WTO and its TRIPS Agreement. Because successful intellectual property enforcement often depends on the existence of an effective enabling environment – which provides crucial preconditions such as consciousness of legal rights, respect for the rule of law, and an effective and independent judiciary[15] – the enforcement provisions in early international intellectual property agreements have not made the local dispute settlement environment more attractive to foreign right holders.

When all of these developments have been taken into consideration, it is difficult not to notice that multilateral agreements such as the Berne and Paris Conventions have had only mixed success in improving multinational intellectual property dispute settlement. Although the national treatment requirement and the adoption of international minimum standards have ensured the provision of a fairer dispute settlement environment to foreign right holders, these right holders continue to demand new alternative mechanisms for resolving multinational intellectual property disputes.

C. STATE-TO-STATE DISPUTE SETTLEMENT

When the WTO was established in Marrakesh in April 1994, it introduced a mandatory process to settle disputes arising from agreements involving the international trading body, including the TRIPS Agreement. That agreement also incorporates the international minimum standards under the Berne and Paris Conventions while creating new substantive standards in other areas, such as geographical indications, plant variety protection, layout designs of integrated circuits, and the protection of trade secrets and other undisclosed information. In addition, the TRIPS Agreement provides a comprehensive set of provisions on intellectual property enforcement, which significantly improve on the rare and piecemeal enforcement provisions in the Berne and Paris Conventions.

Given these improvements, it is no surprise that *Rochelle Dreyfuss* and *Andreas Lowenfeld* singled out the TRIPS Agreement and the mandatory WTO dispute

13. Peter K. Yu, 'Currents and Crosscurrents in the International Intellectual Property Regime', 38 *Loyola of Los Angeles Law Review* (2004), 323, at 355.
14. Examples of these rare and piecemeal enforcement provisions are Articles 13(3), 15 and 16 of the Berne Convention and Articles 9, 10(1), 10*bis* and 10*ter* of the Paris Convention.
15. Robert M. Sherwood, 'Some Things Cannot Be Legislated', 10 *Cardozo Journal of International and Comparative Law* (2002), 37, at 42; Peter K. Yu, 'Intellectual Property, Economic Development, and the China Puzzle', in Daniel J. Gervais (ed.), *Intellectual Property, Trade and Development: Strategies to Optimize Economic Development in a TRIPS Plus Era* (1st edn., Oxford University Press, Oxford, 2007), 213–216; Peter K. Yu, 'TRIPS and Its Achilles' Heel', 18 *Journal of Intellectual Property Law* (2011), 479, at 500.

settlement process as two key accomplishments of the Uruguay Round of Multilateral Trade Negotiations.[16] Policymakers and commentators have also described the latter as a crowning achievement of the WTO (see also Chapter 4).[17] For the purposes of this chapter, this section reviews the strengths and limitations of the SSDS mechanism provided by the WTO.

I. Strengths

As far as the WTO is concerned, its dispute settlement process has provided multinational right holders with several advantages. First, this process has induced legislative changes that are rarely available through domestic litigation in host states, except when courts have found the implicated laws to be unconstitutional. These changes are important because they benefit all foreign intellectual property right holders, not only those prevailing in the disputes. Even better, the WTO dispute settlement process has been highly effective in getting losing respondents to change their laws – except when the losing respondent happens to be the United States.[18] Should compensation be sought, such as through an arbitration proceeding under Article 25 of the Dispute Settlement Understanding, the WTO process may also generate compensation that would ultimately benefit foreign right holders.[19]

Second, although individual right holders cannot file complaints with the WTO Dispute Settlement Body, they can lobby their home governments, or other governments, to do so on their behalves. Such filing will automatically shift enforcement costs to the complaining governments. Even better, countries that have actively participated in the WTO dispute settlement process since its inception, such as the United States and members of the European Union, have amassed highly specialized expertise that would ensure maximum success in the WTO dispute settlement process.[20]

---

16. Rochelle Cooper Dreyfuss and Andreas F. Lowenfeld, 'Two Achievements of the Uruguay Round: Putting TRIPS and Dispute Settlement Together', 37 *Virginia Journal of International Law* (1997), 275.
17. Rachel Brewster, 'Shadow Unilateralism: Enforcing International Trade Law at the WTO', 30 *University of Pennsylvania Journal of International Law* (2009), 1133, at 1134; William J. Davey, 'The WTO Dispute Settlement System: The First Ten Years', 8 *Journal of International Economic Law* (2005), 17, at 32; Ruth Okediji, 'Toward an International Fair Use Doctrine', 39 *Columbia Journal of Transnational Law* (2000), 75, at 149–150.
18. The WTO members found this out painfully in *United States – Section 110(5) of US Copyright Act* and *United States – Section 211 Omnibus Appropriations Act of 1998*. Peter K. Yu, 'Are Developing Countries Playing a Better TRIPS Game?', 16 *UCLA Journal of International Law and Foreign Affairs* (2011), 311, at 337–338.
19. E.g. World Trade Organization, 'United States – Section 110(5) of the US Copyright Act: Recourse to Arbitration under Article 25 of the DSU' (WT/DS160/ARB25/1, 2001).
20. Gregory Shaffer, 'Recognizing Public Goods in WTO Dispute Settlement: Who Participates? Who Decides? The Case of TRIPS and Pharmaceutical Patent Protection', in Keith E. Maskus and Jerome H. Reichman (eds.), *International Public Goods and Transfer of Technology under a Globalized Intellectual Property Regime* (Cambridge University Press, Cambridge, 2005), 900.

Third, WTO complaints help to shield foreign intellectual property right holders from direct confrontation with host state governments. In countries where local governments have taken retaliatory actions, the ability to hide behind their home governments, or other governments, to push for legislative reform is highly appealing. If the complaining governments prevail, the right holders will be able to benefit from the legislative changes demanded by the WTO Dispute Settlement Body. If these governments fail, however, the right holders will still be able to mend their ties with host state governments – perhaps by blaming the complaining governments for taking unnecessary political actions.[21]

Finally, the WTO Dispute Settlement Body resolves state-to-state disputes based on norms that have attained consensus in over 160 WTO members. The WTO panellists and the WTO Appellate Body also utilize rules that have been widely accepted by the international community. To be sure, reports from WTO panels and the Appellate Body have no precedential value.[22] Yet, these institutions have used prior decisions to provide explanation, support or interpretive guidance. As the Appellate Body reasoned in *Japan – Taxes on Alcoholic Beverages*, the use of earlier relevant cases could help to "create legitimate expectations among WTO Members".[23] To a large extent, efforts to settle TRIPS disputes through the mandatory WTO process have provided consistency, predictability and, most importantly, legitimacy.

II. Limitations

Notwithstanding these myriad benefits, the WTO dispute settlement process has significant limitations. First, intellectual property right holders are often at the mercy of the complaining governments. While the right holders may be able to work closely with these governments – through consultation, lobbying or the provision of evidence or financial support[24] – they have no control over the strategies used in the WTO dispute settlement process.

Worse still, if these governments choose not to file WTO complaints – due perhaps to the fear of adverse economic impacts, collateral damage in other trade sectors, or negative political or diplomatic consequences – intellectual property right holders cannot force these governments to take WTO actions on their behalves.[25] Nor does the WTO provide other recourse if the governments settle their disputes.[26] As *Christopher Gibson* observed:

21. Peter K. Yu, 'From Pirates to Partners (Episode II): Protecting Intellectual Property in Post-WTO China', 55 *American University Law Review* (2006), 901, at 931.
22. World Trade Organization, '7.2 Legal Status of Adopted/Unadopted Reports in Other Disputes', <www.wto.org/english/tratop_e/dispu_e/disp_settlement_cbt_e/c7s2p1_e.htm> accessed 14 November 2018.
23. World Trade Organization, 'Japan – Taxes on Alcoholic Beverages: Report of the Appellate Body' (WT/DS8/AB/R, WT/DS10/AB/R, WT/DS11/AB/R, 1996), 14.
24. Christopher Gibson, 'A Look at the Compulsory License in Investment Arbitration: The Case of Indirect Expropriation', 25 *American University International Law Review* (2010), 357, at 408.
25. *Ibid.* at 406–407; Yu, *supra* note 8, at 848–849.
26. Brower and Schill, *supra* note 3, at 480.

> [I]nvestors choosing the WTO forum will be forced to rely upon their government's willingness to bring a claim, which is not a foregone conclusion and may be subject to the vagaries of other considerations in the relations between the two countries concerned. The private investor will thus need considerable political sway to induce its government to initiate the state-to-state dispute.[27]

For instance, despite the wish of Philip Morris and other relevant intellectual property right holders, the United States declined to use SSDS to challenge the tobacco plain packaging regulations in Australia and Uruguay. Likewise, the United States refused to file a WTO complaint against Canada over its use of the so-called "promise doctrine" in patent law to invalidate Eli Lilly's patents on the hyperactivity drug Strattera (atomoxetine) and the anti-psychotic drug Zyprexa (olanzapine).

Second, the WTO dispute settlement process can be very costly. Based on 2004 figures, *Gregory Shaffer* found that "an average WTO claim costs in the range of U.S.$300,000–400,000 in attorneys' fees (although they possibly can be much more)".[28] As *Håkan Nordström* and *Professor Shaffer* later elaborated:

> Under ... back-of-the-envelope calculations, a case of average complexity would cost $100,000 if it ends after the initial consultations because the parties have settled or the complaint is otherwise withdrawn. If the case advanced to the panel stage, it would cost another $320,000. And if the panel decision were appealed, the bill would rise by another $135,000. The total cost would then top one-half of $1 million.[29]

More recently, *Anna Joubin-Bret* stated that "[m]inimum free-market rates for litigating a relatively simple WTO dispute through to the basic panel report stage may range from US$250,000 to US$750,000".[30] Because of the high costs involved in WTO dispute settlement, many developing countries simply cannot afford to take action on behalf of their intellectual property right holders.[31] Nor could the more resourceful countries, including those in the developed world, file WTO complaints as frequently as their right holders prefer.

Third, in difficult cases, WTO panels and the Appellate Body may strive for greater compliance and implementation by striking compromises that would please all of the parties involved – complainants, respondents and participating third parties. A case in point is the first US-China TRIPS dispute.[32] While China won the claim

27. Gibson, *supra* note 24, at 407.
28. Shaffer, *supra* note 20, at 899.
29. Håkan Nordström and Gregory Shaffer, 'Access to Justice in the WTO: A Case for a Small-Claims Procedure?', in Chantal Thomas and Joel P. Trachtman (eds.), *Developing Countries in the WTO Legal System* (Oxford University Press, Oxford, 2009), 205–206.
30. Anna Joubin-Bret, *Establishing an International Advisory Centre on Investment Disputes?* (International Centre for Trade and Sustainable Development and World Economic Forum, Geneva, 2015), 8.
31. Yu, *supra* note 8, at 897–898.
32. World Trade Organization, 'China – Measures Affecting the Protection and Enforcement of Intellectual Property Rights: Report of the Panel' (WT/DS362/R, 2009). On the WTO panel decision, see Peter K. Yu, 'TRIPS Enforcement and Developing Countries', 26 *American University International Law Review* (2011), 727; Peter K. Yu, 'The TRIPS Enforcement Dispute', 89 *Nebraska Law Review* (2011), 1046.

on criminal procedures and penalties, the United States prevailed on the censorship claim. The remaining customs claim was divided between the two parties. With both sides claiming victory in this dispute, neither China nor the United States appealed the decision, and the WTO panel successfully settled the dispute without escalating this bilateral conflict. Although such an outcome seemed diplomatically desirable, it disappointed the US copyright industries, which had lobbied heavily for WTO actions. Adding insult to the injury, the victories the United States secured were mostly paper victories, as opposed to substantive ones.[33]

Finally, the WTO dispute settlement process can be long and arduous. The complaint for the US-China TRIPS dispute discussed earlier was filed on 10 April 2007, with the panel established on 31 August. Although the WTO timetable states that the WTO panel will issue its decision in no more than nine months after the panel's establishment,[34] the decision on that dispute was not handed down until 26 January 2009, more than a year and a half after the United States filed its complaint. The recent WTO case involving Australia's tobacco plain packaging regulation – a key focus of this volume – became even more problematic. The initial complaint was filed on 4 April 2012 – or 13 March 2012, if we start with Ukraine's earlier but subsequently withdrawn complaint.[35] Yet, the WTO panel decision was not released until 28 June 2018. Given the considerable time lag, one has to wonder how appealing it is for multinational intellectual property right holders to rely on their home governments, or other governments, to use the WTO process to resolve international disputes on their behalves. In an area as fast-evolving as intellectual property, six years is a very long time.

D. INVESTOR-STATE DISPUTE SETTLEMENT

In view of the many drawbacks of SSDS, multinational intellectual property industries and their supportive governments have actively pushed for the adoption of a new alternative mechanism known as ISDS to help foreign investors to resolve disputes with host states.[36] Chapter 11 of NAFTA provides a mechanism for settling intellectual property and other disputes arising from the agreement, although the United States–Mexico–Canada Agreement has recently scaled back this mechanism significantly. Chapter 9 of the TPP Agreement, which has now been incorporated into

33. Yu, 'TRIPS Enforcement Dispute', *supra* note 32, at 1081–1103.
34. World Trade Organization, 'The Process – Stages in a Typical WTO Dispute Settlement Case', < www.wto.org/english/tratop_e/dispu_e/disp_settlement_cbt_e/c6s1p1_e.htm > accessed 12 November 2018.
35. World Trade Organization, 'Australia – Certain Measures Concerning Trademarks and Other Plain Packaging Requirements Applicable to Tobacco Products and Packaging: Request for Consultations by Ukraine' (WT/DS434/1, 2012).
36. On ISDS, see Peter K. Yu, 'Conceptual and Institutional Improvements to Investor-State Dispute Settlement', in Christophe Geiger (ed.), *Research Handbook on Intellectual Property and Investment Law* (Edward Elgar Publishing, Cheltenham, 2019); Peter K. Yu, 'Crossfertilizing ISDS with TRIPS', 49 *Loyola University Chicago Law Journal* (2017), 321; Yu, *supra* note 8; Peter K. Yu, 'Investor-State Dispute Settlement and the Trans-Pacific Partnership', in Christophe Geiger, Craig Allen Nard and Xavier Seuba (eds.), *Intellectual Property and the Judiciary* (Edward Elgar Publishing, Cheltenham, 2018).

the CPTPP, also provides for ISDS. This section reviews the strengths and limitations of this dispute settlement mechanism.

I. Strengths

ISDS has a number of strengths that are unavailable in domestic litigation in host states. These strengths compare favourably with the SSDS mechanism provided by the WTO. At times, ISDS also has strengths not found in SSDS, making it particularly attractive to multinational intellectual property right holders.

First, like SSDS, ISDS has the ability to induce countries to change their laws. Such changes will benefit all foreign intellectual property right holders, not only the winning parties in the disputes. While ISDS arbitral panels focus on disputes involving individual right holders, multinational corporations can file follow-up ISDS complaints when other members of the industry have obtained favourable awards against the host states. Successful awards in ISDS cases can therefore send strong signals to local policymakers about the need to change their laws, regulations or administrative practices.

Second, like SSDS, the settlement of ISDS disputes relies on independent and impartial arbitrators. The use of these arbitrators enables the ISDS arbitral process to tackle problems posed by corruption,[37] anti-foreign bias and local protectionism.[38] Although the ISDS process is not as well developed as the WTO dispute settlement process, the use of these arbitrators helps to ensure the provision of a fair dispute settlement environment to foreign right holders.

Third, for businesses wanting to protect confidential information - business or otherwise - the secretive nature of some ISDS proceedings can be highly appealing. By keeping the process secret, these proceedings could help the losing parties to save "face" while preserving the foreign investors' working relationships with local firms or host state governments. Although some ISDS proceedings, such as those conducted through the International Chamber of Commerce and the UN Commission on International Trade Law (UNCITRAL), have remained confidential,[39] the push for greater transparency has made it increasingly difficult for investors to maintain secrecy, especially in arbitrations involving the World Bank's International Centre for Settlement of Investment Disputes (ICSID). To address transparency concerns,

---

37. Hilmar Raeschke-Kessler and Dorothee Gottwald, 'Corruption', in Peter Muchlinski, Federico Ortino and Christoph Schreuer (eds.), *The Oxford Handbook of International Investment Law* (Oxford University Press, Oxford, 2008), 584; Yu, *supra* note 8, at 847.
38. Christoph Schreuer, 'Do We Need Investment Arbitration?', in Jean E. Kalicki and Anna Joubin-Bret (eds.), *Reshaping the Investor-State Dispute Settlement System: Journeys for the 21st Century* (Brill Nijhoff, Leiden, 2015), 883; Office of the US Trade Representative, 'Fact Sheet: Investor-State Dispute Settlement (ISDS)' (2015).
39. Gary B. Born and Ethan G. Shenkman, 'Confidentiality and Transparency in Commercial and Investor-State International Arbitration', in Catherine A. Rogers and Roger P. Alford (eds.), *The Future of Investment Arbitration* (Oxford University Press, New York, 2009), 28; Joubin-Bret, *supra* note 30, at 2.

the TPP Agreement and other recently negotiated bilateral, regional and plurilateral agreements have also included transparency-related language.[40]

Fourth, ISDS can be resolved more quickly than SSDS. From the filing of the complaint on 4 April 2012 to the release of the panel report on 28 June 2018, the WTO dispute concerning Australia's tobacco plain packaging regulation has taken more than six years (not to mention the ongoing appeal by Honduras and the Dominican Republic to the WTO Appellate Body). By contrast, the ISDS case involving Philip Morris and the Australian government took only four years. The notice of claim for that case was filed on 22 June 2011, and the award on jurisdiction and admissibility was released, with sufficient finality, on 17 December 2015. The total time spent on this investor-state dispute is consistent with "[t]he average duration [of] three to five years for an investment treaty case, not taking into account annulment or review".[41]

Finally, should there be damages, right holders will be able to obtain compensation directly. Even though governments that have appeared on the right holders' behalves could share any award they receive through arbitration – such as through a proceeding under Article 25 of the Dispute Settlement Understanding – the governments are not required to turn over the proceeds.[42] Instead, governments are free to allocate the damages as they see fit.

II. Limitations

Notwithstanding its considerable strengths, ISDS, like SSDS, has significant limitations. First, because intellectual property right holders can bring cases against host states themselves, the mechanism no longer shifts enforcement costs to governments. Instead, the right holders bear costs and burdens themselves. According to a study conducted by the Organisation for Economic Co-operation and Development (OECD), the costs of an ISDS arbitration "have averaged over USD 8 million with costs exceeding USD 30 million in some cases".[43] These costs could go up to as high as USD 70 million, like in the highly unusual case concerning Russia's wrongful expropriation of the now-defunct Yukos Oil, which was once the country's biggest oil producer.[44]

Second, because ISDS panels decide cases individually and their awards have no precedential value,[45] ISDS awards could be quite inconsistent and unpredictable.[46] As *Christoph Schreuer* and *Matthew Weiniger* observed:

---

40. For example, Article 9.24.1 of the Trans-Pacific Partnership Agreement requires the host state respondent to make publicly available a variety of documents, including the notice of intent; the notice of arbitration; pleadings, memorials and briefs submitted to the tribunal; minutes or transcripts of hearings of the tribunal; and orders, awards and decisions of the tribunal.
41. Joubin-Bret, *supra* note 30, at 2.
42. Brower and Schill, *supra* note 3, at 480–481.
43. David Gaukrodger and Kathryn Gordon, 'Investor-State Dispute Settlement: A Scoping Paper for the Investment Policy Community', *Organisation for Economic Co-operation and Development, Working Papers on International Investment No. 2012/03* (2012), 19.
44. Joubin-Bret, *supra* note 30, at 2.
45. Yu, *supra* note 8, at 856.
46. Stephan W. Schill, 'The European Commission's Proposal of an "Investment Court System" for TTIP: Stepping Stone or Stumbling Block for Multilateralizing International

> [I]n some cases tribunals did not follow earlier decisions but adopted different solutions. At times, they simply adopted a different solution without distancing themselves from the earlier decision. At other times, they referred to the earlier decision and pointed out that they were unconvinced by what another tribunal had said and that, therefore, their decision departed from the one adopted earlier.[47]

Nevertheless, ISDS arbitrators have followed convincing and well-reasoned prior decisions.[48] As *Cheng Tai-Heng* observed, "although arbitrators in investment treaty arbitration are not formally bound by precedent in the same manner as common-law judges, there is an informal, but powerful, system of precedent that constrains arbitrators to account for prior published awards and to stabilize international investment law".[49]

Third, host states have thus far won most ISDS cases. Drawing on her analysis of about 80 cases and over 100 awards,[50] *Susan Franck* observed, "governments (57.7%) were more likely than investors (38.5%) to win cases and have no damages awarded for alleged treaty breaches".[51] Although the inclusion of the governments from OECD countries in the study has made it difficult to determine whether host states in the developing world will have as much success as their developed counterparts, it is worth noting that the large majority of investors in this study originated from developed countries.[52] The study has also shown no indication that ISDS arbitrators have what *Professor Franck* described as "development bias",[53] which "enables the process to favor the interests of transnational corporations at the expense of host states in the developing world".[54]

Finally, the ISDS mechanism is fraught with procedural flaws. In an earlier article, I identified three types of flaw that are inherent in this mechanism – those relating to the arbitration process, the arbitrators' interpretations and final arbitral

---

Investment Law?', *ASIL Insights* (22 April 2016) <www.asil.org/insights/volume/20/issue/9/european-commissions-proposal-investment-court-system-ttip-stepping>.

47. Christoph Schreuer and Matthew Weiniger, 'A Doctrine of Precedent?', in Peter Muchlinski, Federico Ortino and Christoph Schreuer (eds.), *The Oxford Handbook of International Investment Law* (Oxford University Press, Oxford, 2008), 1196.
48. Marc Bungenberg and Catharine Titi, 'Precedents in International Investment Law', in Marc Bungenberg et al. (eds.), *International Investment Law: A Handbook* (Nomos Verlag, Baden-Baden, Hart Publishing, Oxford, and C.H. Beck Verlag, Munich, 2015); Cheng Tai-Heng, 'Precedent and Control in Investment Treaty Arbitration', 30 *Fordham International Law Journal* (2007), 1014, at 1016; Loretta Malintoppi, 'Independence, Impartiality, and Duty of Disclosure of Arbitrators', in Peter Muchlinski, Federico Ortino and Christoph Schreuer (eds.), *The Oxford Handbook of International Investment Law* (Oxford University Press, Oxford, 2008), 792.
49. Cheng, *supra* note 48, at 1016.
50. Susan D. Franck, 'Empirically Evaluating Claims about Investment Treaty Arbitration', 86 *North Carolina Law Review* (2007), 1, at 24.
51. Susan D. Franck, 'Development and Outcomes of Investment Treaty Arbitration', 50 *Harvard International Law Journal* (2009), 435, at 447.
52. Franck, 'Empirically Evaluating Claims', *supra* note 50, at 26–31.
53. Franck, 'Development and Outcomes', *supra* note 51, at 451.
54. Yu, 'Crossfertilizing ISDS with TRIPS', *supra* note 36, at 339–340.

outcomes.[55] These flaws have led to high volumes of inconsistent arbitral decisions, growing incoherence in the international intellectual property system and considerable inequities suffered by host states in the developing world.[56] Although the TPP investment chapter has provided some helpful upgrades,[57] many flaws remain with the ISDS mechanism,[58] thus calling for reforms explored in Section E.II.

E. THREE OBSERVATIONS

The previous sections have examined three distinct pathways of multinational intellectual property dispute settlement: domestic litigation in host states, SSDS and ISDS. Each pathway is designed with different participants, institutions and objectives in mind. The dispute settlement mechanism used in each pathway also has its strengths and limitations. Because the three previous sections have already closely examined each pathway in turn, this section examines all three pathways together and draws some observations on the overall multinational dispute settlement environment.

I. Balance and Fairness

The first observation concerns the balance and fairness of this environment. With the availability of domestic litigation in host states, SSDS and ISDS, multinational intellectual property right holders can bypass adjudication by local courts to shop for dispute settlement fora that provide more attractive outcomes. Resourceful multinational corporations can also initiate complaints simultaneously in multiple fora. Not only can these complaints impose heavy burdens on host states in terms of both financial resources and technical expertise, but they can also send strong signals to warn these states against introducing undesirable legislation. It is therefore understandable why policymakers and commentators have become increasingly concerned about "regulatory chill"[59] – "a chilling effect that undermines a country's sovereign ability to regulate harmful conducts, including those committed by transnational corporations".[60]

To be sure, right holders rarely use all three dispute settlement mechanisms at the same time. Most intellectual property right holders tend to register grievances with local courts or administrative agencies first. If they fail to satisfactorily resolve their disputes, they will then lobby their home governments, or other governments, to challenge the law before the WTO Dispute Settlement Body. If these governments

55. Yu, *supra* note 8, at 851–864.
56. Yu, 'Crossfertilizing ISDS with TRIPS', *supra* note 36, at 327–341.
57. Yu, *supra* note 8, at 865–875.
58. *Ibid.* at 851–865.
59. On "regulatory chill", see Mouyal, *supra* note 7, at 67–68; Kyla Tienhaara, 'Regulatory Chill and the Threat of Arbitration: A View from Political Science', in Chester Brown and Kate Miles (eds.), *Evolution in Investment Treaty Law and Arbitration* (Cambridge University Press, Cambridge, 2011); UN Conference on Trade and Development, *World Investment Report 2015: Reforming International Investment Governance* (UN Conference on Trade and Development, Geneva, 2015), 128.
60. Yu, *supra* note 8, at 859.

decide against taking actions, settle the disputes or fail to secure favourable outcomes, the right holders will then seek ISDS arbitrations as a last resort.[61]

Practice does not always follow theory, however. Thus far, powerful intellectual property right holders have used multiple dispute settlement mechanisms simultaneously or *ad seriatim*. A case in point concerns Philip Morris' efforts to challenge the Australian tobacco plain packaging regulation. The tobacco giant initially challenged the regulation in local courts. After it had exhausted all local remedies following the negative High Court of Australia decision,[62] it sought ISDS under a bilateral investment agreement between Australia and Hong Kong.[63] Shortly after the filing of that ISDS complaint, Ukraine, Honduras, the Dominican Republic, Cuba and Indonesia also filed state-to-state complaints against Australia under the WTO dispute settlement process.[64] Although Australia eventually prevailed in all three dispute settlement fora – national, ISDS and WTO – one cannot help but sympathize with the country's plight.

One may further wonder whether multinational intellectual property right holders should be able to seek dispute resolution in three different fora. While arguments can certainly be made about the different targets and features of these fora,[65] having three bites at the apple for the same dispute seems unfair by any standard.[66] The right holders' ability to use multiple mechanisms strategically to overwhelm host states, especially resource-deficient ones, also raises questions about the balance of the international intellectual property system – in particular, whether the combined use of these mechanisms has tilted the balance towards the interests of right holders too much.

At some point, it will be worth considering whether rules should be introduced to prevent forum shopping in dispute settlement. For example, Article 28.4.2 of the TPP Agreement states: "Once a complaining Party has requested the establishment of, or referred a matter to, a panel or other tribunal under [the Agreement or another international trade agreement], the forum selected shall be used to the exclusion of other fora". Article 1 of Annex 9-J provides a corollary by prohibiting an investor from using the ISDS mechanism if it "has alleged th[e] breach of an obligation under [the TPP investment chapter] in proceedings before a court or administrative tribunal of Chile, Mexico, Peru or Viet Nam". Although these two provisions do not prevent the right holders' home governments from filing WTO complaints on their behalves, the provisions do prevent "a party from pursuing the same claims both

61. Office of the US Trade Representative, *supra* note 38.
62. *JT International SA v. Commonwealth of Australia* [2012] HCA 43.
63. Agreement between the Government of Hong Kong and the Government of Australia for the Promotion and Protection of Investments, 15 September 1993, 1748 UNTS 385; *Philip Morris Asia Ltd v. The Commonwealth of Australia*, PCA Case No 2012-12, Award on Jurisdiction and Admissibility, 17 December 2015.
64. World Trade Organization, 'Australia – Certain Measures Concerning Trademarks, Geographical Indications and Other Plain Packaging Requirements Applicable to Tobacco Products and Packaging: Report of the Panels' (WT/DS435/R, WT/DS441/R, WT/DS458/R, WT/DS467/R, 2018).
65. Bjorklund, *supra* note 3, at 296.
66. *Ibid.* at 243; Yu, 'Crossfertilizing ISDS with TRIPS', *supra* note 36, at 333.

in ISDS proceedings and domestic courts".[67] The provisions also acknowledge the potential unfairness when right holders file strategic complaints in multiple fora to overwhelm, if not intimidate, host state governments.

II. Potential Improvements

The second observation concerns the potential improvements that have to be introduced to strengthen the existing mechanisms for settling multinational intellectual property disputes. Although each of these mechanisms features varying designs and targets different disputants, the mechanisms share some common challenges. These challenges become especially salient when this section examines SSDS and ISDS side by side.

As the two previous sections have noted, both SSDS and ISDS are very costly. While WTO complaints can cost each party from USD 500,000 to 2 million, depending on the number of claims and complexities involved, investor-state disputes cost each party even more – around USD 4 to 5 million.[68] To make SSDS less cost-prohibitive, *Håkan Nordström* and *Gregory Shaffer* called for the development of streamlined procedures to resolve small claims in the WTO.[69] In an earlier article, I also recommended the extension of this proposal to ISDS.[70]

Another area that is worthy of improvements concerns the need for technical assistance on the part of developing countries and small and mid-sized intellectual property investors. In the WTO context, the Geneva-based Advisory Centre on WTO Law has been crucial in providing developing countries with assistance regarding the WTO dispute settlement process.[71] In the ISDS context, a similar centre could be highly beneficial for host states in the developing world as well as small and mid-sized investors in both the developed and developing worlds. What these potential beneficiaries need is not only financial support, but also technical assistance.

A third area that deserves reform attention pertains to the interplay between SSDS and ISDS. Thus far, investment issues have not figured significantly in the WTO dispute settlement process, due in large part to the WTO members' lack of consensus on international standards for investment. Nevertheless, as international intellectual property issues continue to spill over from the trade regime to the investment regime,[72]

---

67. Office of the US Trade Representative, *supra* note 38.
68. Gaukrodger and Gordon, *supra* note 43, at 19; Matthew Hodgson, 'Costs in Investment Treaty Arbitration: The Case for Reform', in Jean E. Kalicki and Anna Joubin-Bret (eds.), *Reshaping the Investor-State Dispute Settlement System: Journeys for the 21st Century* (Brill Nijhoff, Leiden, 2015), 749.
69. Nordström and Shaffer, *supra* note 29.
70. Yu, *supra* note 8, at 898.
71. Advisory Centre on WTO Law, 'The Services of the ACWL', < www.acwl.ch/download/ql/Services_of_the_ACWL.pdf > accessed 14 November 2018.
72. Rochelle Dreyfuss and Susy Frankel, 'From Incentive to Commodity to Asset: How International Law Is Reconceptualizing Intellectual Property', 36 *Michigan Journal of International Law* (2015), 557; James Gathii and Cynthia Ho, 'Regime Shifting of IP Lawmaking and Enforcement from the WTO to the International Investment Regime', 18 *Minnesota Journal of Law, Science and Technology* (2017), 427.

it is time to strengthen the coordination between the dispute settlement mechanisms in these two regimes.

To provide better coordination, I recently advanced a proposal to cross-fertilize the two regimes by including in ISDS arbitral panels some former WTO panellists, former members of the WTO Appellate Body or other experts who are qualified to serve on WTO panels.[73] That proposal further called for the establishment of an ISDS appellate body that features at least some members with WTO expertise.[74] In the past few years, commentators have also called for greater coordination between ISDS and WTO dispute settlement,[75] including the establishment of an appellate process based on the WTO Appellate Body.[76] As *Andreas Ziegler* observed:

> [I]t may be useful to encourage arbitrators and the members of judicial bodies of multilateral organizations like the WTO and ICSID to refer to each other's case law and engage in a judicial debate. This could avoid the scenario where each system operates in clinical isolation and would certainly be beneficial for the development of an inter-institutional debate on special issues affecting global trade and investment flows.[77]

III. Unintended Consequences

The final observation covers the potential unintended consequences of increased dispute settlement through multiple pathways. With the use of SSDS through the WTO dispute settlement process, intellectual property issues have slowly taken on an unhealthy trade gloss that emphasizes the economic aspects of the disputes while undervaluing the non-economic contributions of intellectual property right holders and users.[78]

While this unhealthy gloss has already been quite problematic for developing countries, especially in relation to public health or in other areas of public interest,

73. Yu, 'Crossfertilizing ISDS with TRIPS', *supra* note 36, at 342–344.
74. *Ibid.* at 344–347.
75. Theodore R. Posner and Marguerite C. Walter, 'The Abiding Role of State-State Engagement in the Resolution of Investor-State Disputes', in Jean E. Kalicki and Anna Joubin-Bret (eds.), *Reshaping the Investor-State Dispute Settlement System: Journeys for the 21st Century* (Brill Nijhoff, Leiden, 2015), 389–391; Andreas R. Ziegler, 'Investment Law in Conflict with WTO Law?', in Bungenberg et al. (eds.), *supra* note 48, 1800.
76. Dreyfuss and Frankel, *supra* note 72, at 601; Yenkong Ngangjoh-Hodu and Collins C. Ajibo, 'ICSID Annulment Procedure and the WTO Appellate System: The Case for an Appellate System for Investment Arbitration', 6 *Journal of International Dispute Settlement* (2015), 308, at 326–330; Ruth L. Okediji, 'Is Intellectual Property 'Investment'? *Eli Lilly v. Canada* and the International Intellectual Property System', 35 *University of Pennsylvania Journal of International Law* (2014), 1121, at 1137.
77. Ziegler, *supra* note 75, at 1800.
78. Ruth L. Okediji, 'Public Welfare and the Role of the WTO: Reconsidering the TRIPS Agreement', 17 *Emory International Law Review* (2003), 819, at 914–915; Peter K. Yu, 'Intellectual Property and Human Rights in the Nonmultilateral Era', 64 *Florida Law Review* (2012), 1045, at 1083–1084; Peter K. Yu, 'The Strategic and Discursive Contributions of the Max Planck Principles for Intellectual Property Provisions in Bilateral and Regional Agreements', 62 *Drake Law Review Discourse* (2014), 20, at 30.

an additional investment gloss has now slowly emerged to colour multinational intellectual property dispute settlement.[79] As policymakers and commentators have lamented, many ISDS arbitrators focus narrowly on the investment aspects of intellectual property rights.[80] According to *Rochelle Dreyfuss* and *Susy Frankel*:

> Because investor rights and IP [intellectual property] rights are both private rights, IP holders tend to equate the investment protectable under these instruments to the private economic value of their IP rights. Further, they see IP rights as reliance interests that are defined by the law at the time they made their investment or, more extremely, when the agreement references TRIPS or its own IP chapter, the law at the time when the investment agreement was made.[81]

Such a narrow focus can become particularly harmful to those host states that have continuously struggled to strike an appropriate balance in the intellectual property system.[82] Given the increasingly globalized environment and the ubiquity of technology-related issues, intellectual property rights can arise in many situations without right holders injecting resources into host states. As *Ruth Okediji* rightly reminded us:

> Intellectual property rights can be held simultaneously in many countries and in some cases, like copyright, without any formalities or other domestic process that would indicate a specific investment purpose. Is merely having authorial works in circulation in a host country sufficient to constitute an "investment in a given country?" Similarly, where patent rights are acquired by mere registration, such as in many least-developed countries, should this alone confer the status of an "investment"? Should requirements of local working conditions that more firmly anchor the patent grant to domestic priorities make a difference in an assessment of a protected investment?[83]

Likewise, some jurisdictions, especially those in the British Commonwealth, have chosen to continue their re-registration system.[84] This type of system recognizes intellectual property rights based on registrations in other countries. If the goal of international investment agreements, or investment chapters in international trade agreements, is to protect foreign investments, it is difficult to understand why intellectual property rights should receive investment protection when foreign investors have not made any investment in the relevant host states.[85]

79. Dreyfuss and Frankel, *supra* note 72, at 566.
80. Yu, 'Crossfertilizing ISDS with TRIPS', *supra* note 36, at 337–338; Yu, *supra* note 8, at 872–873.
81. Dreyfuss and Frankel, *supra* note 72, at 589.
82. Okediji, *supra* note 76, at 1122.
83. *Ibid.* at 1125.
84. Peter K. Yu, 'Foreword', in Li Yahong (ed.), *Patents and Innovation in Mainland China and Hong Kong: Two Systems in One Country Compared* (Cambridge University Press, Cambridge, 2017), xv.
85. Rochelle Dreyfuss and Susy Frankel, 'Reconceptualizing ISDS: When Is IP an Investment and How Much Can States Regulate It', 21 *Vanderbilt Journal of Entertainment and Technology Law* (2018), 377; Yu, *supra* note 8, at 877–887.

IV. Summary

Taken together, these three observations have highlighted the many questions concerning the multiple pathways of multinational intellectual property dispute settlement. Because many of these questions may not emerge until all of these pathways have been holistically studied, policymakers and commentators should examine these different pathways alongside each other more often. Such a holistic examination will provide useful insights into the different ways to improve the overall dispute settlement environment.

F. CONCLUSION

With the proliferation of cross-border intellectual property disputes, a variety of mechanisms have been established for settling multinational intellectual property disputes. Each dispute settlement mechanism has its strengths and limitations. Together, the mechanisms have precipitated additional complications. While it is important to improve the environment for settling multinational intellectual property disputes, especially those involving local firms or host state governments, it is also useful to explore the benefits and drawbacks of allowing intellectual property right holders to make simultaneous use of multiple dispute settlement mechanisms. It is my hope that the comparative analysis provided in this chapter will enhance our understanding of not only the multiple pathways of multinational intellectual property dispute settlement, but also the complexity of the various disputes explored in this edited volume.

PART II:

DISPUTES INVOLVING INTELLECTUAL PROPERTY RIGHTS, NAMELY PLAIN PACKAGING LEGISLATION

CHAPTER 7

Intellectual Property as Investment and the Implications for Industrial Policy

Anselm Kamperman Sanders

A. INTRODUCTION

Bilateral investment treaties (BITs) increasingly serve to allow private parties who are transnational investors to address changes in public policy.[1] This leads to the question to what extent sovereign states have leeway to change public policy in relation to issues covered in trade deals.

Intellectual property is recognised as an investment under BITs. As a result, investors can take national governments to task over issues of direct and indirect expropriation of property. Expropriation has been defined in the *Tecmed v. Mexico* case as follows:

> Although formally an expropriation means a forcible taking by the Government of tangible or intangible property owned by private persons by means of administrative or legislative action to that effect, the term also covers a number of situations defined as de facto expropriation, where such actions or laws transfer assets to third parties different from the expropriating State or where such laws or actions deprive persons of their ownership over such assets, without allocating such assets to third parties or to the Government.[2]

This quote already makes clear that it is hard to distinguish between direct and indirect expropriation, but what actionable acts have in common is that these acts

1. C. Correa, *Bilateral Investment Agreements: Agents of new global standards for the protection of intellectual property rights?* (GRAIN, 2004), online: < www.grain.org >, at 3.
2. *Tecnicas Medioambientales Tecmed S.A. v. United Mexican States*, ICSID Case No. ARB(AF)/00/2, Online: < icsidfiles.worldbank.org/icsid/ICSIDBLOBS/OnlineAwards/C3785/DC4872_En.pdf >, para. 113.

may arguably be a breach of Fair and Equitable Treatment (FET) obligations, which includes any diminishment of the value of an investment contrary to legitimate expectations of the investor.[3] In this context, it is not necessary for there to be an actual transfer of ownership. In *Waste Management v. Mexico* award it was stated that:

> An indirect expropriation is still a taking of property. By contrast, where a measure tantamount to an expropriation is alleged, there may have been no actual transfer, taking or loss of property by any person or entity, but rather an effect on property, which makes formal distinctions of ownership irrelevant.[4]

Contrary to the multilateral trading system's dispute settlement system, Investor-State Dispute Settlement (ISDS) cases are adjudicated by arbitration, often under ICSID or UNCITRAL arbitration rules.[5] The arbitrators are not appointed judges, but professional lawyers who act as representative of parties one day, and as arbitrator the next.

Issues of "expropriation of property" or "diminishment of investments" can also be adjudicated by national (constitutional) courts. ISDS then often leads to a "second bite of the cherry" for undertakings. The cost of litigation is burdensome for states with limited capacity. The case of *Philip Morris v. Uruguay*[6] lasted from 2010 to 2016. In it Philip Morris sought USD 25 million in compensation from Uruguay over introduction of plain packaging tobacco legislation.

In developed nations, public policy decisions may also become subject to ISDS and raise serious public concern. In the case of *Ely Lily v. Canada,*[7] the Canadian patent office adopted a strict(er) application of the "promise doctrine" - which holds that if a patent describes a particular utility but fails to deliver on it, then the patent is invalid. Two of Eli Lily's patents were affected, and it brought action against the Government of Canada under NAFTA arguing that a dramatic change in the law creating the promise doctrine upset its legitimate expectations and that the doctrine was arbitrary and discriminatory.[8] The Tribunal was of the opinion that

---

3. See *Vattenfall AB and others v. Federal Republic of Germany* (ICSID Case No. ARB/12/12), an investor's response to the "Energiewende". See, however, CJEU Case C-284/16 *Slovak Republic v. Achmea*, 6 March 2018, ECLI:EU:C:2018:158:
   "Articles 267 and 344 TFEU must be interpreted as precluding a provision in an international agreement concluded between Member States, such as Article 8 of the Agreement on encouragement and reciprocal protection of investments between the Kingdom of the Netherlands and the Czech and Slovak Federative Republic, under which an investor from one of those Member States may, in the event of a dispute concerning investments in the other Member State, bring proceedings against the latter Member State before an arbitral tribunal whose jurisdiction that Member State has undertaken to accept."
   See also chapter 1 where this issue is addressed further.
4. *Waste Management, Inc. v. United Mexican States*, ICSID Case No. ARB(AF)/00/3, Online: <www.italaw.com/sites/default/files/case-documents/ita0900.pdf>, para. 143.
5. See the tobacco dispute over plain packaging legislation: *Philip Morris Asia Limited v. the Commonwealth of Australia*, (UNCITRAL PCA Case No. 2012-12).
6. *Philip Morris v. Uruguay* (ICSID Case No. ARB/10/7).
7. *Ely Lily v. Canada* NAFTA (ICSID Case No. UNCT/14/2).
8. See M. Seelig, 'Can Patent Revocation or Invalidation Constitute a Form of Expropriation?', 6(2) *Transnational Dispute Management* (2009). Online: <www.transnational-dispute-management.com/article.asp?key=1453>, who argues that post-grant legislative change in (in)validity rules should be assessed by a arbitral tribunal "with a high degree of scrutiny".

the patent law's utility requirement has been subject to gradual development and incremental change, which did not constitute a sudden and dramatic change in law. In addition, the arguments of arbitrary of discriminatory treatment were dismissed. The promise doctrine allows inventors to obtain a patent prior to the demonstration that an invention is useful, based on a sound predictions basis, meaning that the promise doctrine is not unpredictable if such predictions cannot be substantiated. In other words, the ball is entirely in the court of the applicant and the way in which the patentee chooses to present its application. Eli Lilly also argued that there is a causal relationship between the promise doctrine and higher invalidity rates in the pharmaceutical industry. Eli Lilly's expert was, however, not able to substantiate this argument, which was then dismissed. Although Eli Lilly lost the case, it did raise some serious questions on the freedom of states to change IP policy.[9]

This contribution addresses the question to what extent IPRs can be considered investments, and which implications this has for the nature and scope of intangible property.

B. INTELLECTUAL ASSETS AS PROPERTY – BUT DO THEY EQUAL INVESTMENT?

IPRs are by definition considered property and as such they are protected against interference by third parties. This becomes apparent from the WTO panel report in *EC – Trademarks and Geographical Indications*,[10] but even more so in the context of the European Convention on Human Rights (ECHR).

In the case of *Anheuser-Busch v. Portugal*, the European Court of Human Rights (ECtHR) held that the protection provided for by Article 1 of the Protocol No.1 to the ECHR,[11] which guarantees the right to property,[12] is applicable to IP as such.[13] This

9. R. Okediji, 'Is Intellectual Property "Investment"? Eli Lilly v. Canada and the International Intellectual Property System', 35 *University of Pennsylvania Journal of International Law* (2014), 1121–1138.
10. 1992 O.J. (L 208) 1–8.
11. *See* Monica Carss-Frisk, 'A Guide to the Implementation of Article 1 of the Protocol No. 1 to the European Convention on Human Rights', in *Human Rights Handbook* (Eur. Council, Human Rights Handbooks No. 4, 2001), < www.echr.coe.int/LibraryDocs/DG2/HRHAND/DG2-EN-HRHAND-04(2003).pdf > .
12. Convention for the Protection of Human Rights and Fundamental Freedoms Protocol 1 Art. 1, Nov. 4, 1950, 213 U.N.T.S. 222 (European Convention on Human Rights) [hereinafter ECHR]:

    > Every natural or legal person is entitled to the peaceful enjoyment of his possessions. No one shall be deprived of his possessions except in the public interest and subject to the conditions provided for by law and by the general principles of international law.
    > The preceding provisions shall not, however, in any way impair the right of a state to enforce such laws at it deems necessary to control the use of property in accordance with the general interest or to secure the payment of taxes or other contributions or penalties.

13. *Anheuser-Busch Inc. v. Portugal*, App. No. 73049/01, 44 Eur. H.R. Rep. 42, para. 72 (2007) (stating that "Article 1 of Protocol No. 1 is applicable to intellectual property as such," but in the case at hand decided that legitimate regulatory interests may justify interference with the right of property in line with the courts general approach to interference with the right

means that the owner of an intellectual "possession" is protected in respect of: (1) the peaceful enjoyment of property; (2) deprivation of possessions and the conditions thereto; and (3) the control of the use of property by the state in accordance with general interest. Inherent in the convention is the recognition that a fair balance needs to be struck between the demands of the general interests of society and the requirements of the protection of the individual's fundamental rights.[14]

Since 2000, the EU Charter on the Protection of Fundamental Human Rights[15] recognised similar principles that EU citizens can rely on. In *Scarlet Extended v. Sabam*,[16] the CJEU held that:

> The protection of the right to intellectual property is indeed enshrined in Article 17(2) of the Charter of Fundamental Rights of the European Union ("the Charter"). There is, however, nothing whatsoever in the wording of that provision or in the Court's case-law to suggest that that right is inviolable and must for that reason be absolutely protected. ... The protection of the fundamental right to property, which includes the rights linked to intellectual property, must be balanced against the protection of other fundamental rights.

Opinions on how this balance should be struck naturally differ, depending on one's perspective. In a European case involving challenges to restrictions on advertising, branding and trade mark communication in relation to tobacco products, *British American Tobacco*,[17] the CJEU held that restrictions on trade mark use requiring labels to display health warnings by taking up 30% of the front and 40% of the back of a cigarette package[18] amount to a legitimate restriction that still allows for a normal use of the trade mark. The tobacco companies had argued that there is a de facto expropriation of their property in the trade mark. A similar argument was made in the well-publicized constitutional challenge to the Australian Tobacco Plain Packaging

to property). *See also* Anselm Kamperman Sanders, 'Case Comment', Case No. 73049/01 of the Grand Chamber of the ECHR, *Anheuser-Bush Inc. v. Portugal*, 4 Eur. Human Rights Cases (EHRC) 433–437 (2007).

14. *See James v. the United Kingdom*, 8 Eur. H.R. Rep. A98, para. 46 (1986).
15. Charter of Fundamental Rights of the European Union Art. 17, Dec. 18, 2000, 2000 O.J. (C 364) 1, on the right to property provides:
    1. Everyone has the right to own, use, dispose of and bequeath his or her lawfully acquired possessions. No one may be deprived of his or her possessions, except in the public interest and in the cases and under the conditions provided for by law, subject to fair compensation being paid in good time for their loss. The use of property may be regulated by law in so far as is necessary for the general interest.
    2. Intellectual property shall be protected.
16. Case C-70/10 *Scarlet Extended v. Société Belge des auteurs, compositeurs et éditeurs SCRL (SABAM)*, 2011 E.C.R. I-11959.
17. Case C-491/01, *The Queen v. Secretary of State for Health, ex parte British American Tobacco (Investments) Ltd and Imperial Tobacco Ltd.*, 2002 E.C.R. I-11453.
18. Current requirements are even more stringent under Directive 2014/40/EU, of the European Parliament and of the Council of April 3, 2014, on the approximation of the laws, regulations and administrative provisions of the Member States concerning the manufacture, presentation and sale of tobacco and related products and repealing Directive 2001/37/EC, 2014 O.J. (L 127) 1, with Arts. 8–10 amounting to a "75% rule" in terms of the package having to display health warnings.

Act 2011.[19] The High Court of Australia in *BAT v. Commonwealth of Australia*[20] held that there was no acquisition of property that would have required so called "just terms" protection under the Australian constitution. Yet it is the Australian Tobacco Plain Packaging Act 2011 that has also produced two WTO challenges to tobacco plain packaging, by Ukraine,[21] and by a number of other states.[22] Although Ukraine suspended its proceedings on 28 May 2015, the litigation by Honduras, Cuba, Indonesia and Dominican Republic remains unaffected. These cases also raise questions on the remaining policy freedom that nation states have in regulating the use or exercise of IP in light of societal interests, such as public health.

This means that private parties wishing to complain about interference with their property entitlement or investment may have recourse under national law and under investor-state dispute settlement protection. Pluri-lateral and bilateral trade agreements cover the latter option by including investment protection agreements. In addition, private parties may be able to persuade a WTO Member state to act on their behalf.[23] Government actors, being the signatories to the WTO are the sole parties that can bring action before the WTO's Dispute Settlement Body (DSB) under the Understanding on Rules and Procedures Governing the Settlement of Disputes (DSU).[24] The main limitation to this last option lies in the fact that WTO panels can only authorise state-to-state retaliatory measures under the DSU. A private party cannot enforce any direct compensation for the loss suffered, nor is it likely that the facts of a specific individual case of wrongdoing can be assessed. Herein lies the reason for private parties to push for the inclusion of investment protection in bilateral agreements. The inclusion of investment chapters in free trade agreements allow for an investor to bring a claim against a country, provided he is recognised as an "investor" in the agreement, and can bring an action in relation to an "investment" covered by the agreement. Increasingly, intellectual property rights are expressly defined as "investments".[25] As *Peter Yu* noted,[26] this is reinforced by the fact that

19. *See* Tobacco Plain Packaging Act 2011 (Austl.).
20. *British American Tobacco Australasia Limited and Ors v. Commonwealth of Australia*, 2012 250 CLR 1.
21. Complaint by Ukraine, *Australia–Certain Measures Concerning Trademarks, and Other Plain Packaging Requirements Applicable to Tobacco Products and Packaging*, WTO Doc. WT/DS343/1 (13 Mar. 2012).
22. Complaint by Honduras, *Australia–Certain Measures Concerning Trademarks, Geographical Indications and Other Plain Packaging Requirements Applicable to Tobacco Products and Packaging*, WTO Doc. WT/DS435/1 (4 Apr. 2012 [hereinafter *Australia–Certain Measures Concerning Trademarks*); Complaint by Dominican Republic, *Australia–Certain Measures Concerning Trademarks*, WTO Doc. WT/DS441/1 (18 July 2012); Complaint by Cuba, *Australia–Certain Measures Concerning Trademarks*, WTO Doc. WT/DS458/1 (3 May 2013); and Complaint by Indonesia, *Australia–Certain Measures Concerning Trademarks*, WTO Doc. WT/DS467/1 (20 Sept. 2013).
23. As was the case in the WTO tobacco cases, *ibid.*
24. DSU Articles 1–4.
25. J. Mortenson, 'Intellectual Property as Transnational Investment: Some Preliminary Observations', 6(2) *Transnational Dispute Management* (2009). Online: < www.transnational-dispute-management.com/article.asp?key = 1449 > .
26. P. Yu, 'Investment-Related Aspects of IP Rights', 66 *American University Law Review* (2017) 829–910, at 841–842.

policymakers increasingly refer to intellectual property as either exported (from a developed country perspective) or imported (from a developing country perspective) investments. This obfuscates the fact that intellectual property rights primarily serve a public interest, namely to create competitive markets for innovation, cultural arts, and commerce. In a competitive market an intellectual property right, even if defined as an investment, is neither static, nor guaranteed, nor free from regulatory control or intervention based on public policy.[27]

C. INVESTMENT AGREEMENTS AND THE WTO STANDARDS

Bilateral free trade and investment agreements may provide additional protection to investors in relation to their investments that are then considered to be "possessions" in the state where such investments have been made. In order to understand the attraction of bilateral investment agreements, it is also interesting to see to what extent protection granted by means of such agreements changes the legal relations between WTO Members.[28]

This question is not easy to answer, as there seem to be conflicting decisions. The WTO Appellate Body in *Mexico – Taxes on Soft Drinks*[29] rejected the notion that parties can modify WTO obligations by means of an FTA, whereas the WTO Panel in *Peru – Additional Duty*[30] was not so categorically opposed. In the latter case, there are numerous references to Peru's freedom to maintain a price range system (PRS) under an FTA with complainant Guatemala. The WTO Panel, however, observed that the FTA in question was not yet in force, and that its provisions should therefore have limited legal effects on the dispute at hand. Peru's arguments in respect of the FTA were that, even assuming that Peru's PRS was WTO-inconsistent, Peru and Guatemala had modified between themselves the relevant WTO provisions to the extent that the FTA allowed Peru to maintain the PRS. Upon appeal, the Appellate Body stated:

> [W]e are of the view that the consideration of provisions of an FTA for the purpose of determining whether a Member has complied with its WTO obligations involves legal characterizations that fall within the scope of appellate review under Article 17.6 of the DSU.[31]

However, it also considered that WTO Members cannot modify WTO provisions such that these become WTO-inconsistent, even if these changes "merely" operate

27. L. Vanhonnaeker, *Intellectual Property Rights as Foreign Direct Investments: From Collision To Collaboration* (Edward Elgar, 2017), 26.
28. See in this an earlier version of the arguments in this section in A. Kamperman Sanders, 'Geographical Indications as Property: European Union Association Agreements and Investor-State Provisions', in I. Calboli and W. Ng-Loy, *Geographical Indications at the Crossroads of Trade, Development, and Culture* (Cambridge University Press, 2017), 168–185. Online: < doi.org/10.1017/9781316711002 > .
29. Appellate Body Report, *Mexico – Tax Measures on Soft Drinks and Other Beverages*, WTO Doc. WT/DS308/AB/R, (adopted 6 March 2006).
30. Panel Report, *Peru – Additional Duty on Imports of Certain Agricultural Products*, WTO Doc. WT/DS457/R (adopted 27 November 2014) (hereinafter Additional Duty Panel Report).
31. Appellate Body Report, *Peru – Additional Duty on Imports of Certain Agricultural Products*, 5.86 WTO Doc. WT/DS457/AB/R (adopted 20 July 2015).

bilaterally *inter partes* and not amongst all WTO Members. In particular, the Appellate Body held:

> We note, however, that Peru has not yet ratified the FTA. In this respect, it is not clear whether Peru can be considered as a "party" to the FTA. Moreover, we express reservations as to whether the provisions of the FTA (in particular paragraph 9 of Annex 2.3), which could arguably be construed as to allow Peru to maintain the PRS in its bilateral relations with Guatemala, can be used under Article 31(3) of the Vienna Convention in establishing the common intention of WTO Members underlying the provisions of Article 4.2 of the Agreement on Agriculture and Article II:1(b) of the GATT 1994. In our view, such an approach would suggest that WTO provisions can be interpreted differently, depending on the Members to which they apply and on their rights and obligations under an FTA to which they are parties.[32]

In the case at hand, this means that Peru under the FTA is only allowed to maintain a WTO-consistent PRS, which should meet the requirements of Article XXIV[33] of the GATT 1994, which permits certain specific deviations from WTO rules. All such departures require that the level of duties and other regulations of commerce applicable in each of the FTA members to the trade of non-FTA members shall not be higher or more restrictive than those applicable prior to the formation of the FTA.[34]

In *Turkey – Textiles*,[35] the Appellate Body held that the justification for measures that are inconsistent with certain GATT 1994 provisions requires the party claiming the benefit of the defence provided for by Article XXIV GATT 1994 lies in closer integration between the economies of the countries party to such an agreement. It is clear that Peru's PRS measure cannot be interpreted as a measure fostering closer integration; rather, it results in the opposite. Translated into TRIPS obligations, it must be noted that it does not have an equivalent to the relatively open norm of Article XXIV GATT, meaning that any policy freedom must be found within the confines of the TRIPS agreement itself.

In this context it should be noted that in the aftermath of the WTO Agreement, trade negotiations did not result in further progress in terms of establishing a veritable development policy.[36] Instead, developing countries began to oppose higher IP standards,[37] which at the WTO resulted in the Doha Declaration on TRIPS and

32. Additional Duty Panel Report, *supra* note 30, at para. 5.106.
33. GATT 1994 Art. XXIV(5) (providing that parties can form custom unions or free trade areas, subject to certain conditions being met).
34. GATT 1994 Art. XXIV(5)(a).
35. Appellate Body Report, *Turkey – Restrictions on Imports of Textile and Clothing Products*, WTO Doc. WT/ DS34/AB/R (adopted 19 November 1999).
36. A. Kamperman Sanders and D. Shabalala, 'Intellectual Property Treaties and Development', in D. Gervais (ed.), *Intellectual Property, Trade and Development* (Oxford University Press, 2007), 41–72.
37. ICTSD, *The Global Debate on the Enforcement of Intellectual Property Rights and Developing Countries* (ICTSD, 2009), with contributions by C. Fink, 'Enforcing Intellectual Property Rights: An Economic Perspective'; and C. Correa, 'The Push for Stronger Enforcement Rules: Implications for Developing Countries'.

Public Health.[38] Ultimately the WIPO Development Agenda,[39] the result of pressure from civil society and developing countries, is the only tangible set of recommendations that tied into the so-called Millennium Development Goals at the time. The Development Agenda has resulted in closer cooperation between the WTO and the United Nations agencies WIPO and the World Health Organization (WHO).[40] The Development Agenda remains relevant today in that it was established that WIPO member states should:

> Approach intellectual property enforcement in the context of broader societal interests and especially development oriented concerns, with the view that "the protection and enforcement of intellectual property rights should contribute to the promotion of technological innovation in the transfer and dissemination of technology, to the mutual advantage of producers and users of technological knowledge and in a manner conducive to social and economic welfare, and to balance the rights and obligations", in accordance with Article 7 of the TRIPS Agreement.[41]

Article 7 TRIPS is thus the operative provision to address the issue of policy freedom of states in respect of intellectual property in the context of WTO dispute resolution. In the context of investor-state dispute settlement, the question is whether this safeguard can be similarly applied. It can be argued that where such publicly stated norms are widely known, policies to address wider societal social and economic welfare cannot come as a surprise to investors holding IPRs, even if it affects them negatively. BITs, however, can be seen as instruments to counter the move for greater flexibility under the multilateral trading system by taking the dispute away from the national and multilateral sphere and into the realm of private disputes.

D. INTELLECTUAL PROPERTY AS TRANSNATIONAL INVESTMENT

A typical BIT comprises protection against expropriation without compensation and requires fair and equitable treatment (FET) of investments. Included in this package is the adherence to contractual and other legal obligations. Mandatory arbitration allows the investor to take direct action against host governments for any violation of the BIT.

The question is whether intellectual property rights are the type of subject matter suitable for inclusion in BITs. Given the non-physical nature of IPRs, it is not immediately evident that they ought to be included. Many non-physical assets, such as contracts, loan agreements, and other rights to payment have, for example, been

---

38. WT/MIN(01)/DEC/2 (2001), adopted 14 November 2001.
39. WO/GA/31/11 of 27 August 2004.
40. See *Promoting Access to Medical Technologies and Innovation – Intersections between public health, intellectual property and trade* (2012, WTO-WIPO-WHO).
41. The 45 Adopted Recommendations under the WIPO Development Agenda, Cluster F: Other Issues, 45. Online: < www.wipo.int/ip-development/en/agenda/recommendations.html#f >.

excluded.[42] Given the fact that the rationale for the protection of intellectual property rights is often said to lie in providing a property right that enables the holder to obtain a return on investment, the perception that it is indeed an asset that constitutes an investment seems to come naturally.

UNCTAD has made an assessment of the number of intellectual property provisions in international investment arrangements,[43] and noted that industrial and intellectual property rights are increasingly explicitly enumerated.[44] These assets are regularly described not just as "intangible property", but as "intellectual and industrial property rights", or as "copyrights, patents, trade marks, trade names, industrial designs, trade secrets and know-how; and goodwill". Also returns on investment, such as royalty payments or other fees that are subsequently re-invested, fall within the ambit of protected assets.

In order to qualify the extent to which intellectual property rights are protected, the definition of "investment" is of importance. For definitions of industrial property, it may for example be relevant to refer to the definitions provided in Article 1(2) of the Paris Convention, and then enumerate which of the rights listed are included, and whether in registered state when IPRs qualify as property, or also during the pre-grant phase. A failure to do so may result in the decisions of granting authorities, or changes in respect of examination guidelines to be subject to ISDS claims.[45] Applications for registered IPRs after all create an expectation of obtaining an exclusive right, but not a guarantee. In case protection is a right offered pre-grant, provisional rights[46] may give rise to the qualification of such and entitlement as an investment.

---

42. *Salini Costruttori S.P.A. v. Kingdom of Morocco*, Decision on Jurisdiction, ICSID Case No. ARB/00/4 (23 July 2001); *Joy Moning v. Egypt*, Award on Jurisdiction, Case No. ARB/03/11 (6 Aug. 2004); *Mihaly v. Sri Lanka*, Award, ICSID Case No. ARB/00/2 (15 Mar. 2002).
43. UNCTAD, 'Intellectual Property Provisions in International Investment Arrangements', UNCTAD/WEB/ITE/IIA/2007/1, online: <unctad.org/en/docs/webiteiia20071_en.pdf>.
44. L. Liberti, *Intellectual Property Rights in International Investment Agreements: An Overview*, OECD Working Papers on International Investment, 2010/01, (OECD Publishing, 2010) Online: <dx.doi.org/10.1787/5kmfq1njzl35-en>.
45. *Ely Lily v. Canada* NAFTA (ICSID Case No. UNCT/14/2).
46. See, for example in the US Patents Act: 35 U.S. Code § 154:

    (d) Provisional Rights.–

    (1)In general.–In addition to other rights provided by this section, a patent shall include the right to obtain a reasonable royalty from any person who, during the period beginning on the date of publication of the application for such patent under section 122(b), or in the case of an international application filed under the treaty defined in section 351(a) designating the United States under Article 21(2)(a) of such treaty or an international design application filed under the treaty defined in section 381(a)(1) designating the United States under Article 5 of such treaty, the date of publication of the application, and ending on the date the patent is issued–

    (A)

    (i) makes, uses, offers for sale, or sells in the United States the invention as claimed in the published patent application or imports such an invention into the United States; or

    (ii) if the invention as claimed in the published patent application is a process, uses, offers for sale, or sells in the United States or imports into the United States products made by that process as claimed in the published patent application; and

Since many BITs have wide and all-encompassing definitions of investment, such as "every kind of asset", or "rights with respect to ...", exclusions of subject matter from the definition of investment are often the exception, rather than the norm.[47]

In addition, bilateral and regional trade agreements may contain specific standards of protection of IPRs that parties have to adhere to. Nowadays these would be TRIPS-compliant, TRIPS-interpretative, or TRIPS-Plus[48] provisions.[49]

The TRIPS Agreement contains a definition of intellectual property. Article 1(2) TRIPS provides:

> For the purposes of this Agreement, the term "intellectual property" refers to all categories of intellectual property that are the subject of Sections 1 to 7 of Part II.

These are: 1) copyright and related rights; 2) trade marks; 3) geographical indications; 4) industrial designs; 5) patents; 6) layout-designs (topographies) of integrated circuits; and 7) undisclosed information. The list is, however, not exhaustive in that the incorporation by reference of the Paris Convention leads to the inclusion of trade names,[50] and options for alternative forms of protection provided by the TRIPS Agreement itself, such as *sui generis* plant breeder's rights instead of patents. In *US – Section 211 Appropriations Act* (2002), the Appellate Body of the WTO held that:

> The subject of Sections 1 through 7 of Part II deals not only with the categories of intellectual property indicated in each section title, but with other subjects as well. For example, in Section 5 of Part II entitled "Patents", Article 27(3)(b) provides that Members have the option of protecting inventions of plant variety rights by sui generis rights (such as breeder's rights) instead of through patents. Under the Panel's theory, such sui generis rights would not be covered by the TRIPS Agreement. The option provided in Article 27(3)(b) would be read out of the TRIPS Agreement.[51]

Less clear is the mention in the Paris Convention of utility models and protection against unfair competition. Article 11 PC mentions the temporary protection in conformity with domestic legislation and safeguards for priority of utility models only in the context of exhibitions. The protection granted by Article 10*bis* PC in respect of protection against acts of unfair competition contains a non-exhaustive

---

(B) had actual notice of the published patent application and, in a case in which the right arising under this paragraph is based upon an international application designating the United States that is published in a language other than English, had a translation of the international application into the English language.

47. Mortenson, *supra* note 25.
48. R Castro Bernieri, 'Compulsory Licensing and Public Health: TRIPS-Plus Standards in Investment Agreements', 6(2) *Transnational Dispute Management* (2009). Online: <www.transnational-dispute-management.com/article.asp?key = 1455>.
49. L. Liberty, *Intellectual Property Rights in International Investment Agreements: An Overview*, OECD Working Papers on International Investment, 2010/01, (OECD Publishing, 2010) Online: <dx.doi.org/10.1787/5kmfq1njzl35-en>.
50. Article 8 PC: "A trade name shall be protected in all the countries of the Union without the obligation of filing or registration, whether or not it forms part of a trademark."
51. Appellate Body Report, *United States – Section 211 Omnibus Appropriations Act of 1998*, WT/DS176/AB/R (adopted 1 February 2002), at para. 335.

mandatory list of prohibited acts, but lacks a clear definition of the ambit of such legislation. The TRIPS Agreement does not provide minimum standards in respect of these rights,[52] but it is clear that the principles of national and MFN treatment apply. Only intellectual property rights that fall completely outside of the scope of the Paris Convention, Berne Convention, Rome Convention and IPIC Treaty, and the TRIPS Agreement itself are not covered by the principle of national treatment in international treaties. For example, the EU Database Directive contains a reciprocity clause in respect of the *sui generis* database right.[53] For such a right to be part of the protected regime of assets, it would have to be expressly included in the BIT as an investment. It can be argued in this particular context that the definition of the *sui generis* database right lends itself to investment protection, as in order to qualify for protection, the maker has to show "that there has been qualitatively and/or quantitatively a substantial *investment* [emphasis added] in either the obtaining, verification or presentation of the contents to prevent extraction and/or re-utilization of the whole or of a substantial part, evaluated qualitatively and/or quantitatively, of the contents of that database."[54]

E. NATIONAL AND MFN TREATMENT

It is important to realise that once wide definitions of "investment", expropriation, or TRIPS-plus provisions have been included in a bilateral or regional trade agreement, principles of national[55] and most-favoured nation (MFN) treatment will apply unless the application thereof is qualified. This is most notably the case in relation to

52. Panel Report, *Indonesia – Certain Measures Affecting the Automobile Industry*, WT/DS54/R, WT/DS55/R, WT/DS59/R, WT/DS64/R (adopted 23 July1998) at para. 14.275.
53. Directive 96/9/EC of the European Parliament and of the Council of 11 March 1996 on the legal protection of databases, Article 11:
    Beneficiaries of protection under the sui generis right
    1. The right provided for in Article 7 shall apply to database whose makers or rightholders are nationals of a Member State or who have their habitual residence in the territory of the Community.
    2. Paragraph 1 shall also apply to companies and firms formed in accordance with the law of a Member State and having their registered office, central administration or principal place of business within the Community; however, where such a company or firm has only its registered office in the territory of the Community, its operations must be genuinely linked on an ongoing basis with the economy of a Member State.
    3. Agreements extending the right provided for in Article 7 to databases made in third countries and falling outside the provisions of paragraphs 1 and 2 shall be concluded by the Council acting on a proposal from the Commission. The term of any protection extended to databases by virtue of that procedure shall not exceed that available pursuant to Article 10.
54. Directive 96/9/EC of the European Parliament and of the Council of 11 March 1996 on the legal protection of databases, Article 7.
55. L. Choukroune, 'National Treatment in International Investment Law and Arbitration: A Relative Standard for Autonomous Public Regulation and Sovereign Development', in A. Kamperman Sanders (ed.), *The Principle of National Treatment in International Economic Law*' (Edward Elgar, Cheltenham/Northampton, 2014), 183–219.

WIPO-administered treaties, such the Paris and Berne Conventions.[56] In this sense there is a great divide between pre-1994 and post-TRIPS BITs. BITs referencing TRIPS also import the national treatment and unconditional MFN obligations contained in the agreement.

However, the TRIPS Agreement provides for exceptions or derogations from national [Article 3 TRIPS],[57] and MFN [Article 4 TRIPS] treatment, and multilateral agreements on acquisition or maintenance of protection [Article 5 TRIPS] concluded under the auspices of WIPO.[58] The post-TRIPS BITs will typically offer TRIPS-compliant exceptions to national and MFN treatment.[59]

The TRIPS provisions on national and MFN treatment all revolve around the notion that the protection of intellectual property should be non-discriminatory and prevent preferential treatment of one's own nationals or nationals of particular other states that is detrimental to other right holders. The term "protection" of intellectual property is defined in Footnote 3 to Article 3(1) TRIPS, in that it:

> shall include matters affecting the availability, acquisition, scope, maintenance and enforcement of intellectual property rights as well as those matters affecting the use of intellectual property rights specifically addressed in this agreement.

In this context one has to consider what is meant by the terminology "use of intellectual property rights". Intellectual property rights as such do not confer upon the right holder a right to use, but only a right to exclude others from engaging in an activity within the exclusive bundle of rights of the intellectual property right holder. Requirements of use are commonly associated with the maintenance of a trade mark registration.[60] These are covered, therefore, by the enumeration "matters affecting the availability, acquisition, scope, maintenance and enforcement of intellectual property rights". The Article 3(1) TRIPS reference to "use of intellectual property rights specifically addressed in this agreement", should then be read in context of each specific IPR in question. In relation to trade marks this means Art. 20 TRIPS, which addresses the extent to which the use of a trade mark in the course of trade can be made conditional on special requirements, form, or be otherwise limited.[61] In relation to patents, this pertains to the compulsory licensing regime contained in

56. C. Heath, 'National Treatment under the Paris Convention', in Sanders (ed.), *supra* note 55, 223–247; and R. Brauneis, 'National Treatment in Copyright and Related Rights: How Much Work Does It Do?', in Sanders (ed.), *supra* note 55, 248–285.
57. See in this respect A. Kamperman Sanders, 'National Treatment Under the TRIPS Agreement', in Sanders (ed.), *supra* note 55, 286–299.
58. Beneficiaries of and exceptions to National Treatment under Treaties Administered by WIPO can be found in the *Communication from the World Intellectual Property Organization, MTN.GNG/NG11/W/66, 28 February 1990 (see appendix).*
59. For an overview of various BITs incorporating TRIPS standards see Liberty, *supra* note 49.
60. See Art. 19 TRIPS.
61. Art. 20 TRIPS:

    The use of a trademark in the course of trade shall not be unjustifiably encumbered by special requirements, such as use with another trademark, use in a special form or use in a manner detrimental to its capability to distinguish the goods or services of one undertaking from those of other undertakings. This will not preclude a requirement prescribing the use of the trademark identifying the undertaking producing the goods or

Article 31 TRIPS, which deals with use without the authorisation of the right holder and the safeguards for the right holder in relation to such use. The scope of the "use of intellectual property" in the TRIPS Agreement therefore affects the way in which certain state actions can be viewed as expropriation under post-TRIPS BITs.

Similarly, there is the question whether the "use of intellectual property" is "specifically addressed" in the agreement. In this light, there is a school of thought that limits the scope to all that is covered by the agreement itself,[62] whereas another extend this to all that is "contained in the TRIPS Agreement or incorporated by reference".[63] Practically, however, this may not make much of a difference in this context, since the older IP conventions that are incorporated by reference[64] do not contain wider-ranging use-related provisions that could give rise to expropriation arguments. Conversely, as stated before, the exceptions to national treatment and MFN treatment are expressly provided for in Articles 3 and 4 TRIPS.[65]

F. CARVE-OUTS

Carve-out provisions for (indirect) expropriation may therefore be relevant in relation to certain acts. Acts of a predominantly administrative nature are typically the state-related actions that give rise to carve-out provisions. There are multiple administrative acts carried out and decisions rendered by bureaus of intellectual property that are closely related to the acquisition and validity of the right where decisions may be taken that can be framed as an expropriation. The abandoned OECD Multilateral Agreement on Investment contained the following:

> The creation, limitation, revocation, annulment, statutory licensing, compulsory licensing and compulsory collective management of IPRs, and the sharing of remuneration between different holders of IPRs are not expropriation within the terms of this agreement, to the extent that they are not inconsistent with specialised IPR conventions.[66]

The compulsory nature of collective rights management, and the sharing of royalties or remuneration is largely dictated by considerations of economic and distributive efficiency and can therefore be largely legitimized by public interest.[67] Still, the monitoring of such societies by competition authorities and is fundamental to the

---

services along with, but without linking it to, the trademark distinguishing the specific goods or services in question of that undertaking.

62. C. Correa, *Trade-Related Aspects of Intellectual Property Rights: A Commentary on the TRIPS Agreement*, (Oxford University Press, Oxford, 2007), 62.
63. D. Gervais, *The TRIPS Agreement Drafting History and Analysis* (3rd edn., Sweet & Maxwell, London, 1998), 183.
64. See Art. 2 TRIPS
65. See note 37 above and *appendix*.
66. OECD, 'The Multilateral Agreement on Investment: Commentary to the consolidated text' DAFFE/MAI(98)8/REV1 (22 April 1998), Online: <www.oecd.org/investment/internationalinvestmentagreements/multilateralagreementoninvestment.htm>.
67. See in this respect also L. Sermet, 'The European Convention on Human Rights and Property Rights', Human Rights Files, No. 11 rev. (1998, Council of Europe), Online: <www.echr.coe.int/LibraryDocs/DG2/HRFILES/DG2-EN-HRFILES-11(1998).pdf>.

functioning of the market. Exclusive membership clauses and restrictions of the mandates of such societies to the domestic territory effectively result in concerted practices[68] that not only frustrate multi-territorial licensing,[69] but also deprives holders of IPRs the means to effectively collect.

Involuntary use or compulsory licensing of patents for essential pharmaceuticals for least-developed country members to the WTO without production capacity presents a question on expropriation as well. The Doha Declaration on the TRIPS Agreement and Public Health[70] of 14 November 2001 offers all WTO members the autonomy to determine what constitutes a case of national emergency or other circumstances of extreme urgency, especially where public health is concerned. It also introduces a new provision (Art. 31*bis* TRIPS) to the TRIPS Agreement, which although not yet formally in force, is understood to be operational. These forms of compulsory licensing[71] are comprehensively dealt with in Articles 31 and 31*bis*[72] of the TRIPS Agreement.[73] Interesting in this light is the issue of lack of domestic production capacity that many countries face in the pharmaceutical sector, and which has been addressed in the Doha Ministerial Declaration on TRIPS and public health.[74] Despite the fact that, under strict conditions, compulsory licensing can be employed for the purpose of export of essential pharmaceuticals to least developed countries, it also displays that many IPRs in themselves do not constitute an investment. To be more precise, if an IPR is in force in a certain jurisdiction, but there is insufficient capacity to locally work the invention to meet domestic demands, can an investor honestly claim that a compulsory licence amounts to expropriation of an investment?[75] Without the supporting production and absorptive capacity for the related know-how in the jurisdiction, the patent right is merely a legal title to exclude others from working the patent. The compulsory license then also does not amount to a transfer of value, but rather to a limitation on the patentee's right to exclude.[76] Some sectors are subject to heavy state regulation and repeated policy intervention. In the field of pharmaceuticals this is even more pronounced than in other sectors. Regulatory measures, such as clinical testing and marketing approval not only add burdens, but also privileges in the form of supplementary protection certificates or

68. European Commission Decision Of 16-07-2008, Case COMP/C2/38.698 – CISAC
69. See the Digital Single Market policies on modernisation of the EU copyright rules, Online: < ec.europa.eu/digital-single-market/en/modernisation-eu-copyright-rules >.
70. < www.wto.org/english/thewto_e/minist_e/min01_e/mindecl_trips_e.htm >.
71. C. Gibson, 'A Look at the Compulsory License in Investment Arbitration: The Case of Indirect Expropriation', 6(2) *Transnational Dispute Management* (2009). Online: < www.transnational-dispute-management.com/article.asp?key = 1449 >.
72. Not yet in force – General Council (2005), *Amendment of the TRIPS Agreement*, WT/L/641, 1.
73. For a commentary see J. Malbon, C. Lawson and M. Davison, *The WTO Agreement on Trade-Related Aspects of Intellectual Property Rights* (Edward Elgar, 2014), 491–517.
74. WT/MIN(01)/DEC/2.
75. See B. Mercurio, 'Awaking the Sleeping Giant: Intellectual Property Rights in International Investment Agreements', 15(3) *Journal of International Economic Law* (2012), 871–915, at 911.
76. A. Taubman, 'Rethinking TRIPS: "Adequate Remuneration" For Non-voluntary Patent Licensing', 11 *Journal of International Economic Law* (2008), 927–970.

orphan drug status. In all, however, states have an interest in supporting innovation for the purpose of the most efficient treatment of patients. Price controls, regulation of competition, and (the threat of) compulsory licensing are therefore also part of the entire set of regulatory instruments. This means that for the purpose of investment provisions in chapters on intellectual property, sensitive public health related issues are increasingly excluded from ISDS altogether.[77] Even if they are not, however, one may question whether investors in sectors subject to controversy and heavy state regulation can claim that their legitimate expectations have been violated in case of an "indirect, or even direct expropriation".

I. Legitimate Expectations

As indicated above, Fair and Equitable Treatment (FET) in respect of transnational investment protection includes being able to take action in case of any diminishment of the value of an investment contrary to legitimate expectations of the investor. Legitimate expectations can be said to be raised at the time that a transnational investor made the investment. In *International Thunderbird v. Mexico*,[78]a NAFTA dispute conducted under UNCITRAL Arbitration Rules, the panel held that:

> [T]he concept of "legitimate expectations" relates ... to a situation where a Contracting Party's conduct creates reasonable and justifiable expectations on the part of an investor (or investment) to act in reliance on said conduct, such that a failure by the NAFTA Party to honour those expectations could cause the investor (or investment) to suffer damages.[79]

Expectations are, however, not set in stone, and are subject to change over time. In *Saluka v. Czech Republic*,[80] an investor-state dispute also conducted under UNCITRAL Arbitration Rules, the panel held:

> No investor may reasonably expect that the circumstances prevailing at the time the investment is made remain totally unchanged. In order to determine whether frustration of the foreign investor's expectations was justified and reasonable, the host State's legitimate right subsequently to regulate domestic matters in the public interest must be taken into consideration as well.[81]

In light of the fact that very few IP cases have been argued to date,[82] and with none of them successful, it is not that obvious which legitimate expectations in relation to

77. V. Vadi, 'Mapping Uncharted Waters: Intellectual Property Disputes With Public Health Elements in Investor-State Arbitration', 6(2) *Transnational Dispute Management* (2009), Online: < www.transnational-dispute-management.com/article.asp?key = 1456 < .
78. *International Thunderbird Gaming Corporation v. The United Mexican States*, NAFTA, Arbitral Award (26 January 2006), < www.iisd.org/pdf/2006/itn_award.pdf > .
79. *Id.* at 49, para. 147.
80. *Saluka Investments BV (The Netherlands) v. Czech Republic*, Partial Award, (Perm. Ct. Arb. 17 March 2006), < archive.pca-cpa.org/SAL-CZ%20Partial%20Award%20170306ba57.pdf?fil_id = 105 > .
81. *Id.* at 66, para. 305.
82. For an overview see H. Grosse Ruse-Khan, 'Guest Editorial for Special Issue on Intellectual Property and Investment Protection', 19(1) *Journal of International Economic Law* (2016),

intellectual property rights can arise beyond the internationally accepted minimum standards set by the TRIPS Agreement in an investor-state setting. Invalidation rates of patents are, for example, ranging from 50–70% in most jurisdictions.[83] A decision establishing invalidity is therefore something that any transnational investor must recon with. The value of intellectual property is therefore limited if there are no supporting ancillary investments in supporting infrastructure, knowledge base or revenue streams. A negative impact through state intervention can therefore be envisaged by acts tantamount to state induced expropriation by assignment of an IP title, or a complete arbitrary denial of recourse to enforcement only. As long as a state observes international obligations stemming from the TRIPS Agreement, or indeed its bilateral treaty obligations, it remains sovereign in the regulation of domestic matters in the public interest.

In light of the above, it is therefore interesting to consider which state measures or failures to act would potentially be actionable under the principle of expropriation or frustration of legitimate interests. Starting off with trade marks, it is of interest to consider what the essential functions of a mark are and whether investment results in exclusive rights that, where these rights are negatively affected by state measures, would result in such an actionable case. It so happens that the Court of Justice of the European Union has frequently addressed the question what specific interests the proprietor of a trade mark is entitled to protect. The most recent case to date that provides a complete overview of the functions of a trade mark is that of *Mitsubishi v. Duma*.[84] According to the CJEU, the function of a trade mark is not limited to that of the: "essential function of the mark which is to guarantee to consumers the origin of the product or service, but also the other functions of the mark, such as, in particular, that of guaranteeing the quality of the product or service, or those of communication, investment or advertising.[85] As regards those functions, it must be borne in mind that the essential function of a trade mark is to guarantee the identity of the origin of the marked goods or service to the consumer or end user by enabling him to distinguish the goods or service from others which have another origin."[86]

In this context the CJEU also considered the nature of the function of investment of the mark to include: "the possibility for the proprietor of a mark to employ it in order to acquire or preserve a reputation capable of attracting customers and retaining their loyalty, by means of various commercial techniques. Thus, when the use by a third party, such as a competitor of the trade mark proprietor, of a sign identical to the trade mark in relation to goods or services identical with those for which the mark is registered substantially interferes with the proprietor's use of its trade mark

87–90.

83. J. Henkel and H. Zischka, 'Why Most Patents are Invalid – Extent, Reasons, and Potential Remedies of Patent Invalidity' (2015 TUM School of Management, Munich/Center for Economic Policy Research, London) Online: <www.tim.wi.tum.de/fileadmin/w00bcy/www/Research/Publications/Henkel/Henkel_Zischka_Patent_Validity.pdf>.

84. CJEU Case C-129/17, 25 July 2018, *Mitsubishi Shoji Kaisha and Mitsubishi Caterpillar Forklift Europe v. Duma Forklifts NV*, ECLI:EU:C:2018:594.

85. *Ibid.*, at para. 34.

86. *Ibid.*, para. 35.

to acquire or preserve a reputation capable of attracting consumers and retaining their loyalty, the third party's use adversely affects that function of the trade mark."[87]

In all these situations, however, it is clear that the exclusive right that is available to the trade mark holder is to exclude third parties from using a sign that is the same or similar to that which the trade mark owner has registered. In this context the legitimate expectations of a trade mark proprietor as an investor are rather limited in that a positive right to use the trade mark is not part of the investment function, nor of the other above-mentioned functions of the trade mark.

State measures restricting the use of a trade mark in a certain format,[88] or even an absolute prohibition on use of certain marks would not likely lead to an actionable case. Bans on registration of certain trade marks, such as is the case for alcoholic beverages in Iran since the 1979 revolution,[89] may be harder to justify.[90] A complete ban on registration deprives the trade mark holder of the possibility to stop third parties from marketing counterfeit products.[91] The difficulty here lies in the fact that the trade mark holder will not have made any investments as it cannot even legally market its product in such a jurisdiction, and so there cannot be a legitimate expectation in respect of such a ban on trade mark registrations in respect of alcoholic beverages, or other products. It can be said that state sovereignty over moral codes of domestic conduct are recognized, also in business dealings and intellectual property matters.

If the country in question were a WTO Member, which Iran is not, denial of enforcement opportunities for a trade mark holder may be problematic. Such refusal of enforcement by a state is conceivable under the principle of justified retaliatory measures resulting from a WTO decision under the Dispute Settlement Understanding.[92] In such a case, the WTO Member prevailing in a dispute may be placed in a position to suspend rights and obligations under TRIPS as a result of commercial disputes before the WTO up to a prescribed monetary amount. This leads to a situation where traders from the losing WTO Member effectively pay for the lack of compliance of its home country through import tariffs. However, it is also possible that the trade measures result in a cross-retaliation affecting intellectual property rights held by

87. *Ibid.* para. 36, with reference to CJEU case C-323/09, 22 September 2011, *Interflora and Interflora British Unit*, EU:C:2011:604, paras. 60 to 62.
88. See *Philip Morris v. Uruguay, supra* note 6.
89. Iranian Patents, Industrial Designs and Trademarks Registration Act of 12 February 2008, Articles 32(b) and 46 contain Sharia-based morality exceptions, available at <wipolex.wipo.int/en/text/197776> (last visited 10 May 2019). As a result, it is not possible to file under class 33 (Alcoholic beverages) of the Nice classification, see the Iranian Executive Regulation of Patent, Industrial Designs and Trademarks Registration Law, available at <wipolex.wipo.int/en/text/325079> (last visited 10 May 2019). In light of the above, even reliance on Article 6*bis* of the Paris Convention to prevent counterfeit use of well-known trade marks would be problematic.
90. Iran is a member of the Paris Convention, but not of the WTO. Despite being granted observer status, the US has refused to support Iran's full WTO membership since 2007.
91. See <iranintl.com> 29 September 2018 17:08: "Nearly 300 People Poisoned with Counterfeit Alcoholic Drinks", available at <iranintl.com/en/iran/nearly-300-people-poisoned-counterfeit-alcoholic-drinks> (last visited 10 May 2019).
92. See the WTO Dispute Settlement Understanding (DSU). See also Article 64 TRIPS.

rightholders based in the losing WTO Member.[93] This may result in the non-payment if royalties due, as is often the case in relation to copyright works that are exploited, or even in case where there is a refusal to enforce intellectual property rights.[94] In the context of investment law, once can ask what amounts to investments in copyright works in a jurisdiction. Investments such as active distribution efforts rather than passive consumption of copyright works would have to be demonstrated. Similarly, investments in local content production, or investments in tours or performances of copyright works would have to be present. In spite of all this, WTO sanctions may still be levied against royalty income flows.

From the perspective of international investment law, one can argue that this is all part of the rule-based international trading system, meaning that the IP rightholder negatively affected cannot claim a legitimate expectation that its rights will never be affected.[95] What the IP rightholder can legitimately expect, however, is that the retaliatory measures imposed by a WTO Dispute Settlement Body (DSB) are proportionate to the non-compliance measure.[96] This means that such measures are limited in terms of the amount that the WTO may recover,[97] and do not result

93. R. Vargas Amaral, *Cross-retaliation in IP rights: Addressing Member Asymmetries and Compliance at the WTO* (Wolf Publishing, Nijmegen, 2012).
94. See in this respect WT/DS27 EC-Bananas III, in which Ecuador requested authorisation to suspend the obligations under Article 14 TRIPS on protection of artists and performers, producers of holograms and broadcasting organisations, geographical indications and industrial designs. On May 18, 2000 Ecuador was indeed authorised by the DSB to suspend concessions to the EC. Similarly, in WT/DS285 US Gambling, the DSB allowed Antigua to cross-retaliate to under TRIPS in an amount of USD 21 million, which was only not carried though due to a lack of domestic legislation that would effectuate the WTO's DSB authorisation. See also WT/DS267 US Cotton, where Brazil shied away from DSB-sanctioned suspension of concessions under the TRIPS Agreement and instead reached an mutually-agreed solution with the US.
95. Part I of TRIPS, where the national treatment and most-favoured nation provisions can be found (Articles 3 and 4) cannot be suspended. See Article 22.3(f) (iii) DSU of suspension of obligations in various sectors: "for purposes of this paragraph, 'sector' means: ... (iii) with respect to trade-related intellectual property rights, each of the categories of intellectual property rights covered in Section 1, or Section 2, or Section 3, or Section 4, or Section 5, or Section 6, or Section 7 of Part II, or the obligations under Part III, or Part IV of the Agreement on TRIPS;"
96. See WT/DS27 *Ecuador v. EC*: "The Suspension of TRIPS Obligations and the Relation with the Conventions Administered by World Intellectual Property Organisation (WIPO) ... It is not within our jurisdiction as Arbitrators, acting pursuant to Article 22.6 of the DSU, to pass judgment on whether Ecuador, by suspending, once authorized by the DSB, certain TRIPS obligations, would act inconsistently with its international obligations arising from treaties other than the agreements covered by the WTO (e.g. the Paris, Berne and Rome Conventions which Ecuador has ratified). It is, if at all, entirely for Ecuador and the other parties to such treaties to consider whether a specific form chosen by Ecuador for implementing such suspension of certain TRIPS obligations gives rise to difficulties in legal or practical terms under such treaties."
97. Note that although through valuation a price for an intellectual property portfolio may be established, this value may not be commensurate to the actual damages that the countervailing measures allow for. In effect, the only reasonably quantifiable measure is a suspension of the remittance of royalties until the total amount recoverable is reached.

in a permanent inability to exercise and benefit from the intellectual property rights affected.[98] This means that certain industrial property rights, such as trade mark rights,[99] do not lend themselves to measures amounting to a refusal to enforce. The effect of such a measure will after all be that the consumer may be confused as to the commercial origin of the goods, which would be a form of state-sanctioned counterfeiting activity that is likely to result in long-lasting if not permanent damage suffered by the trade mark proprietor.

When considering state measures suspending intellectual property rights, it is relevant to remember that some enjoy only a limited term of protection. Patent rights have a limited term with a maximum of 20 years during which the patentee can recoup investments made in the patented technology. A suspension, however temporary, may have long-term negative effects on the investments made. Furthermore, there may be negative spill-over effects on the competitive technological sector if investment expectations will have to be adjusted by other market participants that are active in the technology sector affected. When considering compulsory licenses in any given technology sector, a patentee must therefore be able to rely on the legitimate expectation that compulsory licenses are granted in accordance with the Paris Convention and/or TRIPS Agreement. Article 5A of the Paris Convention recognizes the Member States' freedom to grant a compulsory license to prevent abuses that may result from a failure to work the invention or a failure to work in on reasonable terms. This has traditionally been understood as amounting to a use of the patent to monopolize importation while also limiting the introduction and dissemination of the use of the patented technology in a country. Failure to work or insufficient working is thus a legitimate ground for state action. The problem, however, is that the Paris Convention does not provide a definition for "failure to work", leaving it up to Member States to decide whether domestic demand can be served by importation, or whether local production is required.[100] What is clear, however, is that when the patentee abuses its patent right, a compulsory license may very well be justified. Article 8 of the TRIPS Agreement exemplifies these grounds further in mentioning state measures for the protection of public health and the promotion of public interests in sectors of vital importance to their socio-economic and technological development. In respect of the interpretation of public health measures, however, WTO Members have even more leeway following the Doha Declaration on TRIPS and Public Health, which offers each Member the right to grant compulsory licenses and the freedom to determine the grounds upon which such licenses are granted.[101] Article 5A(3) of the Paris Convention makes clear that the compulsory license is the prime instrument

98. Article 22, para. 8 DSU states that a suspension must be temporary and must last only until the defaulting party complies with the Dispute Settlement Body's (DSB's) decision, until the measure found to be inconsistent with the WTO agreement is removed or until the parties find a mutually agreed solution to the dispute.
99. In addition, one can think of trade secrets and other badges of trade, such as trade names and geographical indications of origin.
100. See for example Supreme Court of India 12 December 2014, *Bayer Corp. v. Union of India* (Nexavar), available at < www.sci.gov.in/jonew/bosir/orderpdf/2118354.pdf >, rejecting Bayer's appeal to set aside the granted compulsory licence application No. 1 of 2011, *Natco v. Bayer*, Controller of Patents, Mumbai 9 March 2012, IIC 2012, 597.
101. WT/MIN(01)/DEC/2, 20 November 2001, para. 5(b).

to address patent misuse, as forfeiture or revocation of the patent are measures of last resort in case a compulsory licensing has, after a duration of two years, proven to be ineffective in remedying the abuse.

Given this timeline, there can also be a legitimate expectation that investors will not forfeit their patent right or have it revoked due to a state measure, unless it is preceded by a compulsory license. Moreover, prior to the grant of such a compulsory license genuine negotiations that sought to find a mutually agreeable solution to a failure to work, insufficient working, or a public health or other public interest measure must have been undertaken.[102] These regulatory measures may also include price controls for patented products,[103] especially where UN Member states have obligations in respect of providing universal health coverage to their citizens.[104]

Conversely, one can also ask the question whether a patent applicant is entitled to relief if a patent office is responsible for unduly long delays in granting a patent. In the Harvard Oncomouse case, a patent related to mice genetically engineered to have the propensity to develop cancer was filed on 24 June 1985 with a priority date of 22 June 1984. After an initial refusal by the Examination Division and an appeal in 1990,[105] the patent was granted on 13 May 1992.[106] Subsequently no fewer than seventeen oppositions were filed between December 1992 and February 1993 arguing that the invention would be contrary to "ordre public" or morality. The patent was maintained in amended form after oral proceedings. This decision was appealed, with a decision taken on 6 July 2004,[107] amounting to a remission to the Opposition Division with the view to maintain the patent in yet another amended form. Before any decision could be reached, however, the revocation of the patent was published on 16 August 2006 for failure to pay the fees. In short, it took the patentee close to 20 years, the full maximum term of patent protection, to receive a decision that was not even final. One can argue that the patentee can never be certain about the validity of the patent, especially in cases involving controversial subject matter such as in the Harvard Oncomouse case. The failure to deliver a decision within a reasonable timeframe arguably is tantamount a "denial of justice". However, the patent was granted and, despite the uncertainty during all the years of opposition, could

102. Article 31 TRIPS.
103. See in this respect also the actions of the World Health Organization's Fair Pricing Forum and its report on drug pricing; A. Hill, M. Barber, D, Gotham, 'Estimated Costs of Production and Potential Prices for the WHO Essential Medicines List', *BMJ Glob Health* 2018; 3:e000571. doi:10.1136/ bmjgh-2017-00057, concluding that "A wide range of medicines in the EML can be profitably manufactured at very low cost. Most EML medicines are sold in the UK and South Africa at prices significantly higher than those estimated from production costs. Generic price estimation and international price comparisons could empower government price negotiations and support cost-effectiveness calculations."
104. See UN Sustainable Development Goal target 3.8 and the 2008 Human Rights Guidelines for Pharmaceutical Companies in relation to Access to Medicines, available at <www.who.int/medicines/areas/human_rights/A63_263.pdf> (last visited 17 May 2019).
105. EPO board of appeal decision T 19/90 of 3 October 1990 (Onco-Mouse), ECLI:EP:BA:1990:T001990.19901003, holding that whereas animal varieties are excluded of patentability under Article 53(b) EPC, animals (as such) are not.
106. See EP 0169672.
107. EPO board of appeal decision T 0315/03 of 6 July 2004 (Transgenic animals/Harvard), ECLI:EP:BA:2004:T031503.20040706.

conceivably be enforced. In fact, many patentees also attempt to stall the delivery final decisions in order to maintain uncertainty in terms of the freedom to operate for competitors. The case could arguably be different if the patent office does not render a decision on whether to grant or deny the patent in the first place, for example due to enormous backlog in the processing of applications. Still, the question remains what the investment in the given jurisdiction is in those circumstances.

G. CONCLUSION

The protection of transnational investors and investments against direct and indirect expropriation through bilateral investment treaties encompasses intellectual property rights, which are treated as investments. When it comes to indirect expropriation the Fair and Equitable Treatment (FET) principle extends to the protection of legitimate expectations that the host state has raised for a transnational investor. However, an investor cannot expect these expectations to be set in stone. By their very nature, intellectual property rights, being instruments of innovation policy, are by definition subject to policy change. Furthermore, certain sectors of the economy face heavier government regulation than others. In sectors such as pharma, intellectual property rights furthermore operate in tandem with clinical and market approval, or even supplementary protection mechanisms. These markets are fundamentally driven by public interest concerns, which means that transnational investors cannot have high expectations that their intellectual property investment will remain subject to the same policy environment that was operational at the time the investment was made. The FET principle that lies at the heart of investor and investment protection is in this particular context nothing more than a guarantee against discriminatory and arbitrary expropriation.

In order to provide clarity on the scope of BITs, states would do well to articulate more clearly to what extent intellectual property rights are subject to protection, which sectors are excluded, or better still, which policy freedom remains within the sovereign realm of the state.

APPENDIX

Beneficiaries of and exceptions to National Treatment under Treaties Administered by WIPO Communication from the World Intellectual Property Organization, MTN.GNG/NG11/W/66, 28 February 1990

II. LIST OF EXCEPTIONS TO NATIONAL TREATMENT

(a) under the **Paris Convention**

6. The following exceptions to national treatment are contained in the Paris Convention:

- i) the provisions of the laws of each of the countries party to the Paris Convention relating to judicial or administrative procedure and to jurisdiction, which may be required by the laws on industrial property, are expressly reserved (Paris Convention, Article 2(3));
- ii) the provisions of the laws of each of the countries party the Paris Convention relating to the designation of an address for service or the appointment of an agent, which may be required by the laws on industrial property, are expressly reserved (Paris Convention, Article 2(3)).

(b) under the **Berne Convention**

7. The following exceptions to national treatment are contained in the Berne Convention:

- i) where a work is protected in the country of origin solely as an industrial design – and not (also) as a work of applied art, i.e., by copyright law – that work is entitled in another country party to the Berne Convention only to such special protection as is granted in that country to industrial designs – even though copyright protection is available in that country (Berne Convention, Article 2(7), second sentence, first part);
- ii) where a country not party to the Berne Convention fails to protect in an adequate manner the works of authors who are nationals of one of the countries party to the Berne Convention, the latter country may restrict the protection given – on the basis of their first publication in that country – to the works of authors who are, at the date of the first publication thereof, nationals of the other country and are not habitually resident in one of the countries party to the Berne Convention; if the country of first publication avails itself of this right, the other countries party to the Berne Convention are not required to grant to works thus subjected to special treatment a wider protection than that granted to them in the country of first publication (Berne Convention, Article 6(1));
- iii) in the country where protection is claimed, the term of protection shall not, unless the legislation of that country otherwise provides, exceed the term fixed in the country of origin of the work (Berne Convention, Article 7(8));
- iv) the right ("droit de suite"), enjoyed by the author, or, after his death, by the persons or institutions authorized by national legislation, to an interest in

any sale of the work - which is either an original work of art or an original manuscript of a writer or composer - subsequent to the first transfer by the author of the work may be claimed in a country party to the Berne Convention only if legislation in the country to which the author belongs so permits, and to the extent permitted by the country where this right is claimed (Berne Convention, Article 14ter(1) and (2));

v) in relation to the right of translation of works whose country of origin is a country - other than certain developing countries - which, having used the limited possibility of reservations available in that respect*, has declared its intention to apply the provisions on the right of translation contained in the Berne Convention of 1886 as completed by the Additional Act of Paris of 1896 (concerning the restriction, under certain conditions, of the term of protection of the right of translation to ten years from the first publication of the work), any country has the right to apply a protection which is equivalent to the protection granted by the country of origin (Berne Convention, Article 30(2)(b), second sentence).

(c) under the **IPIC Treaty**

8. The following exceptions to national treatment are contained in the IPIC Treaty:

i) any Contracting Party is free not to apply national treatment as far as any obligations to appoint an agent or to designate an address for service are concerned (IPIC Treaty, Article 5(2));
ii) any Contracting Party is free not to apply national treatment as far as the special rules applicable to foreigners in court proceedings are concerned (IPIC Treaty, Article 5(2)).

* Only four States have maintained such a reservation.

CHAPTER 8

Lilly v. Canada: Lessons for International Intellectual Property Law and Policy

Daniel J. Gervais[1]

A. INTRODUCTION

Although this chapter cannot provide a full picture of the case, it presents the aspects of the complaint filed by Eli Lilly & Company against Canada under Chapter 11 of the North American Free Trade Agreement (NAFTA) and the tribunal's findings that are most directly relevant for international intellectual property experts.[2] The case attracted a lot of interest in both international intellectual property law & policy circles and among Investor-State Dispute Settlement (ISDS) experts.[3]

ISDS and intellectual property had not really had a substantive face-to-face before this case, with the possible exception of the recent *Phillip Morris v. Uruguay* tribunal on trade marks and tobacco packaging.[4] ISDS, which emerged in NAFTA, is a mechanism meant to provide multinational corporations investing in a State a right to sue that State in a special arbitration process, provided of course the State is party to an investment treaty (such as bilateral investment treaty or BIT) or a trade agreement containing an investment protection chapter for direct or indirect

1. The author was an expert retained by Canada in the *Lilly v. Canada* arbitration. The views expressed and all mistakes are the author's own.
2. *Eli Lilly and Co. v. The Gov't of Canada* (hereinafter *Lilly v. Canada*), Final Award, 16 March 2017, (hereinafter the Lilly Award). Documents concerning the case including briefs submitted by all parties are available at < www.italaw.com/cases/1625 > (last accessed 27 June 2017).
3. North American Free Trade Agreement, 8–17 December, 1992, 107 Stat. 2057, 32 I.L.M. 605 (hereinafter NAFTA). *Lilly v. Canada*, ICSID Case No. UNCT/14/2.
4. *Philip Morris Brands Sàrl, Philip Morris Products S.A. and Abal Hermanos S.A. v. Oriental Republic of Uruguay*, ICSID Case No. ARB/10/7 (8 July 2016). Available at < bit.ly/2ud8yqP > (last accessed 27 April 2019). For details, see chapter 9 in this book.

expropriation (both types of agreements can be referred to together as international investment treaties (IIAs)).[5] It is more than likely that any given major State will be party to one or more IIAs because, according to UNCTAD, as of 2015 there were 3,304 IIAs, 3,304 agreements (2,946 BITs and 358 other treaties with investment provision (TIPs)).[6]

ISDS was pushed mostly by large US companies in NAFTA. According to a report by the powerful Industry Policy Advisory Committee (IPAC) , "the availability of binding arbitration dispute settlement should ease concerns about due process in Mexico."[7] The central concern that ISDS was meant to address was thus ostensibly to provide an alternative to domestic courts in obtaining remedies against a host government whose courts were not fully trusted by foreign investors.

ISDS clauses in post-NAFTA IIAs, as is further explained in chapters 2 and 3 of this book, is meant to protect investments generally and "intellectual property" specifically. IIAs often mention IP in the definition of "investment" – though this is not the case in NAFTA, at least not directly.[8] The inclusion of intellectual property in the definition of investment can, as Eli Lilly tried to do in the case under review, lead to a challenge to a state's intellectual property and innovation policy.[9] Indeed, a showdown between IP and investment law was to be expected sooner or later as investment protection clauses are now standard in IIAs.[10]

ISDS was and probably still is a good idea to attract foreign investment, especially in countries where the legal system may not be effective at imposing remedies against the state. ISDS is so widespread, however, that it may no longer signal a comparative advantage over states that do not provide it; instead, it might be more accurate to say that states that do *not* have investment protection (including ISDS) are at a comparative *dis*advantage.[11]

The case also highlighted how ISDS can mesh with a state's right to regulate its own public policy and to enforce human or fundamental rights within its borders. Not all limits on state sovereignty are undesirable of course. As Lord Millet noted

5. NAFTA, *supra* note 3. See Vivian H.W. Wang, 'Investor Protection or Environmental Protection? "Green" Development under CAFTA', 32 *Columbia Journal Environmental Law* (2007), 251, at 260.
6. See United Nations Conference on Trade And Development, World Investment Report 2016, at 101. Available at < unctad.org/en/PublicationsLibrary/wir2016_en.pdf > (hereinafter UNCTAD Report), at 101.
7. IPAC, Report on the North American Free Trade Agreement (14 September 1992), at 30. Online: < bit.ly/2uFPjGy > .
8. See e.g. the definitions and Art. 6(5) of the 2012 US Model Bilateral Investment Treaty at < www.state.gov/documents/organization/188371.pdf > . See also Susan K. Sell, 'TRIPS-Plus Free Trade Agreements and Access to Medicines', 28 *Liverpool Law Review* (2007), 41.
9. See Ruth L. Okediji, 'Is Intellectual Property "Investment"? *Eli Lilly v. Canada* and the International Intellectual Property System', 35 *University Pennsylvania. Journal International Law* (2014), 1121, at 1124.
10. See David R. Sedlak, 'ICSID's Resurgence in International Investment Arbitration: Can the Momentum Hold?', 23 *Pennsylvania State International Law Review* (2004), 147, at 147–149
11. For an in-depth discussion on the pros and cons of ISDS compared to other forms of legal redress, see chapter 6 of this book.

in a very different context (the Pinochet case): "No longer is international law a matter which concerns sovereign States alone. It marches with human rights law to protect individuals from State action. The world community has finally decided that the way a sovereign State treats its own nationals is not a purely internal matter".[12] But what happens when international law is used to *limit* the protection of human or fundamental rights that a state (or a supranational body such as the European Union) wants to protect (in the form of, say, a limit on an intellectual property right for public health purposes) because it is alleged to constitute an expropriation of the IP right? ISDS is meant to enforce investment protection and has traditionally had no clear doctrinal mechanism to acknowledge - let alone defer to - human rights and other public interest norms and associated polices that a state might wish to apply in its own territory.

Lilly v. Canada was heard at International Centre for Settlement of Investment Disputes (ICSID) - the forum of choice for NAFTA investor-state disputes - according to UNCITRAL Arbitration Rules.[13] ICSID is known for the confidentiality and effectiveness of its services.[14] Hearings are not public and calls for more transparency have been made, although memorials (briefs) and expert reports as well as tribunal orders are generally made available to the public on the ICSID website.[15]

The Award (decision) of the tribunal was made available in March 2017. All of Lilly's claims were rejected.[16] That said, the tribunal had no difficulty accepting that patents were investments.[17] It also accepted that acts of courts as judicial organs of the State could be scrutinized by an ISDS tribunal but it set the bar quite high, namely only if there was "clear evidence of egregious and shocking conduct".[18] This means that the Award does not necessarily bar future ISDS claims based on patent invalidations, a matter to which the chapter returns below.

---

12. Rt. Hon. Lord Millet, 'The Pinochet Case - Some Personal Reflections', in Malcolm D. Evans (ed.), *International Law* (2nd edn., Oxford University Press, Oxford, 2006), 10.
13. NAFTA, Art. 1120. ICSID was established by the Convention on the Settlement of Investment Disputes between States and Nationals of other States, 18 March 1965, 17 U.S.T. 1270. UNCITRAL is the United Nations Commission on International trade law. As of 1 April 2014, UNCITRAL added to its arbitration rules the UNCITRAL Rules on Transparency in Treaty-based Investor-State Arbitration. See < www.uncitral.org/uncitral/en/uncitral_texts/arbitration/2014Transparency.html > (last accessed 27 June 2017).
14. See Ibrahim F.I. Shihata, 'The Settlement of Disputes Regarding Foreign Investment: The Role of the World Bank, with Particular Reference to ICSID and MIGA', 1 *American University Journal International Law & Policy* (1986), 97, at 103.
15. See J. Anthon VanDuzer, 'Enhancing the Procedural Legitimacy of Investor-State Arbitration Through Transparency and Amicus Curiae Participation', 52 *McGill Law Journal* (2007), 681.
16. Although Lilly did defeat a time-bar (prescription) argument made by Canada.
17. See Lilly Award, para. 167 (referring to "the investments at issue in this arbitration (the Zyprexa and Strattera Patents)".
18. *Ibid.*, para. 224.

B. THE PATENTS AT ISSUE BEFORE CANADIAN COURTS

The two patents issued by the Canadian Intellectual Property Office (CIPO) to Eli Lilly applied to compounds known as atomoxetine and olanzapine, sold under the brand names Strattera and Zyprexa, respectively.[19] Atomotexine was sold as treatment for attention deficit/hyperactivity disorder (ADHD) and olanzapine for the treatment of schizophrenia.

The two patents at issue were not patents on new molecules. The notion of novelty, which is facially central to patent law's equilibrium, is used rather flexibly in the pharmaceutical area. The atomotexine patent was a "new use" patent on a compound that had already been patented twice. The patent on olanzapine was one of the compounds contained in a so-called "genus" patent that covered approximately 15 trillion benzodiazepine derivatives filed in 1975 and which led to the issuance of Canadian patent CA 1,075,687 on 15 April 1980[20]. As this patent was about to expire, between 1995 and 1998 Eli Lilly filed 16 separate patent applications alleging new uses for the compound, but ultimately abandoned them. In 1991, however, Lilly had filed a so-called "selection patent" claiming a selection from within the genus covered by the patent issued in 1980. The selection patent 2,041,113 was issued on 14 July 1998.

In both cases, litigation ensued between Lilly and Canadian pharmaceutical company Novopharm Limited (now Teva Canada Limited) and Novopharm challenged the validity of the patents, as is common in patent proceedings.

In the case of atomotexine, Novopharm challenged the evidence used to claim a new use for the compound using an" impeachment action" under subsection 60(1) of the Canadian Patent Act.[21] The trial court held that Lilly had failed to provide evidence of utility.[22] The only evidence submitted by Lilly was a small, short term study conducted at the Massachusetts General Hospital.[23] The court was "too small in size and too short in duration to provide anything more than interesting but inconclusive data."[24]The matter was appealed to the Federal Court of Appeal, which

19. The description contained in this section of the chapter is based on the author's knowledge of the case but confirmation can be found in Canada's Counter-Memorial (brief) filed on 27 January 2015, pages 11–28, available at <bit.ly/2rnGMaI> (last accessed 27 April 2019).
20. In 1980, patents in Canada were still protected for 17 years for the date of *issue*, which means that this patent expired on 15 April 1997. Canada has since moved, in keeping with the rule contained in the TRIPS Agreement, to a term of 20 years from the date of *filing*.
21. This is essentially asking the court for a declaration that the patent is invalid. *Novopharm Ltd. v. Eli Lilly and Co.*, 2010 FC 915.
22. *Ibid.*, at paras. 112–113. Utility is one of the three main patentability criteria in both Canadian and United States patent law. In most other jurisdictions, an equivalent (but not identical) notion of industrial applicability is used instead. Both are allowed under Article 27.1 of the TRIPS Agreement (and the footnote to that article).
23. See *ibid.*
24. *Novopharm v. Lilly, supra* note 21, para. 113.

basically confirmed the trial court's decision, and leave to appeal was then refused by the Supreme Court of Canada.[25]

The olanzapine proceedings were a more traditional infringement/defense of invalidity scenario but they took a number of twists and turns. The trial court first held the patent invalid on several grounds, namely, obviousness, anticipation, double- patenting, inutility, and insufficiency.[26] The Federal Court of Appeal remanded the case to the trial court on the issues of utility and insufficiency, and the Supreme Court of Canada refused Novopharm's leave to appeal the remand.[27] Interestingly, in opposing the leave to appeal, Lily argued that Canada's law on utility, which it would later claim changed "surprisingly" before the ISDS tribunal, was "well settled".[28] On remand, the trial court noted that "the promise of the 113 patent is that olanzapine is substantially better ('marked superiority') in the clinical treatment of schizophrenia (and related conditions) than other known antipsychotics, with a better side-effects profile, and a high level of activity at low doses".[29] The court considered whether there was, at the filing date of the patent, sufficient evidence of utility. Only one human study was disclosed in the patent and it showed no decreased side effects. That study included ten patients (not treated for schizophrenia) over four weeks, and then only seven patients completed the study.[30] The case went back up to the Federal Court of Appeal, which affirmed the trial court's judgment, and again leave was sought but denied at the Supreme Court of Canada.[31]

C. THE COMPLAINT

An ISDS case involving intellectual property might not be controversial if it were limited to an actual expropriation (e.g. state A takes the title to a patent or copyright belonging to company B to keep it or transfer it to a third party without adequate compensation). Actual expropriation is not the fact pattern in *Lilly v. Canada*, however. As explained above, the Lilly case relates to the invalidation of two Canadian patents on its drugs Zyprexa and Strattera (atomoxetine and olanzapine) by Canadian courts for failure to meet one of the core patentability criteria, namely the utility requirement.[32] The claimant (Lilly) contended that the adoption of a "new, radically different standard for determining whether inventions fulfil that requirement" (this is a reference to the "promise of the patent" doctrine discussed below) amounted to

25. *Eli Lilly and Company v. Teva Canada Limited*, 2011 FCA 220; leave to appeal refused, 34396 (8 December 2011).
26. *Eli Lilly Canada Inc. v. Novopharm Limited*, 2009 FC 1018.
27. *Eli Lilly Canada Inc. v. Novopharm Limited*, 2010 FCA 197, leave to appeal refused 33870 (10 February 2011).
28. See Expert Report of Ronald E. Dimock, 26 January 2015, para. 167, available at <www.italaw.com/sites/default/files/case-documents/italaw4138.pdf> (last accessed 27 April 2019).
29. *Eli Lilly Canada Inc. v. Novopharm Limited*, 2011 FC 1288, para. 124.
30. *Ibid.*, paras. 144–145.
31. *Eli Lilly Canada Inc. v. Novopharm Limited*, 2012 FCA 232, leave to appeal to SCC refused, 35067 (16 May 2013).
32. Claimants Memorial, at 1.

an "uncompensated expropriation, in violation of Article 1110 of NAFTA".[33] Claimant alleged that the promise of the patent doctrine violated the intellectual property chapter (Chapter 17) of NAFTA, which "requires Canada to provide patents to inventions, in all fields of technology, that are 'new, result from an inventive step, and are capable of industrial application [i.e., have utility]'", arguing that if "Canada can *unilaterally* reinterpret a core legal term in such a stark manner and with such severe consequences, legally operative words in NAFTA with internationally-accepted meanings could be susceptible to *unilateral* re-definition, such that NAFTA will no longer establish foundational requirements for patent protection".[34]

Put differently, Lilly was trying to use the investment chapter of NAFTA to challenge the compatibility of the application of a patentability criterion by Canadian courts (in which it undeniably received due process) with Canada's substantive IP obligations in the patent section of chapter 17 of NAFTA, which are broadly similar to the TRIPS Agreement.[35] The word "unilateral" used twice in the short quotation above betrays Lilly's thinking: a routine exercise of state sovereignty is framed here as an unacceptably "unilateral" measure.

A second strand of Lilly's argument was that the interpretation of the notion of utility by Canadian courts violated Canada's obligations to afford "fair and equitable treatment" (FET) to Lilly's investments under Article 1105 of NAFTA.[36] Specifically, Lilly alleged that the promise utility doctrine violated: (i) protection against arbitrary treatment (the doctrine is completely unpredictable and unreasonably difficult to satisfy); (ii) protection of legitimate, investment-backed expectations; and (iii) protection against discriminatory treatment.[37]

Lilly also argued that it "relied on Canada's patent law when it sought patent protection for Zyprexa and Strattera and launched those drugs in Canada" and that the patents had been issued "after a careful review by Canada's patent examiners in light of Canada's utility".[38] These last two arguments, it seems, could be rephrased as arguing that *any invalidation* by a court of an issued patent amounts to expropriation and that any significant change in the interpretation of a patentability criterion could also amount to expropriation under NAFTA.

D. CANADA'S COUNTER-MEMORIAL

In its Counter-Memorial, the Government of Canada noted, first, that Claimant received due process before Canadian courts (a fact not in dispute) and was simply disappointed with the outcome of two patent trials. That did not amount to a breach of the relevant obligations. Rather, according to Respondent, "[t]he threshold for a violation by a court of the minimum standard of treatment" is set "extremely high"

33. *Ibid.*, at 1–2.
34. *Ibid.*, at 5–6.
35. For a discussion see Expert Report of Daniel J. Gervais (26 January 2015) 18–20 (hereinafter First Report).
36. Claimant's Memorial, at 6.
37. *Ibid.*, 6–7.
38. *Ibid.*, 7.

under customary international law[39]. Specifically, Canada alleged that Claimant had failed "to prove that the theory of 'legitimate expectations' has become a rule of customary international law" protected by NAFTA Article 1105(1) and, moreover, that "regardless of its status generally in international law, it is a doctrine which fundamentally cannot be applied to judgments of the domestic judiciary acting in an adjudicative function of domestic statutory interpretation".[40]

On the issue of the alleged change in the interpretation of the utility requirement by Canadian courts, Canada countered on several fronts. It noted that even if the theory of legitimate expectations is now a rule of custom protected under Article 1105(1),

> Claimant could not have had a "legitimate expectation" of how a court would rule in the future in light of the law, facts, evidence and other considerations presented before the court at the time of challenge. To assert otherwise would give every disappointed litigant an automatic remedy in international law against any adverse domestic ruling that it "expected" to win.[41]

The United States, in a submission made (as NAFTA Parties not involved in a dispute can do under NAFTA Art. 1128) noted along similar lines that:

> The concept of "legitimate expectations" is not a component element of "fair and equitable treatment" under customary international law that gives rise to an independent host State obligation. An investor may develop its own expectations about the legal regime governing its investment, but those expectations impose no obligations on the State under the minimum standard of treatment. The United States is aware of no general and consistent State practice and *opinio juris* establishing an obligation under the minimum standard of treatment not to frustrate investors' expectations ... Moreover, the concept of "legitimate expectations" is particularly inapt in the context of judicial measures.[42]

Canada also argued that the "promise of the patent" doctrine was not new in Canadian law, as Canadian academics and a well-known Canadian expert retained by the government of Canada demonstrated.[43] A quote from a 1981 Supreme Court of Canada opinion should suffice to illustrate the strength of Canada's argument[44]:

> There is a helpful discussion in *Halsbury's Laws of England*, (3rd ed.), vol. 29, at p. 59, on the meaning of "not useful" in patent law. It means "that the invention will not work, either in the sense that it will not operate at all or,

39. Government of Canada Counter Memorial, 27 January 2015 at 94.
40. *Ibid.*, 115.
41. *Ibid.* See also Henning Grosse Ruse-Kahn, 'Litigating Intellectual Property Rights in Investor State Arbitration: From Plain Packaging to Patent Revocation', University of Cambridge Faculty of Legal Studies Research Paper Series, Paper No. 52/2014, (2014), 27, available at <papers.ssrn.com/sol3/papers.cfm?abstract_id=2463711>.
42. Submission of the United States of America, 18 March 2016, at 4–5.
43. See E. Richard Gold and Michael Shortt, 'The Promise of the Patent in Canada and Around the World', 30(1) *Canadian Intellectual Property. Review* (2014), 35; and Expert Report of Ronald E. Dimock 26 January 2015.
44. *Consolboard v. MacMillan Bloedel (Sask) Ltd.*, (1981) 1 SCR 504 at paras. 36 and 37 (Can.).

more broadly, *that it will not do what the specification promises* that it will do". ... The discussion in *Halsbury's Laws of England* ... continues:

> [T]he practical usefulness of the invention does not matter, nor does its commercial utility, *unless the specification promises commercial utility*, nor does it matter whether the invention is of any real benefit to the public, or particularly suitable for the purposes suggested. [Footnotes omitted.]

and concludes:

> ... it is sufficient utility to support a patent that the invention gives either a new article, or a better article, or a cheaper article, or affords the public a useful choice. [Footnotes omitted.]

Canadian law is to the same effect.[45]

The tribunal agreed with Canada on that point.[46]

Canada's Counter-Memorial also noted in this context that *even if* the promise of the patent doctrine was considered to change the interpretation of the utility criterion, changes in the interpretation of patentability criteria by courts in all three NAFTA parties are common, and sometimes significant.[47] This happened in several opinions of the United States Supreme Court for example.[48] Here again, the tribunal agreed.[49]

Lilly argued that the notion of utility in Canada should be defined basically the same way that it is in the United States (and therefore practically non-existent as a substantive threshold). Canada countered that (a) the US definition is not internationally binding on other nations and (b) that the notion of utility does different normative work (if any) in the United States because the notions of written description and enablement (which do not exist as such in Canadian law) perform essentially the same function as the Canadian notion of utility.[50] Relatedly, Lilly argued, as Valentina Vadi explains, that it faced "more arduous patent standards in Canada than a Canadian investor might face in other jurisdictions, such as the United States and Europe".[51] As Vadi also notes "this form of extraterritorial analogy is highly unusual in national treatment claims before arbitral tribunals, given the regulatory diversity of IP laws across the globe, and is likely not going to be accepted by the Arbitral Tribunal".[52] Indeed, the Tribunal opined that it was "difficult to see

45. *Ibid.* (emphasis added).
46. See Lilly Award, paras. 318–323.
47. US: Expert Report of Timothy R. Holbrook, 26 January 2015; Mexico: Expert Report of Hedwig Lindner, 26 January 2015.
48. See e.g. *Alice Corp. Pty. Ltd. v. CLS Bank Int'l*, 134 S. Ct. 2347 (2014); *Association for Molecular Pathology v. Myriad Genetics, Inc.*, 133 S. Ct. 21707 (2013); *Mayo Collaborative Services. v. Prometheus Laboratories, Inc.*, 132 S. Ct. 1289 (2012) (R-110); *Bilski v. Kappos*, 561 U.S. 593; and *KSR International Co. v. Teleflex, Inc.*, 550 U.S. 398 (2007).
49. See Lilly Award, at para. 310 (noting that "evolution of the law through court decisions is natural, and departures from precedent are to be expected") and para. 386 (referring to "incremental and evolutionary changes" in the interpretation of the utility criterion).
50. See Counter-Memorial at 5.
51. Valentina S. Vadi, 'Towards A New Dialectics: Pharmaceutical Patents, Public Health And Foreign Direct Investments', 5 *NYU Journal Intellectual Property. & Entertainment Law* (2015), 113, at 181.
52. *Ibid.*, 181–182.

how a comparison across jurisdictions can demonstrate a change over time within a single jurisdiction".[53]

E. THE CONNECTION BETWEEN CHAPTERS 11 AND 17

Canada disagreed both that there was a violation of the substantive intellectual property chapter (Chapter 17) of NAFTA and that the ISDS tribunal should consider that alleged violation to begin with. The patent-related provisions contained in that chapter, which was negotiated at about the same time as the TRIPS Agreement, are largely similar to those found in TRIPS[54]. Lilly's argument was not about investment protection proper but about the compatibility of Canadian law with obligations undertaken vis-a-vis other States (Mexico and the United States).

It is important to understand how Lilly couched its argument. Normally, a disagreement on the application of intellectual property norms contained in the TRIPS Agreement or NAFTA would be subject to a state-to-state dispute under the relevant agreement.[55] ISDS in this context was viewed as a way to achieve indirectly what a corporation cannot do directly (because it cannot convince its host state to file a WTO case).[56] Lilly's argument hung on a provision in NAFTA that seems to exclude precisely this type of situation from the purview of investor-state disputes. That provision is Article 1110(7), which reads as follows:

> This Article [investor-state arbitration] does not apply to the issuance of compulsory licenses granted in relation to intellectual property rights, or to the revocation, limitation or creation of intellectual property rights, *to the extent*

53. Lilly Award, at para. 377.
54. TRIPS Agreement Arts. 27–34. First Report at paras. 18–20.
55. For NAFTA, this is provided under chapter 20, and specially Art. 2004, which provides in part that "the dispute settlement provisions of this Chapter shall apply with respect to the avoidance or settlement of all disputes between the Parties regarding the interpretation or application of this Agreement". See Laurinda L. Hicks and James R. Holbein, 'Convergence of National Intellectual Property Norms in International Trading Agreements', 12 *American University Journal of International Law & Policy* (1997), 769, at 799–800.
The TRIPS Agreement provides that disputes between WTO Members shall be settled "under the provisions of Articles XXII and XXIII of GATT 1994 as elaborated and applied by the Dispute Settlement Understanding". TRIPS Agreement, art 64.1. See also Understanding on Rules and Procedures Governing the Settlement of Disputes (DSU), 15 April 1994, Marrakesh Agreement Establishing the World Trade Organization, Annex 2, Legal Instruments--Results of the Uruguay Round, 33 I.L.M. 1125. For a discussion, see Daniel Gervais, *The TRIPS Agreement: Drafting History and Analysis* (4th edn., Sweet & Maxwell, London, 2012), 669–675.
56. See Gaetan Verhoosel, 'The Use of Investor-State Arbitration under Bilateral Investment Treaties to Seek Relief for Breaches of WTO Law', 6 *Journal International Economic Law* (2003), 493, at 503–506. It is true that there have been few TRIPS disputes and that many did not provide relief for the corporations that had requested that the cases be brought. See Joost Pauwelyn, 'The Dog that Barked but Did Not Bite: 15 Years of Intellectual Property Disputes at the WTO', 1 *Journal of International Dispute Management* (2010), 389, at 393–395

> *that such issuance, revocation, limitation or creation is consistent with Chapter Seventeen* (Intellectual Property).[57]

Lilly's argument in this respect was that it had "demonstrated that Canada's measures were cognizable expropriations because they violated Canada's obligations in Chapter 17 of NAFTA (a basis for liability that Article 1110(7) contemplates)".[58] Basically, the argument rested on the fact that, if the investor can demonstrate that the revocation (or other measure) mentioned in Article 1110(7) was not "consistent with Chapter Seventeen", then it was fair game under Chapter 11 (ISDS).

Canada disagreed. It noted in its rejoinder that:

> The inference that Claimant is asking the Tribunal to draw is a logical fallacy, known as the fallacy of denying the antecedent. In essence, the problem with the reasoning is that it ignores the other reasons why something may or may not have occurred. The most classic example involves the following syllogism: "If it is raining, then the streets are wet". [ ] Applied to this case, the relevant conditional statement would be: "If a measure is consistent with Chapter 17, then it is consistent with Article 1110". From this, one cannot infer, as Claimant suggests, that because a measure is inconsistent with Chapter 17, it is inconsistent with Article 1110. There could be many other reasons why the measure is consistent with Article 1110. Claimant's interpretation perverts the logic of Article 1110(7) by transforming what was intended to be a shield for the NAFTA Parties in a sensitive area into a sword for disappointed patent litigants to wield.[59]

Mexico and the United States agreed. The US submission noted that:

> Article 1110(7) therefore should not be read as an element of an investor's claim under Article 1110(1) or as a jurisdictional hook that allows a Chapter Eleven tribunal to examine whether alleged breaches of Chapter Seventeen by a NAFTA Party constitute an expropriation of intellectual property rights. Nor should Article 1110(7) be read as an invitation to review a NAFTA Party's measures, each time they arise, for consistency with Chapter Seventeen.[60]

Article 1110(7) has a straightforward object and purpose, namely to exclude certain elements from an investor-state arbitration panel's jurisdiction. Indeed, had Lilly's interpretation been accepted, it would have seemed injurious to the object and purpose of the treaty. In contrast, Canada's argument that it is a shield meant to protect States and not a sword meant to help investors seemed inescapable. Put differently, it is not because a measure is inconsistent with chapter 17 that it is an expropriation or an FET violation. The shield in question is, however, limited in scope. If this is correct, an investor is thus free to try to show that the shield does not apply because the IP measure under scrutiny is inconsistent with chapter 17. This, in turn, means that the ISDS panel would have to engage on chapter 17 consistency. At the same time, as the US submission notes, that is not the purpose of the ISDS provisions in NAFTA. Perhaps the answer lies, to use evidentiary standards, in requiring that

57. NAFTA, Art. 1110(7). Emphasis added.
58. Memorial at 108.
59. Rejoinder at 99.
60. United States Submission, at 16.

an investor show a significant probability of inconsistency instead of a mere 51/49 threshold. In other words, to validly attack an IP measure of the type targeted by Article 1110(7) under chapter 11, the violation of chapter 17 should be fairly clear.

This approach of requiting a high bar to allow a chapter 11 to proceed in the case of compulsory licensing, revocation, limitation or creation of an IP right seems consisted with the tribunal's remark that the "decision of a court, or other judicial conduct, that falls so far below accepted minimum standards - in the words of counsel for Respondent, that 'had a result that was so surprising that propriety and competence had to be questioned' - might engage the liability of the respondent State. The Tribunal agrees with this acknowledgment by Respondent."[61]

This raises an interesting doctrinal question: can an investment tribunal disregard the fact that all parties to the "contract" called NAFTA agree on its meaning - in this case the meaning and intent behind Article 1110? After all, it has been said that "states which are bound by [a treaty] at the relevant time, own the treaty", which is consonant with Art. 31of the Vienna Convention, because the parties' understanding both illuminates the "object and purpose" of the treaty and may provide evidence of the subsequent practice of the parties.[62] True, it has also been argued that tribunals should ignore the parties' views when the text is clear, also on the basis of the VCLT, assuming of course that meaning is clear and unambiguous from the text itself.[63] The answer is that an ISDS tribunal is not formally bound by the parties' submissions, but it should think long and hard before ignoring them.[64] Indeed, the Tribunal did pay great heed to the American and Mexican submissions.[65]If the Parties provide convincing evidence of their intention *at the time of entering into the treaty*, then that should have significant force because, using Vienna Convention (Art. 31(1)) terminology, it provides powerful evidence of the object and purpose of the agreement. Evidence of uniform subsequent practice should also matter, and in practice it has, in an arbitral context.[66] This method of determining object and purpose and subsequent practice matters because, even though Article 32 of the Vienna Convention allows use of "preparatory work of the treaty and the circumstances of its conclusion" as supplementary means of interpretation,[67] an empirical analysis has shown that arbitral

61. Final award at para. 219.
62. Article 31(1) of the Vienna Convention on the Law of Treaties Arts. 31–32, 23 May 1969, 1115 U.N.T.S. 331 (entered into force 27 January 1980) provides that a treaty "shall be interpreted in good faith in accordance with the ordinary meaning to be given to the terms of the treaty in their context and in the light of its purpose". See UNCTAD, Interpretation of IIAs: What States Can Do, IIA Issues Note, No. 3, 3, UNCTAD/WEB/DIAE/IA/2011/10 (11 January 2012); and James Crawford, 'A Consensualist Interpretation of Article 31(3) of the Vienna Convention on the Law of the Treaties', in Georg Nolte (ed.), *Treaties and Subsequent Practice* (Oxford University Press, Oxford, 2013), 29, 31.
63. See Kenneth J. Vandevelde, 'Treaty Interpretation from a Negotiator's Perspective', 21 *Vanderbilt Journal of Transnational Law* (1988), 281, at 296.
64. See Margie-Lys Jaime, 'Relying Upon Parties' Interpretation in Treaty-Based Investor-State Dispute Settlement: Filling the Gaps in International Investment Agreements', 46 *Georgetown Journal of International Law* (2014), 261, 293.
65. Lilly Award, at para. 158.
66. See Iran–United States Claims Tribunal, Case No. B1, Interlocutory Award No. ITL 83-B1-FT (Iran–U.S. Cl. Trib. 2004)
67. VCLT, *supra* note 62, Art. 32.

tribunals rarely if ever have recourse to such supplementary means, especially the *travaux*.[68]

F. LILLY'S CHANGE OF APPROACH

In its Memorial, Lilly argued that, as "Robert Armitage, Lilly's former General Counsel, explains, the utility requirement is "*substantially harmonized* across jurisdictions".[69] The Author's initial report to the tribunal demonstrated in no uncertain terms that the harmonization argument was a red herring.[70] Every effort to agree on a definition of utility pre and post NAFTA, including in the Patent Law Treaty discussions, failed to produce consensus.[71]

In its Reply Memorial, Lilly changed its approach. It abandoned the harmonization argument, even denying, despite having made it very openly as can be seen above from the mouth of its own General Counsel, that it had ever claimed there had been substantive harmonization of patent law.[72] One of Lilly's experts hired in support of its Reply--a former WIPO patent official--argued instead that "the industrial applicability (utility) standard is, as further discussed below, applied in a manner that is *remarkably similar* around the world".[73] He further noted that "my experience has also taught me that there are equally important areas where *the practices of member states are consistent*. I disagree with Professor Gervais's attempt to place industrial applicability (utility) in the first category (of divergence) *rather than the second category (of consistency)*".[74]

The second report prepared by the Author of this chapter, in reply to Lilly's expert, quoted, *inter alia*, a report prepared by WIPO, indeed by the very Division of which their WIPO expert was director when the report was produced.[75] This WIPO document noted the following:

> Information received by [WIPO] members, reveals that *there is a wide range of differences among SCP members concerning the interpretation and practice relating to the "industrial applicability/utility" requirement*. It also shows that

68. See Baiju S. Vassani and Anastasiya Ugale, 'Travaux Préparatoires and the Legitimacy of Investor-State Arbitration', in Jean E. Kalicki and Anna Joubin-Bret (eds.), *Reshaping the Investor-State Dispute Settlement System* (Brill, Leiden, 2015), 150–171. One could contrast this approach with the more holistic view to the Vienna Convention interpretive process adopted by the WTO Appellate Body, for example in *United States – Continued Existence and Application of Zeroing Methodology: Report of the Appellate Body,* WTO doc. WT/DS350/AB/R (4 February 2009), at para. 268.
69. Memorial, at 132.
70. See First Report 7–12.
71. *Ibid.*
72. Reply Memorial, 11 Sept. 2015, at 5.
73. Expert Report of Philip Thomas, Sept. 2015, at 4.
74. *Ibid.* at 12 (emphasis added).
75. Lilly's expert noted in his report that "[i]n 1990, I joined the World Intellectual Property Organization ('WIPO') as a Senior Legal Officer. Over the next 20 years, I served in a range of senior positions, including as Director of the PCT Legal Development Division and Director of the Patent Policy Department. I retired in 2010 as Senior Director-Advisor (PCT and Patents)". *Ibid.*, at 2.

> the industrial applicability/utility requirement is closely linked, or sometimes overlaps, with other substantive patentability requirements, such as the sufficient disclosure (enablement) requirement, inventive step, exclusions from patentable subject matter and the definition of "invention".[76]

Unfortunately, the Tribunal neither discussed nor opined on the multilateral harmonization question.

G. REGULATORY FLEXIBILITY

A significant disagreement between the parties in the Lilly case concerned the flexibility of States to implement international obligations. Lilly's argument tugged directly on the "tension between the private interests of foreign investors and the regulatory autonomy of the host state".[77] Indeed, the issue of regulatory flexibility is often a major issue in the ISDS context. Recall that this was not a case of actual or direct expropriation; instead, the notion of *indirect expropriation* was used to challenge the judicial application of a patent doctrine to specific inventions, thus arguably amounting to a challenge by a private non-state actor to Canada's sovereign ability to regulate its substantive patent law and evolve its patent law through court interpretations. As noted above, multinational investors want to limit regulatory flexibility and ISDS can provide them with a powerful tool to do so. At bottom, this became an argument about state sovereignty. Canada's Reply Memorial noted the following in this respect:

> [A]s Claimant itself acknowledges, the NAFTA Parties have flexibility in deciding how to implement the obligations of NAFTA Chapter Seventeen. Accordingly, even if NAFTA Article 1709(1) required the NAFTA Parties to impose the specific "low threshold" utility standard Claimant alleges (it does not), it has nothing to say about how the NAFTA Parties are permitted to implement the requirement, particularly with regard to issues of evidence and disclosure.[78]

Parties to a treaty can agree to definitions that must then be applied in the event of a dispute according to the Vienna Convention rules, but there is no definition of "utility" in either NAFTA or TRIPS. Hence, Canada was correct to argue that NAFTA left to each Party "the flexibility to define and implement the specific legal standard under each of the enumerated criteria of novelty, non-obviousness or inventiveness, and utility or industrial applicability. It does not adopt any one particular meaning for any of the terms".[79] Canada's argument followed the Vienna Convention because the VCLT considers: (1) the ordinary meaning of the terms "useful" and "capable of industrial application" as understood in the patent law field in the NAFTA Parties; (2) the context of Article 1709(1); (3) the subsequent practice of the NAFTA Parties; (4)

---

76. WIPO, The Practical Application of Industrial Applicability/Utility Requirements under National and Regional Laws, April 2001, quoted in Second Report, *supra* note 49, at 15 (emphasis added).
77. Vadi, *supra* note 51, at 119.
78. Reply Memorial, at 64–65 (notes omitted).
79. *Ibid.*, at 65.

other relevant rules of international law; and (5) to the extent necessary to eliminate ambiguity, any relevant supplemental means of interpretation.[80]

Canada argued that none of these points supports Lilly's argument that a single or baseline notion circumscribing the meaning of utility or other patentability criteria (including those not named in NAFTA such as enablement) bound the NAFTA Parties or their domestic courts. The Tribunal agreed with Canada that ISDS tribunals were not courts of appeal of domestic courts but noted that courts are organs of the state and that egregious errors by a court could be subject to an ISDS proceeding, thus refusing a categorical exclusion. This is not altogether surprising. After all, one of the key justifications for ISDS is that it removes the "*home field advantage* that sovereigns may enjoy via their national court systems".[81] This concern informed the stance taken by multinational companies during the NAFTA negotiations, but it was in respect of Mexico, not Canada (which also had a pre-existing free trade agreement with the United States).[82] Yet allowing a private party who received full due process (which was not denied by Lilly) to use the ISDS process to reverse a reasonable court decision goes several steps beyond "removing home field advantage". It is, in effect, providing an appeal from domestic court decisions. This is clearly not what ISDS is meant to be.

This means that a court decision, to form the basis for a successful ISDS case, should normally be the result of a demonstrable absence of due process. Though a categorical exclusion of all cases in which the investor received due process is inconsistent with the award in the Lilly case, it seems hard to imagine a case in which a decision reached by court after genuine due process would be so egregious as to trigger either a finding of expropriation or violation of FET. The proper standard here, this chapter suggests, is the one proffered by Canada and accepted by the tribunal, namely "so surprising that propriety and competence had to be questioned".[83] The tribunal referred with approval to a previous and quite well-known ISDS case, *Glamis Gold*, which had noted that Article 1105 of NAFTA requires "an act that is sufficiently egregious and shocking – a *gross denial of justice, manifest arbitrariness, blatant unfairness, a complete lack of due process, evident discrimination, or a manifest lack of reasons* – so as to fall *below accepted international standards*."[84] The bar above which a NAFTA investor can challenge a domestic court decision is thus quite high indeed. In the case of an IP revocation, invalidation or compulsory license, it seems it must also show a probable violation of chapter 17 to pierce the "shield" of Article 1110(7).

80. VCLT, *supra* note 62, Arts. 31–32; Reply Memorial at 65.
81. See Timothy J. Feighery 'Rule of Law in the Emerging Development Agenda: On Finding the Optimal Role for Investment Treaties', 21 *Southwestern Journal of International Law* (2015), 297, at 299.
82. *Supra* note 7.
83. Lilly Award, at para. 219. See also Berk Demirkol, *Judicial Acts and Investment Treaty Arbitration* (Cambridge University Press, Cambridge, 2018), 186–187.
84. *Glamis Gold, Ltd. v. United States*, UNCITRAL, Award, 8 June 2009 quoted in Final Award at para. 222.

H. THE CONNECTION WITH HUMAN RIGHTS

Patents are rights to prohibit use of protected material (inventions). If seen as a form of property, they may benefit from fundamental or human rights to the protection of private property. This is so even in the absence of a viable market. To that extent, they are, like other property rights, rights to exclude. Yet, the denial of access to patented pharmaceuticals to patients who cannot afford them, when they, or their government, could afford those products at a generic rate (that is, without the patent rent) is sometimes seen as an affront to another human right, namely the right to health.

There is a dual basis for this view. First, the Preamble to the WHO Constitution provides that the "enjoyment of the highest attainable standard of health is one of the fundamental rights of every human being without distinction of race, religion, political belief, economic or social condition".[85] Then, the right to health appears in Article 12 of the ICESCR, which recognizes "the right of everyone to the enjoyment of the highest attainable standard of physical and mental health".[86] According to General Comment 14, this right to health requires access to at least certain medicines.[87] The right also rests on Article 25.1 of the 1948 Universal Declaration of Human Rights:

> Everyone has the right to a standard of living adequate for the health and well-being of himself and of his family, including food, clothing, housing and *medical care* and necessary social services, and the right to security in the event of unemployment, sickness, disability, widowhood, old age or other lack of livelihood in circumstances beyond his control.[88]

This creates a potential problem when making policy in areas such as patent protection of pharmaceuticals that affect public health. As Valentina Vadi notes, pharmaceutical protection reflects both private and public interests, namely the private interest of the patent owner (that is, exclusive rights for the term of the patent and possible extensions) but also the public interest.[89] The public interest portion is protected both by access to (new) life-saving or life-improving medicines and by the possibility afforded by the patent disclosure for other innovators to build on inventions disclosed to develop their own, including in markets where no patent is in force and in which there is thus no need to wait for the expiration of the patent.[90]

---

85. Constitution of the World Health Organization, 22 July 1946, 62 Stat. 2679, 14 U.N.T.S. 185. Preamble.
86. ICESCR, Art.12.
87. Committee on Economic, Social and Cultural Rights (CESCR), General Comment 14: The Right to the Highest Attainable Standard of Health (Article 12), para. 17, UN Doc. HRI/GEN/Rev.9 (Vol. I) (2000), < www.unhchr.ch/tbs/doc.nsf/(symbol)/E.C.12.2000.4.En >. See also Helen Keller and Lena Grover, 'General Comments of the Human Rights Committee and Their Legitimacy', in Helen Keller and Geir Ulfstein (eds.), *UN Human Rights Treaty Bodies: Law and Legitimacy* (Cambridge University Press, Cambridge, 2012), 116, at 132.
88. Universal Declaration of Human Rights, G.A. Res. 217, U.N. GAOR, 3d Sess., U.N. Doc. A/810 (1948).
89. Vadi, *supra* note 51, 121.
90. *Ibid.* On the value of patent information, see Sean B. Seymore, 'The Teaching Function of Patents', 85 *Notre Dame Law Review* (2010), 621, at 661.

A number of commentators had foreseen the looming conflicts. Professor Sornarajah suggested that conflicts between private and public interests are more likely in an ISDS context than in multilateral trade law.[91] Kate Myles wrote in the same vein that there is "little room for the consideration of the public interest in a regime so heavily weighted towards investor protection".[92] Then Professor Susy Frankel noted in that connection that,

> Investment tribunal arbitrators when making decisions (including the interpretation of the agreements at issue) are likely to focus on the function of IP as a set of property rights rather than as equally important parts of the international IP structure, which enables tailoring of those rights to reward innovation appropriately (rather than excessively) and to maintain regarding interests, such as when property rights need to be balanced with affordability and availability of medicines ... [T]hat does not require and should not result in detaching the property aspects of IP from its other functions and objectives.[93]

True, "property" in the patent field does not mean quite the same thing as in real property.[94] For example, property rights are sometimes described as absolute.[95] Intellectual property by contrast has inherent limitations (e.g. term) and exceptions (e.g. compulsory licensing) that are built into the system. They are "part of the framework of rights, rather than being something that gnaws away at them"[96] Those broader societal objectives related to innovation and access provide "both boundaries and the framework of the scope of the property rights".[97]

Then the grant of a patent right has a specific purpose, and that purpose, seen teleologically (from a policy perspective), is primarily an instrument to create an incentive that will be in the (private) interest of the patent holder but for the greater public interest in access to innovation.[98] The public interest component present to a certain extent at least in state-to-state dispute-settlement, is not the same when a party to the dispute is a multinational company. As Susan Sell notes, despite all

91. See Muthu-Cumaraswamy Sornarajah, 'Evolution or Revolution in International Investment Arbitration? The Descent into Normlessness', in Chester Brown and Kate Miles (eds.), *Evolution In Investment Treaty Law And Arbitration* (Cambridge University Press, Cambridge, 2011).
92. Kate Myles, 'Reconceptualizing International Investment law: Bringing the Public Interest into Private Business', in Meredith Kolsky Lewis and Susy Frankel (eds.) *International Economic Law and National Autonomy* (Cambridge University Press, Cambridge, 2010), 295, at 296.
93. Susy Frankel, 'Interpreting the Overlap of International Investment and Intellectual Property Law', *Journal of International Economic Law* (2016), 1, at 5.
94. See Jakob Cornides, 'Human Rights and Intellectual Property: Conflict or Convergence?', 7 *Journal of World Intellectual Property* (2004), 135, at 143.
95. See Robert P. Burns , 'Blackstone's Theory of the "Absolute" Rights of Property', *University of Cincinnati Law Review* (1985), 54, at 67.
96. Frankel, *supra* note 93, 14.
97. *Ibid.*, 16.
98. See Christophe Geiger, 'The Social Function of Intellectual Property Rights, or How Ethics can Influence the Shape and Use of IP Law' (Max Planck Institute for Intellectual Property and Competition Law, Working Paper No. 13-06, 2013).

the rhetoric of economic competitiveness, states are not firms.[99] Firms "only have to worry about one thing--shareholder value. The bottom line is always to earn a profit, and they have one clear goal--to increase shareholder value. Policymakers face a much more complicated array of issues and priorities".[100]

If patent owners use of ISDS to challenge regulatory measures adopted by host states can directly impact regulatory autonomy, including the state's ability to make and change innovation polices and to protect human rights, the risk extends to a possible disruption of "regulations governing everything from public health, energy, finance, education, privacy, and free expression. Under these provisions investors can attack domestic social bargains and, if successful, override legitimate sovereign regulatory discretion".[101]

In sum, in an ISDS context regulatory autonomy may be threatened due to the very fuzzy interface with both human rights law and the right to regulate. Panels in ISDS disputes can and often do consider human rights arguments put forward by a party as they would any other argument brought to their attention. Is that a sufficient guarantee? The answer is certainly not a clear yes.[102]

At its most basic level, the human rights balance argument is thus as follows: when the patent holder cannot reasonably hope to have a significant market in a territory for a product that has life-saving potential, there is no legitimate reason to prevent access to that product if someone (a public or private entity) is willing to produce it at a cost that the country can afford. There are legitimate concerns on the part of patent holders about re-exportation, and those should be adequately addressed, as they have been at the WTO.[103]

That being said, it must be emphasized that the problem of severe diseases affecting least-developed countries does not lie entirely with patents, far from it. In several African countries where patent protection would be available, antiretroviral drugs have not been patented. Least-developed nations have until 2033 to adopt pharmaceutical patent protection under WTO rules.[104] Problems often lie elsewhere, such as in the absence of a capacity of production and the lack of an efficient medical infrastructure and distribution networks. The latter can be solved, though with colossal efforts, by setting up distribution mechanisms, local clinics, etc. Concerns

99. Susan K. Sell, 'Remarks', 8 *American Society of International Law Proceedings* (2014), 317.
100. *Ibid.*, 318.
101. Sell, *supra* note 99, 317.
102. See Lone Wandhal Mouyal, *International Investment Law and the Right to Regulate: A Human Rights Perspective* 223 (Routledge, New York, 2016) at 9.
103. See World Trade Organization, Ministerial Declaration of 14 November 2001 on the TRIPS Agreement and Public Health, WT/MIN(01)/DEC/2, 41 I.L.M. 755 (2002), para. 6; and Marla L. Mellino, 'The TRIPS Agreement: Helping or Hurting Least Developed Countries' Access to Essential Pharmaceuticals?', 20 *Fordham Intellectual Property Media & Entertainment Law Journal* (2010), 1349, at 1388.
104. Some commentators believe that this flexibility is "merely academic" because many sub-Saharan countries comply with TRIPS even if they are under no obligation to do so. See Poku Adusei, 'Right to Health and Constitutional Imperatives for Regulating the Exercise of Pharmaceutical Patent Rights in Sub-Saharan Africa', 21:2 *African J International and Comparative Law* (2013), 250, at 262.

about interrupted treatments and the possible emergence of more aggressive viruses must be taken very seriously.

In some cases, patents do remain part of the obstacles that must be dealt with appropriately to ensure adequate access. Hence, the ripple effects of the clash between patents and human rights are far from over. The WHO, for example, has actively entered the field and broadened the discussion to the entire financing of pharmaceutical research, questioning the predominance of private, profit-driven enterprises. The WHO is not alone. The United Nations has generally taken a dim view of the interface between trade and human rights, especially when ISDS is factored in. A report presented in 2015 to the UN General Assembly concluded that ISDS "should be abolished as a fundamentally flawed system having adverse human rights impacts".[105]

I. CONCLUSION

Lilly lost the gamble it played when filing its CAD 500 million investor-state dispute against Canada. The case did however provide scholars and the investment law community with a unique opportunity to reflect on the balancing of intellectual property, investment, human rights and regulatory autonomy. This Chapter reviewed the arguments made by parties, the Award, and the normative and doctrinal gaps between intellectual property, human rights, and investment law.

The case made yet have a chilling effect on courts knowing that, despite its unambiguous loss, Lilly and others might bring new ISDS-based challenges to court decisions even if they received full due process. That said, the standard of egregiousness set by the Lilly panel - based on solid precedential foundations - discussed in this chapter is a high threshold indeed. Still, in the wake of Canada's win, the Supreme Court of Canada reversed the jurisprudence it has itself established on the notion of utility and ejected the promise of the patent doctrine from Canadian law, in a decision that specifically footnotes the Lilly Award.[106] Whether this was, even in part, motivated by Lilly's challenge is of course anyone's guess.

105. UN General Assembly, Promotion of a democratic and equitable international order: Note by the Secretary-General, UN Doc A/70/285 (5 August 2015).

106. *AstraZeneca Canada Inc. v. Apotex Inc.*, 2017 SCC 36 (30 June 2017). Referring to the argument made by the appellant in the case that the promise of the patent doctrine violated NAFTA and TRIPS, the court noted in footnote 1: "This argument was advanced prior to the final arbitration award in *Lilly v. Canada* rendered by the International Centre for Settlement of Investment Disputes under NAFTA (I.C.S.I.D. Case No. UNCT/14/2), March 16, 2017." The court nonetheless concluded as follows: "The Promise Doctrine in its operation is inconsistent with the purpose of s. 27(3) of the Act which calls on an inventor to "fully describe the invention and its operation or use". Thus, the Promise Doctrine undermines a key part of the scheme of the Act; it is not good law."(*ibid.*, at para. 51).

CHAPTER 9

The Tobacco Plain Packaging Legislation Before Investor-State Tribunals: *Philip Morris Asia v. Australia* and *Philip Morris et al. v. Uruguay*

Iveta Alexovicova

A. INTRODUCTION

Two prominent cases on tobacco control legislation with significance beyond these particular disputes have been brought and relatively recently decided by international investment tribunals – *Philip Morris v. Australia*[1] and *Philip Morris v. Uruguay*.[2] In both cases, the respondent state prevailed, be it on different grounds, and the tobacco giant Philip Morris lost on all points of importance. While the order to pay the costs of proceedings[3] must have been inconvenient even for a multinational corporation

1. *Philip Morris Asia Limited v. The Commonwealth of Australia ("Philip Morris v. Australia")*, PCA Case No 2012-12, Award on Jurisdiction and Admissibility of 17 December 2015 ("Australia Award").
2. *Philip Morris Brands Sàrl, Philip Morris Products S.A. and Abal Hermanos S.A. v. Oriental Republic of Uruguay ("Philip Morris v. Uruguay")*, ICSID Case No. ARB/10/7, Award of 8 July 2016 ("Uruguay Award").
3. In the dispute against Uruguay, Philip Morris was ordered to bear its own costs (almost USD 17 million), to pay all fees and expenses of the tribunal and the ICSID as administering institution (almost USD 1.5 million) and to compensate Uruguay's costs in the amount of USD 7 million (out of USD 10.3 million spent by Uruguay). The tribunal applied the "loser pays" principle in this case, using its discretionary power under Article 61(2) of the (applicable) ICSID Convention. It reduced the amount of Uruguay's costs to be compensated by Philip Morris on the basis of Uruguay's unsuccessful jurisdictional objections. – Uruguay Awards, paras. 583–590. The amount of compensation awarded to Australia was long unknown, just like all other costs and fees spent in relation to this

with an annual revenue higher than one of the states involved,[4] it is the significance of the loss of the battle against tobacco control legislation as such, with its world-wide implications, that must have hurt the most.

When the two requests for arbitration were filed, there were some concerns that (one of the) two tribunals could find in favour of Philip Morris.[5] Such an outcome was not inconceivable given the vagueness of at least one of the invoked standards of investment protection, the fair and equitable treatment (FET) contained in the relevant investment treaties and far from consistent case law, with some tribunals interpreting and/or applying this standard in an extensive manner also when it comes to regulatory measures.[6]

The fears have not materialised. Arguably, both tribunals were well-aware of the extremely high stakes in these disputes, with neither of them willing to put the entire investor-state dispute settlement (ISDS) system into a risk of an outright rejection that would have inevitably followed a decision even slightly favourable to the tobacco multinational. Criticism of investment arbitration decisions condemning states to payment of high compensation for legislation negatively affecting foreign investments, including those taken in times of (severe) economic crisis, would have been trivial compared to the outrage that would have arguably followed if either Australia or Uruguay were obliged to compensate a producer of a product as harmful

---

dispute. The Final Award Regarding Costs of 8 July 2017 redacted all relevant references to costs, fees and proportion of compensation. – Final Award Regarding Costs available at < www.italaw.com/sites/default/files/case-documents/italaw9212.pdf > . The Government of Australia itself refused to publicly disclose how much it spent on defending the plain packaging legislation against Philip Morris but it has been argued that the figure could be as high as AUD 50 million (USD 37 million). See Jarrod Hepburn and Luke Nottage, 'A Procedural Win for Public Health Measures', 18 *Journal of World Investment and Trade* (2017), 307–319, at 315–316. Very recently, however, in March 2019 Australia released unredacted excerpts of the Australia award regarding costs in the dispute with Philip Morris, following a request by Investment Arbitration Reporter made under Australia's freedom of information legislation. According to the award, the tribunal accepted as reasonable the amount claimed by Australia for its legal representation in the dispute standing at AUD 23 million (USD 16 million). The costs for the arbitration proceedings were above EUR 1.3 million. It is now also clear that Philip Morris was ordered to compensate 50% of costs incurred by Australia, including both its share of arbitration costs and its legal representation. See Investment Arbitration Reporter, Documents Downloads, *Philip Morris v. Australia Unredacted Excerpt of Costs Award*, award paras. 103–105, and Jarrod Hepburn, *Final costs details are released in Philip Morris v. Australia following request by IAReporter*, 21 March 219, both available at < www.iareporter.com/ > , last visited on 21 March 2019.

4. Financial Times has reported that annual revenues of Philip Morris International is more than USD 80bn across 180 countries, while Uruguay's gross domestic product is closer to USD 50bn. < www.ft.com/content/1ae33bc8-454e-11e6-9b66-0712b3873ae1 > .
5. Margaret Chan, *The Changed Face of the Tobacco Industry*, Speech delivered at the 15th World Conference of Tobacco and Health, Singapore, 20 March 2012, available at < www.who.int/dg/speeches/2012/tobacco_20120320/en/ > and cited in Matthew Rimmer, 'The Chilling Effect: Investor-State Dispute Settlement, Graphic Health Warnings, The Plain Packaging Of Tobacco Products, and the Trans-Pacific Partnership', 7(1) *Victoria University Law and Justice Journal*, 77.
6. See, for example, Federico Ortino, 'The Obligation of Regulatory Stability in the Fair and Equitable Treatment Standards: How Far Have We Come?', 21 *JIEL* (2018), 845–865.

as tobacco for losses (or, to be precise, lesser profits) incurred as a result of legislation aimed at the protection of humans health and life from such product, or even to withdraw the challenged legislation or refrain from applying it to the tobacco giant, as requested by Philip Morris in these two disputes.[7]

This is not to say that the tribunals were biased against Philip Morris' claims as from the start. This was not argued by the investors and is not the opinion of the author of this contribution (who could certainly not substantiate such a claim). However, it can hardly be doubted that the eyes of both supporters of tobacco control measures as well as opponents to the ISDS and foreign investment protection regime in general were watching the disputes carefully, with guns fully prepared to fire should the investor succeed against the legislation adopted for such important public purpose. It has also been argued that certainly the dispute brought against Uruguay, a country with a relatively small resources but sufficiently large tobacco market, were a testing ground for Philip Morris to learn how far it could go in using investment arbitration[8] in its fight against tobacco control legislation in general and, more importantly, to deter – or at least to delay – adoption of similar measures in other countries, thereby producing the so-called regulatory chill effect.[9] Even a temporary chill of a few years duration may well have been worth the effort and costs in exchange of years of unhampered advertising of Philip Morris' products in

7. In the Uruguay dispute, Philip Morris' first plea to the tribunal was to order Uruguay to withdraw the measures at issue or not to apply them to its investments. In the alternative, Philip Morris requested compensation of damages of almost USD 23 million plus compound interest. – Uruguay Award, para. 12. While in the dispute against Australia, Philip Morris did not ask for withdrawal of Australia's plain packaging legislation, it did request suspension of its enforcement against its investment as well, plus compensation for damages. Here, too, an alternative claim for compensation was included, with the amount of damages "to be quantified but of the order of billions of Australian dollars". – Australia Award, para. 8.
8. It should be noted that tobacco companies have been challenging tobacco control measures also in other fora, including domestic courts and other international fora. – See the other chapters of this book. An interesting analysis of domestic litigation is provided in Sarah L. Steele, Anna B. Gilmore, Martin McKee and David Stuckler, 'The Role of Public Law-based Litigation in Tobacco Companies' Strategies in High-income, FCTC Ratifying Countries, 2004–14', 38(3) *Journal of Public Health* (2016), 516–521. On international litigation, see for example Sergio Puig, 'Tobacco Litigation in International Courts', 57(2) *Harvard International Law Journal* (2016), 383–432.
9. Oft-cited Todd Weiler, '*Philip Morris vs. Uruguay*, An Analysis of Tobacco Control Measures in the Context of International Investment Law', *Report #1 for Physicians for a Smoke Free Canada*, 28 July 2010, < www.smoke-free.ca/eng_home/2010/PMIvsUruguay/Opinion-PMI-Uruguay.pdf >, footnote 54 on p. 17 and p. 36. See also Tania Voon, 'Big tobacco vs Australia's plain packaging', *Columbia FDI Perspectives*, 5 September 2018, < pursuit.unimelb.edu.au/articles/big-tobacco-vs-australia-s-plain-packaging >. Philip Morris itself confirmed in a reaction to the Uruguay award that "The arbitration concerned an important, but unusual, set of facts that called for clarification under international law, which the parties have now received". – < www.ft.com/content/1ae33bc8-454e-11e6-9b66-0712b3873ae1 >. This confirms that at least the Uruguay case was of a more systemic interest to Philip Morris than a recovery of damage cost by the challenged measures.

countries considering adoption of similar tobacco control measures, but waiting for the outcome of this dispute.[10]

From a legal perspective, the most interesting is to observe how the two tribunals got out of the potentially dangerous situation where, as put by Nottage, the "'big bad company' [claimed] against a government trying to pass a 'good law'",[11] given the fact that the disputes were brought under a legal regime set up to protect companies against state action with little, if any, explicit regard for other societal interests. While the two tribunals did, as they were supposed to, base their judgment on legal instruments and arguments, broader implications for the potential survival of the existing architecture for the protection of foreign investments through international treaties and international arbitration was clearly on the arbitrator's minds when interpreting and applying the relevant law. This chapter looks at the two disputes from this perspective.

B. *PHILIP MORRIS V. AUSTRALIA*

Initiated in 2010, *Philip Morris v. Uruguay* was the first of the two disputes against tobacco control legislation brought before an international investment tribunal, although the second dispute, brought a year later against Australia, was eventually decided first.[12] This may be due to the fact that Australia prevailed on (preliminary) jurisdictional grounds while the Uruguay case proceeded with the merits after Uruguay's jurisdictional objections had been rejected.[13] This is also why, although

---

10. The Guardian reported that the dispute against Uruguay delayed adoption of tobacco control measures in at least Costa Rica, Paraguay and New Zealand. – Cecilia Olivet and Alberto Villareal, 'Who Really Won the Legal Battle Between Philip Morris and Uruguay?', *The Guardian*, 28 July 2016, available at < www.theguardian.com/global-development/2016/jul/28/who-really-won-legal-battle-philip-morris-uruguay-cigarette-adverts > , last visited on 22 February 2019. It has also been argued that Uruguay itself faced pressure to relax the application of the measures challenged by Philip Morris after the initiation of the dispute. – 'Uruguay to Relax Tobacco Laws to Combat Philip Morris Claim', *Global Arbitration Review*, 28 July 2010, available at < globalarbitrationreview.com/article/1029479/uruguay-to-relax-tobacco-laws-to-combat-philip-morris-claim > , last visited on 22 February 2019.
11. Luke Nottage, 'Investor-state Arbitration Policy and Practice after Philip Morris v. Australia', *The University of Sydney – Japanese Law and Asia Pacific Blog*, 3 August 2011, available at < blogs.usyd.edu.au/japaneselaw/2011/07/isa_claim.html > , last visited on 22 February 2019.
12. While these are the only two disputes litigated before international investment tribunals, tobacco companies have resorted – and continue to do so – to many other fora to challenge tobacco control measures increasingly adopted by countries around the world, including national (supreme and constitutional) courts as well as the dispute settlement system of the World Trade Organization (WTO). For an overview of litigation against tobacco control measures world-wide, see the chapters of this book, and Tobacco Control Laws website, maintained by lawyers, that provides access to both legislation and dispute settlement decisions from around the world, incl. fact sheets and legal analysis: < www.tobaccocontrollaws.org/ > , last visited on 22 February 2019.
13. *Philip Morris Brands Sàrl, Philip Morris Products S.A. and Abal Hermanos S.A. v. Oriental Republic of Uruguay*, ICSID Case No. ARB/10/7, Decision on Jurisdiction, 2 July 2013 ("Uruguay Decision on Jurisdiction").

the 2015 jurisdictional award in *Philip Morris v. Australia* was undoubtedly a big relief, it was only with the award in *Philip Morris v. Uruguay* that states could relax and consider stringent tobacco control legislation without fear of ISDS proceedings. Nonetheless, given its own implications for ISDS, a brief account of *Philip Morris v. Australia* is worth mention.[14]

The dispute was brought by Philip Morris Asia Ltd. under the terms of the bilateral investment treaty (BIT) concluded between Hong Kong and Australia in 1993[15] and the Arbitration Rules of the United Nations Commission on International Trade Law (UNCITRAL Arbitration Rules)[16], with the Permanent Court of Arbitration (PCA) servicing the proceedings given the fact that the UNCITRAL Arbitration Rules are only a set of procedural rules with no machinery to administer them. This means that parties select an institution, such as the PCA, to provide administrative support for the proceedings. They also choose arbitrators serving on the tribunal. In principle, each party to the dispute appoints one member of the tribunal, with the third – presiding – member being appointed by an agreement of the two party-appointed arbitrators. In this dispute, the two party-appointed arbitrators failed to agree on the tribunal's presiding member and so, in accordance with the relevant rules, it was left for the PCA Secretary-General to do so.[17]

Before turning the merits of the case, the tribunal had to address a number of procedural issues Philip Morris and Australia disagreed upon, including the place of arbitration, bifurcation of proceedings (i.e. separation of jurisdictional and merits stage) and confidentiality.[18] With regard to the latter, arguably the most interesting among the three, the UNCITRAL Arbitration Rules provide very little guidance and stipulate only that both hearings and the award are confidential, unless both disputing parties agree otherwise.[19] While Australia was in favour of transparency for the proceedings in this dispute, Philip Morris argued against it referring to the need to ensure manageability of the proceedings and protection of confidential and

14. For an analysis of merits of the case, not addressed by the tribunal, see Tania Voon and Andrew D. Mitchell, 'Time to Quit? Assessing International Investment Claims Against Plain Tobacco Packaging in Australia', 14(3) *Journal of International Economic Law* (2011), University of Melbourne Legal Studies Research Paper No. 560, also available at SSRN: < ssrn.com/abstract = 1906560 >, last visited on 22 February 2019.
15. Agreement between the Government of Hong Kong and the Government of Australia for the Promotion and Protection of Investments, singed on 15 September 1993, available at < investmentpolicyhub.unctad.org/Download/TreatyFile/152 >, last visited on 22 February 2019.
16. Arbitration Rules of the United Nations Commission on International Trade Law, United Nations General Assembly Resolution A/31/98, available at < www.uncitral.org/pdf/english/texts/arbitration/arb-rules/arb-rules.pdf >, last visited on 22 February 2019.
17. Article 9 of the UNCITRAL Arbitration Rules and Australia Award, paras. 13, 16 and 17. The members of the tribunal were: an eminent and one of the most often appointed investment arbitrators Prof. Gabrielle Kaufmann-Kohler (appointed by Philip Morris), Prof. Donald M. McRae from Canada (appointed by Australia) and Prof. Karl-Heinz Böckstiegel from Germany, serving as the president of the tribunal.
18. See tribunal's Procedural Order Nos. 3–5 but also subsequent orders, available at < www.italaw.com/cases/851 >, last visited on 22 February 2019, and the reproduction of the procedural history of this case in the award, starting at para. 11.
19. Articles 28(3) and 34(5) of the UNCITRAL Arbitration Rules.

sensitive information. Using its discretionary power, the tribunal eventually decided that all hearings and meetings (incl. their minutes) will be kept confidential but that each party will remain free to disclose its submissions to the public, subject to appropriate reductions. At the same time, the tribunal's orders, decisions and awards were to be – and were – published by the PCA.[20]

The measures at issue in this dispute were the Australian Plain Packaging Act and implementing regulation enacted in 2011, prohibiting the use of logos, brand imaginary or other promotional text on tobacco products packaging and requiring packaging uniform in size, colour and format. Philip Morris argued that such plain packaging barred the use of its intellectual property on tobacco products resulting in a substantial reduction of the value of its investments in Australia.[21] Australia in turn rejected the claims on the merit and raised a number of jurisdictional objections, one of them successfully.[22]

The claimant in the case, Philip Morris Asia Ltd., is a subsidiary of a US multinational Philip Morris International Inc. (PMI) headquartered in New York, with subsidiaries and affiliates in various parts of the world, including Australia. In September 2010, PMI initiated a complex corporate restructuring of several companies within the PMI Group, resulting in Philip Morris Australia (then owned by Philip Morris group companies incorporated in Switzerland) being transferred to Philip Morris Asia (incorporated in Hong Kong) in February 2011,[23] only two months before the adoption of the legislation challenged in this dispute. Given the fact that Australia has no BIT with Switzerland but concluded one with Hong Kong, the corporate restructuring and, in particular, the transfer of PM Australia from Swiss companies to Philip Morris Asia opened the door for Philip Morris' legal action against Australia under its BIT with Hong Kong.

Concluded in 1993, the Hong Kong–Australia BIT belongs to the "old" generation of investment treaties much criticised for one-sided focus on foreign investment protection and notable ignorance of host state's regulatory autonomy to pursue other important policy objectives, such as public health or environmental protection. As most investment agreements of that generation, the BIT contains typical standards of foreign investment protection, including protection against (indirect) expropriation without compensation, the (most controversial) obligation of fair and equitable treatment (FET), the obligation of full protection and security as well as an umbrella

---

20. Procedural Order No. 5, part V. Decision, available at < www.italaw.com/sites/default/files/case-documents/italaw1216.pdf >, last visited on 22 February 2019. Interestingly, as noted by Hepburn and Nottage, despite pushing for transparency, Australia eventually did not make its submissions on merits public. – Jarrod Hepburn and Luke R. Nottage, 'Case Note: Philip Morris Asia v Australia', 18(2) *Journal of World Investment and Trade* (2017), 307–319, at 317; also available as Sydney Law School Research Paper No. 16/86 at < ssrn.com/abstract = 2842065 > or < dx.doi.org/10.2139/ssrn.2842065 >, 8.
21. Australia Award, para. 7.
22. The tribunal dismissed Australia's two other objections – illegality of the claimant's investment in Australia under the country's foreign investment laws and a lack of *ratione temporis* jurisdiction based on the argument that the dispute had arisen before the claimant's investment was made in Australia. – Australia Award, part VI.C and D.
23. *Ibid.*, paras. 141–143.

clause. Philip Morris alleged a breach of all these obligations[24] and while Australia was ready to defend its measures on merits, as mentioned above, merits of this dispute were not substantially addressed by the tribunal.

After rather lengthy proceedings of no less than 4 years,[25] in a relatively long award on jurisdiction the tribunal declared Philip Morris' claims inadmissible and declined to exercise its jurisdiction. The inadmissibility was based on the tribunal's conclusion that Philip Morris had engaged in an abuse of rights through corporate restructuring that led to the acquisition of Philip Morris Australia by Philip Morris Asia so as to benefit from the Australia–Hong Kong BIT. Disagreeing with Philip Morris that there was a sound business case for the restructuring, the tribunal considered an abuse of rights to be evidenced by the fact that this restructuring took place "at a time when there was a reasonable prospect that the dispute would materialise and as it was carried out for the principal, if not sole, purpose of gaining Treaty protection".[26] This approach is not unique in investment arbitration and is in fact in line with previous case law, although it has been argued that by requiring merely "a reasonable prospect" of the dispute materialising rather than its actual existence or something very close to it, the tribunal sided with less stringent arbitrators as opposed to those insisting on a "very high probability" of a dispute at the time of restructuring.[27]

In that regard it is worth noting that the decision was unanimously endorsed by all three members of the tribunal. While keeping in mind that - disregarding the governing rules and the administering forum - investment arbitration decisions carry no precedent weight and future tribunals may - and sometimes do - adopt different approaches towards similar or even identical issues (and situations), the unanimous support for the rejection of Philip Morris actions in the case against Australia may indicate that a "reasonable" rather than a "very high" prospect of a dispute may become the standard required for an abuse of rights objections of host states against investor's treaty shopping attempts in the future. This would seem more in line with a changing spirit in international investment law and arbitration since 2012, rebalancing host state's and investors' rights and obligations under international law.[28]

---

24. In addition, Philip Morris also claimed unreasonable impairment of the investment's use under Art. 2(2) of the BIT. All claims can be found in Written Notification of Claim Australia/ Hong Kong Agreement for the Promotion and Protection of Investments, submitted by Philip Morris to the Government of Australia on 27 June 2011, available at < www.ag.gov.au/Internationalrelations/InternationalLaw/Pages/Tobaccoplainpackaging.aspx >.
25. See the discussion of the remarkable length of the proceedings, see Hepburn and Nottage, *supra* note 20.
26. Australia Award, para. 588.
27. *Ibid.*, paras. 538–554. See also Hepburn and Nottage, *supra* note 20.
28. Note that the most stringent approach of "a very high probability" adopted by the tribunal in *Pam Rim* case and referred to by *Philip Morris v. Australia* tribunal dates back to 2012 - *Pac Rim Cayman Llc v. El Salvador*, ICSID Case No. ARB/09/12, Decision on the Respondent's Jurisdictional Objections, para. 2.99.

C. *PHILIP MORRIS V. URUGUAY*

As mentioned above, Philip Morris' defeat against Australia undoubtedly boosted the spirit of anti-tobacco lobby and policy makers. However, it was only the dismissal of Philip Morris' substantial claims in the dispute against Uruguay that is considered to have "significant implications for tobacco control in particular and public health more generally" confirming "the potential for public health measures to withstand legal challenge at the international level on the merits",[29] making *Philip Morris v. Uruguay* a landmark case. Together with the subsequent ruling of the World Trade Organization (WTO) on the consistency of Australia's plain packaging legislation with WTO law[30] where, just like Uruguay in the ISDS case, Australia prevailed on merits, the decision in *Philip Morris v. Uruguay* removed the arguable "chilling" effect of foreign investment protection law on other countries considering the adoption of similar tobacco control measures.[31]

I. Procedural Issues

The case against Uruguay was brought by three PMI subsidiaries under the terms of the bilateral investment treaty between Switzerland and Uruguay of 1988, in force from 1991.[32] Unlike the (subsequent) challenge of Australian plain packaging legislation, the dispute against Uruguay could have been – and was – brought under the terms of the Convention on the Settlement of Investment Disputes between States and Nationals of Other States (ICSID Convention)[33] pursuant to Article 10 of

---

29. Tania Voon, 'Philip Morris v. Uruguay: Implications for Public Health', 18(2) *Journal of World Investment & Trade* (2017), 320–331, at 321.
30. Panels Reports, *Australia – Certain Measures Concerning Trademarks, Geographical Indications and Other Plain Packaging Requirements Applicable to Tobacco Products and Packaging*, WT/DS435/R, WT/DS441/R, WT/DS458/R and WT/DS467/R (this is a single document constituting four separate Panel Reports issued in four cases brought against the same measures by four different countries: Honduras, the Dominican Republic, Cuba and Indonesia), 28 June 2018. At the time of writing, two of the four reports were under appeal (filed by Honduras and the Dominican Republic). Therefore, it remains to be seen whether the WTO Appellate Body upholds these reports. The other two reports were adopted by the WTO Dispute Settlement Body.
31. Indeed, a number of countries have introduced plain packaging for tobacco products in the meantime. Plain packaging for tobacco products exists by now in the United Kingdom, France, Ireland, Norway, New Zealand, with Hungary and Israel to follow in 2019, and Slovenia and Thailand (first Asian country) in 2020. Other countries are making steps in the same direction, including Canada, Finland, Belgium, Chile, South Africa, Singapore and Taiwan. See, for example, information provided by Clean Air Nederland available at <www.cleanairnederland.nl/component/tags/tag/89-plain-packaging>, last visited on 22 February 2019.
32. Agreement between the Swiss Confederation and the Oriental Republic of Uruguay on the Reciprocal Promotion and Protection of Investments, singed on 7 October 1988, available at <investmentpolicyhub.unctad.org/Download/TreatyFile/3121>, last visited on 22 February 2019.
33. Convention on the Settlement of Investment Disputes between States and Nationals of Other States, concluded on 18 March 1965, UNTR No. 8359, available at <treaties.un.org/

the Switzerland–Uruguay BIT which did not specify arbitration forum to be used. In contrast thereto, Article 10 of the Australia–Hong Kong BIT explicitly requires investment disputes to be resolved through arbitration under the UNCITRAL Arbitration Rules.[34]

By choosing the ICSID as arbitration forum for its case against Uruguay, Philip Morris made use of the most important advantage of the ICSID Convention over other international arbitration fora, which relates to enforcement of awards. According to Articles 53 and 54 of the ICSID Convention, awards are not only subject to no appeal and binding upon the parties to the dispute but – as far as pecuniary remedies are concerned, which are sought in most cases – also directly enforceable in all 154 state parties to the ICSID Convention. Unlike under the New York Convention on the Recognition and Enforcement of Arbitral Awards of 1958 (New York Convention),[35] which applies to the enforcement of awards rendered by other ISDS fora, ICSID awards do not need to undergo a domestic recognition process in the enforcing country. All ICSID contracting states are bound to enforce awards rendered as if they were final judgments of their courts.[36] This not only saves investors the trouble (and time and costs), it also prevents that the award is refused recognition, and thus enforcement, if considered to be contrary to its public policy by the country in which enforcement is sought. This may happen under the 1958 New York Convention[37] and would not be inconceivable in the case of an award ordering a state to pay compensation to a tobacco company for a legislative measure adopted for the purposes of protecting public health from a product as harmful as tobacco. Therefore, it is understandable that Philip Morris made use of the wording of the applicable BIT and brought the case against Uruguay to the ICSID.[38]

---

doc/Publication/UNTS/Volume%20575/volume-575-I-8359-English.pdf>, last visited on 22 February 2019.

34. It must also be noted that Hong Kong is not a party to the ICSID Convention. Therefore, a dispute initiated under an investment agreement to which Hong Kong is a party, such as the Australia–Hong Kong BIT, could not be brought to the ICSID on this ground, too, although Australia is a party to the ICSID Convention. This is because Article 25 of the ICSID Convention requires both the home and the host state of the investor to be a contracting party for the ICSID to have jurisdiction. In the case *Philip Morris v. Uruguay*, both Switzerland and Uruguay are parties to the ICSID Convention. See the ICSID database of its member states available at <icsid.worldbank.org/en/Pages/about/Database-of-Member-States.aspx#>, last visited on 22 February 2019.
35. Convention on the Recognition and Enforcement of Foreign Arbitral Awards, concluded on 10 June 1958, UNTR No. 4739, available at <treaties.un.org/doc/Publication/UNTS/Volume%20330/volume-330-I-4739-English.pdf>, last visited on 22 February 2019.
36. ICSID Convention, Article 54(1).
37. New York Convention, Article V(2)(b). There are also other grounds for the refusal to recognize and enforce an award under this Convention, mentioned in Article V. They relate to procedural matters, such as the composition of the arbitration tribunal being not in accordance with the agreement of the parties to the dispute.
38. Indeed, the ICSIS is by far the most popular ISDS forum. According to the most recent available data (31 July 2018), out of the total of 904 known cases, almost a half (488) was brought to the ICSID, with 280 cases brought to UNCITRAL, 57 cases to the ICSID Additional Facility (not benefitting from Article 54 of the ICSID Convention), 46 cases to the Stockholm Chamber of Commerce and just a few cases to each other forum. UNCTAD

As for the tribunal, the disputing parties agreed on the way in which it was to be composed.[39] Accordingly, Philip Morris appointed a US national, the prominent arbitrator Gary Born, while Uruguay chose Prof. James Crawford, an Australian eminent public international law expert and now a judge at the International Court of Justice. Following a failure of the two appointed arbitrators to appoint the third – presiding – member of the tribunal, the ICSID Secretary-General appointed an international investment law expert and arbitrator Prof. Piero Bernardini from Italy to serve as President.[40] The composition of the tribunal by these most prominent and vastly experienced international (investment) law experts clearly reflected the very high stakes present in this dispute.

II. Challenged Measures and Philip Morris' Claims

Philip Morris' challenge against Uruguay concerned two regulations adopted by this Latin American country in 2008 and 2009, known as "Single Presentation Regulation" and "80/80 Regulation". These regulations were the latest in a row of tobacco control measures taken by Uruguay over the past decades under its increasingly stringent anti-smoking policy which, as acknowledged by the tribunal, got "an important push from its current President … who in his earlier career was an oncologist".[41] Indeed, with one of the Latin America's highest rate of smokers and high economic impact of smoking (both in terms of smoker's own spending and health care costs), Uruguay has long been at the forefront of the fight against smoking.[42]

The challenged Single Presentation Regulation required each brand of tobacco products to have a single presentation, thereby prohibiting marketing of more than one variant of a single brand family of cigarettes. This meant, for example, that Philip Morris' best known Malboro brand could no longer be offered in its four variants sold in Uruguay previously (Malboro Fresh Mint, Malboro Red, Malboro Blue and Malboro Gold). The requirement aimed at preventing false information communicated to consumers by the producer that some variants are less harmful than others.[43] The second challenged measure, the 80/80 Regulation, imposed a requirement to cover 80% of the front and of the back of each cigarettes package

---

Investment Dispute Settlement Navigator available at >investmentpolicyhub.unctad.org/ISDS/FilterByRulesAndInstitution<, last visited on 22 February 2019.

39. Article 37(2)(a) of the ICSID Convention and Uruguay Award, para. 17.
40. Uruguay Award, paras. 17–18.
41. *Ibid.*, para. 77.
42. For details on Uruguay's tobacco control policy and legal framework, see *ibid.*, paras. 74–84 and 96–107.
43. *Ibid.*, paras. 112 and 403–404. As explained for example by Freeman, Chapman and Rimmer, in countries that have banned descriptions on tobacco products such as "light" and "mild", the producers resorted to other practices aiming at the same goal, namely tricking smokers into believing that some brands are lower or higher yielding. An example is Philip Morris' substitution for colour coding under which red colour equals full strength, blue and gold are mild and grey means light. – Becky Freeman, Simon Chapman and Matthew Rimmer, 'The case for the plain packaging of tobacco products', 103(4) *Addiction*, 580–590, also available at SSRN under <papers.ssrn.com/sol3/papers.cfm?abstract_id=1004646>, last visited on 22 February 2019.

with health warnings, increasing the coverage of such warnings from previous 50% to 80%. The 80/80 regulation thus left tobacco companies with as little as 20% of the cigarettes package for their branding.[44] That being said, unlike the plain packaging requirement in Australia, the Uruguay measures did not ban branding of tobacco products on their packages entirely. Nonetheless, given the crucial importance of packaging for marketing and sale of products as homogenous as cigarettes,[45] Philip Morris challenged the Uruguay regulations, first in domestic courts[46] and subsequently in investment arbitration.

Similar to the dispute against Australia, Philip Morris argued that the two challenged measures breached Uruguay's BIT obligations concerning indirect expropriation, fair and equitable treatment, unreasonable and discriminatory impairment of the investment's use and enjoyment, and the BIT's umbrella clause, with an additional claim of denial of justice resulting from two contradictory judgments of Uruguayan courts. Unsurprisingly, Uruguay denied all claims and, as is a good habit in investment arbitration, also put forward a number of challenges regarding the tribunal's jurisdiction to hear this case.[47] The tribunal however disagreed and confirmed its jurisdiction.[48]

III. Tribunal's Assessment

1. *Limited Trade Mark Protection*

When assessing the substantive claims, the tribunal addressed first an issue crucial to the dispute as a whole, concerning the nature of trade mark protection. The question was whether a trade mark conferred a positive right (to use the registered mark), as argued by Philip Morris, or a negative right ("only" to prevent others from using the same mark), as argued by Uruguay. Having considered parties' arguments, national, regional and international legal frameworks for trade mark protection and

44. Uruguay Award, paras. 121–123.
45. On the crucial importance of packaging for marketing of a product as homogenous as cigarettes, see also Freeman, Chapman and Rimmer, *supra* note 43.
46. More detail on these claims is provided below.
47. Uruguay argued that the claimants had not met the requirement of Article 10 of the applicable BIT to negotiate for 6 months and litigate in domestic courts for 18 months before resorting to ISDS; that health measures were outside the scope of the BIT on the basis of Article 2 which recognised each party's right not to allow economic activities for reasons of, *inter alia*, public health; and that the claimants' activities in Uruguay were not "investment" within the meaning of Article 25 of the ICSID Convention because they did not contribute to Uruguay's economic development. – Uruguay Decision on Jurisdiction, paras. 31–54, 151–162, 176–182 and 211–220.
48. The tribunal found that Philip Morris had met its obligations under Article 10 of the BIT by communicating with the Uruguayan government and challenging measures at dispute before domestic courts; that Article 2 of the BIT only applied to the pre-establishment phase of foreign investments, not to investments already made; and that Article 25 of the ICSID Convention did not require investments' contribution to the host states' development as a condition for ICSID jurisdiction. – *Ibid.*, in particular paras. 113, 129, 148, 174–175, 208–210 and 234–235.

opinions of a number of intellectual property law experts, the tribunal rejected Philip Morris' argument that trade marks lead to a positive right of use[49] but emphasised the following:

> In the Tribunal's view, both Parties have focused on a dichotomy between a right to use and a right to protect. However, it may be more fruitful to view the case as a question of an absolute versus exclusive right to use. Ownership of a trademark does, in certain circumstances, grant a right to use it. It is a right of use that exists vis-à-vis other persons, an exclusive right, but a relative one. It is not an absolute right to use that can be asserted against the State *qua* regulator.[50]

The tribunal focused on the question whether trade mark owners' right ("an exclusive right to exclude third parties from the market so that only the trademark holder has the possibility to use the trade mark in commerce")[51] was absolute or relative and concluded that the latter was the case given the fact that it was subject to the regulatory power of the relevant state.[52] Although the tribunal subsequently agreed with Philip Morris that, despite being negative rights, trademarks did constitute property capable of being expropriated,[53] its conclusion that there was no "carve-out of trademarks from the legitimate realms of regulation"[54] was a clear prelude to what was coming. It set a tone followed like a red line throughout the award, with only minor variations here and there depending on the standard of investment protection under consideration. And so, to continue with the first substantive right, the tribunal found that no expropriation of Philip Morris' intellectual property right took place as neither of the two challenged measures had a substantive effect on Philip Morris' business in Uruguay. The tribunal stressed that the business remained profitable, dismissing the argument that it could have been more profitable in the absence of the challenged measures as irrelevant.[55]

2. *"Cementing" States' Regulatory Autonomy in* Obiter Dictum *on Expropriation*

Interestingly, while expressly recognising no need for further analysis of the expropriation claim, the tribunal added an *obiter dictum* expressing its view that "the

49. Uruguay Award, paras. 264–266. Two years later, in June 2018, the same conclusion was reached by WTO Panels hearing the cases brought against the Australian tobacco plain packaging measures to the WTO. Panels Reports, *Australia – Certain Measures Concerning Trademarks, Geographical Indications and Other Plain Packaging Requirements Applicable to Tobacco Products and Packaging*, WT/DS435/R, WT/DS441/R, WT/DS458/R and WT/DS467/R, paras. 7.1978–7.1980.
50. Uruguay Award, para. 267.
51. *Ibid.*, para. 271.
52. *Ibid.*, paras. 267–271.
53. *Ibid.*, para. 274.
54. *Ibid.*, para. 270. Upreti argues that this is a clear sign of a move towards a new intellectual property system for health. – Pratyush Nath Upreti, 'Philip Morris v Uruguay: A Breathing Space for Domestic IP Regulation', 40(4) *European Intellectual Property Review* (2018), 277–284, at 284.
55. Uruguay Award, paras. 276, 284–286.

adoption of the Challenged Measures by Uruguay was a valid exercise of the State's police powers, with the consequence of defeating the claim for expropriation".[56] The tribunal continued this *obiter dictum* by an extensive analysis of its understanding of the state's police powers doctrine and its role in interpretation of international investment agreements disregarding whether they explicitly incorporate this doctrine or not. The tribunal considered the doctrine to be a part of general international law and thus, in accordance with the Vienna Convention on the Law of Treaties (VCLT), indispensable for investment treaties' interpretation, despite the lack of initial recognition of this doctrine by early investment arbitrators.[57] Applying the doctrine to the dispute at hand, and in particular to the expropriation claim, the tribunal further analysed Uruguay's measures and held that they complied with all conditions required by the doctrine in order not to constitute indirect expropriation (good faith, the purpose of protecting the public welfare, non-discrimination and proportionality).[58]

The effort of the tribunal spent on the extensive analysis of the state's police doctrine, its role in international investment law and subsequent application to Uruguay's tobacco control measures leaves no doubt about the tribunal's intention to "cement", if possible, what it believed to be "a consistent trend in favour of differentiating the exercise of police powers from indirect expropriation"[59] in ISDS case law. Perhaps the tribunal also simply wished to prevent future challenges of similar tobacco control measures in making in other countries. While many of us may have great sympathy for this - what could arguably be called arbitrators' activism - and may agree with it, just like in previous ISDS case law here too one would wish a more solid legal authority providing evidence for the existence of customary international law for non-compensatory taking of aliens' property.[60]

---

56. *Ibid.*, para. 287.
57. *Ibid.*, paras. 290–301. The tribunal included an extensive list of references to the police powers doctrine, such as the 1961 Harvard Draft Convention on the International Responsibility of States for Injury to Aliens, the Third Restatement of the Foreign Relations Law of the United States of 1987, the 2004 OECD working paper '"Indirect Expropriation" and the "Right to Regulate" in International Investment Law', a series of investment arbitration awards, the 2004 and 2012 US as well as Canada Model BITs, the recent EU-Canada Comprehensive Economic Trade Agreement (CETA) as well as EU-Singapore FTA.
58. Uruguay Award, para. 305, with the analysis of each condition in the subsequent paras. An interesting issue to note is that of the standard required to prove the rational of the measure under consideration, i.e. its contribution to the achievement of the objective sought. Recognizing a potential difficulty in some instances, the tribunal considered it sufficient that that the challenges measures were introduced as a part of a larger tobacco control regulatory framework in Uruguay, directed at a reduction of smoking incidents especially among young people and capable of achieving this end. - para. 306.
59. *Ibid.*, para. 295.
60. It should be noted that the tribunal referred to the same sources as this tribunal itself referred to, such as awards in *Tecmed v. Mexico*, ICSID Case No. ARB(AF)/00/2, Award of 29 May 2003, para. 119 and *Saluka Investments BV v. Czech Republic*, UNCITRAL, Partial Award of 17 March 2006, paras. 255, 260, 262. They all invoked i.a. the Harvard Draft Convention on the International Responsibility of States for Injury to Aliens of 1961 and the American Law Institute's *(Third) Restatement of Foreign Relations Law of the United States* of 1987, as well as OECD documents. One could have doubts about the authoritativeness of these

With that being said, modern international investment treaties leave no doubt that states do not – if they ever did – intend to surrender their regulatory autonomy to the interests of foreign investors and so that harm inflicted upon the later by regulatory choices of the former are not to be considered indirect expropriation *per se*. The tribunal in *Philip Morris v. Uruguay* indeed referred to these modern treaties to confirm the existence of customary international law on state's police power doctrine[61] though, as pointed out by Sornarajah, neither these treaties nor other authorities provide much guidance for making a distinction between regulatory takings that are non-compensable and compensable takings, a distinction that is not always easy to make.[62] As mentioned above, the tribunal in *Philip Morris v. Uruguay* relied in this regard on criteria developed in the past case law (such as good faith and proportionality) and found that they all were met in the present case.

It is notable that the tribunal used contemporary developments (i.e. wording of a few recent US and EU investment (model) treaties) to determine the status of customary international law (concerning police powers doctrine) and used this to interpret an aged investment treaty.[63] When doing so, the tribunal did not argue evolution of the customary international law. Although it recognised that the police powers doctrine was not immediately acknowledged by investment tribunals, it proclaimed that the doctrine had always been a part of international law, which to some extent is contradictory. The tribunal then referred to the existence of a consistent trend in investment arbitration case law from 2000 onwards, which is more in line with the doctrine, and expressed a belief that the modern investment treaties may well incorporate this concept *ex abundanti cautela*.[64]

It is clear that the tribunal made the effort to ensure that the police powers doctrine is applied without opposition also to old generation treaties, despite their silence about states regulatory autonomy qualifying obligations undertaken therein vis-à-vis foreign investors. After all, most ISDS disputes are still initiated by recourse

---

sources, given the fact that they are either an unadopted (and disputed) draft attempting to codify international rules with no success, or unilateral documents of (a group of like-minded) states. For an interesting article on the development of international law on state responsibility and liability, distinguishing the two concepts (linking the former to a breach of international obligation by a state and the latter to liability for harm resulting from lawful acts by a state): Sompong Sucharitkul, 'State Responsibility and International Liability under International Law', *Loyola of Los Angeles International and Comparative Law Review* (9 January 1996), available at <digitalcommons.lmu.edu/cgi/viewcontent.cgi?referer=&httpsredir=1&article=1400&context=ilr>, last visited on 22 February 2019.

61. Uruguay Award, para. 300.
62. M. Sornarajah, *The International Law on Foreign Investment* (4th edn., Cambridge, 2017), see especially pp. 460–475.
63. The tribunal used Article 31(3)(c) of the Vienna Convention on the Law of Treaties which mandates interpretation of international treaties in the light of all relevant rules of international law. – Uruguay Award, para. 290.
64. Out of an abundance of caution.

to these older treaties,[65] a trend that is likely to continue for some time to come.[66] A more pro-state interpretation of the provisions of those treaties is what the tribunal in this dispute considered to be the present trend to follow. Indeed, despite the difficulty faced by the tribunal to identify a solid legal authority proving the existence of the customary international law rule concerning the police powers doctrine long before the conclusion of new generation investment treaties, it seems highly unlikely that any state would oppose application of this doctrine to the interpretation of investment treaties at present, disregarding whether they are old or new treaties. Even foreign investors no longer argue against the doctrine itself, rather against its application to specific circumstances of their case. This is where differences in opinion will persist, just as they did in the present dispute, with the tribunal eventually finding that the exercise of the regulatory power by Uruguay when adopting the challenged measures did not breach the conditions required by the doctrine.

3. *High FET Threshold*

Apart from indirect expropriation of its trade marks, Philip Morris also claimed that Uruguay's measures breached the country's obligation under Article 3(2) of the BIT to provide fair and equitable treatment to its investment due to their arbitrariness and their failure to protect Philip Morris' legitimate expectations and legal stability in Uruguay. Here, too, the tribunal denied all claims. It agreed that arbitrariness, protection of legitimate expectations and legal stability were a generally recognised part of this further "far from settled" standard of investment protection[67] but found that Uruguay did not engage in any breach. While in many investment disputes, the issues of legitimate expectations and legal stability are most controversial, in this case it was the claim of arbitrariness that was most extensively dealt with by the tribunal and, as discussed below, caused a friction among its members.

The tribunal unanimously agreed that "the requirements of legitimate expectations and legal stability as manifestations of the FET standard do not affect the State's rights to exercise its sovereign authority to legislate and to adapt its legal system to changing circumstances".[68] Therefore, as long as legislative changes are a normal exercise of the host state's regulatory power to pursue public interests, they are not a breach of the FET standard. The tribunal did accept that modifications of the regulatory framework existing at the time of an investment "outside of the acceptable margin of change" would be problematic[69] but did not further elaborate on

---

65. According to the latest available data, 673 out of 904 known IIA-based investment disputes were initiated under IIAs concluded between 1990 and 1999. Data are retrieved from online UNCTAD Investment Policy Hub available at <investmentpolicyhub.unctad.org/ISDS/FilterByApplicableIia>, last visited on 22 February 2019.
66. This is due, inter alia, to the so-called sunset clauses contained in many old generation IIAs prolonging the life of these treaties in case of their termination for a long period of time, typically 10 or 15 years.
67. Uruguay Award, paras. 320–324.
68. *Ibid.*, para. 420. The tribunal referred to a large number of awards by "more recent investment tribunals" to support its view.
69. *Ibid.*, para. 423.

this qualifier since it considered this was not at issue in this case, given the limited impact of the change on Philip Morris' business mentioned earlier.

More importantly, the tribunal concurred with previous case law that legitimate expectations depended on specific representations by the host state inducing investors into making an investment, stressing that this could not be done by generally applicable legislation such as the one at issue. As Philip Morris did not provide evidence of specific representations by Uruguay, it could have no legitimate expectation that tobacco control laws in Uruguay would not change. Rather, given internationally recognised concerns about harmfulness of tobacco, Philip Morris could have expected increasingly more stringent tobacco control legislation.[70]

The tribunal also rejected Philip Morris' argument that Uruguay's measures were "breaking new ground". When based on a rational basis and not discriminatory, states may adopt novel measures without infringing upon anyone's legitimate expectations or country's legal stability, according to the tribunal.[71] Since no discrimination was at issue in this case, it was the reasonableness of Uruguay's measures that required most of the tribunal's attention when analysing the FET claim.

The analysis of this issue was marked by a number of notable elements. When assessing Philip Morris' claim that Uruguay's measures lacked sufficient rationale and were therefore unreasonable and thus arbitrary,[72] the tribunal relied heavily on *amicus curiae* briefs submitted by the World Health Organization (WHO) and Pan-American Health Organization (PAHO) and fully accepted their assessment of Uruguay measures' rationale.[73] *Amici curiae* are indeed no longer a stranger in investment arbitration proceedings, although the discretion of the tribunal to decide whether and to what extent it will allow their submission remains significant.[74] In this case, apart from the WHO and PAHO, two other organizations requested permission to submit *amicus curiae* briefs, the Avaaz Foundation ("Avaaz")[75] and the Inter-American Association of Intellectual Property (ASIPI). Unlike the WHO and PAHO, however, Avaaz and ASIPI were denied the possibility of filing their submissions. The tribunal used its discretion under ICSID Arbitration Rule 37(2) to find that Avaaz was unlikely to offer a perspective, knowledge or insight different from those put forward by the disputing parties and that ASIPI lacked independence

70. *Ibid.*, paras. 424–430.
71. *Ibid.*, para. 430.
72. Philip Morris argued that the measures were arbitrary due to their unreasonableness: "adopted without a scientific evidence of their effectiveness, without due consideration by public officials and with no reasonable connection between the objectives pursued by the State and the utility of the chosen measure". – Summary of the claimants' argument by the tribunal, Uruguay Award, para. 389.
73. Uruguay Award, para. 391.
74. On *amicus curiae* in investment arbitration and related recent developments, see for example Gabriele Ruscalla, 'Transparency in International Arbitration: Any (Concrete) Need to Codify The Standard?', 3(1) *Goettingen Journal of International Law* (2015), especially part IV, and also A. Saravanan and S.R. Subramanian, 'The Participation of Amicus Curiae in Investment Treaty Arbitration', 5(4) *Journal of Civil & Legal Sciences* (2016).
75. Avaaz is an online activist network that describes itself as "a global web movement to bring people-powered politics to decision-making everywhere". See Avaaz website available at < www.avaaz.org/page/en/about/ >, last visited on 22 February 2019.

from Philip Morris whose lawyers served on the ASIPI management board and in its thematic committees.[76]

On the other hand, WHO's and PAHO's submissions were given great weight by the tribunal in assessing the existence of a rational connection between Uruguay's measures and their public health objectives, these measures' effectiveness as well as Uruguay's good faith in adopting them.[77] Although it discussed each of the specific issues brought forward by Philip Morris, such as the effectiveness of the increase of the coverage of health warnings from 50 to 80%, the tribunal generally accepted that relevant international evidence existed and guided the WHO (with its Framework Convention on Tobacco Control (FCTC)) when recommending states what types of measures to take. The tribunal reasoned that states were allowed to follow such recommendations without conducting additional studies, in particular when it comes to states with limited technical and economic resources, like Uruguay.[78] The tribunal hereby embraced international cooperation and encouraged countries, particularly but arguably not just those with limited means, to engage in implementation of broadly supported international agreements without a fear of investment arbitration. Accepting that measures based on evidence behind such international agreements are reasonable, without requiring further proof for their rationale – or their actual effectiveness[79] – was itself no less than reasonable. After all, globally supported international agreements such as the FCTC[80] do not come to life easily and when they do, it means that their parties agree that what they sign up to is needed and suitable for addressing issues covered by the agreement.

In this context it is understandable that, as mentioned, the tribunal also did not require proof of actual effectiveness of the specific measures adopted. Apart from this not always being possible, certainly with novel measures, the tribunal held that the standard to be applied is the measures' reasonableness at the time of their adoption, to be assessed by looking at whether they endeavour to address a real public policy concern, are not disproportionate and are adopted in good faith.[81] In the tribunal's view, any other consideration is within the discretion of governments making public policy determination, and it is not for arbitration tribunals to second guess governments' choices but rather to accept their "margin of appreciation".[82] This explains why the (majority of the) tribunal approved of Uruguay's single presentation regulation, despite the fact that such measure was not specifically referred to in the FCTC (or its Guidelines), and why it approved of the 80% coverage of health

76. Uruguay Award, paras. 52–55. There was also an additional reason for denying both petitioners the possibility to file *amicus curiae* briefs, namely a late submission of both petitions.
77. *Ibid.*, para. 391.
78. *Ibid.*, paras. 393–396.
79. *Ibid.*, para. 409.
80. At present, the FCTC has 181 parties (including the EU) covering more than 90% of the world population. Official website of the FCTC available at <www.who.int/fctc/cop/en/>, last visited on 22 February 2019.
81. Uruguay Award, para. 409.
82. *Ibid.*, paras. 388 and 398–400.

warning without the FCTC setting that precise limit.[83] As emphasised by the tribunal, it is for the state's government to strike a balance between various considerations when deciding upon matters of general public interest, whereby the FET standard of investment protection "is not a justifiable standard of good government, and the tribunal is not a court of appeal".[84] By using this catchy phrase, the tribunal clearly showed its mindfulness of the host states' right to regulate in the general public interest, the already mentioned red line visible throughout the entire award.

This decision was not supported by all three arbitrators, however. Gary Born, arbitrator appointed by Philip Morris, disagreed with the majority of the tribunal that one of the challenged measures, the single presentation regulation, found support in the WHO FCTC. This is because such measure is specifically mentioned neither in the FCTA nor in the FCTC Guidelines. The arbitrator argued that this absence did not support the reasonableness of Uruguay's measure but rather its unreasonableness, given the fact that the measure was not included in the extensive and well thought through list of measures required or recommended by the FCTC.[85] Born also dissented on the point of "margin of appreciation", disagreeing that this concept, developed by the European Court of Human Rights, applied to interpretation of investment treaties, although he did agree that a substantial degree of difference is to be applied for regulatory choices made by governments.[86] Nonetheless, Born insisted on "a minimum level of rationality and proportionality"[87] being required for state measures aimed at achieving legitimate policy objectives arguing that "deference to sovereign measures is the starting point, but not the ending point".[88] The dissenting arbitrator pled for an *objective* analysis of disputed measures' rationale, implying there were limits to host states' regulatory autonomy and their subjective policy choice of means to be employed for the fulfilment of various policy objectives, confined to those that were "fair and equitable".[89] Unlike the majority of the tribunal, the dissenting arbitrator Born believed that, on the basis of the evidence presented by both parties, including the FCTC and its Guidelines, an objective rationale behind the single presentation requirement, challenged by Philip Morris in this dispute, did not exist. The requirement was therefore arbitrary and disproportionate, in breach of FET standard of protection.[90]

4. *Denial of Justice Denied*

The tribunal's pro-state regulatory autonomy approach in this case was not shaken by the three remaining claims of Philip Morris relating to the allegation that the disputed measures impaired the use and enjoyment of Philip Morris' investments in

83. Article 11 of the FCTC Guidelines recommend more than 50% of the principal display area with the aim to cover as much as possible. – See Uruguay Award, para. 412.
84. *Ibid.*, para. 418.
85. Concurring and Dissenting Opinion, paras. 193–194.
86. *Ibid.*, para. 137.
87. *Ibid.*, para. 139.
88. *Ibid.*, para. 142.
89. *Ibid.*, especially para. 144.
90. *Ibid.*, paras. 146–196.

Uruguay, that they were in breach of Uruguay's obligation to observe its commitments entered into with respect of trade marks, and that Philip Morris was denied justice by two contradictory judicial decisions by Uruguay courts. Most interesting of the three is the last one on denial of justice.[91] Here the tribunal's pro-state attitude is visible most prominently.

Philip Morris' claim concerned two contradictory decisions, one by Uruguay's Supreme Court and one by Uruguay's Administrative Tribunal, on the meaning of a statutory provision on which the 80/80 Regulation was based. The statutory provision at issue was Article 9 of Law 18,256, according to which tobacco products packages must contain health warnings and images describing products' harmful effects on "at least 50% (fifty percent) of the total exposed primary surfaces". Philip Morris argued that "at least 50%" in Article 9 meant "no less than 50%", but not "50% or more". Therefore, this provision did not authorize the executive branch to increase the coverage of health warning beyond 50% and the 80/80 Regulation was unlawful. It was undisputed that if the opposite reading of Article 9 were to be adopted, i.e. as authorizing a coverage of health warnings beyond 50%, Law 18,256 would be unconstitutional due to an excessive delegation of legislative authority to the executive. According to Uruguay's Constitution, fundamental rights, thus including property rights, could only be limited by law and not by an executive act.

Relying on the submissions presented by the Uruguay's Legislature and the State Attorney General, the Supreme Court ruled that Article 9 of Law 18,256 was not in breach of the country's Constitution since it did not authorize health warnings beyond 50% of tobacco product's packaging surface. Therefore, the Supreme Court rejected Philip Morris's claim, which on this basis challenged the legality of the 80/80 Regulation before Uruguay's Administrative Tribunal, arguing the regulation (authorizing 80% coverage) was in breach of Article 9 of Law 18,256 (that only authorized a maximum of 50% of coverage). Despite the clear and well-reasoned decision of the Supreme Court, and without providing reasons, the Uruguay's Administrative Tribunal refused to follow the interpretation adopted by the Court, but also the Uruguay's Legislature and the State Attorney General, and ruled that Article 9 of Law 18,256 did authorize an increase of the required surface coverage for health warnings beyond 50% (thus to 80%). Consequently, Philip Morris' claims were, once again, dismissed.[92] The third and final dismissal of its complaints came

91. The claim alleging impairment of the use and enjoyment of Philip Morris' investments in Uruguay was rejected on the same basis as the arbitrariness claim under the FET, given the fact that the relevant BIT provision only prohibited impairment by "unreasonable or discriminatory measures" and Philip Morris argued a breach of this standard on the same factual and legal basis as the FET standard (with regard to arbitrariness based on unreasonableness). Similarly, the claim under the umbrella clause (obliging BIT parties to observe other commitments entered into with regard to foreign investments) was rejected by reference to the tribunal's earlier finding that trademarks were not absolute positive rights. On this basis the tribunal held that trademarks were not commitments (they were "not a promise by the host state to perform an obligation") and thus outside the scope of the BIT umbrella clause. – Uruguay Award, paras. 444–446 and 481–482.

92. See the insightful explanation of the factual and procedural background of the Philip Morris claim of denial of justice provided by the dissenting arbitrator Born – Concurring and Dissenting Opinion, paras. 13–35.

from the investment arbitration tribunal before which Philip Morris argued that justice was denied to it by Uruguay and its courts.

By rejecting Philip Morris' claim, the arbitration tribunal contradicted its own standard to be applied to the denial of justice claims. According to the tribunal, "[a]n elevated standard of proof is required for finding a denial of justice due to the gravity of a charge which condemns the State's judicial system as such."[93] While stressing that "it is not enough to have an erroneous decision or an incompetent judicial procedure, arbitral tribunals not being courts of appeal", the tribunal did acknowledge that "a decision [that] was clearly improper and discreditable" and "'grave procedural errors' may result in a denial of justice depending on the circumstances of each case".[94] When applying this standard to the facts of Philip Morris' challenge of the 80/80 Regulation before two Uruguay's highest courts, however, the tribunal found these courts' squarely contradictory rulings only "unusual" and "surprising" but "not shocking".[95]

Under the circumstances of this particular case, where the Uruguay's Administrative Tribunal is obliged by law to follow Supreme Court's rulings such as the one at issue but departs from it by only "a brief and largely unreasoned decision",[96] while at the same time both contradictory decisions are applied to the party to the proceedings to deny it a relief against the government action that is at issue, with no means of judicial recourse,[97] the tribunal's conclusion is hard to digest. One is more likely to agree with the dissenting arbitrator Gary Born that the situation is "the antithesis of the rule of law" and "a classic denial of access to justice".[98] Oddness of the situation was well summarized in Gary Born's dissent and is worth quoting:

> the contradictory interpretations of law are both applied by a state's courts to deny a party relief against governmental actions. Here, the Supreme Court rejected Abal's [Philip Morris' subsidiary] claims by holding that Law 18,256 was constitutional because it *did not* authorize a requirement of graphic warnings larger than 50% of the surface of tobacco packaging, and the TCA rejected Abal's claims by holding that Decree 287/009 and Ordinance 466 were valid because Law 18,256 *did* authorize a requirement of graphic warnings larger than 50% of the surface of tobacco packaging.[99]

Philip Morris' claims on the same matter were thus rejected by the two courts on entirely contradictory grounds. This was not disputed by the tribunal. The fact that there was nowhere else Philip Morris could go to challenge this clearly incorrect decision of the Administrative Tribunal – and, given the insufficiency of its reasoning

93. Uruguay Award, para. 499.
94. *Ibid.*, paras. 500–501, quoting previous case law.
95. *Ibid.*, para. 529.
96. Concurring and Dissenting Opinion, para. 58. Indeed, the Administrative Tribunal did not provide reasons for not following the earlier ruling of the Supreme Court, or on which basis it concluded that the provision at issue authorized increase of the required coverage of health warnings. Rather, it resorted to policy reasons for which an increase in the coverage should be seen, in line with the FCTC.
97. See *ibid.*, paras. 58–64.
98. *Ibid.*, paras. 57 and 64.
99. *Ibid.*, para. 61.

and clear contradiction with the binding decision by the Supreme Court, which was to be followed, arguably even "improper and discreditable" decision, it is more arguable than not that Philip Morris did not get effective access to an appropriate judicial forum and was therefore denied justice. As noted by the dissenting arbitrator, had there been a possibility to reopen proceedings before the Supreme Court whose decision was not followed by the Administrative Tribunal, the situation would have been different.[100] This was however not the case.

It was also not just an incorrect decision one could disagree with. Indeed, as stressed by the tribunal, this is not the standard to be applied since investment arbitration tribunals are not courts of appeal.[101] However, in this case, the two decisions in question were also not "just" divergent judicial decisions sometimes rendered by different courts in similar cases until a higher court sooner or later brings unity into the question. As repeatedly stressed by the dissenting arbitrator, these were two contradicting decisions rendered in regard of an identical measure, identical subject matter and identical party to the proceedings, a contradiction which will remain unresolved indefinitely due to the deficiency in the judicial system of Uruguay.[102] As a result, the claimants' right to an appropriate and enforceable decision at the end of the process was breached. It seems undisputed that such right constitutes an element enshrined in the principles of access to justice, fair procedure and the prohibition of denial of justice.[103]

It could indeed be argued that the tribunal's assessment of Philip Morris' access to Uruguay's courts was overly formalistic. Yes, the claimant had its day in court, and yes, there was an available judicial body hearing the challenge to the 80/80 Regulation. However, and contrary to the view expressed by the arbitration tribunal,[104] it could be argued that a relevant judicial body did *not* give a properly reasoned decision. Moreover, as mentioned, there was no judicial body available to hear the claimant's complaint about a clear contradiction between two rulings applying to the same case. Although one cannot impose a system of judicial organization on sovereign states, one can require that if the country's courts fails to arrive at an unambiguous decision in a specific case, and one of them clearly breaches domestic law in a blatant way, the judicial system of the country is capable of remedying injustice done. The refusal of the *Philip Morris v. Uruguay* tribunal to acknowledge the existence of denial of justice in this case, and thus to rule in favour of Philip Morris and order an appropriate remedy,[105] can hardly be explained otherwise than by the tribunal's

100. *Ibid.*, para. 76.
101. Uruguay Award, para. 528.
102. Concurring and Dissenting Opinion, for example paras. 63 and 76.
103. Rudolf Dolzer and Christoph Schreurer, *Principles of International Investment Law* (2nd edn., Oxford, 2012), 179.
104. Uruguay Award, para. 527.
105. While the tribunal would be unlikely to substitute the judgment of Uruguay courts by its own judgment and decide which of the two courts reached a correct decision, it is clear that – disregarding which decision was correct – Philip Morris would have won, either because Law 18,256 was inconsistent with the Constitution or because the 80/80 Regulation was inconsistent with Law 18,256. In any case, Philip Morris would then be entitled to at least compensation for damages caused by application of either unconstitutional or unlawful act to its investments in Uruguay, though restitution cannot

mindfulness of the systemic impact of a ruling in an exemplary dispute brought by a tobacco multinational against a small country that wants to protect health and life of its population from a deadly product.

D. CLOSING REMARKS

There is hardly another product as harmful as tobacco, killing a great number of its users, yet allowed on the market in most countries. It appears that prohibition of this product is, for various reasons, unfeasible and perhaps undesirable even in the long term. The best protection a great majority of countries seem to believe in are measures aimed at increasing awareness of the lethal nature of tobacco consumption, especially among the youth, rather than its outright prohibition. It is expected that such approach will eventually lead to the significant reduction of the tobacco consumption and, who knows, the product may even vanish from the market one day due to insufficient demand. Until then, however, no doubt, tobacco producers and suppliers will continue to search for new ways to promote tobacco products so as to protect their profitable business.

After the victory of Australia and Uruguay in investor-state disputes initiated by a tobacco giant Philip Morris, one of the avenues used by the tobacco industry seems to have closed.[106] As this contribution shows, states' autonomy to regulate in the interest of their population prevailed in full over obligations owed to foreign investors under international investment agreements. These obligations were interpreted and applied by the two tribunals restrictively, following a trend in more recent investor-state arbitration practice, keen on reading more balance into the foreign investment protection regime than was the case in the past. This contribution argues that choices made by the two tribunals were made not merely on the basis of *de lege lata* but also in full cognizance of the systemic implications of their decisions for the legitimacy and perhaps also survival of investor-state dispute settlement.

When assessing the corporate restructuring of Philip Morris, done at the time when the adoption of the challenged measures was foreseeable, the Australia tribunal chose not to follow a line of previous case law insisting on a very high probability of a dispute. Instead, it was satisfied with a fair prospect of the dispute to find abuse of rights by Philip Morris, permitting it to declare all claims inadmissible. The Uruguay tribunal followed a clear and consistent line throughout its analysis of Uruguay's

---

be excluded. If the latter were to be awarded, Uruguay would need to take appropriate steps to remove unconstitutionality of Law 18,256 or unlawfulness of the 80/80 Regulation and thus revoke the single presentation requirement, at least until it complies with the requirements of its domestic legal framework. In the meantime, it would have to compensate Philip Morris for damages suffered during the period of application of the regulation until its revocation. Usually, the host state may also select compensation over restitution. Whatever remedy would be applied in this case, it would likely come down to the same effect as if the 80/80 Regulation were found in breach of the BIT, despite the fact that the tribunal considered this was not the case.

106. Recall the reaction of Philip Morris on the Uruguay award: "The arbitration concerned an important, but unusual, set of facts that called for clarification under international law, which the parties have now received", available at <www.ft.com/content/1ae33bc8-454e-11e6-9b66-0712b3873ae1>, last visited on 22 February 2019.

measures, involving a significant difference to the regulatory autonomy of the state. It stuck to it even at the point where a violation of an international obligation by Uruguay was more arguable than not, for its two unfortunate decisions that denied the claimant a relief for the entirely opposite reasons. This must have been a hard choice to make, denying full respect to the rule of law for the sake of a just decision.

No doubt, any other outcome, disregarding its legal soundness, would have resulted in a further backlash against both the investor-state dispute settlement system as well as the international legal framework for the protection of foreign investments generally. While the initiation of the two disputes by Philip Morris contributed to worsening of the already existing negative image of the system and it is uncertain whether the dismissal of all claims will change anything in the public perceptions, the strong difference of the two tribunals, composed of prominent arbitrators, towards the state and its policy choice fully confirm the trend of a more balanced approach towards interests of all stakeholders in the system, not just those of foreign investors.

At the same time, in particular the Uruguay award clearly shows that worrying uncertainty remains.[107] This is not merely due to the strong dissent by one of the prominent arbitrators who is likely to sit on future ISDS tribunals. It is also because most disputes continue to be brought to investment arbitration under the old generation of investment treaties with broadly worded and largely undefined standards of protection which in some instances, such as in cases of denial of justice, are to be – but are not very much – helped by equally undefined and unascertainable rules of public international law. The discretion of arbitration in interpreting and perhaps even more so in applying such rules is necessarily broad. As demonstrated by the Uruguay dispute, this may lead to different arbitrators coming to different conclusions with regard to the same matter. Such legal uncertainty continues to be detrimental to the system at large. If it is to survive, reform efforts should to be stepped up and pay sufficient attention to the existing body of the old generation of international investment agreements as well as to thorough drafting of the new generation of treaties.

To some extent, this is already happening. Many newly concluded treaties with investment protection provisions contain explicit recognition of the states' police powers doctrine, definitions of a number of standards of investment protection (such as FET), numerous clarifications, exceptions, and carveouts for (usually) tobacco control measures. All this applies, *nota bene*, also to the new investment treaty between Australia and Hong Kong, concluded as recently as on 26 March 2019. Upon its entry into force, this investment treaty will replace the 1993 BIT under which Philip Morris brought its claims against Australia's Plain Tobacco Packaging legislation to the international investment arbitration.[108] The fact that new investment treaties continue to be agreed upon, also by states that have paid a high price for defending public interest in investment arbitration, reveals that the existing international system

107. See also Voon, *supra* note 29, in particular 330–331.

108. Jarrod Hepburn, 'After Australia Fends off Philip Morris Claim under Hong Kong BIT, Australia and HK Agree to Overhaul of Treaty Terms', *Investment Arbitration Reporter*, 26 March 2019, available at < www.iareporter.com/articles/after-australia-fends-off-philip-morris-claim-under-hong-kong-bit-the-two-countries-release-a-new-treaty-including-tobacco-exception/ >, last visited on 29 March 2019.

of foreign investment protection is here to stay. The economic stakes are simply too high. At the same time, governments have learned their lesson, and while most are not ready to abandon the system, they do – and are likely to continue to – exercise more caution when drafting the terms of protection offered to foreign investors.

It remains to be seen how resistant new treaty provisions will be towards claims against states' regulatory actions. It is this author's view that yet a considerably more precise definition of most controversial standards of protection and exceptions, as well as broader carveouts (beyond tobacco control measures) may be needed. For example, the two currently prevailing approaches towards the delineation of the content of the FET standard, one linking it to the customary international law minimum standard of treatment of aliens, and the other listing type of treatment to be covered by the standard, provide little – if any – clarity, and continue leaving broad discretion to arbitration tribunals in this standard's application in specific cases. This is because neither the customary international law nor the type of treatment to be covered, such as denial of justice, have a plainly ascertainable content themselves that could be applied with a high degree of predictability and legal certainty. Therefore, to (re) gain broader support and legitimacy, and to prevent that another "big bad company" will sue a country for making legitimate policy choices, the system will need to do still better than it does at present.

CHAPTER 10

The WTO Disputes Regarding Tobacco Plain Packaging: Selected TRIPS Findings from the Panel Stage

Wolf R. Meier-Ewert[1]

A. INTRODUCTION AND OVERVIEW

The WTO panel decision upholding Australia's tobacco plain packaging (TPP) measures is the culmination of a series of national and international legal challenges[2] brought against Australia's tobacco control measures since their introduction in 2011. In what has been called "one of the most highly anticipated reports ever",[3] the panel[4] decision released in June 2018 explored governments' regulatory leeway in the area of

1. Counsellor in the Intellectual Property, Government Procurement and Competition Division of the WTO Secretariat. The views presented in this paper are the responsibility of the author alone, and should not be attributed to the WTO Secretariat, the WTO or its Members. Comments by Antony Taubman and Hannu Wager are gratefully acknowledged.
2. See *JT International SA v. Commonwealth of Australia, British American Tobacco Australasia Limited v. The Commonwealth* [2012] HCA 43 and *Philip Morris Asia Limited v. The Commonwealth of Australia*, UNCITRAL, PCA Case No. 2012-12, Award on Jurisdiction and Admissibility, 17 December 2015.
3. WorldTradeLaw.net Dispute Settlement Commentary (DSC).
4. For convenience, in this paper "the Panel" refers to the five separate panels established pursuant to the five separate complaints by Ukraine, Honduras, the Dominican Republic, Cuba and Indonesia, but maintains the plural for the plain packaging *disputes*. The term "Panel Report" will refer to the panels' reports that are issued in the form of a single document constituting four separate panel reports: WT/DS435/R, WT/DS441/R, WT/DS458/R, and WT/DS467/R. For the procedural history see section A.II below.

tobacco control under the WTO's TBT[5] and TRIPS Agreements[6] against a background of complex and contentious legal and policy questions. While maintaining coherence between different and interconnected international intellectual property (IP) regimes is a familiar theme in TRIPS disputes,[7] the significance of the WHO Framework Convention on Tobacco Control (FCTC) – which encourages plain packaging and partly motivated Australia's introduction of the TPP measures[8] – for the assessment under the TBT and TRIPS Agreements, presented less familiar territory. Different views about the effectiveness of plain packaging as a public health measure were reflected in the vast amount of statistical and behavioural evidence submitted to the Panel, the assessment of which was further complicated by the fact that Australia had been the first to introduce such measures.[9]

From the perspective of the IP community – the main addressee of this factual summary – the central issue in this dispute was how the Panel would assess the compatibility of the TPP measures' limitations on the use of certain trademarks with the relevant TRIPS obligations. In this regard, the Panel's interpretation and application of Article 20 TRIPS – one of the few TRIPS provisions addressing trademark use, and one with regard to which little prior jurisprudence existed[10] – was awaited particularly eagerly. Similar curiosity extended to the Panel's views on the related, but substantively distinct, question of whether TRIPS and Paris Convention provisions regulating the *registration* and *protection* of trademarks (such as Article 15 and 16 of the TRIPS Agreement, and Article 6*quinquies* of the Paris Convention) could provide a basis to challenge the TPP's limitations on trademark *use* – in other words, whether they contained or implied some entitlement to using one's own trademark. This line of argument has often, and somewhat simplistically, been referred to as the "right to use" a trademark.[11]

5. WTO Agreement on Technical Barriers to Trade.
6. WTO Agreement on Trade-Related Aspects of Intellectual Property Rights. Complainants also brought a claim under Article IX:4 of GATT 1994.
7. On the regular practice of TRIPS-related dispute settlement panels to request factual background information on provisions of WIPO Convention invoked in WTO disputes see, inter alia, *US – Section 110(5) Copyright Act*, WT/DS/160/R, para. 4.1; *EC – Trademarks and Geographical Indications*, WT/DS/174/R, para. 2.16; *China – Intellectual Property Rights*, WT/DS/362/R, para. 2.7. In *US – Section 110(5) Copyright Act*, WT/DS/160/R, para. 6.66 and 6.70, the panel discusses "the need to interpret the Berne Convention and the TRIPS Agreement in a way that reconciles the texts of these two treaties and avoids a conflict between them, given that they form the overall framework for multilateral copyright protection."
8. Section 3(1)b) of Australia's Tobacco Plain Packaging Act 2011 (Cth) states that one of its objects is "to give effect to certain obligations that Australia has as a party to the Convention on Tobacco Control."
9. For the Panel's examination of the evidence commissioned or relied upon for a critique of the literature supporting the design and effectiveness of TPP measures see Panel Report, paras. 7.522–7.645. For the examination of the evidence regarding the application and impact of the TPP measures see Appendixes A-E of the Panel Report.
10. See only *Indonesia – Autos*, paras. 14.277–14.278 and 14.282.
11. See, among many others, Suzy Frankl, Daniel Gervais, 'Plain Packaging and the Interpretation of the TRIPS Agreement', 46(5) *Vanderbilt Journal of Transnational Law* (2013); Mark Davison, 'The Legitimacy of Plain Packaging Under International Intellectual Property

Somewhat outside the spotlight occupied by the foregoing topics, the Panel's engagement with the complainants' multiple TRIPS claims resulted in a number of further significant findings and clarifications relating, *inter alia*, to the systemic relationship between the Paris Convention's trademark provisions and the TRIPS Agreement, to Article 15 of the TRIPS Agreement, and to the incorporation and interpretation of Article 10*bis* of the Paris Convention into the TRIPS Agreement under its Article 2.1.

This paper provides a brief overview of the procedural history for the different complainants in the plain packaging disputes, and a factual summary of selected TRIPS-related findings by the Panel.

I. Discussions in the TRIPS Council

Since 2011, even before the TPP legislation entered into force in Australia in 2012, the TPP measures were raised and discussed in the TRIPS Council by the complainants in the subsequent disputes, and discussions on Australia's and other countries' envisaged tobacco control measures continued well into 2015. This is noteworthy since – in contrast to the transparency requirements under the TBT Agreement which require the notification of WTO Members' *proposed* technical regulations to the TBT Committee at an appropriate early stage when amendments can still be introduced and comments taken into account – notification obligations under TRIPS only require the notification of *legislation*,[12] and discussions of *prospective* IP measures are therefore very unusual in the TRIPS Council.[13]

After Australia's notification of the proposed measures to the TBT Committee[14] in April 2011, the TPP Bill 2011 and its compatibility with the TRIPS Agreement was first raised in the TRIPS Council in June 2011.[15] Between June 2011 and November 2012, when the measures entered into force in Australia, the topic was raised in the Council three times, each time specifically focusing on Australia's Tobacco Plain Packaging Bill 2011.[16] In these discussions, some of the subsequent complainants developed a number of the arguments regarding TRIPS compatibility of the TPP

Law: Why There is No Right to Use a Trademark Under Either the Paris Convention or the TRIPS Agreement', in A. Mitchell, T. Voon and J. Liberman (eds.), *Public Health and Plain Packaging of Cigarettes: Legal Issues* (Edward Elgar, 2012). See Annette Kur, 'The Right to Use One's Own Trade Mark: A Self-evident Issue or a New Concept in German, European, and International Trade Mark Law?', 4 *EIPR* (1996), 198. Note that most complainants in the plain packaging disputes denied claiming such a right – see *infra* note 163.

12. See Article 63.1 and 2 TRIPS Agreement.
13. See however the TRIPS Council discussions, beginning in 2010, on the Anti-Counterfeiting Trade Agreement (ACTA), before and after its signature.
14. In accordance with Article 2.9 of the TBT Agreement, Australia notified the "Tobacco Plain Packaging Bill 2011" and the "Plain Packaging of Tobacco Products Consultation Paper" to the TBT Committee on 8 April 2011 (See WTO document G/TBT/N/AUS/67).
15. Item K: "Australia: Tobacco Plain Packaging Bill 2011 and its compatibility with the TRIPS Agreement", IP/C/M/66, para. 166 *et seq.*, raised by the Dominican Republic.
16. The same item was put on the agenda of the TRIPS Council meeting in October 2011 at the request of Ukraine (see IP/C/M/67, para. 373 *et seq.*) and in February 2012 at the request of the Dominican Republic (see IP/C/M/69, para. 155 *et seq.*).

measures later raised in their submissions and – until mid-2012 – urged Australia to take these concerns into account. Interventions in the TRIPS Council – and in the TBT Committee – by WTO Members that shared concerns on the TPP measures' impact also provide information on the economic importance of tobacco production and trade – and hence the dimension of the feared economic consequences – in their respective economies. Australia's interventions in defence of the TPP measures elaborate its justifications for the scope and design of the measures and give a successive account of the consultative and legislative process – including amendments and delays applied in response to consultations – leading up to the Act's entry into force in 2012.

After March 2013, the focus of these TRIPS Council discussions shifted to similar tobacco-control measures that were being proposed by New Zealand, the European Union, the United Kingdom or Ireland, or referred more generally to Members that had implemented, or were considering, plain packaging for tobacco products.[17] In February 2014, Cuba, supported by the other complainants and some other delegations, urged other countries to refrain from adopting plain packaging measures before the WTO dispute on the legality of the Australian measures had been decided.[18] Australia countered that pending dispute settlement proceedings should not be used to demand legislative delays in other countries' policy decisions.[19]

The World Health Organization (WHO), an observer in the TRIPS Council, intervening at Council meetings where plain packaging had been added to the agenda, provided information on the health impact of smoking and on the WHO's view on tobacco advertising.[20] Its interventions also provided information on the FCTC that had entered into force in 2005, and whose implementation guidelines referred to plain packaging as a means to implement the signatories' commitment to undertake a comprehensive ban of all tobacco advertising, promotion and sponsorship.[21]

17. See, *inter alia*, TRIPS Council agenda item "Proposed Measure by New Zealand: Notification Circulated in Document G/TBT/N/NZL/62, Dated 24 July 2012, on a Proposal to Introduce Plain Packaging of Tobacco Products in New Zealand" raised by the Dominican Republic in March 2013 (IP/C/M/72); discussions under Other Business at the TRIPS Council meetings of June (IP/C/M/73 and Add.1) and October 2013 (IP/C/M/74 and Add.1) regarding the proposal for an EU directive on tobacco products and the Irish legislative programme including generic packaging of tobacco products; February 2014, Cuba "Concerns with Respect to Measures Related to Plain Packaging of Tobacco Products and Their Compatibility with the TRIPS Agreement" (IP/C/M/75 and Add.1); October 2014, Ukraine and the Dominican Republic: "Concerns with Respect to Measures Related to Plain Packaging of Tobacco Products and Their Compatibility with the TRIPS Agreement" (IP/C/M/77 and Add.1); February 2015, the Dominican Republic: "Concerns with Respect to Proposals for Plain Packaging of Tobacco Products in the United Kingdom and Ireland" (IP/C/M/78 and Add.1).
18. IP/C/M/75/Add.1, para. 495.
19. *Ibid.*, para. 517.
20. See IP/C/M/66, paras. 216 *et seq.*
21. *Ibid.*, paras. 219–227.

II. Procedural History

The timing of the procedural steps required to initiate formal WTO dispute settlement procedures – beginning with the request for consultations, followed by the request for establishment of a panel, and the actual composition of the panel[22] – is largely at the discretion of the initiating party, and thus influenced by the strategic, tactical, and often practical considerations of each individual complainant. This was also true for the five plain packaging disputes.

While the first complainant, Ukraine, moved relatively quickly from its request for consultations in March 2012[23] to requesting the Dispute Settlement Body (DSB) to establish a panel for its dispute in August of the same year,[24] the two next complainants, Honduras and the Dominican Republic, waited for over 16 months after the first step[25] before moving forward.[26] Cuba and Indonesia, the last two complainants, filed requests for consultations in 2013 and did not move to request panel establishment until 2014.[27]

In April 2014, Australia and the five complainants reached a procedural agreement[28] which facilitated the selection of panellists and ensured that harmonized procedures could be used for the five procedurally distinct panels which, the parties agreed, related to the same matter.[29] After the establishment of the remaining panels on 25 April 2014,[30] the composition of the five panels (collectively "the Panel") with the same panellists was determined on 5 May 2014 – about three years after the issue had first been raised in the TBT Committee.

---

22. On the procedural steps required to initiate panel proceedings under the WTO Dispute Settlement Understanding (DSU) please see *A Handbook on the WTO Dispute Settlement System* (Cambridge University Press, 2017).
23. WT/DS434/1.
24. WT/DS434/11. The DSB established the panel in DS434 at is meeting in September 2012.
25. Honduras requested consultations with Australia on 4 April 2012 (WT/DS435/1). The Dominican Republic requested consultations with Australia on 18 July 2012 (WT/DS441/1).
26. Although Honduras and the Dominican Republic requested the DSB to establish a panel for its dispute with Australia, respectively, on 15 October 2012 (WT/DS435/16) and 9 November 2012 (WT/DS441/15), they did not – after the DSB's deferral of panel establishment at the next meeting in 2012 – put their requests on the DSB's agendas again until September 2013 and April 2014, respectively. The DSB established the panel in DS435 (Honduras) at its meeting on 25 September 2013 and the panel in DS441 (Dominican Republic) on 25 April 2014.
27. Cuba requested consultations on 3 May 2013 (WT/DS458/1). Indonesia requested consultations on 20 September 2013 (WT/DS467/1). The establishment of their respective panels was requested by Indonesia on 3 March 2014 (WT/DS467/15) and by Cuba on 4 April 2014 (WT/DS458/14). For the establishment of these two panels see the minutes of the DSB meeting on 25 April 2014 (WT/DSB/M/344).
28. WT/DS535/17 WT/DS434/12, WT/DS435/17, WT/DS441/16, WT/DS458/15, WT/DS467/16 dated 28 April 2014.
29. The parties' agreement that the five disputes related to "the same matter" within the meaning of Article 9.2 DSU facilitated the selection of the same panellists for the five separate panels.
30. See minutes of the DSB meeting on 25 April 2014 (WT/DSB/M/344).

One year into its work the Panel, upon the request of Ukraine, suspended its work on Ukraine's complaint on 29 May 2015.[31] Since the parties did not resume work on that dispute, the authority for establishment of Ukraine's panel lapsed in May 2016[32] and proceedings in the plain packaging disputes continued only with respect to the remaining four complainants. Even though Ukraine's first written submission and associated evidence[33] had been referred to, incorporated[34] and relied upon[35] by the remaining four complainants, Ukraine's withdrawal from the case did not cause procedural complications, since under the Panel's working procedures, Ukraine's submission remained on the record in the remaining four disputes as a third-party submission.[36]

The high interest in the substance of the disputes was reflected in the large number of over 60 WTO Members participating in the Panel's proceedings as third parties,[37] and the record number of over 35 *amicus curiae* submissions received by the Panel.[38]

After substantive meetings with the parties in June and October 2015, the Panel issued its interim report on 2 May 2017, and its final Panel Report was issued to the parties on 25 September 2017. The Panel Report was circulated to Members in the three official WTO languages on 28 June 2018.[39]

B. SELECTED PANEL FINDINGS

I. Australia's TPP Measures at Issue in the Disputes

Extensive press coverage and commentary on Australia's plain packaging laws, and the introduction of similar measures by several countries since, have ensured that most readers will be well informed about the details of Australia's TPP measures that were at issue in the WTO plain packaging disputes. Against this background,

---

31. Australia agreed to this request on 29 May 2015. See Communication from the Chairperson of the Panel (WT/DS434/16, dated 3 June 2015). For more background to Ukraine's request for suspension see 'Yatsenyuk mulls end to challenge of Australia's plain packaging law', *Kyiv Post*, 22 May 2015.
32. Article 12.12 of the DSU. See Note by the Secretariat, Lapse of authority for the establishment of the Panel (WT/DS434/17, dated 30 June 2016).
33. This included an expert report by Professor Dinwoodie, on which Cuba and Honduras relied. See Panel Report, para. 7.1990, fn 4461, and fn 4345.
34. See, for example, for Cuba para. 7.1736, fn 4054.
35. See Panel Report, para. 7.1990, fn 4461, and fn 4345.
36. See Panel Report, paras. 1.51–1.54.
37. For an overview of third parties to the five different disputes see, Panel Report, paras. 1.11, 1.15, 1.19, and 1.23.
38. See Panel Report, paras. 1.46–1.50.
39. Circulation of panel reports to Members – which marks the end of the panel stage, and which enables the consideration for adoption of the report by the Dispute Settlement Body – requires translation into the three official WTO languages (English, French and Spanish). Given the increasing volume of panel reports – in this case over 880 pages, excluding annexes – this requirement can lead to significant delays in the formal resolution of disputes.

this paper provides only a brief description of the relevant aspects of the measures introduced by the Tobacco Plain Packaging Act 2011 (Cth) (TPP Act), the Tobacco Plain Packaging Regulations 2011 (Cth), as amended (TPP Regulations); and the Trade Marks Amendment (Tobacco Plain Packaging) Act 2011 (Cth), (TMA Act) - which were the measures at issue in the plain packaging disputes (collectively referred to as the "TPP measures").

Under the TPP measures, all tobacco products and their retail packaging offered for sale in Australia as of 1 December 2012[40] must comply with requirements regarding their appearance and the use of trademarks. The most recognizable requirements regarding the standardized appearance of tobacco products and retail packaging were that the outer surface of cigarette packaging is to be of a single colour, the "drab dark brown" Pantone 448C, that virtually no variation (such as round edges or embossing) is permitted in the physical features of cigarette packaging, and that no additional imagery and design is permitted on the packaging. This standardization of tobacco packaging is partly motivated by the desire to increase the effectiveness of graphic health warnings (GHWs) - for which expanded, and more prominent, use on tobacco products was introduced at the same time as the TPP measures[41] - but this related measure was not challenged in the plain packaging disputes at the WTO.[42]

Regarding trademarks, the TPP measures permit, on retail *packaging* of tobacco products, the use of word marks that denote the brand, business or company name, or the name of the product variant, provided that they appear in the orientation and form prescribed by the TPP Regulations - i.e. in Lucida Sans font in the colour Pantone Cool Gray 2C. They prohibit the use of stylized word marks, composite marks and figurative marks. In respect of tobacco *products*, the TPP measures prohibit the use of all trademarks on cigarettes. In respect of cigar bands, they permit the use of trademarks denoting the brand, business or company name, or the name of the product variant, as well as the country of origin, so long as they appear in the form prescribed by the TPP Regulations.[43]

In the context of trademark law, the TPP measures contain several legal provisions surrounding trademark use that are intended to "preserve a trade mark owner's ability to protect a trade mark, and to register and maintain registration of a trade mark".[44] These provisions, stipulated in Section 28 of the TPP Act, essentially aim to prevent certain legal consequences under trademark law that could normally follow from non-use of a trademark - such as to reject or revoke the registration of a trademark - where such non-use is caused by the operation of the TPP Act.[45]

40. Products produced in Australia had to comply already from the 1 October 2012.
41. Panel Report, para. 2.54.
42. For an overview of other tobacco control measures applied in Australia, see section 2.2 of the Panel Report.
43. For a full description of the requirements please see Panel Report, section 2.1.2.
44. TPP Bill Explanatory Memorandum, cited at Panel Report, para. 7.2574.
45. The operation of s. 28 TPP Act ultimately only played a minor role in the Panel's findings. For a brief discussion, and the Panel's finding that it does not prevent cancellation of registered trademarks on the basis of subsequent loss of distinctiveness, see Panel Report, paras. 7.2034–7.2037.

II. The Complainants' Main Claims and Arguments

The complainants' complex and multi-faceted challenges of the TPP measures in these disputes can be roughly categorized in two general lines of argument: under the first approach, the complainants argued that the TPP measures were *ineffective* with respect to their stated goal - to ultimately reduce tobacco consumption - and were thus *more trade-restrictive than necessary* within the meaning of Art. 2.2 of the TBT Agreement and *unjustifiable* within the meaning of Art. 20 of the TRIPS Agreement. A second line of argument claimed that the TPP measures' restrictions on the use of certain distinctive signs were incompatible with a number of TRIPS rules on trademark registration and protection - and were thus contrary to Art. 6*quinquies* of the Paris Convention, Art. 15.4, Art. 16.1 and 16.3, Paris Convention Arts 10*bis*(1), 10*bis*(3)(1) and 10*bis*(3)(3), and TRIPS Art. 22.2(b) and 24.3. The complainants also raised a claim under Art. IX:4 GATT 1994.[46]

Given that the complainants used the same evidence in respect of their claims under Art. 2.2 TBT Agreement and Art. 20 TRIPS, this paper will first give a brief summary of the Panel's considerations and findings under the TBT claims before moving on to a factual summary of the Panels treatment of the main TRIPS claims, beginning with Art. 20.

III. Summary of the Panel's Considerations under the TBT Claims

The TBT Agreement requires Members to ensure that technical regulations are not prepared, adopted or applied with a view to, or the effect of, creating unnecessary obstacles to international trade.[47] For that purpose, the central obligation of the TBT Agreement in Art. 2.2 requires that

> [T]echnical regulations shall not be more trade-restrictive than necessary to fulfil a legitimate objective, taking account of the risks non-fulfilment would create.

Since TBT disputes, mostly addressing this provision, make up a significant share of the over 600 WTO disputes to date, there is well-established jurisprudence[48] on the methodology how to assess whether a technical regulation is "more trade-restrictive than necessary". This assessment requires first a "relational analysis" involving (1) the degree to which measures contribute to a legitimate objective, (2) their trade-restrictiveness, and (3) the nature and gravity of the risks that non-fulfilment of the objective would create. This first step is then followed, as relevant, by a "comparative analysis" in which complainants - who bear the burden of showing unnecessary trade-restrictiveness - may indicate possible alternative measures that may be reasonably available to the respondent, and which would make an equivalent contribution to the objective while being less trade-restrictive.

---

46. For a full explanation of the Panel's order of analysis of all claims see Panel Report, section 7.1, paras. 7.1-7.14.
47. Art. 2.2, first sentence, TBT Agreement.
48. For a full coverage of the extensive jurisprudence on the methodology under Article 2.2 TBT Agreement see the WTO Analytical Index available at < www.wto.org >.

The Panel concluded overall that the TPP's objective of improving public health by reducing the use of, and exposure to, tobacco products is legitimate, and that the TPP measures are apt to, and do, make a meaningful contribution to this objective. While it found that the TPP measures are trade-restrictive to the extent that they result in a reduction in the total volume of imports, it concluded that since the nature of the risks that would arise from the non-fulfilment - not reducing of tobacco use and exposure - are particularly grave, and none of the alternatives proposed by the complainants would contribute to the objective to an equivalent degree,[49] the TPP measures were not more trade-restrictive than necessary to fulfil a legitimate objective, within the meaning of TBT Art. 2.2.[50]

The Panel's analysis under the TBT claims engages with the complainants' complex arguments on each step of the above assessment, as well as with the extensive volume of evidence relating to the design and the operational impact of the TPP measures. Given this paper's focus on the main TRIPS-related claims of the disputes, however, only two elements of the TBT analysis - those that are relevant for the subsequent analysis under Art. 20 TRIPS - will receive more than a brief summary here.

The first element is the significance of the FCTC as a justification for Australia's measures. Under Art. 2.5 TBT Agreement, technical regulations that are prepared, adopted or applied "in accordance with relevant international standards" shall be "rebuttably presumed not to create an unnecessary obstacle to international trade" - a considerable privilege in light of the above-mentioned rigorous analysis otherwise applied under Art. 2.2 TBT.

Although the relevant obligations under the treaty text of the FCTC - to implement measures against misleading or deceptive tobacco product packaging (Art. 11) and to undertake a comprehensive ban of all tobacco advertising, promotion and sponsorship (Art. 13) - did not themselves specify plain packaging, the implementation guidelines for these articles, unanimously adopted[51] by the FCTC parties, recommend it as a means to implement the treaty obligation. The guidelines regarding Arts. 11 and 13 FCTC provide that

> Parties should consider adopting measures to restrict or prohibit the use of logos, colours, brand images or promotional information on packaging other than brand names and product names displayed in a standard colour and font style (plain packaging)...[52]

> Packaging and product design are important elements of advertising and promotion. Parties should consider adopting plain packaging requirements to eliminate the effects of advertising or promotion on packaging.[53]

49. For the Panel's analysis of the complainants four proposed alternative measures, see Panel Report, section 7.2.5.6.
50. Panel Report, paras. 7.1724 - 7.1732.
51. 'WHO's Framework Convention on Tobacco Control ... saving lives', WHO 2010, available at: < www.emro.who.int/images/stories/tfi/documents/wntd-2011/WHO_Framework_Convention_on_Tobacco_Control_EN.pdf?ua = 1 > .
52. Guidelines to Article 11 FCTC.
53. Guidelines to Article 13 FCTC.

Since its measures had been adopted "in accordance" with what it claimed to be a relevant international standard, Australia argued that its TPP measures should thus benefit from the presumption in Art. 2.5 TBT.[54] The Panel examined the FCTC guidelines against the definition of a "standard" in Annex 1.2 of the TBT Agreement,[55] and relevant Appellate Body jurisprudence,[56] and engaged in particular detail with the definition's criteria as to what a relevant "document" must fulfil for an assessment to determine whether a challenged measure was in accordance with that standard.[57]

While the Panel ultimately found[58] that Australia had not been successful in showing that the Guidelines on Arts. 11 and 13 FCTC constitute a standard within the meaning of Annex 1.2 of the TBT Agreement, it recognized that they provide important guidance to FCTC parties in addressing packaging, and, as relevant, implementing plain packaging as an element of a comprehensive scheme of effective tobacco control policies.[59] It also stressed that its finding under Art. 2.5 TBT – rejecting it as an international standard – should not be read as an assessment of the FCTC's relevance for other considerations or claims in these disputes – notably those under Art. 20 TRIPS.[60]

The second element of the TBT analysis that is also relevant for the claim under Art. 20 TRIPS, is the assessment of evidence which the Panel analysed under the question whether the TPP measures – in the manner they were designed and in which they operated – actually contributed to the "legitimate objective" of improving public health.[61] Given the detailed analysis necessary under this step in the TBT

54. Panel Report, paras. 7.254–7.257.
55. Annex 1.2 of the TBT Agreement, which under Art. 15.5 TBT constitutes "an integral part of the agreement", defines a standard as a "document approved by a recognized body, that provides, for common and repeated use, rules, guidelines or characteristics for products or related processes and production methods, with which compliance is not mandatory. It may also include or deal exclusively with terminology, symbols, packaging, marking or labelling requirements as they apply to a product, process or production method."
56. For the Panel's full examination on the meaning of "relevant international standard" in Art. 2.5 TBT see Panel Report, paras. 7.265–7.289.
57. Panel Report, para. 7.331: "In making this determination, as described above, we are not suggesting that a "document", for the purposes of meeting the definition of "standard" in Annex 1.2 (and, specifically, constituting a "relevant international standard" under the second sentence of Article 2.5), could not be contained within an instrument that simultaneously addresses other issues or, together with various other instruments, form part of a broader context or framework. Rather, what is relevant is that all relevant product requirements, or other specifications related to the specific subject matter that is claimed to be the object of the "relevant international standard" (in the present case, "tobacco plain packaging") be identifiable with sufficient clarity to allow a "comparative assessment" to be properly conducted, to determine whether the challenged measure is "in accordance with" that international standard." (footnotes omitted).
58. Panel Report, para. 7.402.
59. Panel Report, para. 7.397.
60. Panel Report, paras. 7.403–7.405.
61. For the Panel's identification and assessment of the objective of the TPP measures for the purposes of the TBT analysis, see Panel Report, section 7.2.5.1.1. "In light of the above, we understand the objective pursued by Australia by means of the TPP measures to be to improve public health by reducing the use of, and exposure to, tobacco products." Panel Report, para. 7.232.

analysis, a precise identification of the objective of the measure in question, and of the operative mechanisms it employed to achieve them, is necessary in order to enable an assessment of the degree of contribution, and a review of potentially less trade-restrictive alternative measures.

Australia explained that, by design, the TPP measures were intended to operate on the basis of a "causal chain model"[62] whereby the standardized appearance and packaging would reduce the appeal of tobacco products and increase the effectiveness of graphical health warnings, which in turn would affect smoking behaviour, such as uptake or quitting, and thus contribute to long-term public health outcomes such as reduced smoking prevalence and reduction in tobacco-related disease and deaths.

In challenging the effectiveness of the measure, the complainants presented evidence seeking to undermine the credibility of the extensive pre-implementation evidence - studies and research on the effects of standardized appearance on the appeal of tobacco products, and on the relationship between appeal and behavioural changes - on which Australia had based the operational design of its first-of-its-kind measure. They consequently argued that plain packaging was - by its design - not capable of contributing to the intended objective.[63]

The parties also presented post-implementation empirical evidence on the application of TPP since its entry into force. The complainants sought to show that the actual application of plain packaging did not have the intended effect, and that therefore the measure did not contribute to its intended objective within the meaning of Art. 2.2.[64]

Based on extensive analysis, the Panel concluded that the studies submitted as pre-implementation evidence came from respected and qualified sources, focused on relevant outcomes, and had not been shown to be, overall, so methodologically flawed that they should be dismissed in their entirety as an unreliable evidentiary base in support of tobacco plain packaging.[65] It considered that credible pre-implementation evidence from recognized sources had been presented supporting the hypothesis that the TPP measures would indeed be capable of contributing to Australia's objective of improving public health through the mechanisms employed.[66] Having assessed the post-implementation statistical evidence on TPP application, the Panel concluded that the TPP measures, together with the enlarged graphic health warnings introduced at the same time but not challenged in the proceedings, did - among other things - statistically reduce the appeal of cigarettes among adult smokers and increase the noticeability of health warnings.

Statistical evidence also showed that the general trend of decrease in both overall smoking prevalence and cigarette sales continued - and accelerated - after the introduction of the TPP measures in Australia.[67] Overall, the Panel therefore

62. Panel Report, para. 7.488.
63. See the Panel's extensive engagement with over 60 studies of pre-implementation evidence at Panel Report, paras. 7.518–7.931.
64. See the Panel's engagement with the statistical post-implementation evidence relating to the application of the TPP measures at Panel Report, paras. 7.932–7.986 and Appendices A–E.
65. Panel Report, para. 7.639 et seq.
66. Panel Report, paras. 7.929- 7.931.
67. See Panel Report, paras. 7.972 and 7.979.

concluded that the evidence before it, taken in its totality, supported the view that the TPP measures, in combination with other tobacco-control measures maintained by Australia (including the enlarged graphic health warnings introduced simultaneously with TPP), "are apt to, and do in fact, contribute to Australia's objective of reducing the use of, and exposure to, tobacco products."[68]

IV. Claims under Article 20 TRIPS[69]

The complainants claimed that the TPP measures were inconsistent with Art. 20 TRIPS because they imposed "special requirements" that "encumber" the "use" of trademarks "in the course of trade" – and that such use was "unjustifiably" encumbered. Given the structure of the obligation expressed in Art. 20, that "use of a trademark in the course of trade shall not be unjustifiably encumbered by special requirements" – and particularly the use of the negative form to describe one of the elements of the obligation – the parties first of all disagreed about who bore the burden of proof regarding the element of "unjustifiability" of the encumbrance.[70]

1. *Burden of Proof*

While the complainants agreed, in line with the principle that the party asserting the affirmative of a particular claim or defence bears the burden of proof thereof, that they had to show that the plain packaging measures amounted to special requirements that encumber the use of trademarks in the course of trade within the meaning of Article 20,[71] they argued that these elements established a general prohibition of encumbrances, and that if a Member wished to overcome this "presumption in favour of unencumbered use" it was incumbent on that Member to show that the encumbrance was justifiable.[72]

In rejecting this argument, the Panel found that the first sentence of Art. 20 establishes a single obligation – not to "unjustifiably encumber" – rather than an obligation and exception thereto. It was therefore for the complainants to present a *prima facie* case for all elements of Art. 20, including that the use of a trademark in the course of trade is unjustifiably encumbered by the special requirements.[73]

68. Panel Report, para. 7.1025.
69. As pointed out above, the Panel's order of analysis treated the TRIPS claims in the order that the relevant provisions appeared in the TRIPS Agreement. Given the focus of interest on the claims under Art. 20 TRIPS, we will summarize these findings first, before turning to other TRIPS claims.
70. Panel Report, para. 7.2162.
71. Panel Report, paras. 7.2158 and 7.2161.
72. Panel Report, para. 7.2161.
73. Panel Report, para. 7.2169. For the Panel's full reasoning on burden of proof see 7.2163 – 7. 7.2171. The Panel emphasized that the "this allocation of the initial burden of proof does not address the standard of proof required to make a *prima facie* case, nor does it exhaust the respective responsibilities of the parties in the production of proof and evidence in the course of the proceedings." Panel Report, para. 7.2170; and that "[t]o the extent, therefore, that the respondent considers that, contrary to the complainants' assertions, any encumbrances arising under the challenged measures are not "unjustifiable", it will

The Panel then considered Australia's claims that certain aspects of the TPP measures were not covered by Art. 20 and could therefore not be found to violate that provision: specifically, the Panel considered whether the TPP measures constituted "special requirements" that "encumber" the "use" of a trademark "in the course of trade".

2. *Special Requirements that Encumber*

While Australia agreed that the TPP measures impose "special requirements" on the use of trademarks, insofar as they require that any word marks used on tobacco products and their retail packaging must appear in certain form, they contended that the term "special requirements" in Art. 20 does not encompass those aspects of the TPP measures that *prohibit* the use of trademarks on tobacco retail packaging and products. They argued that if domestic law prohibits the "use" of certain trademarks altogether, then those trademarks are not being "use[d] ... in the course of trade" and Art. 20 is not engaged, and pointed to the examples of a "special requirement" contained in the first and second sentences of Art. 20 – which refer to *how* a trademark may be used when it is used, rather than to *whether* it can be used – in support of this line of their argument. The complainants argued that "encumbrances" include any requirements that hinder or restrain trademark use,[74] and include complete prohibitions of use as the "ultimate encumbrance".[75]

The Panel considered that the term "special requirements" refers to a condition that must be complied with, has a close connection with or specifically addresses the "use of a trademark in the course of trade", and is limited in application. Based on the textual analysis of the provision, it found that this may include a requirement not to do something, in particular a prohibition on using a trademark.[76]

The Panel noted that – interestingly, and for different reasons – all parties agreed that general regulatory measures, such as an advertising ban, would not fall under the disciplines of Article 20. While the complainants reached this conclusion – arguing that general regulatory measures that do not specifically concern, but only *incidentally affect*, use of a trademark, are not "*special* requirements" – Australia came to the same conclusion, arguing that *prohibitions* on the use of trademarks are not covered by Article 20.[77] While the Panel expressly refrains from making a ruling in this regard, it emphasizes that

> nothing in our findings should be taken as suggesting that the kind of trademark use that may be affected by measures falling within the scope of Article 20 is

---

be incumbent upon it to present the arguments and evidence sufficient to disprove any *prima facie* case established by the complainants in this respect.", Panel Report, 7.2171.

74. For an overview of the complainants' arguments in this regard see Panel Report, paras. 2.2176–2.2203.
75. That term is employed by Honduras (See Panel Report, para. 6.78, fn 420) and picked up by Malawi, Zambia and Zimbabwe in their third-party submissions (Panel Report, paras. 7.2212, 17.2218, 7.2219).
76. Panel Report, para. 7.2231.
77. Panel Report, para. 7.2233.

necessarily limited to use in the form of application of a trademark on a product presented for sale.[78]

As regards the meaning of "encumber", the Panel was not persuaded that the terms of Art. 20 imply that only "special requirements" that would determine *how* a trademark may be used, to the exclusion of special requirements entirely disallowing the use of a trademark, may be considered to "encumber the use" of such trademarks. Encumbrances arising from special requirements may range from limited encumbrances, such as those resulting from the specific types of requirements mentioned in the first and second sentences of Art. 20, to more extensive encumbrances, such as a prohibition on the use of a trademark in certain situations.[79]

3. *Use in the Course of Trade*

Based on divergent views on the interpretation of the term "in the course of trade" and on what constitutes relevant "use" of a trademark for the purposes of Art. 20, the parties also disagreed whether the TPP measures encumber the use of trademarks "in the course of trade".

Australia took the view that "in the course of trade" refers to acts undertaken during the buying and selling of goods for profit, which necessarily "culminates" at the point of sale. Given that Australia maintains bans on tobacco advertising at retail premises and on point-of-sale display of cigarettes[80] – so that packaging and products are not visible to consumers at retail – it argued that the plain packaging measures did not affect the use of trademarks "in the course of trade".[81]

The Panel, taking into account text, context,[82] and the different language versions of the TRIPS Agreement,[83] found that the phrase is not, on its face, limited to "trade" in the sense of "buying and selling" but more broadly covers the process

---

78. *Ibid.*
79. Panel Report, para. 7.2239. "We also agree with those complainants and third parties who argue that it would be 'counterintuitive' to consider that a measure that restricts the use of a trademark would be subject to the disciplines of Article 20 while a more far-reaching measure to prohibit such use would not." Para. 7.2238.
80. "A typical point-of-sale display ban in Australia requires that tobacco products be kept in an opaque, closed cabinet that is inaccessible to consumers and is behind the counter of a retail outlet." Panel Report, para. 2.67.
81. Panel Report, para. 7.2252.
82. "We note that the phrase "in the course of trade" is used, in addition to Article 20, in two other provisions of the TRIPS Agreement that are the subject of separate claims in these proceedings, namely Article 16.1 of the TRIPS Agreement and Article 10*bis*(3)(3) of the Paris Convention (1967), as well as Article 24.8 of the TRIPS Agreement and Article 10*bis*(3)(2) of the Paris Convention (1967). ... Harmonious interpretation requires that same or similar terms in different provisions of the same agreement should be presumed to have the same or similar meaning, much as the use of different terms creates a presumption that the terms were intended to have a different meaning." Para. 7.2262.
83. "The corresponding French phrase 'au cours d'opérations commerciales' and Spanish phrase 'el curso de operaciones comerciales' also connote a meaning that more broadly relates to commercial activities." Panel Report, para. 7.2261.

relating to commercial activities, and that at least some commercial activities taking place after the retail sale were covered by the phrase.[84]

Regarding the relevant "use", Australia argued that it was the use *to distinguish* the goods and services of one undertaking from those of other undertakings that was relevant for the Art. 20 analysis, and that encumbrances on the use of a trademark for *other purposes* (such as advertising or promotion) were not relevant under Art. 20.[85]

The Panel rejected these arguments, finding that the general language in Art. 20 does not qualify the nature of relevant "use" or otherwise circumscribe this obligation in terms of any particular uses, other than such use being "in the course of trade".[86] It found that, as reflected in prior WTO jurisprudence, the manner in which the exploitation of TRIPS-protected subject-matter takes place, and how to extract economic value from it, was essentially a matter for the right holder to decide.[87] Like in other TRIPS provisions mentioning trademark use,[88] what was relevant was the *objective fact* of use "in the course of trade", i.e. in the course of commercial activities, rather than seeking to distinguish types of uses on the basis of *function or purpose of such use*, which, in any case, may often overlap with each other in practise.[89]

4. *Meaning of the Term "Unjustifiably"*

The Panel considered extensive arguments related to the meaning of "unjustifiably" and the methodology for determining whether it applied to an encumbrance on use. It found the ordinary meaning[90] of the first sentence of Art.20 connoted a situation where the use of a trademark is encumbered by special requirements in a manner that lacks a justification or reason sufficient to support the resulting encumbrance. This, it considered, implies in turn that there may be circumstances in which good reasons exist that sufficiently support the application of encumbrances on the use of a trademark in a reasonable manner.[91] Assessing the context of other TRIPS and WTO provisions in this respect, the Panel was guided in part by Articles 7 and 8 TRIPS,[92] and para. 5 of the 2001 Doha Declaration on TRIPS and Public Health (the "Doha Declaration").[93]

---

84. Panel Report, paras. 7.2263–7.2264.
85. Panel Report, paras. 7.2265–7.2271. Australia further argued that the trademark definition in Art. 15.1 also focuses on the distinguishing function.
86. Panel Report, para. 7.2280.
87. Panel Report, para. 7.2285.
88. Such as Arts. 15.3 and 19 TRIPS.
89. Panel Report, para. 7.2284. "As we noted in the context of our analysis of the complainants' claims under Article 16.1 of the TRIPS Agreement, the "use" of a trademark that is relevant for the acquisition and maintenance of distinctiveness is not limited to use on packaging of a product, but rather extends to a wider range of commercial, advertising and promotion activities." Panel Report, para. 7.2285.
90. The general rule of interpretation (VCLT Art. 31.1) provides: "A treaty shall be interpreted in good faith in accordance with the *ordinary meaning* to be given to the terms of the treaty in their *context* and in the light of its *object and purpose*."
91. Panel Report, paras. 7.2395–7.2396.
92. Panel Report, paras. 7.2399–7.2406.
93. WT/MIN(01)/DEC/W/2.

Referring to previous WTO jurisprudence,[94] the Panel considered that Art. 8.1 TRIPS reflected the drafter's intention to preserve Members' ability to pursue certain legitimate societal interests while recognizing their potential impact on IP rights.[95] It considered that the specific objectives mentioned in Art. 8.1 – while not limiting the scope of what could be the basis of justifiability – could help identify the types of recognized "societal interests", including public health, that might justify measures under Art. 20.[96] The Panel saw this view confirmed by para. 5 of the Doha Declaration, which it considered a "subsequent agreement" of WTO Members within the meaning of Art. 31(3)(a) of the Vienna Convention on the Law of Treaties.[97]

Reviewing the use of similar (e.g. "unjustifiable") or different (e.g. "unnecessary") terms in the TRIPS Agreement and other WTO agreements, the Panel concluded that while the emphasis should be on establishing the proper meaning of a term as used *in the provision*, rather than determining its meaning *in opposition* to any other term, such context was relevant and suggested – in this case – a deliberate choice designed to convey different meanings. The TRIPS context, where use of the term "necessary" is pervasive,[98] supports the implication of a deliberate choice of a distinct term "unjustifiably" which should not be assumed to be synonymous with "unnecessarily",[99] nor with the meaning of "unjustifiable" in Art. XX GATT.[100]

While observing that Art. 20 did not itself grant exceptions to rights, nor expressly refer to a notion of "legitimate interest", the Panel considered that due account needed to be taken of the TRIPS context. This meant taking account of the

94. Panel Report, *Canada – Pharmaceutical Patents*, para. 7.26.
95. "Specifically, the principles reflected in Article 8.1 express the intention of drafters of the TRIPS Agreement to preserve the ability for WTO Members to pursue certain legitimate societal interests, at the same time as it confirms their recognition that certain measures adopted by WTO Members for such purposes may have an impact on IP rights, and requires that such measures be "consistent with the provisions of the [TRIPS] Agreement", Panel Report, para. 7.2404.
96. Panel Report, para. 7.2406.
97. This categorization of the ministerial declaration has systemic significance in the context of the WTO's legal architecture. For the full consideration see Panel Report, paras. 7.2407–7.2411.
98. "We note that the term "necessary", by contrast, is used in a number of other provisions of the TRIPS Agreement, namely in Articles 3.2, 8.1, 27.2, 39.3, 43.2, 50.5 and 73(b), as well as Article 11(3) of the Paris Convention (1967) and Article 17 of the Berne Convention (1971) as incorporated by reference into the TRIPS Agreement. The term is also used in paragraphs 1 and 3 of Article 31*bis* of the TRIPS Agreement, as well as in paragraphs 1(a) and 2(b)(i) of the Annex to the TRIPS Agreement." Panel Report, para. 7.2419.
99. Panel Report, para. 7.2419. The complainants' argument to assimilate the meaning of "unjustifiably" to the term "unnecessary" implied also applying the equivalent methodology as in Art. 2.2 TBT – including the consideration of alternative measures that would make an equivalent contribution while providing less of an encumbrance on trademark use. See below under section B.IV.5.c).
100. Panel Report, 7.2420–7.-2421. The Panel rejected the Australian argument that – in reference to the Appellate Body's interpretation of the terms "arbitrary and unjustifiable" in Art. XX GATT in *Brazil–Retreaded Tyres* and *EC–Seal Products* – Art. 20 should be interpreted to mean that trademark use is "unjustifiably" encumbered only if there is *no* rational connection between the imposition of the special requirements and a legitimate public policy objective.

legitimate interest of the trademark owners in using its trademark in the course of trade – recognized in previous WTO jurisprudence[101] under Art. 17 TRIPS – and how that is affected by the encumbrances to be justified.[102] Overall, the Panel concluded, Art. 20 reflects the balance intended by the drafters of the TRIPS Agreement between the existence of a legitimate interest of trademark owners in using their trademarks in the marketplace, and the right of WTO Members to adopt measures for the protection of certain societal interests that may adversely affect such use.[103]

On the basis of its general interpretative analysis, including the considerations summarized above, the Panel enunciated – for the first time in WTO jurisprudence[104] – the standard of review it would apply to the term "unjustifiably" in Art. 20. Under that standard, a determination of whether the use of a trademark in the course of trade is being "unjustifiably" encumbered by special requirements, should involve a consideration of the following factors:

a) the nature and extent of the encumbrance resulting from the special requirements, bearing in mind the legitimate interest of the trademark owner in using its trademark in the course of trade and thereby allowing the trademark to fulfil its intended function;
b) the reasons for which the special requirements are applied, including any societal interests they are intended to safeguard; and
c) whether these reasons provide sufficient support for the resulting encumbrance.[105]

The different interests at issue were to be "weighed and balanced" on a case-by-case basis, in light of the particular circumstances of the case.

Before applying the standard of review to the TPP measures, the Panel first considered the complainants' claim that the Panel need not engage in a detailed consideration of the extent to which the measures contribute (or not) to their stated objectives, since the TPP measures were *per se* – by their "very nature" – unjustifiable. This claim was based on the argument that:

- the prohibition of use of certain trademarks rises to a level of restrictiveness that cannot be justified under any circumstances;[106]
- Australia did not assess the justifiability of the requirements in respect of individual trademarks and their individual features;[107]

---

101. "As also expressed by the panel in *EC – Trademarks and Geographical Indications,* this interest reflects the function of trademarks in the marketplace, which benefits trademark owners as well as consumers." Panel Report, para. 2428. See also Panel Report, *EC – Trademarks and Geographical Indications (Australia)*, paras. 7.662-7.663 (quoting Panel Report, *Canada – Pharmaceutical Patents*, para. 7.69).
102. Panel Report, para. 7.2428.
103. Panel Report, para. 7.2429.
104. The panel in *Indonesia – Autos* did not address this question.
105. Panel Report, para. 7.2430.
106. For the detailed treatment of this argument by Honduras and Indonesia, see Panel Report, paras. 7.2436–7.2442.
107. For the detailed treatment of this argument see Panel Report, paras. 7.2443–7.2508.

- Australia had failed to follow its own domestic regulatory procedures in adopting them;[108] and
- the TPP measures fall within the illustrative list of measures in Art. 20 and, therefore, are "presumptively invalid".[109]

While the Panel engaged with – and rejected – all of these claims individually, only a few findings of note are summarized here.

Conceptually in line with its earlier determination that the notion of "encumbrance" also included the ultimate encumbrance of prohibition, the Panel saw nothing in Art 20 that would make a highly restrictive measure inherently unjustifiable, and thus would remove the need to assess its justifiability under the standard of review the panel had just developed.[110]

Regarding the question of "individual assessment", the Panel pointed out that the use of the singular in Art. 20 ("use of a trademark") was a drafting convention also employed elsewhere in the TRIPS Agreement. While decisions under domestic law on eligibility for protection, registration and invalidation, as well as enforcement of rights conferred, were necessarily taken in respect of individual trademarks, this did not imply that special requirements under Art. 20 would have to be formulated – or their justifiability be assessed – in respect of individual trademarks. Rather, the extent to which an assessment of the unjustifiability of specific encumbrances would require an assessment of individual trademarks and their specific features will depend on the circumstances of each case. Where a Member applies such requirements to a class of trademarks or to some specific types of situations rather than to the specific features of particular trademarks, the assessment of their unjustifiability may concentrate on the overall rationale as it relates to the reason for adopting them.[111]

On the basis of a textual analysis in English and French,[112] confirmed by the negotiating history[113] of the provision, the Panel found that Art. 20 enumerated examples of "special requirements," – rather than examples of special requirement that would be presumptively unjustifiable. The examples in the illustrative list in the first sentence of Art. 20 were thus subject to the same standard as other special requirements, namely that they shall not unjustifiably encumber the use of a trademark in the course of trade.[114]

108. For the detailed treatment of this argument by Indonesia see Panel Report, paras. 7.2509–7.2514.
109. For the detailed treatment of this argument by Cuba see Panel Report, paras. 7.2514–7.2528.
110. Panel Report, para. 7.2442.
111. Panel Report, para. 7.2505.
112. Panel Report, para. 7.2525.
113. Panel Report, para. 7.2527.
114. Panel Report, para. 7.2526.

5. *Application of the Standard of Review in Article 20 to the TPP Measures*

a) *Nature and Extent of the Encumbrance*

The Panel noted three issues when applying the first leg of the standard of review it had developed concerning the nature and extent of the encumbrance. First, it pointed out that while Art. 16.1 TRIPS provides for a registered trademark owner's right to prevent certain uses by unauthorized third parties under the conditions set out in the first sentence of Art. 16.1,[115] Art. 20 was an additional undertaking by Members not to unjustifiably encumber trademark use by special requirements. It further recalled its earlier finding that the relevant trademark "use" for the purposes of Art. 20 is not limited to the use for the specific purpose of distinguishing the goods and services of one undertaking from those of other undertakings. Against this background, the focus of its analysis under this leg of the standard was on the implications that the TPP requirements have in the marketplace, both on a trademark's ability to distinguish goods and services in the course of trade and on an owner's ability to extract economic value from the use of its trademark, as well as how these requirements affect consumers.[116]

The Panel recognized the importance of trademark use, that marks can serve to distinguish products in the marketplace,[117] and the legitimacy of the owner's interest in using its trademark for various purposes, including to identify the source of the product and communicate benefits of the product, whether functional or intangible.[118] It acknowledged that by disallowing the use of design features in trademarks, the TPP measures prevent a trademark owner from using such features to convey any messages about the product, whether functional or intangible, and deriving any economic value from the use of such features.[119]

The Panel considered the TPP measures' prohibitions on the use of figurative elements to be far-reaching[120] in terms of the trademark owner's possibilities to extract economic value from the use of such features.[121] It also noted that the practical implications of those prohibitions were partly mitigated by the fact that the TPP measures allow tobacco manufacturers to use word marks, including brand and variant names, to distinguish their products from each other. The Panel noted further that the complainants had not sought to demonstrate that consumers had in

115. Since in the Panel's order of analysis, its findings on Art. 16 preceded the Art. 20 analysis, the Panel was able to "recall" its discussion of Art. 16, which, in the context of this article, follows below.
116. Panel Report, paras. 7.2533 and 7.2563.
117. Panel Report, para. 7.2561.
118. Panel Report, para. 7.2522.
119. Panel Report, para. 7.2562.
120. Panel Report, para. 7.2557.
121. "Figurative elements, combinations of colours, and combinations of signs, form part of the definition of the protectable subject-matter under Article 15.1. Their inclusion in this definition suggests that the drafters of the TRIPS Agreement considered that it is possible to use such non-word trademark content to distinguish the goods of one undertaking from those of other undertakings." Panel Report, para. 7.2557.

fact been unable to distinguish tobacco products of one undertaking from those of other undertakings, as a result of the TPP-related encumbrances.[122]

As regards the extent of the encumbrance, the Panel recalled the analysis of empirical evidence it had completed under the analysis of the TBT claim.[123] As regards price competition, the empirical evidence relating to cigarette prices, to the total value of the retail market and to the total value and volume of cigarette imports does not validate the complainants' argument that the TPP measures would lead to an increase in price competition and a fall in prices, and consequently to a decrease in the sales value of tobacco products and the total value of imports.[124]

With respect to downward substitution or "downtrading",[125] the Panel considered that there is some evidence, albeit limited, that, together with enlarged GHWs introduced on the same date, the TPP measures appear to have had a negative impact on the ratio of higher- to low-priced cigarette wholesale sales. However, the Panel was not persuaded that the decrease in consumption and imports of premium products was exclusively the result of "downtrading", given that the overall consumption of tobacco products had decreased, and that the two market segments had evolved on the basis of distinct trends even before the implementation of the TPP measures.[126]

b) *Reasons for the TPP Measures*

In examining the reasons for which Australia applied the TPP measures the Panel recalled its determination under the TBT analysis that Australia's principal objective was improving public health by reducing the use of, and exposure to, tobacco products. The Panel noted that the parties were in agreement about the importance of public health as a policy concern, and of effective tobacco control measures to reduce the public health burden resulting from tobacco use. It noted, in particular, that Australia's statements on the impact of tobacco use, including the following, remained uncontested by complainants[127]:

> Tobacco use continues to be the leading global cause of preventable death. It kills approximately six million people and causes hundreds of billions of dollars of economic damage worldwide each year ... if current trends continue, by 2030

122. Panel Report, para. 7.2570. The Panel notes "that some of the evidence before us suggests that the potential impact of plain packaging on brand recall, i.e. the ability to recognize a brand, was considered in some of the plain packaging studies and concluded that "for young smokers at least, plain packaging would not affect brand recall". Stirling Review, (Exhibits AUS-140, HND-130, CUB-59), section 4.6.3, p. 82.", see fn 5210.
123. See above section B.III.
124. Panel Report, para. 7.2572.
125. Downward substitution from higher- to low-priced brands means that some consumers buy a cheaper brand than the brand that they bought before the TPP measures were introduced. Complainants argued that the elimination of differentiating features would lead to consumers being less loyal to their former brands and lower their willingness to pay for their former brand and thus switch to a cheaper brand.
126. Panel Report, para. 7.2573.
127. Panel Report, para. 7.1307.

> tobacco will kill more than eight million people worldwide each year, with 80 percent of these living in low- and middle-income countries.
>
> ...
>
> Tobacco smoking remains one of the leading causes of preventable death and disease among Australians, killing over 15,000 Australians every year.[128]

It further noted the Appellate Body's recognition that the preservation of human life and health as a value that is "both vital and important in the highest degree",[129] and recalled its consideration that the specific identification of public health as a societal interest in Art. 8.1 was relevant for the interpretation of Art. 20, as confirmed by para. 5 of the Doha Declaration.[130] WTO Members had further emphasized the importance of public health as a legitimate policy concern in paragraph 4 of the Doha Declaration.

A further element in the Panel's considerations of relevant reasons was Australia's explanation that the decision to introduce the TPP measures was made in the context of a comprehensive range of tobacco control measures, including advertising and promotional bans, excise taxes, GHWs, and investments in anti-smoking initiatives, and Australia's intention to give effect to certain obligations under the FCTC through the TPP measures, as well as its explanations of how the TPP measures are reflected in the Art. 11 and Art. 13 FCTC Guidelines.[131]

c) *Whether the Reasons Provide Sufficient Support for the Resulting Encumbrance*

In completing the final leg of the analysis under the Art. 20 standard of review it had established - namely assessing the health concerns underlying the TPP measures against their implications for the use of trademarks, taking into account the nature and extent of the encumbrance - the Panel first noted it was undisputed that the grounds on which the TPP measures were applied address an exceptionally grave domestic and global health problem involving a high level of preventable morbidity and mortality.[132] The fact that the special requirements, as part of the overall TPP measures and in combination with other tobacco-control measures maintained by Australia, had been found to contribute to Australia's objective of improving public health by reducing the use of, and exposure to, tobacco products, suggested, in its view, that the reasons for which these special requirements were applied provided sufficient support for the application of the resulting encumbrances on the use of trademarks.

It recalled its review of the evidence[133] that the removal of design features on retail packaging and cigarettes is apt to reduce the appeal of tobacco products and

---

128. Panel Report, para. 7.1308.
129. Panel Report, para. 7.2587, citing the Appellate Body Report, *EC – Asbestos*, para. 172.
130. Panel Report, para. 7.2588.
131. The FCTC preamble recognizes that "the spread of the tobacco epidemic is a global problem with serious consequences for public health that calls for the widest possible international cooperation and the participation of all countries in an effective, appropriate and comprehensive international response." Panel Report, para. 7.2589.
132. Panel Report, para. 7.2592.
133. See above section B.III.

increase the effectiveness of GHWs, and that uniformity of features is an integral part of the approach underlying the TPP measures. In keeping with its nuanced finding under the TBT analysis – that the FCTC, despite not qualifying as an international standard under Art. 2.5 TBT, constituted nevertheless important guidance under other claims and provisions – the Panel considered the fact that Australia pursues its domestic public health objective in line with its commitments under the FCTC – which "was developed in response to the globalization of the tobacco epidemic" and had been ratified by 180 countries – underscored the importance of the public health reasons for which the trademark-related special requirements under the TPP measures are applied.[134]

Mirroring the discussion on the meaning of "unjustifiably" referred to above,[135] the complainants argued that the standard of review of "unjustifiably" should include a consideration of whether "an alternative measure could have been deployed that would make an equivalent contribution, while imposing a lesser or no encumbrance on trademark use". Australia contended that the ordinary meaning of the term "unjustifiably" does not support the view that only the "least restrictive" encumbrance of "reasonably available" alternatives would pass the test.[136]

The Panel concluded that the term "unjustifiably" provides a degree of latitude to a Member to choose an intervention to address a policy objective, as long as the reasons sufficiently support any resulting encumbrance. It did, however, not close the door on the relevance of alternative measures that involve a lesser or no encumbrance on the use of trademarks. The availability of such measures could still inform an assessment of whether the reasons for which the special requirements are applied sufficiently support the resulting encumbrance. However, the measures proposed by the complainants already in the context of the TBT analysis – and again under Art. 20 – had already been found by the Panel to be inapt to contribute to Australia's objective in a manner equivalent to that of the TPP measures.[137]

Thus, while alternative measures could be relevant for the analysis under Art. 20, the Panel was not persuaded that the alternatives proposed by the complainants in this case called into question the sufficiency of the reasons Australia had given for the TPP trademark restrictions, given the contribution that the TPP measures make to Australia's objective of improving public health. The Panel was thus "... not persuaded that the complainants have demonstrated that Australia has acted beyond the bounds of the latitude available to it under Article 20 to choose an appropriate policy intervention to address its public health concerns in relation to tobacco products".[138]

In its conclusion, the Panel emphasized its recognition that trademarks "have substantial economic value" and that the TPP measures have a far-reaching impact on the trademark owners' possibilities to extract economic value from the use of figurative or stylized features of trademarks.[139] It then recalled the main considerations – apart

134. Panel Report, para. 7.2596.
135. See above section B.IV.4.
136. Panel Report, para. 7.2597.
137. Panel Report, para. 7.2600 referring to the Panel's TBT analysis.
138. Panel Report, para. 7.2604.
139. *Ibid.*

from the gravity of the public health problem - why it still found these measures to "not unjustifiably encumber" the use of trademarks under Art. 20. In pointing out once again that the TPP measures' trademark restrictions are "an integral part of Australia's comprehensive tobacco control policies, and designed to complement the pre-existing measures" the Panel considered it significant that Australia had already exhausted most other conventional tobacco control measures - such as banning advertising in retail spaces and point-of-sale display, prohibition of smoking in public places and taxation measures.[140]

The Panel found that in this already highly-regulated policy area, Australia - as the first country to implement tobacco plain packaging - pursued its domestic public health objective in line with the emerging multilateral public health policies in the area of tobacco control as reflected in the FCTC and the guidelines developed under its auspices. Finally, Australia's chosen measures - the special requirements as part of the TPP measures - had been found to in fact contribute to Australia's objective of improving public health, which suggested to the Panel that "the reasons for which these special requirements were applied provided sufficient support for the application of the resulting encumbrances on the use of trademarks".[141]

V. Highlights from other TRIPS Claims

Turning to other TRIPS claims advanced by one or more of the complainants, this article will now outline some findings and clarifications that are of particular systemic relevance for the TRIPS Agreement. The claims under Art. 15.4 provided an opportunity for the Panel to highlight the operation of Art. 15, including the definition of "trademark" - which was a significant substantive addition that the TRIPS Agreement provided to the, hitherto mostly procedural, international trademark law under the Paris Convention.

1. Highlights from the Claim under Article 15.4

Under Art. 15.4 TRIPS, the complainants claimed that permitting *acquired* distinctiveness through use for trademark registration under Art. 15.1, third sentence - as Australia had opted to permit - was incompatible with restricting the use of certain signs which could therefore not acquire distinctiveness for certain products and are thus prevented from being registered.[142] As the TPP measures mandated such use restriction *based on the nature of the goods* to which the marks would be applied, this - they argued - constituted an obstacle to trademark registration in contravention of Art 15.4. In other words, the complainants argued that, because the TPP measures prevent signs, which are not inherently distinctive and have not yet acquired distinctiveness through use - but are *capable* of acquiring distinctiveness through

140. See Panel Report, section 2.2 for a description of Australia's other tobacco control measures in place.
141. Panel Report, para. 7.2604.
142. Panel Report, para. 7.1789.

use – from acquiring distinctiveness through use for tobacco products, these measures constitute an obstacle to registration *based on the nature of the product.*[143]

In its general interpretative analysis, the Panel elaborated that the term *trademark* in Art. 15.4 refers to signs or combinations of signs that meet the distinctiveness requirement set out in Art. 15.1, first sentence, and which Members are therefore under an obligation to consider as "capable of constituting trademarks".[144]

The complainants argued that signs that are not inherently distinctive, and have not (yet) acquired distinctiveness through use, might nevertheless be *capable* of constituting a trademark in that they may acquire distinctiveness through use, and should therefore be covered by the term "trademark" in Art. 15.4 – thus benefitting from its prohibition of obstacles to registration that are based on the nature if the goods to which they will be applied. In response, the Panel elaborated that the definition in Art. 15.1 refers to signs that, *at that particular moment*, are capable of distinguishing goods and services and that are, therefore, considered as capable of constituting a trademark, and does not cover signs that only have *the potential to develop this capacity* in the future.[145] Referring to the negotiating context of Art. 15.1, it suggested the term had been employed in order to accommodate the two main approaches to trademark registration salient at the time:

> (1) The *first-to-use* approach, mostly employed in common law traditions, in which registration always depended on use, and trademarks therefore already distinguished goods and services in the market at the moment of applying for registration, and (2) the *first-to-file* approach, common in civil law countries, where use was not a condition of registration, and distinctive signs could therefore be registered as trademarks even if they had never been used in the market. The formulation of the distinctiveness requirement chosen in Article 15.1, first sentence, covers both scenarios by requiring that signs are "*capable* of distinguishing" goods or services from different undertakings if they were applied to goods and services in the market at that moment. In that respect, the TRIPS Agreement maintained the neutrality of the Paris Convention (1967).[146]

Consequently, the Panel concluded that the term "trademark" as used in Art. 15.4 does not encompass signs that do not meet the "distinctiveness" requirement in Art. 15.1, and that the obligation in Art. 15.4. does therefore not extend to signs that are not inherently distinctive and have not yet acquired distinctiveness through use.

The complainants further argued that where a Member exercises the option under Art. 15.1, third sentence, to make registrability of non-inherently distinctive signs depend on distinctiveness *acquired through use*, such a Member would violate Art. 15.4, if, at the same time, it restricts the ability of an applicant to use the sign on a particular good in order to acquire distinctiveness solely because of the nature of the good. In response to this argument, the Panel confirmed that Art. 15.1, third sentence indeed provides *the option*[147] for Members to make registrability dependent

143. Panel Report, para. 7.1816.
144. Panel Report, para. 7.1831.
145. Panel Report, para. 7.1864.
146. Panel Report, para. 7.1868, fn 4237.
147. Panel Report, para. 7.1889.

on distinctiveness acquired by use. However, it found no indication that a Member's exercise of that option would modify the scope of the definition of "trademark" and thus extend the scope of the prohibition in Art. 15.4, for the relevant Member, so as to include signs that are not inherently distinctive and which have not yet acquired distinctiveness through use.[148]

Finally, Cuba argued that the restriction on the use of signs under the TPP measures reduces *the protection* Australia provides to tobacco-related trademarks - that flows from trademark registration - and thereby violates the governing principle of Article 15.4, namely to confer *protection* to trademarks on the same terms and conditions notwithstanding the nature of the product.[149] In engaging with this argument, the Panel elaborated on the Appellate Body's assessment in *US - Section 211 Appropriations Act*, of the relationship between the trademark provisions in the Paris Convention and the TRIPS Agreement.[150] In that regard, the Art. 15 provisions, together with Article 6(1) of the Paris Convention (1967) set the conditions under which Members may, or may not, deny the act of registration of specific signs "as a trademark", which is distinct from the extent of the rights that flow from such registration, once it is granted.[151]

While the Panel noted that registration is the "gateway to substantive protection" of a trademark, as it is the condition for the rights defined in Article 16 to be accorded to the owner of a registered trademark, this does not imply that the obligation in Article 15.4 in relation to the conditions for "registration" of a trademark should be read to apply more generally to substantive protection of a trademark once it is registered.[152] The provisions governing the procedural step of registration are therefore only relevant for the *availability* of protection, while the *scope and content* of the substantive protection itself, once granted, are governed by other provisions, including Article 16 of the TRIPS Agreement and, to the extent that they offer enhanced protection within their jurisdiction, the domestic laws of WTO Members.[153] While not providing minimum standard trademark rights to marks on certain products might therefore constitute a violation of *Art. 16.1*, the Panel clarifies that *Art. 15.4* does not stipulate an obligation that the scope and content of trademark protection that flows from registration has to be the same regardless of the nature of the goods or services to which trademarks are or may be applied.[154]

As in past WTO disputes on TRIPS issues, the Panel emphasized its understanding that the TRIPS provisions operate in harmony with other parts of the

148. *Ibid.*
149. Panel Report, para. 7.1898.
150. See Panel Report, paras. 7.1841-7.1855 and 7.1904-7.1912.
151. Panel Report, para. 7.1904.
152. Panel Report, para. 7.1905.
153. Panel Report, para. 7.1906.
154. Panel Report, para. 7.1908. Although the interesting question whether different levels of trademark *protection* - beyond the level required by Art. 16.1 - according to different product groups would be compatible with the TRIPS Agreement was not before the Panel, it is clear from the Panel's reasoning here that any such non-discrimination requirement as to trademark *protection* could not be derived from the prohibition on obstacles to *registration* based on the nature of the product under Art. 15.4.

international intellectual property system[155] by confirming its finding with reference to the "underlying approach" of the Paris Convention (1967), which did not itself aim to provide substantive protection standards, but focused on permitting Convention nationals access to the protection systems provided by the Convention countries' domestic legal systems.[156] It further noted support for its interpretation from the negotiating history of Art. 7 Paris Convention (1967), on which Art. 15.4 is based, which had been changed from the original reference to obstacles to the "filing" of a trademark, to the current "registration", at the 1925 Hague Revision Conference, but which did not include "renewal", whose inclusion had been expressly rejected at the 1958 Lisbon Revision Conference.[157]

2. *Highlights from the Claim under Article 16.1*

As highlighted at the outset, one main line of the complainants' arguments had been to imply that ensuring some degree of trademark use constituted a central element of the concept of "protection" required under different provisions of the Paris Convention and the TRIPS Agreement itself, namely under Art. *6quinquies* Paris Convention (1967),[158] and Articles 16.1[159] and Article 16.3[160] TRIPS.

In their claims under Art. 16.1, the complainants argued that a trademark owner's ability to demonstrate confusion in the market, and thus infringement, correlates with the degree of distinctiveness, or "strength" of the trademark which, they argued, is intrinsically linked to the trademark owner's ability to use it in the market. They asserted that because the TPP measures' prohibition of certain uses of certain marks results in a reduction of the trademark's distinctiveness, these measures eroded the trademark owners' ability to prevent third parties from using similar or identical marks on similar goods in a manner that creates a "likelihood of confusion". Honduras argued that Art. 16 obliges Members to guarantee a minimum level of private rights to trademark owners that allows them to successfully protect the distinctiveness and source-indicating function of their marks in infringement proceedings. The remaining complainants submitted that Art. 16.1 obliges Members to *refrain from regulatory conduct* that undermines or eliminates the distinctiveness that is essential to exercising trademark rights.[161]

Particularly in the later part of the proceedings the complainants' rooted their argument in the trademark owner's *legitimate interest in using the trademark* that had been recognized by the Appellate Body,[162] and which they saw as an important consideration with respect to their claims under Art. 16.1. Honduras, the Dominican Republic and Indonesia expressly clarified, however, that they did not argue that

155. See the panel's approach in *US – Section 110(5) Copyright Act*, cited *supra* note 7.
156. Panel Report, para. 7.1906 (footnotes omitted).
157. Panel Report, para. 7.1911.
158. See Panel Report, paras. 7.1233–7.1775 for the Panel's full analysis under this claim.
159. See Panel Report, paras. 7.1914–7.2051 for the Panel's full analysis under this claim.
160. See Panel Report, paras. 7.2052–7.2130 for the Panel's full analysis under this claim.
161. Panel Report, para. 7.1966.
162. Panel Report, *EC – Trademarks and Geographical Indications (Australia)*, para. 7.664.

Art. 16.1 conferred a positive "right to use" a trademark.[163] Cuba argued further that the principle of effective treaty interpretation ("effet utile") requires Members to provide a minimum opportunity to use a trademark, as otherwise the minimum rights conferred by Art. 16.1 are not guaranteed.

In its general interpretative analysis of Art. 16.1[164] the Panel, on the basis of textual analysis and earlier rulings, confirmed that Art. 16.1 does not establish a *right to use* a registered trademark, but provides for a registered trademark owner's *right to prevent* certain activities by unauthorized third parties under the conditions set out in Art. 16.1, first sentence.[165]

The complainants essentially argued that the TPP measures would reduce the distinctiveness of certain registered tobacco-related trademarks and, as a consequence, there would be fewer instances in which a "likelihood of confusion" with unauthorized uses of similar signs on similar or identical products would occur. This reduction in the occurrences of a "likelihood of confusion", they argued, constituted a violation of Art. 16.1. The Panel expressed its doubts regarding the complainants' factual allegation in this regard,[166] but focused on the second part of the argument - namely whether causing the instances in which the infringement criterion of "likelihood of confusion" may arise to be reduced constitutes a violation of Art. 16.1.

The Panel's analysis of the role of Art. 16.1 in this regard illustrates the unique operation of the TRIPS Agreement as an international treaty addressing obligations to Members and their governments with the purpose of regulating the private rights of IP rightsholders, who retain full discretion on whether to create, register, or defend against infringement, the individual IP assets they may own. The Panel found that nothing in the text of Art. 16.1, first sentence, suggests that Members must not only *provide protection* where likelihood of confusion does arise, but also *maintain market conditions* that would enable the circumstances set out in this provision, including a likelihood of confusion, to *actually occur* in any particular situation. Rather, Members must ensure that *in the event that these circumstances do arise*, a right to prevent such use is available to the right holder in accordance with Art. 16.1.[167]

The exclusive right conferred by Art. 16.1 reflects the purpose of enabling the right owner to protect the source-identifying function of the trademark against actual infringements by third parties.[168] It is "not intended to protect that function against

163. Panel Report, para. 7.1966. See fn 4428 for the variety of formulations used in the complainants' submissions over time. Cuba, in its responses to the Panel's questions, had suggested that Art. 16.1 recognized a right to use a trademark.
164. Panel Report, paras. 7.1970–7.1981.
165. Panel Report, para. 7.1978.
166. See Panel Report, paras. 7.1989–7.1993.
167. Panel Report, para. 7.2000: "In other words, whether unauthorized third parties actually use similar or identical signs on similar goods or services in the market, and whether such use actually does or does not result in a 'likelihood of confusion' among consumers, is immaterial to the assessment of whether a Member ensures that a trademark owner has at its disposal the right to prevent such acts by third parties, in compliance with Article 16.1."
168. Panel Report, para. 7.2001 and 7.2011, referring to Appellate Body Report, *US – Section 211 Appropriations Act*, para. 186 and Panel Report, *EC – Trademarks and Geographical Indications (Australia)*, para. 7.246.

waning distinctiveness due to other reasons, such as changing market conditions, inaction of the right owner, or changing consumer perception."[169] There is no indication in the text of Art. 16.1, first sentence, of an obligation on Members to maintain the distinctiveness of registered trademarks, or to refrain from regulatory conduct that might negatively affect the distinctiveness of such trademark through use.

As regards the complainant's emphasis on the owner's legitimate interest in preserving the distinctiveness of its trademark – which includes the interest in using the trademark in connection with the relevant goods and services of its own or authorized undertakings – the Panel points out that this finding[170] was made in the context of Art. 17. It confirms that these interests need to be taken into account – not *protected* as a *right* – when considering whether an exception in a Member's domestic law to the exclusive *right to prevent* conferred by Art. 16.1 meets the criteria for permissible exceptions as contained in Art. 17. However, the recognition of this legitimate interest under Art. 17 does not create a general obligation under Art. 16.1 to refrain from measures that would undermine the distinctiveness of trademarks.[171]

The Panel also dismissed[172] the argument based on the principle of effective treaty interpretation ("effet utile"), which requires a treaty interpreter to give a legally operative meaning to all applicable provisions harmoniously, in a manner that does not reduce whole clauses or paragraphs of a treaty to redundancy or inutility.[173] It found that that the absence of a minimum opportunity to use a trademark does not render Art. 16.1 "legally inoperative" – as Cuba had claimed – since Art. 16.1 rights were available even in the absence of use,[174] and assuming such an obligation would create tension with other provisions that expressly provide conditions under which use can be encumbered (Art. 20) and which address the consequences of obstacles to use (Art. 19).[175]

In adopting the trademark provisions in Section 2 of Part II of the TRIPS Agreement, the Panel clarified, Members have not taken on a general responsibility for safeguarding the distinctiveness of signs, either before or after such signs have been registered as trademarks.[176] The obligation in Article 15.1 to consider distinctive signs as registrable does not imply that Members have the responsibility to permit non-distinctive signs to acquire or maintain distinctiveness, and does not create a "right to distinctiveness" for trademark owners. It is the responsibility of applicants to

169. Panel Report, para. 7.2011.
170. Panel Report in *EC – Trademarks and Geographical Indications (Australia)*, para. 7.664.
171. Panel Report, para. 7.2008.
172. Panel Report, paras. 7.2019–7.2030.
173. Panel Report, para. 7.2022, referring to Appellate Body Report, *Argentina – Footwear (EC)*, para. 81, Appellate Body Report, *US – Gasoline*, p. 23, DSR 1996:I, 3, p. 21, and the Appellate Body Report, *Canada – Dairy*, para. 133.
174. Panel Report, para. 7.2025.
175. Panel Report, para. 7.2029.
176. Panel Report, para. 7.2028. See also para. 7.2026 "Considering that trademark distinctiveness varies according to a variety of market factors – including those beyond the control of Members' governments or trademark owners – it is not plausible to assume that Members would have taken on such a general responsibility" (footnotes omitted).

choose, or – if permitted[177] – to develop through use, signs that fulfil the condition of distinctiveness in the context of variable market conditions, in order to trigger Members' obligation to consider them for registration as trademarks under Article 15.1.[178]

Similarly, the obligation to confer certain rights to owners of registered trademarks under Art. 16.1 *assumes* distinctiveness of that mark – since that is a condition for registration under Art. 15.1. By providing a right to trademark owners to prevent situations that fulfil the infringement criteria, Article 16.1 does not make Members responsible for the conditions in which those infringement criteria such as a "likelihood of confusion" can be fulfilled, let alone obligated to refrain from regulatory conduct that might impair a trademark owner's ability to maintain the distinctiveness of a sign in order to satisfy the "likelihood of confusion" criteria.[179]

A trademark owner's commercial interest in a market situation in which its registered trademark can be successfully used to stop as many signs as possible from being used on similar or identical goods or services, and the corresponding interest in using its trademark, including for the purpose of maintaining or further strengthening its distinctiveness, is not *a right* under Art. 16.1. It is, however, recognized in the TRIPS Agreement as *a legitimate interest* that needs to be taken into account in considering the permissibility of domestic exceptions to the exclusive rights under Art. 17, and may be relevant for assessing whether the use of a trademark in the course of trade is unjustifiably encumbered by special requirements within the meaning of Art. 20.[180]

3. *Highlights from the Claim under Article 10bis Paris Convention, as Incorporated into the TRIPS Agreement by Article 2.1*

In their claims under Article 10*bis* Paris Convention (1967), as incorporated into the TRIPS Agreement by its Art. 2.1, the complainants pursued arguments related to two aspects. Cuba alone argued that the TPP measures themselves constitute an act of unfair competition on the grounds that they create unfair conditions for competition. Cuba and other complainants also claimed that the TPP measures compel market actors to engage in the types of acts of unfair competition against which Australia is obliged to assure effective protection pursuant to para. 1, or to prohibit under paras. 3(1) or 3(2) of Art. 10*bis*.

The Panel rejected these claims after a thorough engagement with the complainants' detailed arguments, and the Panel's analysis is particularly instructive on the interoperation of the separate subsections of the provision. This paper will summarize only two elements of the Panel's analysis – the scope of incorporation

177. If a Member has exercised the option under Article 15.1, third sentence, to permit registration on the basis of distinctiveness acquired through use.
178. Panel Report, para. 7.2009: "We further recall our finding in that context that, outside the scope of express obligations set out in the TRIPS Agreement, the Agreement does not in our view oblige Members to ensure that private parties are in a position to fulfil the criteria under Article 15.1, or to refrain from regulations otherwise not inconsistent with the covered agreements that may affect relevant market conditions."
179. Panel Report, para. 7.2010.
180. Panel Report, para. 7.2011.

of Art. 10*bis* into the TRIPS Agreement and the Panel's interpretation of the term "unfair competition" - which for the first time in WTO dispute settlement practice comprehensively delineate the TRIPS obligations regarding the protection against unfair competition.

a) The Scope of Incorporation of Art. 10bis Paris Convention (1967)

The parties disagreed on whether Art. 10*bis*, as incorporated into the TRIPS Agreement by its Art. 2.1, covers both the requirements within the TPP measures that affect the use of trademarks, geographical indications and other categories of IPRs on tobacco retail packaging and products ("trademark requirements"), and the requirements that concern other physical features of tobacco retail packaging and products ("format requirements"). While the Dominican Republic and Indonesia considered that the reference in Art. 2.1 to Parts II, III and IV of TRIPS does not limit WTO Members' obligations in respect of the incorporated articles of the Paris Convention (1967), Australia took the view that, to the extent that this provision applied to the TPP measures, Art. 2.1 TRIPS read in conjunction with Art. 10*bis* Paris Convention (1967) could only be applied to the TPP "trademark requirements" that are the subject of Parts II, III and IV of TRIPS.[181]

Previous WTO jurisprudence on this matter had been inconclusive in this regard. In *US – Section 211 Appropriations Act* the panel had interpreted the terms "[i]n respect of" in Article 2.1 to mean that "Members have to comply with Articles 1 through 12 and 19 of the Paris Convention (1967) 'in respect of' what is covered by those parts of the TRIPS Agreement identified therein"[182] and had hence found against a TRIPS obligation to protect trade names - which must be protected under Article 8 of the Paris Convention (1967) - because these are not a category of IP covered by the TRIPS Agreement.[183] The Appellate Body overturned this finding on the grounds that the words "in respect of" in Art. 2.1 should not be read to "condition" the scope of Members' obligations under the Paris Convention provisions incorporated into the TRIPS Agreement, in a manner that would not cover trade names.[184] The panel in *EC – Trademarks and Geographical Indications* - in deciding a complainant had not made a *prima facie* case under Art. 10*bis* Paris Convention (1967) - emphasized that this did not imply any view on "whether and in what respects" this provision has been incorporated into the TRIPS Agreement.[185]

Following the Appellate Body's reasoning in US - Section 211 Appropriations Act that "in respect of" in Art. 2.1 should not be read as "conditioning" Members'

181. Panel Report, para. 7.2621. Honduras and Cuba argued that Part II of TRIPS, referred to in Art. 2.1, covers seven areas of IPRs, and that the TPP format requirements have an actual or potential bearing on several categories of IPRs covered in Part II
182. Panel Report, *US – Section 211 Appropriations Act*, para. 8.30.
183. Panel Report, *US – Section 211 Appropriations Act*, para. 8.41. The panel had analysed the negotiating history of the TRIPS Agreement and had been of the view that it confirmed its view. See paras. 8.31-8.40.
184. Appellate Body Report, *US – Section 211 Appropriations Act*, para. 337.
185. See Panel Report, *EC – Trademarks and Geographical Indications (Australia)*, paras. 7.719–7.728.

obligations under the provisions incorporated, the Panel found further support for this view in the express references to Art. 10*bis* in other TRIPS provisions, which did not themselves regulate acts of unfair competition - such as Art. 22.2(b), Art. 39.1, and Article 4 of the Treaty on Intellectual Property in Respect of Integrated Circuits (1989), as incorporated into the TRIPS Agreement by Art. 35. The reference in Art. 39.1, in particular, confirmed the view of the Panel that the obligation to provide effective protection against unfair competition pursuant to Article 10*bis* of the Paris Convention (1967) is intended to be incorporated through Article 2.1 of the TRIPS Agreement.[186]

In light of the above considerations, the Panel found that, pursuant to the second sub-clause of Art. 2.1, Members are required to comply with Art. 10*bis* of the Paris Convention (1967), and that the term "in respect of" in the first sub-clause of Art. 2.1 does not have the effect of conditioning the scope of incorporation of the obligation under Paris Art. 10*bis* to cover only those acts of unfair competition that relate to the types of subject-matter addressed in Parts II, III or IV of TRIPS.[187]

In light of the previous lack of clarity in this regard, this unequivocal finding is significant in that it confirms protection against unfair competition in all areas of "industrial and commercial matters" - not just "in respect of" intellectual property rights - as a TRIPS obligation.

b) The Meaning of "Unfair Competition" in Art. 10bis Paris Convention (1967)

Developing a general interpretation of Art. 10*bis*, the Panel began with a textual analysis of the definition and read the terms "an act of unfair competition" in para. 2 of Art. 10*bis* to refer to "something that is done by a market actor to compete against other actors in the market in a manner that is contrary to what would usually or customarily be regarded as truthful, fair and free from deceit within a certain market."[188]

Regarding the relationship between the separate paragraphs, the Panel understood that the obligation in para. 1 required Members, in the process of assuring effective protection against acts of unfair competition within the meaning of para. 2, to prohibit the types of practices in industrial and commercial matters that fall under para. 3.[189] Supported by the negotiating history of the Paris Convention in this regard, it further interpreted the provision to oblige Members to provide effective protection against all acts falling more generally within the scope of its para. 2 - not just against the specific types of acts identified in para. 3.[190]

186. Panel Report, para. 7.2629.
187. Panel Report, para. 7.2631.
188. Panel Report, para. 7.2667.
189. Panel Report, para. 7.2669.
190. Panel Report, para. 7.2679.

Considering a WIPO commentary of 1994,[191] and analysing WTO jurisprudence on the similar concept of "public morals",[192] the Panel understands that no single "clear-cut, universally accepted standard of behaviour" applies in determining whether a commercial practice is "honest" under para. 2.[193] Rather, the manner in which industrial and commercial matters are usually or customarily carried out differs from market to market, as do the perceptions of and the standards for determining what constitutes "honest" commercial practices. The standard relevant under para. 2 should therefore be interpreted with reference to standards of honest conduct habitually applied and maintained *in the domestic market at issue*, which in turn needs to be determined based on the circumstances of a particular case.[194]

The Panel emphasizes that the fact that the concept of "honest practice" may vary from market to market does not render the obligation discretionary. If certain acts objectively fall within what is considered, within the domestic market at issue, "contrary to honest practices in industrial or commercial matters", then they will constitute an act of unfair competition subject to the obligation in Article 10*bis*.[195]

The Panel notes further that protection against unfair competition serves to protect competitors as well as consumers, together with the public interest, and that when determining "honesty" in business dealings, all these factors have to be taken into account – as reflected in the balance of societal interests mentioned in Art. 7 of the TRIPS Agreement. Consequently, a determination of what amounts to an act that is contrary to honest practices in commercial matters – beyond the examples in para. 3 – may, depending on the circumstances, reflect a balancing of these interests.[196]

---

191. International Bureau of WIPO, *Protection Against Unfair Competition: Analysis of the Present World Situation*, World Intellectual Property Organization (Geneva, 1994). This commentary was provided in response to the Panel's request for factual background information on the Paris Convention provisions invoked in these disputes – see above fn 7 on this practice.
192. Panel Report, para. 7.2673, citing Panel Report, *US – Gambling*, para. 6.465 and Panel Report, *China – Publications and Audiovisual Products*, para. 7.763.
193. Panel Report, para. 7.2672.
194. Panel Report, para. 7.2675.
195. Panel Report, para. 7.2675. See fn 5359: We also note that the Guide to the Paris Convention by Bodenhausen refers to notions of honesty not only as prevailing in a Member's jurisdiction but also as established in international trade: "[a]ny act of competition will have to be considered unfair if it is contrary to honest practices in industrial or commercial matters. This criterion is not limited to honest practices existing in the country where protection against unfair competition is sought. The judicial or administrative authorities of such country will therefore also have to take into account honest practices established in international trade." Bodenhausen, Full text, (Exhibit DOM-79), p. 144. In the circumstances of a particular case, honest practices established in international trade, if discernible, should therefore also inform the meaning of "[a]ny act of competition contrary to honest practices in industrial or commercial matters" under paragraph 2 of Article 10*bis*.
196. Panel Report, para. 7.2680.

C. CONCLUSION

I. Appeals by Honduras and the Dominican Republic

On 17 July 2018, Honduras appealed the findings of the panel under Art. 2.2 of the TBT Agreement and under Arts. 16.1 and 20 of the TRIPS Agreement,[197] followed by the Dominican Republic on 23 August 2018.[198] The Appellate Body consolidated the two appeals into one proceeding, but had to inform the Chair of the DSB that "due to the exceptional size and complexity of these consolidated proceedings" – and with reference to the current backlog of pending appeals, resulting "in part from the reduced number of Appellate Body Members"[199] – it would not be able to submit its report within the usual timeframes.[200]

Cuba and Indonesia did not lodge appeals and the panel reports in their respective disputes were adopted by the Dispute Settlement Body (DSB) at its meeting on 27 August 2018.

The appeals by Honduras and the Dominican Republic on Art. 2.2 TBT and Arts. 16.1 and 20 TRIPS are pending at the time of writing. The Panel's other findings – notably with respect to Arts. 15.4 and 16.3 of the TRIPS Agreement, and Arts. 6*quinquies* and 10*bis* of the Paris Convention – are final.

II. Conclusion

The Panel's interpretations of the TRIPS and Paris Convention provisions invoked in this case, including in the selected findings summarized above, entailed balancing an array of interests. These included the interplay of government obligations and regulatory space with the protection of private rights of right holders, the interaction of the mostly procedural foundations of the Paris Convention with the substantive protection standards added in the TRIPS Agreement, and the legitimate interest of trademark owners in using their trademarks in the marketplace with the right of WTO Members to adopt measures for the protection of certain societal interests that may adversely affect such use. These findings, in respect of some of which appeals are pending, provide important contributions to TRIPS jurisprudence that may be useful reference points for future cases.

In the comparatively short, but eventful, history of WTO TRIPS disputes, the plain packaging decision further demonstrates the concrete ways in which the objectives of IP protection and public health can be reconciled – itself a long-standing

197. Notice of Appeal WT/DS435/23, dated 25 July 2018.
198. Notice of Appeal WT/DS441/23, dated 28 August 2018. The Dominican Republic limited its appeal to the findings under Art. 2.2 TBT and Art. 20 TRIPS.
199. For a view on the issues underlying the current crisis regarding appointments of new Appellate Body Members, see the Farewell speech of Appellate Body Member Ricardo Ramírez-Hernández on 28 May 2018, on <www.wto.org/english/tratop_e/dispu_e/ricardoramirezfarwellspeech_e.htm>.
200. See Communication from the Appellate Body, WT/DS435/24, WT/DS441/25, dated 20 September 2018. Art. 17.5 DSU provides that proceedings should be completed within 90 days.

concern for TRIPS law and policy. Earlier TRIPS cases focused on transitional matters, on the scope of exceptions, on the application of non-discrimination provisions, and on the meaning of the enforcement obligations.[201] In this case, the Panel was called upon to give practical effect to the seemingly hortatory statement expressing the principle in Article 8.1 of the TRIPS Agreement – namely how a Member may take measures to protect public health that are consistent with the provisions of this Agreement. While still subject to appellate review, the Panel's decision illustrates how a close analysis of the TRIPS guarantees of trademark protection need not stand in conflict with a government's initiatives in this area.

201. For a recent overview of TRIPS cases, see Graham Cook and Hannu Wager, 'Adjudicating intellectual property disputes at the GATT/WTO: Are there general lessons for the investor-state dispute settlement system?', in Christophe Geiger (ed.), *Research Handbook on Intellectual Property and Investment Law* (Edward Elgar Publishing, Cheltenham (UK)/ Northampton, MA (USA), forthcoming 2019).

CHAPTER 11

Unpacking Constitutional Protection for Trade Marks: The Plain Packaging Disputes Before National Courts

Robert Burrell

A. INTRODUCTION

The introduction of plain packaging for cigarettes and other tobacco products has led to legal challenges before both national and international tribunals. These challenges have all attracted comment and analysis, but among trade mark scholars it is the disputes brought against Australia before the WTO by tobacco-producing countries that have attracted most attention[1]. This is hardly surprising given that the WTO cases have clarified the nature and scope of trade mark rights under the TRIPS Agreement. It is important, however, not to underestimate the importance of the domestic litigation. For example, the 2012 decision of the High Court of Australia in *JT International SA v. Commonwealth*[2] was the most significant constitutional case involving trade marks in Australia since the "Union Label" decision of 1908.[3] The equivalent litigation in the UK, *R (on the Application of BAT) v. Secretary of State for*

1. Five cases were brought against Australia's plain packaging regime before the WTO, four of which proceeded to a determination. See DS435, DS441, DS458, DS467 *Australia — Certain Measures Concerning Trademarks, Geographical Indications and Other Plain Packaging Requirements Applicable to Tobacco Products and Packaging* (28 June 2018).
2. [2012] HCA 43.
3. *Attorney-General (NSW) v. Brewery Employees' Union of NSW* (1908) 6 CLR 469. In that case the High Court held that the term "trade mark" as used in s 51(xviii) of the Australian Constitution did not include so-called "workers" trade marks (that is, an indication that goods were produced by unionised labour. For discussion see S. Ricketson, 'The Union Label Case: An Early Australian IP Story', in A. Kenyon et al. (eds.), *Landmarks in Australian Intellectual Property Law* (Cambridge University Press, Melbourne, 2009).

Health, produced decisions at first instance[4] and before the Court of Appeal[5] that are perhaps less obviously of seminal importance, but which nevertheless deal with a raft of important issues. Courts in both jurisdictions were forced to confront the question of what it means to own a trade mark. It is this aspect of the domestic litigation that is worthy of further attention. This is particularly the case since although the outcomes in the two national cases were similar there are notable points of difference in the reasoning.

This essay suggests that the willingness of courts in both jurisdictions to look beyond the narrow confines of the trade marks register when identifying the nature of the property that enjoys constitutional protection is to be welcomed. It also suggests that this broader approach can be justified by reference to traditional trade mark theory, that is, its legitimacy does not rest on an acceptance of the idea that the protection offered by trade mark law should extend beyond guaranteeing trade origin. Insofar as it takes issue with the reasoning in the cases under consideration, it is around the question of whether there was an expropriation or a taking of the claimant's property. It is suggested that the indication from the High Court of Australia that the plain packaging legislation did result in a taking is more convincing than the contrary conclusion reached by courts in the UK. This is not to suggest that the outcome reached in the UK was necessarily wrong, since there were other ways that the same ultimate conclusion might have been justified – as the court at first instance recognised.

B. THE AUSTRALIAN PLAIN PACKAGING LITIGATION

I. Background and Context

Australia was the first country in the world to introduce "plain" or "standardised" packaging for tobacco products. The Australian regime is set out in the Tobacco Plain Packaging Act 2011 (Cth) (TPPA) and associated Tobacco Plain Packaging Regulations 2011 (Cth) (TPPR). The effect of this regime is that the colour and shape of tobacco retail packaging and the imagery used thereon are placed under the control of the state, with the packaging being designed to look as unappealing as possible. As part of this regulatory scheme, the TPPA contains a general prohibition on the use of trade marks on packaging[6] or on the goods themselves.[7] The TPPA also provides that "[n]o part of the retail packaging of tobacco products may make a noise, or contain or produce a scent, that could be taken to constitute tobacco advertising and promotion".[8] Manufacturers are, however, permitted to use a "brand, business or company name for the tobacco products, and any variant name for the tobacco products".[9] The TPPA and TPPR go on to spell out in fine detail how the brand

4. [2016] EWHC 1169 (Admin).
5. [2016] EWCA Civ 1182.
6. TPPA, s 20(1).
7. TPPA, s 26(1).
8. TPPA, s 24. "Tobacco advertising and promotion" bears the same meaning under the TPPA as under the Framework Convention on Tobacco Control: TTPA, s 4(1).
9. TPPA, s 20(3)(a).

and variant name are to appear. To take cigarette packs as an example, the TPPA provides that the brand and variant name can appear once only on the front, top and bottom outer surfaces.[10] The TPPR specify that the brand and variant name can be rendered only in a particular typeface, in a particular shade of grey, with the first letter capitalised and no other upper-case characters.[11] A brand, business or company name must be in no larger than 14 point font, while a variant name must be in no larger than 10 point font.[12]

The effect of the plain packaging regime is that tobacco companies are now prohibited from exploiting many of their established trade marks in any meaningful sense. Any mark that includes a device, or that consists of a word rendered in a special form, can no longer be used on retail packaging. It might be possible to employ some of these marks on letterhead or on wholesale packaging, but it is no longer possible to use them in a manner which builds consumer recognition. Moreover, any mark that relates directly to the get-up of the goods (as with trade marks that relate to appearance of a cigarette packet) cannot even be used even in this limited manner. This formed the context for the constitutional challenge. However, before turning to consider this challenge in detail, it is worth saying something about how the issue of non-use has been addressed.

Without special provision, many tobacco marks might in due course become vulnerable to being removed on the grounds of non-use.[13] In a similar vein, applications for new tobacco marks might be successfully opposed on the grounds of no intent to use[14] or refused at the examination stage or opposed on the basis that use of the mark would be contrary to law.[15] As an aside, it is worth noting that from the perspective of the integrity of the trade mark register, this is precisely what *ought* to happen, a point that has become lost in most of the discussion of the plain packaging regime.[16] However, the Australian Government took the view that tobacco companies needed to be given the right both to preserve their existing marks and to apply for new marks. In taking this view, the Government may well have had half an eye on the inevitable constitutional challenge, but seems to have been more directly motivated by the requirements of TRIPS. Specifically, TRIPS Art 15(4), which provides that "[t]he nature of the goods or services to which a trademark is to be applied shall in no case form an obstacle to registration of the trademark", and TRIPS Art 19, which provides that "[c]ircumstances arising independently of the will of the owner of the trademark which constitute an obstacle to the use of the trademark, such as... government requirements for goods or services protected by the trademark, shall be recognized as valid reasons for non-use". Consequently, in order to avoid the non-use "problem" the TPPA made special provision to ensure that tobacco trade marks remain registrable and valid. Specifically, s 28(1) TTPA provides that an applicant

10. TPPA, s 21(2).
11. TPPR, reg 2.4.1(a), (d)–(f).
12. TPPR, reg 2.4.1(b)–(c).
13. In Australia this would be pursuant to s 92(4)(b) of the Trade Marks Act 1995 (Cth) (TMA).
14. Pursuant to s 59 of the TMA.
15. Pursuant to s 42(b) of the TMA.
16. But see T. Stevens, 'The Impact of Plain Packaging Legislation on Australian Trade Mark Law', FICPI World Congress, Melbourne, 15–17 April 2012, <ficpi.org/wp-content/uploads/2013/09/3-2-Stevens-Trevor.pdf>.

is taken to intend to use the mark "if the applicant would intend to do so but for the operation of this Act". The provision is worded so as to exclude one of the usual grounds of opposition to a mark under Australian law, namely, that the owner does not intend to use, or authorise the use of, the trade mark in Australia.[17] Similarly, as regards removal proceedings, 28(4) TPPA provides that an allegation of non-use is taken to have been rebutted if the owner can establish that it would have used the trade mark but for the TPPA.

The constitutional challenge was launched within a few months of the TPPA receiving Royal Assent. The case was brought by Japan Tobacco International SA (JTI) and British American Tobacco Australasia Limited (BAT), with Philip Morris Ltd, Van Nelle Tabak Nederland BV and Imperial Tobacco Australia Ltd intervening in support. The plaintiffs argued that the legislation was invalid as being incompatible with s 51(xxxi) of the Australian Constitution. There are two peculiarities of this provision that are worth noting. The first is that s 51(xxxi) does not create a constitutional guarantee of the right to property *per se*. The Australian Constitution does not contain a Bill of Rights. However, it has a number of provisions that in practice serve to safeguard important interests from encroachment by the state and s 51(xxxi) fits this pattern.[18] In form this provision confers a power on the Commonwealth (i.e. federal) Parliament to acquire property. Specifically, Parliament is authorised to "make laws for the peace order, and good government of the Commonwealth with respect to...the acquisition of property on just terms from any state or person for any purpose in respect of which the Parliament has the power to make laws". Importantly, however, this provision also serves as a limit on government action irrespective of the source of the power. Insofar as some other head of legislative power might be thought to give rise to a right to acquire property (for example, the power to legislate in relation to the construction of railways[19] or lighthouses[20]), then any such right is to be read down to the scope of what is permitted by s 51(xxxi). This approach is unsurprising. However, more difficult questions of interpretation arise where the nature of the property in question is highly regulated and, above all, where property rights have been set up and conferred under legislation, as is the case with intellectual property rights.[21]

The second peculiarity of the Australian Constitutional framework is that it relates to the "acquisition" and not merely the "taking" of property. The distinction between these concepts is not obvious as a matter of ordinary construction. Nor is it one to which any consideration appears to have been given by the Framers during

17. Cf. TMA, s 59.
18. See also Australian Constitution s 80: trial on indictment shall be by jury; s 116: Commonwealth not to legislate in respect of religion; ss 7, 24, 64, 128: creating an Implied "freedom of political communication" as to which see, in particular, *Lange v. Australian Broadcasting Corporation* (1997) 189 CLR 520. The limited nature of the guarantee of freedom of expression in Australia helps explain why this did not form part of the Constitutional challenge. However, it might also be noted that s 16 TPPA seeks to foreclose a free speech challenge in any event.
19. Australian Constitution, s. 51(xxxiv).
20. Australian Constitution, s. 51(vii).
21. See Australian Constitution, s. 51(xviii) (giving the Commonwealth Parliament the power to legislate in respect of "copyrights, patents of inventions and designs, and trade marks").

the Constitutional Conventions of the late 1890s. The distinction is nevertheless one that is long-established and it was reiterated and affirmed in the plain packaging litigation. As Chief Justice French explained, "Taking involves deprivation of property seen from the perspective of its owner. Acquisition involves receipt of something seen from the perspective of the acquirer".[22] The effect of this distinction is that the destruction of property or the extinguishing of property rights is not enough to trigger the Constitutional prohibition. The state or some other party must gain some form of interest in the property.[23] This second peculiarity, in particular, had important implications for the way the case was argued before the High Court and for the way in which the outcome was justified.

II. The Case Before the High Court of Australia

The first step for the plaintiffs was to identify the property that they claimed to have lost as a consequence of the plain packaging regime. JTI claimed loss of rights in its trade marks and get-up for its "Camel" cigarettes. BAT claimed loss of rights in its "Winfield" and "Dunhill" registered and unregistered trade marks and associated goodwill. BAT also claimed loss of copyright, registered design rights and patent rights over various elements of its cigarette packs. The second step was to demonstrate how the test of "acquisition" of rights was satisfied. The plaintiffs' principal contention was that the Commonwealth had acquired the power to determine the appearance of the packaging and this provided the Government with the opportunity to promote the "Quitline" service using a device mark owned by the Anti-Cancer Council of Victoria.

Significantly, a majority of the High Court was persuaded of the view that the new regime effected a taking of the plaintiffs' trade mark rights.[24] Importantly, this view was not underpinned by anything other than an orthodox understanding of the nature and function of trade marks. During the litigation the Commonwealth made much of the fact that trade marks are purely negative in character, arguing that provided the trade mark owner retains the right to exclude others from using the mark, no taking could be said to have occurred. There is therefore a suggestion in the judgment that the characterisation of trade mark rights as "positive" or "negative" might be determinative of the legitimacy of the plain packaging regime. The idea that this characterisation issue might play a central role is also one that seems to have gained traction in discussions regarding compliance with TRIPS. Moreover, Australia is an interesting jurisdiction in which to test the characterisation issue, since

22. *JT International SA v. Commonwealth*, [42].
23. It is generally emphasised that the interest gained need only be "slight or insubstantial". It must, however, be "proprietary in character".
24. French CJ, Gummow J and Heydon J reached this conclusion expressly. In their joint judgment Hayne and Bell JJ declined to reach a definite view on this issue, but noted that the proposition that the plain packing regime effects a taking of property "seems hard to deny". Crennan J was more equivocal and her judgment is open to the interpretation that she would not have been inclined to find that there had been a taking. For further analysis of the positions taken by members of the High Court see S. Ricketson, 'Plain Packaging Legislation for Tobacco Products and Trade Marks in the High Court of Australia', 3 *QMJIP* (2013), 224 and D. Fletcher, 'JT International SA v Commonwealth: Tobacco Plain Packaging', 35 *Syd LR* (2013), 827.

the idea that trade mark rights ought to be regarded as positive is one that seems to draw support from the TMA. Specifically, s 20 TMA gives the registered owner the exclusive right to use the mark, and to authorise others to do so.[25] Despite this provision, the High Court agreed with the Commonwealth that trade mark rights should be characterised as being essentially negative in character. This conclusion is not, however, all that it seems, since the argument that trade mark registration should be conceptualised as conferring a positive right did not form part of the plaintiff's case, a point that is in danger of becoming overlooked.[26]

The High Court's decision should therefore not be taken as a case in which the characterisation issue was properly tested. In many respects, however, this makes the High Court's conclusion on the taking point of greater significance. The majority took the view that the legislation effected a taking despite proceeding on the basis that trade mark rights turn on the right to exclude; the Court's conclusion on the taking point did not turn on the wording of an introductory provision of the domestic statute. Although expressed in different ways, the members of the court who were prepared to accept that the plain packaging regime effected a taking were clearly interested in the commercial reality confronted by the plaintiffs. The TPPA stripped them of their most important means of attracting new customers and left them with bare legal title to trade indicia that they could never in practice employ, either directly or by way of a licensing arrangement.[27] Use of the marks other than on retail packaging was clearly regarded as more hypothetical than real. Indeed, much the same could be said even of the argument that the tobacco companies could bring an infringement action against third parties who used their device marks. Put simply, they would have no need to do so, because any potential defendant would be operating in violation of the criminal provisions of the TTPA such that enforcement could be left to the state.

It was the second step that caused the plaintiffs to stumble, that is, they were unable to persuade the Court that either the Commonwealth or some other person had acquired a proprietary interest or benefit of a proprietary character as a consequence of the TPPA. The plaintiffs' strongest argument under this head was that the Commonwealth had acquired for itself the power to dictate the messages that tobacco packaging would communicate to consumers. By dictating the entirety of the appearance of the packaging the Commonwealth had commandeered the space. To express this idea another way, we might say that the device marks served to advertise the goods.[28] In stripping the tobacco companies of ownership of these marks the Government had provided itself with the opportunity to reorient the advertising function performed by the appearance of the packaging towards its

25. Reference might also be made to s 122(1)(e), which provides that a registered owner has a defence to a claim for registered trade mark infringement, but this provision was not mentioned during the litigation.
26. See JTI's Submissions, fn 43 and accompanying text, available at: <www.hcourt.gov.au/assets/cases/s409-2011/JT_Plf.pdf>.
27. The loss of the ability to license or assign the trade mark was a matter that figured particularly heavily in Gummow J's conclusion as to why the legislation should be regarded as having effected "a taking".
28. Cf. F. Schechter, 'The Rational Basis of Trademark Protection', 40 *Harv. L. Rev.* (1927), 813.

own preferred message. Ultimately, however, Heydon J was the only member of the Court who was persuaded that this was sufficient to trigger s 51(xxxi). For the other members of the Court there was insufficient symmetry between the deprivation of the plaintiffs' trade marks and any benefit that the Commonwealth received and, in any event, the benefit to the Commonwealth that the plaintiffs were relying upon was not proprietary in nature.

It is difficult to avoid agreeing with the majority that the plaintiffs' argument on acquisition represented a significant stretch. But from a comparative perspective, the key point, and one that is worth reiterating, is that the majority of the High Court signalled that the TPPA did involve a taking. There is, moreover, one other thing that is worth drawing out of Heydon J's dissenting judgment. It concerns that general manner in which the Court should approach a claim under s 51(xxxi) and it is also one that has a wider significance. Like those in the majority, Heydon J recognised that the plaintiffs were running a novel argument. This did not, however, mean that the Court should approach the plaintiffs' claim with the customary degree of caution. Faced with legislation that stripped the plaintiffs of valuable rights in order to further public ends, Heydon J concluded that the presumption had to be in favour of extending the operation of s 51(xxxi).

C. THE UK PLAIN PACKAGING LITIGATION

I. Background and Context

It is perhaps a matter of some surprise that the UK decided to introduce plain packaging when it did, as one might have expected that the UK would have awaited the outcome of the proceedings against Australia before the WTO. This would also have given the UK more time to evaluate evidence from the Australian experience as to the efficacy of plain packing in reducing smoking rates over time. Many other European Member States certainly took this view. The Government, however, relied on a version of the precautionary principle, concluding that the evidence was that plain packing stood a reasonable chance of reducing smoking rates and that if it failed to act immediately a number of young people would take up an addictive and harmful habit in the interim. The Government therefore decided to press ahead and introduced plain packaging by means of the Standardised Packaging of Tobacco Products Regulations 2015 (SPTPR).

The SPTPR were closely modelled on the Australian scheme, to the extent that some provisions of the SPTPR were lifted directly from the Australian legislation with only the most minor amendments.[29] The provisions relating to trade marks required more extensive modification to make them compatible with the European trade mark regime – there is, for example, no standalone "no intent to use" ground of opposition in the EU – but the overall thrust of the scheme is identical, in that it preserves the registration of tobacco trade marks while drastically curtailing the opportunities that tobacco companies have to exploit their marks. The domestic basis for the SPTPR

29. See, for example, the provisions of the SPTPR dealing with packaging that produces a noise or a scent or that changes after retail sale.

was s 94 of the Children and Families Act 2014. This provision affords the Secretary of State for Health a broad power to make regulations controlling the appearance of the retail packaging of tobacco products, provided that he or she considers that the regulations will contribute to the health or welfare of people under the age of 18. In addition, however, the SPTPR was intended to implement the 2014 Tobacco Products Directive,[30] such that the Regulations were also said to be made pursuant to s.2(2) of the European Communities Act 1972.[31] One line of attack was for the industry to mount a challenge to the legality of the Tobacco Products Directive. This challenge that was dismissed by the Court of Justice in May 2016,[32] leaving the path clear for the English High Court to hand down its decision.

---

30. Directive 2014/40/EU of the European Parliament and of the Council of 3 April 2014 on the approximation of the laws, regulations and administrative provisions of the Member States concerning the manufacture, presentation and sale of tobacco and related products.
31. See the Preamble to the SPTPR.
32. EUGC, decision of 4 May 2016, Case C-547/14 *Philip Morris Brands SARL and Others v. Secretary of State for Health*. The English High Court decided to stay the proceedings and to refer, *inter alia*, the following questions to the Court of Justice for a preliminary ruling:
    "(1) Is [Directive 2014/40] invalid in whole or in part because Article 114 TFEU does not provide an adequate legal basis? In particular:
    (a) In relation to Article 24(2) of [Directive 2014/40]:
    (i) on its proper interpretation, to what extent does it permit Member States to adopt more stringent rules in relation to matters relating to the "standardisation" of the packaging of tobacco products; and,
    (ii) in light of that interpretation, is Article 24(2) invalid because Article 114 TFEU does not provide an adequate legal basis?
    (b) Is Article 24(3) [of Directive 2014/40], which allows Member States to prohibit a category of tobacco or related products in specified circumstances, invalid because Article 114 TFEU does not provide an adequate legal basis?
    (c) Are the following provisions invalid because Article 114 TFEU does not provide an adequate legal basis:
    (i) the provisions of Chapter II of Title II [of Directive 2014/40], which relate to packaging and labelling;
    (ii) Article 7 [of Directive 2014/40], in so far as it prohibits menthol cigarettes and tobacco products with a characterising flavour;
    (iii) Article 18 [of Directive 2014/40], which allows Member States to prohibit cross-border distance sales of tobacco products; and,
    (2) In relation to Article 13 [of Directive 2014/40]:
    (a) on its true interpretation, does it prohibit true and non-misleading statements about tobacco products on the product packaging; and,
    (b) if so, is it invalid because it violates the principle of proportionality and/or Article 11 of the [Charter]?
    (3) Are any or all of the following provisions of [Directive 2014/40] invalid because they infringe the principle of proportionality:
    (a) Article 7(1) and (7), in so far as [it] prohibit[s] the placing on the market of tobacco products with menthol as a characterising flavour and the placing on the market of tobacco products containing flavourings in any of their components;
    (b) Articles 8(3), 9(3), 10(1)(g) and 14, in so far as they impose various pack standardisation requirements; and,
    (c) Article 10(1)(a) and (c), in so far as [it] require[s] health warnings to cover 65% of the external front and back surface of the unit packaging and any outside packaging?"

The mixed domestic and European legislative underpinnings of the SPTPR lent significant complexity to the litigation and allowed the industry to bring a plethora of administrative law challenges to the validity of the UK regime. A further complicating factor was that the expert evidence on which the parties sought to rely was fiercely contested and stretched across a number of academic disciplines, from behavioural psychology to economics to sociology. For present purposes, however, the most important part of the tobacco industry's case was the argument that the SPTPR effected an expropriation of property without compensation that was unlawful by virtue of both Article 1, Protocol 1 of the European Convention on Human Rights (ECHR) and Article 17 of the Charter of Fundamental Rights ("Charter"). These arguments were reinforced by an argument about the nature of property rights at common law and an alleged duty at common law to pay compensation.

II. The Case Before the English High Court

The tobacco industry's challenge was heard by Mr Justice Green, a highly experienced administrative law judge. Green J rejected all of the industry's arguments. In so doing, he handed down a thousand-paragraph judgment that the Court of Appeal later acknowledged as a *tour de force,* even as they criticised it for being unnecessarily long. In relation to elements of the judgment that are of interest for present purposes, it should be noted that the common law aspect of the case was disposed of relatively easily. Respect for property rights was a bedrock of the common law and of the traditional British Constitution. Justice Spigelman, writing in his extra-judicial capacity, has gone so far as to argue that there was a "Common Law Bill of Rights" of which the right to property formed a key component.[33] However, the rights recognised at common law acted primarily as a rule of statutory interpretation: courts would require clear and unambiguous language in order to conclude that a statute interfered with vested property rights or alienated property without compensation. Building on this idea, the tobacco industry argued that the common law contains a right to "full indemnification" in the event of a property right being curtailed. This right can, of course, be curtailed by Parliament – no other conclusion would be compatible with the traditional Diceyan account of the nature of Parliamentary sovereignty that remains the bedrock of the British Constitution – but in this case the legislation underpinning the plain packaging regulations was silent on the question of compensation. Interestingly, Green J cut through this argument and declined to deal with the historical position in detail. Instead he relied on the Human Rights Act 1998, concluding that irrespective of what the position may have been historically,

The European Court of Justice in its decision affirmed the lawfulness of the Directive. While this was an important stepping stone for the Member States to go ahead with the implementation of the Directive, it should be recalled that the Directive did not mandate a plain packaging regime, and that neither the questions referred nor the decision of the Court concerned any aspects of trade mark law that deserve an analysis in the context of this chapter.

33. J. Spigelman, *The Common Law Bill of Rights: Statutory Interpretation and Human Rights* (University of Queensland Press, 2008). Available at SSRN: <ssrn.com/abstract=1806775>.

the common law could not now be treated as conferring a more extensive right to compensation than that would arise under the ECHR.

In relation to the other claims, Green J concluded that Article 1, Protocol 1 of the ECHR and Article 17 of the Charter are essentially coterminous. This conclusion is unsurprising both as a matter of common sense and legal history. It is nevertheless important because there are aspects of the Charter that might point to Article 17 providing a stronger degree of protection and this is a point that the plaintiffs pushed. One problem lies in the wording of Article 17, which provides as follows:

> 1. Everyone has the right to own, use, dispose of and bequeath his or her lawfully acquired possessions. No one may be deprived of his or her possessions, except in the public interest and in the cases and under the conditions provided for by law, subject to fair compensation being paid in good time for their loss. The use of property may be regulated by law in so far as is necessary for the general interest.
>
> 2. Intellectual property shall be protected.

The unqualified nature of Article 17(2) raises the question of whether intellectual property rights are entitled to a higher degree of protection than "possessions". On one reading the juxtaposition between Article 17(1) and 17(2) suggests that whereas Article 17 sets up restrictions on when a deprivation can occur, the absence of similar conditions in Article 17(2) means that no deprivation can ever be justified. This was not the drafters' intention. Rather, the aim was to ensure that intellectual property rights are treated as "possessions". The intention was that the language of "*intellectual property shall be protected*" should be interpreted as meaning "protected within the terms of Article 17(1)". That this was not made clearer is obviously unfortunate. The argument that Article 17(2) provides unqualified protection for intellectual property rights is not a point that the plaintiffs seem to have pushed during the hearing. Nevertheless, the general approach to interpreting Article 17 adopted by Green J makes it clear that such an argument would also have been destined to fail. More generally, it seems reasonable to assume that any court is likely to baulk at the suggestion that rights over, say, a patented industrial chemical enjoy a greater degree of constitutional protection than rights over, say, a wedding ring or family home.[34] This is not, however, to say that Article 17(2) will not give rise to further difficulties of interpretation in the future. As an aside, it might be noted that in taking steps to ensure that intellectual property rights attract constitutional protection, the drafters were seeking to signal that Community Courts should follow the lead of the European Court of Human Rights and give "possession" an expansive interpretation. But by only making express reference to intellectual property rights in Article 17(2) there is a question as to whether other types of intangible asset are implicitly *excluded* from the scope of Article 17. Again, this was almost certainly not the drafters' intention, but the point appears to be open on the text of the provision.

A second avenue by which it can be argued that the Charter provides for broader protection is by reference to Article 52. This provision, which deals with the "Scope

34. Cf. M. Radin, 'Property and Personhood', 34 *Stan. L. Rev.* (1982), 957 (pointing out that we have very varied levels of emotional attachment to things that we label as "property").

of guaranteed rights", provides in subsection 1 that "Any limitation on the exercise of the rights and freedoms recognised by this Charter must be provided for by law and respect the *essence* of those rights and freedoms". The argument run by the plaintiffs was that the italicised words mean that the fundamental rights guaranteed by the Charter have an irreducible core and that any restriction or limitation placed on a fundamental right can only be justified if this core is left undisturbed. In support of this position the plaintiffs cited a number of EU decisions. The most significant of these cases was arguably the decision of the General Court in *Trabelsi,*[35] a case involving the freezing of assets owned by Tunisian nationals following the Arab Spring. In that case the Court set up the test for when a limitation on the exercise of the right to property would be compatible with EU law. In so doing, the Court seemed to suggest that the "essential content" of the right must always be preserved.[36] Green J was of the view that as a policy matter there was little to be said for the plaintiffs' interpretation of Article 52 and he pointed out that it would produce nonsensical outcomes.[37] Equally, however, he recognised that the state of the case law was such that the plaintiffs' interpretation was still open. He therefore resolved this aspect of the case on the basis that even if the plaintiffs' argument were to be accepted there was still no breach of Article 17. If the owner of a trade mark enjoys an irreducible core of protection then that can lie only in the right to exclude, a right left unaffected by the plain packaging regime.

The argument that the Charter provides broader protection could therefore be set aside and the core issue became whether there was any breach of Article 1, Protocol 1 of the ECHR. One key issue that confronted the Court was whether the plain packaging regime amounted a "deprivation" or a mere "control of use". Following ECHR jurisprudence, it was recognised that this is a multifaceted inquiry that looks to the substance rather than the form of the measure. Green J concluded that the regulations effected a mere "control of use". A significant part of the reasoning was tied to the question of how the property rights in question should be identified. The plaintiffs pushed the argument that the word marks and the device marks needed to be treated entirely separately. Since they could no longer make any use of the device marks they submitted that the regime could only be conceptualised as effecting a deprivation. Green J was, however, unconvinced. The plaintiffs had made much of the fact that when determining the impact of the plain packing regime (for the purposes of deciding whether there had been a deprivation or a mere control of use) the tribunal was obliged to look beyond legal form to the commercial reality. But for his Lordship this approach also had to be extended to the process of identifying the property in the first place: in a "world where substance and not form matters… the word and figurative marks are used in conjunction with each other to convey a collective message to consumers".[38]

Treating the word and the device marks in combination was central to the outcome under Article 1 Protocol 1. Once this stride has been taken it is then only a short step to conclude that there had been no expropriation but merely a control of

35. Case T-187/11 (28 May 2013).
36. *Ibid.*, [81].
37. At [825].
38. At [747].

use. This means that the test for whether compensation should be payable is one of "fair balance". Given the health risks associated with smoking it is then only another short step to say that a fair balancing analysis favours the denial of compensation. At the heart of the different conclusions on the taking/expropriation point reached by the Australian and the English Court we therefore find a different process of identification. That there can be disagreement over what the property "is" tells us much about the confusion and untested assumptions that surround the way in which we think about trade marks as items of property. Greater conceptual clarity around the nature of property in trade marks is therefore essential if we are to build consensus about the appropriate limits of constitutional protection for trade mark proprietors. These issues form the focus of the analysis section of this essay, but it is necessary first to make some brief comments about the Court of Appeal's decision.

III. The Case Before the Court of Appeal

The appeal was heard by Lewison LJ; Beatson LJ and Sir Stephen Richards. The Court of Appeal handed down a unanimous judgment on 30 November 2016. The grounds of appeal were broad and the Court had to address most of the issues that had been tested before Green J. Given the complexity of the case and the range of issues covered, there were remarkably few points of difference between the Court of Appeal and the judge at first instance. The only real area of disagreement concerned Green J's attempt to produce a set of guidelines on how to deal with expert evidence in judicial review proceedings. Although the appellate court was sympathetic to the scale of the task faced by the court at first instance, it concluded that the judge had acted unwisely in seeking to lay down a process for dealing with technical evidence. Rather, the Court of Appeal signalled that courts hearing applications for judicial review should endeavour to avoid getting drawn into the resolution of technical disputes. Insofar as possible they should focus on whether the material before the primary decision-maker (that is, the executive agency whose decision is being challenged) was sufficient to underpin the decision made, with this assessment forming a key component of the proportionality enquiry.

In relation to the challenges around expropriation of property, the differences between Green J and the Court of Appeal were more ones of nuance than anything else. In relation to the common law argument, the Court of Appeal was seemingly reluctant to dispose of the case on the basis that the common law could not go beyond the ECHR. Here the Court was perhaps mindful of the note of caution struck by the Supreme Court, which has emphasised the importance of not overlooking the common law or in turning too readily to the Human Rights Act to solve all matters of interpretation.[39] For the Court of Appeal the matter could be disposed of instead on the basis that the common law interpretive principle only arises in cases where property has been appropriated. Since the Court concluded that the plain packaging regime only imposed a control on use and did not amount to an expropriation the common law claim could be dismissed. This underscores the central importance of the question of whether there had been an expropriation.

39. See, e.g., *Kennedy v. The Charity Commission* [2014] UKSC 20, [46].

Turning to the question of whether the Charter provides greater protection than the ECHR, the Court of Appeal dealt with this argument in almost identical terms to Green J. The Court was obviously unconvinced by the argument that the Charter carves out an irreducible core of protection for property (and other) rights, but could dismiss this part of the plaintiff's case on the narrower ground that any such irreducible core of protection could only be equated with the right to exclude.

The heart of the case thus became whether there had been an expropriation. Applying principles that are well-established in Strasbourg jurisprudence, the Court of Appeal noted that although retention by the claimant of legal title to the property counted against a finding that there had been an expropriation, it was not determinative of the issue. For the Court of Appeal there were two other factors that led to the conclusion that the plain packaging regime established a mere control of use. The first was that the Court was persuaded by the argument that the trade mark rights retained a not inconsequential set of functions and hence sufficient value to conclude that no expropriation had occurred. The Court focused, in particular, on the possibility of using the marks against counterfeiters, on wholesale materials and to prevent the sale of unauthorised e-cigarettes. The Court therefore concluded that even if the claimants were correct that each mark had to be taken in isolation there had still been no expropriation. However, the Court also signalled its approval of the way in which Green J had approached the question at first instance. The Court noted that there was a strong argument that the correct approach was to look beyond individual marks to the way in which they are exploited alongside word marks. Since word marks can still be used, albeit in a restricted manner, the regime looks much more like one that sets up a mere control of use.

D. ON TRADE MARKS, INVESTMENT, GOODWILL AND PROPERTY

I. Expropriation as Destruction of Goodwill

Academic and judicial discussions of trade marks as a species of property often suffer from a lack of precision. The question of whether we are concerned with property in the sign, property in the brand or ownership of goodwill is often left unspecified, and slippage between these ideas can and does occur. One reason for the seeming lack of precision is that each of these understandings of the nature of the property in a trade mark can be relevant at different times and for different purposes. For example, if two parties are negotiating the sale of a single registered trade mark that has not yet been put to use by its proprietor, the transaction can only be thought of as concerning property in a sign. If, however, two parties are negotiating for the sale of an established business any registered mark that forms part of the sale will be understood primarily as one of the anchors of brand value and goodwill.

Given that trade mark scholars are often vague about the nature of the "*res*" that the law protects and given that different understandings would seem to make most sense for different purposes, it is unrealistic to expect a court hearing a constitutional case not to struggle with the precise nature of the property at issue. Moreover, the analysis would also have to be sensitive to the facts at hand. If, for example, the state were to forcibly transfer title to a series of marks that were as yet unused (but before they were vulnerable to cancellation for non-use) it would only make sense to think of property in the signs. Some degree of constitutional protection must therefore be given to property in signs. However, the scope of such protection must be narrow. Trade marks only perform a valuable economic and social function once they are in use.[40] Provided legal title to an unused mark remains in the hands of its proprietor expropriation ought to be difficult to establish.

The real value of trade marks lies in their ability to connect consumers to the goods and services they wish to acquire. It is as repositories for goodwill, famously described as "the attractive force that brings in custom".[41] If we accept that trade marks attract constitutional protection as a protected form of intangible asset then if such protection is to be meaningful it must extend to protect the commercial magnetism of the mark, the thing that brings consumers into the owner's shop or onto its website. To be clear, this is not to suggest that this means that constitutional protection has to be thrown around all brand value. As Dev Gangjee has noted, the value of a brand is a complex phenomenon produced by many different actors. There are good reasons not to allow trade mark owners control over all attempts to change the meaning of a brand or give them the right to prevent the brand being associated with values that the trade mark owner finds objectionable.[42] However, even if we stick to traditional trade mark theory, namely, that trade marks act as a badge of origin to allow consumers to identify the products they want quickly and cheaply, there is a strong argument that we should protect the resulting benefit that this provides to trade mark owners, that is, their goodwill.

Commercial magnetism or goodwill does not necessarily attach to individual signs: traders can change individual elements of their branding without damaging their goodwill. In this respect, the willingness of courts in both Australia and the UK to look beyond the individual marks recorded on the register to consider how marks are exploited as a package is entirely appropriate. In many cases, such an analysis might well support the conclusion reached by the UK courts: taken as a sign, property remains in the hands of the trade mark owner; viewed in terms of the protection of goodwill, provided the owner can continue to exploit other significant elements of its branding, the loss of its ability to exploit individual marks is of much less significance and looks much more like a "control of use" than an expropriation.

There is, however, one important consideration that distinguishes plain packaging from the hypothetical considered at the end of the previous paragraph. Plain packaging regimes do not merely seek to restrict the range of signs that tobacco companies can employ, leaving them free to exploit other elements of their branding. Rather, the point of a plain packing regime is to destroy the tobacco industry's goodwill. This objective will not be achieved overnight, but it is the ultimate and unabashed aim of a plain packaging regime. The point is to delegitimise tobacco products; to ensure that consumers do not have any positive association with tobacco companies; to ensure that there is no attractive force to bring in business.

---

40. W. Landes and R. Posner, 'The Economics of Trademark Law', 78 *TMR* (1988), 267, 280.
41. *Inland Revenue Commissioners v. Muller & Co's Margarine Ltd* [1901] AC 217, 224 (HL, Lord Macnaghten.
42. See also D. Gangjee, 'Property in Brands: The Commodification of Conversation', in H. Howe and J. Griffiths (eds.), *Property Concepts in Intellectual Property Law* (CUP, Cambridge, 2013).

A plain packaging regime is thus best analogised to a slow and steady government programme to destroy an old and established building of huge proportions, with the state's response to the expropriation claim being that the residents are free to reside in the rooms that remain while the work is being carried out. The decision of the Australian High Court can be understood on the back of this analogy: due to a quirk of the Australian Constitution the mere destruction of property does not give rise to a claim for compensation.

In contrast, the decisions of the UK courts on the "expropriation" point are harder to defend. To be fair, the Court of Appeal did note that insofar as the claimants were seeking to rely on ownership of goodwill their claim was not properly particularised. Equally, however, the Court did not consider the consequences of its conclusion that the constitutionally protected locus of trade mark rights is not the individual signs recorded on the register. Once one goes beyond those signs to look at the commercial reality as the Court indicated (quite rightly) one should, then it is also necessary to think about the nature of what is being protected in more detail, something that the Court did not do in this case.

II. Tobacco Really is Different

The thing that is missing from the analysis thus far is any consideration of the unique nature of tobacco and the position of the tobacco industry. The analysis in the previous section was motivated in part by a normative consideration, namely, that we ought to be cautious about allowing Government to set out to destroy a company's goodwill without having to provide compensation. That a rule requiring compensation might emerge from human rights principles would, in any other circumstances, strike most lawyers and legal academics as entirely unsurprising. This is not to say that there would not be opposition to the establishment of such a rule - some would no doubt conclude that such a rule would unduly constrain governmental action - but it would be the *type* of rule whose emergence would strike us as entirely within the bounds of what we might expect. Moreover, even critics would probably have to concede that the practical impact of a rule requiring compensation would probably be relatively modest because Governments are not in the habit of seeking to destroy the goodwill of established businesses.

The question of whether there ought to be a legal entitlement to compensation when a Government sets out to destroy the goodwill of a business is, in other words, exactly the sort of area where one would expect careful and considered analysis, with contributions from experts across a number of legal fields and recognition, on all sides, that finely balanced interests are at stake. A similar observation can be made about the WTO dispute. Given the importance of the issues at stake, one might have expected sober analysis of all of the arguments being put forward by tobacco producing countries. This was not, however, the pattern. For some engaged in the debate about plain packaging, any attempt to put the case for the tobacco industry is beyond the pale. This has led to a level of personal animosity developing between academic commentators that is largely unprecedented in the normally staid world of intellectual property scholarship.

The reason that passions run high in this area is that tobacco really is different from other types of product. Smoking related disease kills almost 6 million people every year and the average life expectancy for a smoker is about 10 years less than for a non-smoker.[43] It must also be borne in mind that smoking is highly addictive. Tobacco companies therefore depend on selling a product that consumers will struggle to stop using and that will very likely shorten their lifespan. Moreover, the industry had a long and disgraceful history of seeking to conceal what it knew about the health risks of smoking. In the three decisions examined here, this background was only fully considered by Green J. One question that has not attracted sufficient attention concerns what level of compensation would have been appropriate if the tobacco industry had been able to make out its case. Here, both the Australian and the UK Governments argued that even if the tobacco companies were entitled to succeed, the "fair" level of any compensation would be "zero" given the unique nature and history of the tobacco industry.

To find that the state had interfered with property rights to a degree that would generally demand compensation, but then to deny compensation on broader policy grounds is clearly not a step to be taken lightly. It was certainly not a step that Heydon J in the High Court of Australia was prepared to countenance. For His Honour this would have opened the door on such an argument being run in every case in which property had been expropriated, since the state would always be able to point to some countervailing consideration of public policy to justify refusing to pay compensation.[44] There is something to this concern. Any exception to the duty to pay compensation would therefore have to be confined to circumstances where highly unusual considerations are in play. But this describes the position of the tobacco industry.

The issue is not merely that the level of harm to public health caused by smoking is staggering or even that the state has to bear much of the resulting cost. If these considerations were sufficient it would not be difficult to draw analogies with other very different types of case. For example, one might point out that flooding can cause a very significant threat to life as well as enormous economic damage and that the state has to bear many of the costs of recovery following a natural disaster. Most of us would not, however, be likely to regard these considerations as sufficient to avoid the duty to pay compensation should the state decide to expropriate coastal properties in order to strengthen flood defences. The consideration that really sets plain packaging apart is that the property rights that have been expropriated are the things that help attract consumers to the product in the first place. The property seized actually helps cause the harm (and resulting costs to the state) that the plain packaging regime is trying to alleviate. That goodwill still resides to the extent that it does is in no small part due to the concerted efforts of the tobacco industry to mislead consumers of the nature of the risks attached to smoking. Moreover, the harm in question is inevitable and is a natural consequence of the underlying product being used as intended. This makes the plain packaging regime quite different from legislation prohibiting, say, the possession of firearms or other products where the risk to public health is attached to unlawful, reckless or unusual uses. It is therefore worth reflecting on the fact that Green J did conclude that the circumstances of the

43. Centers for Disease Control and Prevention, 'Smoking & Tobacco Use', available at: < www.cdc.gov/tobacco/data_statistics/fact_sheets/fast_facts/index.htm > .
44. *JT International SA v. Commonwealth*, [236].

tobacco industry are so unusual that an exception to the duty to provide compensation could be justified. To the author's mind that would probably have been a safer basis on which to dispose of the case than the conclusion that there had been no breach of Article 1, Protocol 1 at all.

E. CONCLUSION

The legal disputes around plain packaging look set to continue for many years. The outcome of the WTO case will obviously be extremely important, but it also seems safe to assume that there will be a constitutional challenge to plain packaging legislation in almost every country that seeks to introduce such a regime. There is sufficient variation in the nature and scope of constitutional guarantees of property (to say nothing of differences in judicial sentiment) that the outcome in the Australian and UK cases may well not be a safe guide to what happens elsewhere. The point that this essay has tried to make is that we should not necessarily welcome the conclusion that plain packaging regimes do not give rise to a *prima facie* duty to compensate. Those who are outraged by the attempt of the tobacco industry to seek compensation for loss of their trade mark rights should recognise that this is because the tobacco industry is almost entirely underserving of sympathy. It is not because the state setting out to destroy the goodwill of established businesses is something about which we should be sanguine in general.

Index

IEEM SERIES ON INTERNATIONAL INTELLECTUAL PROPERTY LAW

1. Intellectual Property in the Digital Age – Challenges for Asia
   Christopher Heath and Anselm Kamperman Sanders (eds.)
   Published by Kluwer Law International 2001
   ISBN 90-411-9847-4

2. Intellectual Property in the Bio-Medical Age – Challenges for Asia
   Christopher Heath and Anselm Kamperman Sanders (eds.)
   Published by Kluwer Law International 2003
   ISBN 90-411-9926-8

3. New Frontiers of Intellectual Property Law
   Christopher Heath and Anselm Kamperman Sanders (eds.)
   Published by Hart Publishing 2005
   ISBN 1-84113-538-0

4. Intellectual Property and Free Trade Agreements
   Christopher Heath and Anselm Kamperman Sanders (eds.)
   Published by Hart Publishing 2007
   ISBN 978-1-84113-801-5

5. Spares, Repairs and Intellectual Property Rights
   Christopher Heath and Anselm Kamperman Sanders (eds.)
   Published by Kluwer Law International 2009
   ISBN 978-90-411-3136-2

6. Landmark Intellectual Property Cases and Their Legacy
   Christopher Heath and Anselm Kamperman Sanders (eds.)
   Published by Kluwer Law International 2011
   ISBN 978-90-411-3343-4

7. Intellectual Property Liability of Consumers, Facilitators and Intermediaries
   Christopher Heath and Anselm Kamperman Sanders (eds.)
   Published by Kluwer Law International 2012
   ISBN 978-90-411-4126-2

8. Employees, Trade Secrets and Restrictive Covenants
   Christopher Heath and Anselm Kamperman Sanders (eds.)
   Published by Kluwer Law International 2017
   ISBN 978-90-411-8379-8

9. Intellectual Property Rights as Obstacles to Legitimate Trade?
   Christopher Heath, Anselm Kamperman Sanders and Anke Moerland (eds.)
   Published by Kluwer Law International 2018
   ISBN 978-94-035-0330-1

10. Intellectual Property and International Dispute Resolution
Christopher Heath and Anselm Kamperman Sanders (eds.)
Published by Kluwer Law International 2019
ISBN 978-90-411-9097-0